THAILAND'S
SUSTAINABLE
BUSINESS
GUIDE

THAILAND'S
SUSTAINABLE
BUSINESS
GUIDE

HOW TO **FUTURE PROOF**
YOUR BUSINESS IN THE NAME
OF A **BETTER WORLD**

EDITIONS DIDIER MILLET

Editor-in-Chief
Nicholas Grossman

Editors
Bhimsupa Kulthanan
Max Crosbie-Jones
Nina Wegner

Special Advisor
Yvan Van Outrive

Contributing Editor
Will Baxter

Project Consultants
Alex Mavro
Nick Pisalyaput
Sarinee Achavanuntakul

Picture Researcher
Grissarin Chungsiriwat

Art Directors
Benjapa Sodsathit
Luxana Kiratibhongse
Patinya Rojnukkarin

Designers
Siree Simaraks
Nichapat Chaokchaingamsangh
Sirikul Raddudsadee

Project Coordinator
Jaruphan Phan-in

Production Manager
Annie Teo

For a list of all writers and contributors, see pages 342–343.

First published in 2017 by
Editions Didier Millet (EDM)

Email: **edm@edmbooks.com.sg**
www.edmbooks.com

Bangkok office
Room 1310, 3rd Floor
8, Sukhumvit 49/9, Klongton Nua
Wattana, Bangkok 10110
Thailand
Tel: +66-2018-7808

Singapore head office
75 Jalan Hitam Manis
Singapore 278488
Tel: +65-6265-7644

Cover design by
Palotai Design Co., Ltd.
www.palotaidesign.com

FSC
www.fsc.org
MIX
Paper from
responsible sources
FSC™ C103447

Color separation by
PICA DIGITAL, Singapore

Printed by
Sirivatana Interprint Public Co., Ltd.

ISBN 978-981-4610-56-8

Table of Contents

A Note on Sources

The statistics and information in this book
were derived from a range of sources,
including the business sector and companies
themselves, international organizations such
as the World Bank, and Thai government
ministries. The editorial team attempted to
identify the most reliable source and check
against other sources whenever necessary.
In many cases, the source is cited. However,
we felt it would be tedious reading to cite
within the text every reference and source
for the large amount of information gathered
here. Please see References on page 334 for
a more comprehensive list.

Directory of Case Studies

Directory of Interviews

This project was inspired by the launch of the

and it was made possible thanks to the financial support of the following organizations:

We would also like to recognize our project partner:

Page 5: Wind turbines in Chiang Mai province at sunset. Page 9: Aerial view of Victory Monument in Bangkok. Page 10: Aerial view of cargo containers at Khlong Toei Port, Bangkok's main port. Page 13: A fisherman who supplies the Fisherfolk brand hauls in his catch by hand.

FOREWORD

The concept of sustainable development has come into vogue among companies in Thailand. This shift is significant. It demonstrates that Thai companies are concerned not just about their future viability in a fast-changing business environment, but also about their greater responsibility to the world at large.

There are many business factors fueling this rise: intensifying public scrutiny, fierce competition, increasing industry regulation, and heightened stakeholder engagement across many groups. In addition, there is the growing recognition, or alarm, that so-called "megatrends" such as climate change, rapid technological advancement, and demographic shifts are occurring so rapidly that businesses that do not act to meet these challenges will see their own existence threatened.

All of these factors are creating demand for a new way of doing business, a more responsible approach that is transparent and prevents corruption, that addresses any negative external impacts of a company's products or operations, that develops employee capacities while seeking productive public partnerships, and that sincerely applies a long-term vision that is inclusive of all stakeholders. In short, many Thai businesses are adopting new business ethics and mindsets.

These ethics have special resonance here because they were long espoused by His Majesty King Bhumibol Adulyadej and exemplified through his life's work, which was then formalized in his Sufficiency Economy Philosophy (SEP). While SEP may have its roots in Buddhist principles and His Majesty's agricultural projects, it can be readily applied to private sector practice as well. Indeed, it was the devastating economic events of the 1997 Asian Financial Crisis that focused more public attention on SEP in the first place.

Yet 20 years later, most of the Thai private sector may still not fully appreciate how SEP and the concepts of sustainability can be applied and how truly transformative they can be for a business. That's why the Thailand Sustainable Development Foundation and the publisher EDM have collaborated to create *Thailand's Sustainable Business Guide*. This third book in our series on sustainable development spotlights the best practices and great opportunities available to Thai businesses through the sustainability movement. Here, we provide informative insights from executives, case studies, and practical recommendations across many sectors to show how SEP and sustainable development can be put into practice and the business value they may create.

This publication doesn't dwell on past problems, but instead offers objective analysis and positive solutions in the name of guiding the business sector and Thailand overall toward a prosperous future, where the concepts and principles of SEP and sustainability are the new "business as usual." On behalf of the Thailand Sustainable Development Foundation and the many contributors to this publication, I hope you will discover much value in *Thailand's Sustainable Business Guide*.

Dr Prasarn Trairatvorakul
Chairman of the Editorial Advisory Board
and a Director of the Thailand Sustainable
Development Foundation (TSDF)

EDITOR'S NOTE

Thailand's Sustainable Business Guide is the third in a series of books by EDM and its partner, the Thailand Sustainable Development Foundation, that examine the sustainable development movement in Thailand. The focus of this volume is on the rapidly changing and innovating private sector, because the success of the whole sustainability movement depends on it.

In the name of helping businesses look forward, as they must constantly do, we don't focus on past crises, scandals, and problems in the Thai private sector, but present forward-looking recommendations and solutions to current challenges. These ideas encompass applications of Thailand's Sufficiency Economy Philosophy, the United Nations' Sustainable Development Goals (SDGs), and the key guiding concepts of corporate sustainability in general, such as sustainability strategies and reporting, corporate governance, risk and sustainable supply chain management, human resources development, product life cycles, and more.

We also look at sustainability issues from an industry sector perspective because Thailand's economy faces some unique challenges. Its agribusiness industry, for example, is extremely vulnerable to both climate change and global price fluctuations; its fisheries industry has recently faced the threat of trade sanctions due to exploitative labor practices; and its manufacturing sector risks spinning its wheels due to a lack of innovation, a skills shortage, and loss of competitiveness. All sectors are fraught with the contemporary tensions of doing "business as usual" and the social and environmental damage such behavior could have on our collective future. These existential threats could all be solved, it can be argued, through the application of the sustainability principles discussed in these pages.

The editorial team conducted hundreds of interviews to form the "Insights," recommendations for "Take Action," and other key texts that you will discover throughout this book. We also visited and spoke with many companies in order to create a "Case Study" that shows how some businesses are, in their own unique way, advancing the sustainability movement in Thailand.

Writing about businesses in Thailand can be a sensitive undertaking. We did our best to gather information from the most reputable sources, including through direct engagement with the businesses themselves in the vast majority of cases. We would like to note that the inclusion of a company in these pages does not mean we endorse it and all of its practices. Inclusion simply means that we found the practices described noteworthy and hopefully interesting to readers.

This project had some corporate sponsors who helped us pay for its costs. The best practices of some of these companies are featured, but the content was not created by them, and many other companies who did not support this project have been highlighted. Our goal was to present a diverse selection of businesses and projects, both big and small; however, in a field that is evolving so rapidly it would be impossible to be comprehensive. We are aware that some businesses featured here have received criticism and are looking to improve their record and performance. We would like to give them that opportunity too.

Most of all, we are hopeful that the book will prove valuable to its readers and we look forward to further dialogue as Thailand continues to grapple with the great potential of the sustainability movement.

THAILAND OVERVIEW

PEOPLE

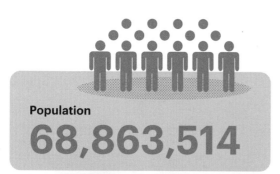

Population

68,863,514

38
Median Age

75.1
Life Expectancy

ECONOMY

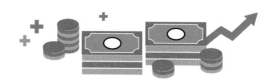

▶ Gross Domestic Product (GDP, US$)

$407 Billion

▶ Average annual GDP Growth

3.2%

▶ Gross National Income (US$ Per Capita)

$5,640

▶ Exports of goods and services (% of GDP)

69%

▶ Imports of goods and services (% of GDP)

54%

▶ Income Level

Upper-middle Income

Source: World Bank, 2015

TOTAL AREA

Land use

Agriculture	46%
Forest	31%
Other	23%

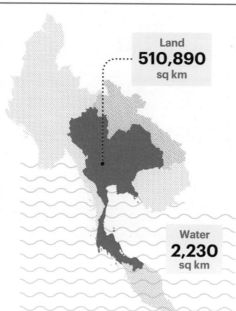

Land
510,890
sq km

Water
2,230
sq km

Borders

Myanmar	**2,401 km**	(West)
Cambodia	**798 km**	(Southeast)
Lao PDR	**1,810 km**	(Northeast)
Malaysia	**647 km**	(South)

Source: Office of Agricultural Economics, Thailand

CARBON DIOXIDE EMISSIONS

CO_2 emissions per capita (tons) in ASEAN countries

THAILAND 4.6

Brunei	**24**	Lao PDR	**0.2**	Philippines	**0.9**
Cambodia	**0.3**	Malaysia	**7.8**	Singapore	**4.3**
Indonesia	**2.3**	Myanmar	**0.2**	Vietnam	**2.0**

Source: United Nations Development Programme Human Development Report 2015 for Thailand

HUMAN DEVELOPMENT RANKING

(Out of 188 countries) Thailand is listed among those countries with high levels of human development. Rankings of other Asian nations include:

 THAILAND 87

Malaysia	59		China	90
Sri Lanka	73		Philippines	116
Vietnam	115		Myanmar	145

Source: United Nations Development Programme Human Development Report 2016

POVERTY

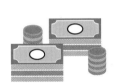

0.6% Population living below **$1.90 a day**

This is the international poverty line as determined by the World Bank.

Source: United Nations Development Programme Human Development Report 2015

THAILAND IS AN AGEING SOCIETY

The year when approximate number of young people and seniors will be the same. **2025**

Source: United Nations Development Programme Human Development Report 2015

SOCIAL PROGRESS RANKING

61 (Out of 133 countries)

Social progress includes nutritional and basic medical care, access to basic knowledge, health and wellness, as well as access to information, communications, and personal safety.

Source: Social Progress Index 2016

EDUCATION

7.3
Mean Years of Schooling

in comparison to

13.5
Expected Years of Schooling

Source: United Nations Development Programme Human Development Report 2014

CORRUPTION

Corruption remains a problem in much of Asia Pacific, including Thailand.

Over 63%
of the region's countries ranked in the bottom half of Transparency International's Corruption Perception Index.

Source: Corruption Perceptions Index 2016

THE BUSINESS LANDSCAPE

ECONOMIC PERFORMANCE

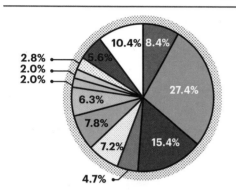

Economic Structure by Sector (% share of supply-side GDP, 2016)

- Agriculture & Fishing
- Manufacturing
- Retail & Wholesale
- Hotels & Restaurants
- Transport & Communication
- Financial Intermediation
- Real Estate
- Health
- Other Social & Domestic Services
- Electricity, Gas, Water Supply
- Construction & Mining
- Public Administration & Education

Source: World Bank Thailand Economic Monitor, August 2017

GROSS CORPORATE PROFITS

Corporate Profit as Percent of National Income
(% of national income)

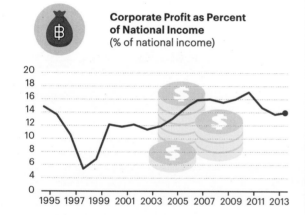

Source: NESDB

INVESTMENT TRENDS

Both public and private investments have yet to recover to pre-1997 Asian Financial Crisis levels.

- Public
- Private
- Gross fixed capital formation

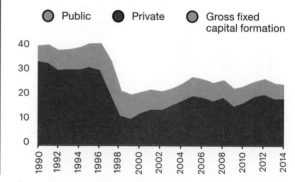

Source: NESDB

EASE OF BUSINESS

According to the World Bank's Ease of Doing Business Report, it is now becoming easier to do business in Thailand.

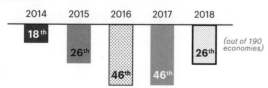

2014 — 18th
2015 — 26th
2016 — 46th
2017 — 46th
2018 — 26th

(out of 190 economies)

Source: World Bank Thailand Country Diagnostic 2017

TIME REQUIRED TO START A BUSINESS

26 days

TOP 10 OBSTACLES TO DOING BUSINESS

 Government instability/coups

 Inadequately educated workforce

 Corruption

 Access to financing

 Inefficient government/bureaucracy

 Inadequate supply of infrastructure

 Political Instability

 Complexity of tax regulations

 Insufficient capacity to innovate

 Poor work ethic in labor force

Source: World Bank, World Economic Forum's Executive Opinion Survey 2016

COMPETITIVENESS

 Asia-Pacific's top 9 countries in terms of global competitiveness

Singapore	3			**Thailand**	**32**
Japan	9		Indonesia	36
Hong Kong SAR	6		Philippines	56
Malaysia	23		Vietnam	55
China	27		*(Global rankings out of 138 economies)*	

Source: The Global Competitiveness Index 2016-2017

R&D EXPENDITURE

Business R&D Expenditure/GDP

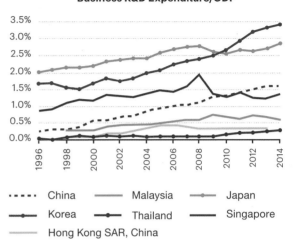

- - - - - China   Malaysia   Japan
Korea   Thailand   Singapore
Hong Kong SAR, China

Source: National Science Technology and Innovation Policy Office, Thailand Business R&D and Innovation Survey 2015

The petroleum industry is the largest spender on R&D and innovation, with green products being a major investment. This is followed by the food and chemicals industries.

Petroleum	4,905
Food	4,097
Chemicals	3,672
Aluminum and Glass	2,157
Office equipment	1,930
Machinery	1,705
TV and Radio	1,008
Rubber and Plastic	963
Automotive	739
Metals	617

(million baht)

Source: National Science Technology and Innovation Policy Office, Thailand Business R&D and Innovation Survey 2015

THAILAND AND THE GLOBAL GOALS

THE 10 PRINCIPLES OF THE UNITED NATIONS GLOBAL COMPACT

Human Rights

Principle 1: Businesses should support and respect the protection of internationally proclaimed human rights

Principle 2: make sure that they are not complicit in human rights abuses

Labor

Principle 3: Businesses should uphold the freedom of association and the effective recognition of the right to collective bargaining

Principle 4: the elimination of all forms of forced and compulsory labor

Principle 5: the effective abolition of child labor

Principle 6: the elimination of discrimination in respect of employment and occupation

Environment

Principle 7: Businesses should support a precautionary approach to environmental challenges

Principle 8: undertake initiatives to promote greater environmental responsibility

Principle 9: encourage the development and diffusion of environmentally friendly technologies

Anti-Corruption

Principle 10: Businesses should work against corruption in all its forms, including extortion and bribery

THAILAND'S PERFORMANCE ON THE SUSTAINABLE DEVELOPMENT GOALS

THAILAND

Overall SDG Performance	Global Rank	Score or Value	East and South Asia Regional Average
SDG Index	55 (of 157)	69.5	63.3
Comparison with other development metrics			
Human Development Index, 2016	77 (of 157)	74.0	67.1
Subjective Well-Being, 2016	35 (of 133)	61	51
GDP per capita, PPP, 2015	64 (of 153)	US$15,347	US$12,194
Global Competitiveness Index, 2016/17	32 (of 134)	66.3	61.6
Environmental Performance Index, 2016	86 (of 157)	69.5	61.1

SELECT COUNTRIES

● Overall rank ● Overall score

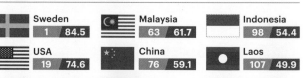

Sweden — 1 / 84.5	Malaysia — 63 / 61.7	Indonesia — 98 / 54.4
USA — 19 / 74.6	China — 76 / 59.1	Laos — 107 / 49.9
Singapore — 25 / 72.7	Vietnam — 88 / 57.6	Myanmar — 117 / 44.5
THAILAND — 61 / 62.2	The Philippines — 95 / 55.5	Cambodia — 114 / 58.2

THAILAND'S PROGRESS ON THE SDGS

SDG		Thailand's Score	East & South Asia Regional Score*
Goal 1	No Poverty	100	83.66
Goal 2	Zero Hunger	55.0	47.09
Goal 3	Good Health and Well-being	76.2	61.24
Goal 4	Quality Education	76.2	70.06
Goal 5	Gender Equality	65.7	55.76
Goal 6	Clean Water and Sanitation	95.1	80.97
Goal 7	Affordable and Clean Energy	76.9	58.49
Goal 8	Decent Work and Economic Growth	85.2	59.55
Goal 9	Industry, Innovation and Infrastructure	39.8	24.27
Goal 10	Reduced Inequalities	64.8	68.64
Goal 11	Sustainable Cities and Communities	75.1	56.28
Goal 12	Responsible Consumption and Production	70.4	39.86
Goal 13	Climate Action	73.0	69.84
Goal 14	Life Below Water	45.0	37.29
Goal 15	Life on Land	63.2	46.22
Goal 16	Peace, Justice and Strong Institutions	58.0	56.37
Goal 17	Partnerships for the Goals	62.6	21.18

(Green = achieved / Yellow & Orange = "caution lane" / Red = significant improvement needed)

THAILAND'S NOTABLE SUCCESSES AND CHALLENGES

	Value	Rating
Poverty headcount ratio at US$1.90 per day (%)	0	
Registered births (%)	99.4	
Freshwater withdrawal (%)	13.1	
Access to electricity (%)	100	
Unemployment rate (%)	0.6	
Terrestrial sites, completely protected (%)	71.7	
Traffic deaths (per 100,000)	36.2	
PM2.5 in urban areas (μm/m3)	25.8	
CO_2 emissions from energy (tCO_2/capita)	4.5	
Climate change vulnerability (0-1)	0.2	
R&D expenditures (% of GDP)	0.5	
Women in national parliaments (%)	6.1	
Homicides (per 100,000)	3.9	
Prison population (per 100,000)	398	

Source: The rankings and scores on these pages come from the SDG Index (2017), which tracks global progress on the SDGs. The full report, including explanations of its methodologies, can be downloaded at wwww.sdgindex.org.

PART 1

Introduction: The Business Case for Sustainable Development

How can the Thai private sector respond to national and global calls to action on sustainability? As Thai businesses start to truly grapple with the challenges of the Sustainable Development Goals and awaken to societal demands for more and better corporate responsibility, they must now put their sustainability commitments into action.

Thai businesses can be a force for innovation and leadership in this fast-changing climate. They have the power to spearhead dramatic changes away from business-as-usual, short-term practices and toward a long-term perspective that accounts for all dimensions of the 'triple-bottom line': people, planet, and profit. They also have the rather unique opportunity to follow the local wisdom of their own sustainability framework known as the Sufficiency Economy Philosophy.

But are they doing enough? What is the level of awareness and engagement among Thai businesses on sustainability today? For companies that have already embarked on this journey, what lessons can be drawn?

Even more importantly, what would be the costs and risks of inaction? From micro and small- or medium-sized enterprises to the large-scale multinational conglomerates, there is opportunity to be realized for all in creating a balanced and sustainable future path for business.

This introductory essay lays bare the deep questioning and transformation occurring within the private sector, and the stark choice between doing business-as-usual or pursuing a new path defined by a more sustainable approach to business.

At Mitr Phol's Innovation and Research Center, a researcher checks samples related to sugarcane tissue culture development.

Sustainability means different things to different companies. For some, sustainability may be about mere survival or the idea of enduring through the complicated times ahead. Efforts are focused on future-proofing the business against rising uncertainty, risk, and rapid change. Other companies are integrating practices associated with sustainability because they must meet new regulatory requirements, conform to higher expectations among consumers, or they fear the potential losses of not acting. More dedicated businesses are overhauling their operational models and processes in a real commitment to 'green' practices, for the benefit of not only their bottom line but also the environment and society at large; while still others are reorienting their entire business models to take advantage of what they see as the market opportunities offered by the green economy and other emerging trends. Then there are the new players, some with new models: sharing, circular, lean service, big data, and social enterprises. Likely, all of these businesses are excited by the potential branding and public relations opportunities sustainability initiatives offer.

In Thailand, as evidenced by the 18 major companies listed on the Dow Jones Sustainability Index, the many social enterprises and eco-oriented businesses, the active discussion of the United Nations' Sustainable Development Goals (SDGs or 'Global Goals'), and the constant seminars and news reports on the subject, there is sincere engagement already with the ideas of sustainability and the sustainable development movement. A further impetus is the Sufficiency Economy Philosophy (SEP), a development framework created by the late Thai monarch, His Majesty King Bhumibol Adulyadej. It shares many of the same principles as the SDGs. Like the SDGs, SEP is focused on guiding individuals, businesses, communities, and the nation itself toward more holistic and balanced – and less capricious – growth.

Anxieties about Thailand's economic competitiveness, the readiness of its workforce for 21st-century challenges, and the health of its environment are also spurring companies to question the long-term benefits of purely profit-driven, business-as-usual practices. Without a strong Thailand, all business prospects may dim. Indeed, natural disasters, corruption, rapid technological advancement, social divisions, and political unrest have created much uncertainty for both large and small companies in Thailand over the last decade. SMEs have been particularly negatively impacted. Farmers are still struggling, essential infrastructure investment is consistently stalled, and big companies are worried about a shortage of skilled labor. Thailand has also seen its share of corporate scandals, some originating from corporate headquarters and others found more remotely in supply chains but still just as damaging. Entire sectors such as the fisheries industry have come under scrutiny and risk of overseas boycotts for their labor practices. In addition, traditional industries across a broad spectrum – from publishing to energy – have been upended by innovation.

In this volatile environment, it is not surprising that the word 'sustainability' has begun to attract the ear of anxious and responsible executives. The notion of a 'business case' for corporate sustainability has been increasingly trumpeted by the corporate sector, environmental organizations, and consultancies, to seek justification for sustainability strategies within companies. The 2017 report 'Better Business, Better World' by the Business & Sustainable Development Commission states:

"The business case for sustainable development is strong already: it opens up new opportunities and big efficiency gains; it drives innovation; and it enhances reputations. With a reputation for sustainability, companies attract and retain employees, consumers, B2B customers and investors, and they secure their license to operate. That's why sustainable companies around the globe are thriving and delivering attractive returns to shareholders."

"The business case for sustainable development is strong already: it opens up new opportunities and big efficiency gains; it drives innovation."

Certainly there is untapped potential for Thailand as well. The same report estimates that achievement of the United Nations' 17 SDGs could create almost 380 million jobs and open up US$121 trillion of market opportunities in four key economic systems worldwide: food and agriculture, cities, energy and materials, and health and wellbeing, representing 60 percent of the real economy. These market opportunities cover topics as diverse as technological innovations used in small-scale farming to reducing food and packaging waste, from energy-efficient buildings to expansion of renewables, from healthcare training to car sharing. Thailand has strong opportunities across the board. The commission argues:

"To capture these opportunities in full, businesses need to pursue social and environmental sustainability as avidly as they pursue market share and shareholder value. Moving business to a sustainable growth model will be disruptive, with big risks as well as opportunities at stake. It will involve experimenting

Transparency or greenwashing? Public scrutiny is forcing businesses to act.

A protest against new coal projects in Thailand. Coal is symbolic of the private sector's resistance to change.

with new 'circular' and more agile business models and digital platforms that can grow exponentially to shape new social and environmental value chains. Knowing how to move first and fast is critical; so is reducing exposure to the risk of assets being stranded by the shift to low-carbon, more automated economies."

In practice, firms, predominantly in the West, already recognize the need to manage corporate sustainability within their businesses. Today, most managers have accepted corporate sustainability as a precondition for doing business. A group of concerned business leaders formed the World Business Council for Sustainable Development (WBCSD) in order to facilitate the dialogue with politicians about the means of achieving sustainability. The WBCSD had, as of 2016, grown to a coalition of about 200 international companies. Numerous firms in the West and increasing numbers in Thailand have also appointed Corporate Sustainability Officers, published sustainability reports, and incorporated sustainability into their corporate communication strategies.

Of all the key sustainability tools, the concept of corporate governance has attracted worldwide attention as an approach to sustain long-term corporate success. It is increasingly seen as fundamental to the operations of any contemporary corporation because it can help better manage and meet the expectations of a company's wide range of stakeholders. For many, good corporate governance aims to create sustainable enterprises, and prevent

fraud and damaging scandals. It requires enterprises to be administered in transparent, ethical ways to maintain the confidence of investors and other stakeholders. Following the 1997 Asian Financial Crisis and through a push by the Stock Exchange of Thailand (SET), Securities Exchange Commission (SEC), Bank of Thailand (BOT), and later the Thai Institute of Directors (IOD), corporate governance has gained traction in the kingdom as well.

Meanwhile, numerous scholars around the world have been seeking an alternative framework to the prevailing business model that promotes a short-term, shareholder-focused approach and arguably does not lead to sustained business success. They argue that this approach to capitalism and business is seriously flawed, and does not bring the quality of life to individuals and societies that the public desires. Management guru Warren Bennis even asserts that the emphasis solely on financial results is reckless and leads to short-termism, lying and scandals, all of which undermine the prospect of true corporate sustainability and the overall sustainable development of a nation.

What are some other alternatives?

In Europe, the Rhineland capitalism model is seen as an alternative approach to corporate sustainability. In Rhineland capitalism, an enterprise is an institution that serves anyone who directly or indirectly 'holds a stake' in its operation, specifically: clients, suppliers, employees, stockholders, and the surrounding social community.

Consistent with the stakeholder theory, Rhineland capitalism is concerned with the long-term sustainability of an enterprise and its relationships with many interest groups, not just with shareholders. More recently, professors Gayle Avery and Harald Bergsteiner have introduced the 'Honeybee' leadership concept, a resilient and humanistic approach to organizational sustainability. They present an evidence-based view of how the 23 Honeybee leadership principles facilitate outputs that go beyond what is typically referred to as the triple bottom line – environmental sustainability, social responsibility, and financial success.

The quest for corporate sustainability also exists in Asia. Southeast Asian businesses, for example, often work under a model that relies on governments taking an active role in creating, shaping and directing markets. They require firms to take considerable responsibility for the social welfare of their employees. Most businesses here have adopted a short-term, shareholder-focused approach to business, a major reason many went bankrupt in the 1997 Asian Financial Crisis.

Most businesses here have adopted a short-term, shareholder-focused approach to business, a major reason many went bankrupt in the 1997 Asian Financial Crisis.

Thailand's answer to corporate sustainability, as mentioned earlier, is known as the Sufficiency Economy Philosophy (SEP). It was formally introduced by His Majesty King Bhumibol Adulyadej in the 1990s as a way for many different stakeholders in Thailand to adopt a more realistic and holistic growth model. The Sufficiency Economy Philosophy approach also facilitates outputs that go beyond just the triple bottom line by highlighting the need for cultural sustainability (see sidebar on page 26 for a detailed explanation). Evidence shows that applying the principles of the Sufficiency Economy Philosophy or sustainability does not lead to a sacrifice of profits or shareholder value. On the contrary, it leads to better business results. In a review of 200 studies on sustainability and corporate performance, Oxford University and Arabesque Partners, an investment management firm, concluded that 90 percent of studies found that high environmental, social, and governance (ESG) standards reduced companies' cost of capital, and that 80 percent show a positive correlation between stock price performance and good sustainability practices.

In 2011, business researchers Sooksan Kantabutra and Thomas Siebenhüner quantitatively examined the relationships between Sufficiency Economy business practices and the corporate sustainability performance of 112 business organizations in Thailand, of which 78.8 percent traded within Thailand and 43 percent were SMEs. The study concluded that Sufficiency Economy practices are associated with sustainability outcomes and have the capacity to deliver competitive performance, endure crises (i.e., resilience), and maintain market leadership.

In 2014, Dr Sooksan confirmed his 2011 findings by identifying corporate sustainability predictors in a much larger sample of 294 randomly chosen business organizations. The findings are largely consistent with the previous study's findings, suggesting that businesses practicing the Sufficiency Economy Philosophy enhanced their corporate sustainability prospect via a capacity to deliver strong performance, endure crises, and deliver public benefits.

In general, these two quantitative studies endorse the Sufficiency Economy Philosophy as a viable approach to corporate sustainability, with many of its underlying concepts linked to an improvement in the capacity for corporate sustainability.

Despite some challenges associated with adapting the Sufficiency Economy Philosophy to the business sector, research provides clear evidence that it can be an effective approach to corporate sustainability. Over a decade of research at the Thailand Research Fund has indicated that businesses adopting SEP bring about the following:

- **A stable and competitive performance in the long run**

- **Low risk with an ability to effectively respond to the changing environment**

- **Innovative goods, services, and procedures, enabling them to always maintain market leadership**

- **Brand loyalty, assuming that the company continues to deliver benefits to the public**

Thailand's Sustainable Business Guide provides wide-ranging examples to demonstrate how small, medium-sized and large companies from different industries and settings, listed and non-listed, are adopting, to varying extents, both sustainable development and SEP best practices in their strategy, policies, and operations to create value and solve challenges.

The publication starts by introducing key management tools, including some best practices derived from businesses dedicated to sustainable development or the

BUSINESS APPLICATION OF THE SUFFICIENCY ECONOMY PHILOSOPHY

"Sufficiency Economy is a philosophy that stresses the middle path as the overriding principle for the appropriate conduct and way of life of the entire populace. It applies to the conduct and way of life of an individual, family and at community levels. At the national level, the philosophy is consistent with a balanced development strategy that would reduce the vulnerability of the nation to shocks and excesses that may arise as a result of globalization. 'Sufficiency' means moderation and due consideration in all modes of conduct, and incorporates the need for sufficient protection from internal and external shocks. To achieve this, the prudent application of knowledge is essential. In particular, great care is needed in the application of theories and technical know-how and in planning and implementation. At the same time, it is essential to strengthen the moral fiber of the nation so that everyone, particularly public officials, academics, business people, and financiers adhere first and foremost to the principles of honesty and integrity. A balanced approach combining patience, perseverance, diligence, wisdom, and prudence is indispensable to cope appropriately with critical challenges arising from extensive and rapid socio-economic, environmental and cultural change occurring as a result of globalization."

– Written statement provided by HM the King Bhumibol Adulyadej in 1999 [unofficial translation from the Thai]

The Key Characteristics of a Sufficiency Economy Business

In business terms, the Sufficiency Economy Philosophy (SEP) is similar to the stakeholder theory of the West. Stakeholder theory is an organizational management and ethics theory that emphasizes values and morality as basic tenets of sound organizational management. Enterprises applying stakeholder theory attempt to meet the demands of their stakeholders as a way of not only avoiding possible pressures and risks but also to create a better society. Businesses in Thailand that adopt SEP are different from other Thai businesses and many Western businesses...very different. They tend to be characterized by moderation, and a willingness to invest for the future, even if doing so may limit their short-term profitability. They place an emphasis on ethics, and do not take advantage of their employees, customers, shareholders, or the rest of society. They are concerned about the impacts their operations could have on future generations. These businesses are well-rounded, anticipate changes in the environment, and invest to prepare themselves for those changes, thereby immunizing themselves to external shocks. Internally, they regard their employees as a core asset, investing in them heavily and retaining them even in times of financial crisis. SEP businesses have strong organizational cultures. This widely shared organizational culture is only possible when a company does not have a high staff turnover rate, and does not lay off employees whenever the top management team needs to cut costs.

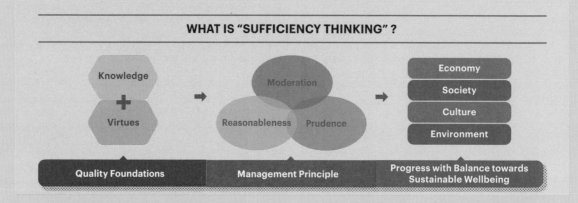

WHAT IS "SUFFICIENCY THINKING"?

Knowledge + Virtues → Moderation / Reasonableness / Prudence → Economy / Society / Culture / Environment

Quality Foundations | Management Principle | Progress with Balance towards Sustainable Wellbeing

His Majesty King Bhumibol Adulyadej during one of his many upcountry field visits. The late monarch's research led him to develop many ideas about how to create sustainability in Thailand.

Sufficiency Economy. These tools range from the strategic level to the operational level, covering sustainability strategy, corporate governance and leadership, risk management, human resources and organizational culture, resource efficiency, supply chain management, product and services management, collaboration and private-public partnerships, technology management, and reporting and disclosure.

It must be pointed out here that although some of these tools appear similar to the tools that already exist in the West, the Thai context, local examples, challenges, and values are highlighted consistently. As the book shows, Thai business leaders and companies are increasingly using these tools, but many could be more effectively applied in the name of sustainability.

Thailand's Sustainable Business Guide also examines the sustainability opportunities and challenges encountered in different sectors in the kingdom, ranging from agribusiness, food and beverage, energy, manufacturing, state-owned enterprises, fisheries and marine resources, tourism, retailing, real estate, healthcare, financial services, transportation, and SMEs. If sustainable development is to be truly achieved, businesses in the same sector must

Thai business leaders and companies are increasingly using these tools, but many could be more effectively appplied in the name of sustainability.

begin to cooperate and act with unity on some fronts in order to move their entire industries toward a more sustainable model. As the Business & Sustainable Development Commission states in 'Better Business, Better World':

"Business as usual will not achieve this market transformation. Nor will disruptive innovation by a few sustainable pioneers be enough to drive the shift: the whole sector has to move. Forward-looking business leaders are working with sector peers and stakeholders to map their collective route to a sustainable competitive playing field, identifying tipping points, prioritizing the key technologies and policy levers, developing new skill profiles and jobs, quantifying new financing requirements, and laying out the elements of a just transition."

Some challenges, lessons and themes run throughout the executive testimonials, case studies, and analyses found in

BUSINESS OPPORTUNITIES AND THE SDGS

Private sector engagement on the SDGs continues unabated. Since their announcement in 2015, today you'd be hard-pressed to find businesses that are not adopting the SDGs in one form or another. For starters, this could mean embedding the SDGs into long-term business objectives, developing initiatives to respond to specific SDGs, and mapping progress against the goals in sustainability reports. Stakeholder pressures and national policies are powerful shapers of this upward trend. Drawing from an assessment of 124 listed businesses in eight industry sectors, the Thaipat Institute's Corporate SDG Index reveals the top three SDGs receiving most business response in Thailand in order of rank:

However, when zooming out to the global level, sustainability professionals unanimously agree that society's progress on sustainable development and the SDGs "has been poor," according to survey results conducted by GlobeScan and SustainAbility of more than 500 individuals. Business leaders new to the SDGs who wish to make good on such opportunities can begin by heeding these six recommendations from the Business & Sustainable Development Commission:

- Build support for the SDGs as being the right growth strategy

- Regain society's trust and secure the license to operate

- Incorporate the SDGs into company strategy

- Drive the transformation to sustainable markets

- Push for a financial system oriented toward longer-term sustainable investment

- Work with policymakers to pay the true cost of natural and human resources

Thailand's Sustainable Business Guide. They are suggestive of some larger recommendations and conclusions that may be drawn about the application of sustainability and SEP in Thailand. These are:

- **Sustainability is first and foremost a mindset based on a belief in the values, social benefits, and business opportunities that applying its principles will create.**

- **Sustainability initiatives in many Thai companies are scattered and lack unity. Sustainability should inform every aspect of corporate strategy, from board appointments, talent management, and capital allocation to reporting efforts.**

- **Sustainability and SEP are not a luxury for only large companies to indulge in. SMEs stand to benefit as much as listed companies from the market opportunities and best practices, if not more so.**

- **Sustainability and SEP cannot be applied without proper leadership from the CEO and board of directors. Strong ethics and values must be reflected by top management and communicated clearly to employees for the whole organization to be successful.**

- **The creation of a dedicated sustainability team may be one step toward sustainability but all departments (from risk to human resources) and staff (from management to entry-level hires) should be engaged and work to manage the material issues and contribute to the larger sustainability goals of a company.**

- **There is a lot of activity in the sustainability movement in Thailand, but one of the common challenges is increasing cooperation and creating effective partnerships so that the lessons and values are more widely shared and implemented. This means that more private sector partnerships with NGOs, government ministries, and universities must be created.**

- **Businesses should cooperate with each other to raise standards on an industry-wide scale. The private sector in Thailand is well positioned and empowered to shape government policy on such issues.**

- **Sustainability often relies on innovation. A lack of investment in research and development is limiting Thailand's potential, and a lack of investment in human resource development is exacerbating the skills shortage among the workforce. Companies must continuously invest in both their people and their operations to remain competitive in the future.**

The launch of the Sustainable Development Goals (SDGs) or 'Global Goals' by the United Nations in 2015 has galvanized action around the world.

Innovations do not need to be focused solely on technological improvements, but can be incremental and occur within many departments of a business.

- Both consumers and employees, especially the younger generation, are eager for both products and jobs with a sense of social or environmental purpose. This generation will drive the future of sustainability in your organization.

- Supply chains offer both risk and opportunities. Companies must take responsibility for the behavior of their suppliers and can also reap the benefits and new value of improving the performance of suppliers to spread sustainability throughout the value chain.

- Overall, much effort is expended on the "form" of sustainability in Thailand. Companies are branding products and creating reports to herald their green credentials and receive awards or recognition. However, the real successes of sustainability can only be measured through the real value they create for a company's business, its people, society, and the environment. Once more Thai businesses achieve more meaningful successes in this area, other companies are sure to follow in their path.

- The risk of not acting may be too great. Food safety and security, climate change, corruption, and other issues put the entire Thai private sector and economy at risk.

Even if you think you know all about corporate sustainability, even if you think your corporate practices are perfect, and even if you are totally confident in Western management philosophy and practices, we invite you to take a careful look at the application of the Sufficiency Economy Philosophy and the sustainability practices and principles featured here. We trust that being open-minded, you will be rewarded with some practical examples relevant to your context, and can adapt them to your own circumstances to ensure greater corporate sustainability in your organization and for the benefit of future generations.

PART 2

How to Implement Sustainability in your Company

How can companies begin their sustainability journey? This should start at the very top with sustainability strategy formulation and corporate governance, and a push for improvements in resource management efficiency and sustainable supply chain management, collaborating through partnerships, creating shared value – and finally, reporting on performance.

In this section, we provide practical guidance on how companies can integrate sustainability into various aspects of their organization. Each of the **ten articles** feature **toolboxes** of useful resources, **insights** from practitioners and business executives, **case studies** of sustainability in practice, and lastly, list ways that companies can **take action** going forward.

By presenting a balance of approaches commonly adopted by Thai companies and international best practices, these "how to" guidelines are tangible means through which Thai businesses can build their own sustainable enterprise.

Sustainability Strategy

- *To ensure the successful implementation of a sustainability strategy, a company must achieve 'buy-in' across the entire organization. This is most easily achieved when led from the top.*

- *As sustainability practices often already exist in a company, it is not necessary to start from scratch when fleshing out a sustainability strategy.*

- *Conducting a materiality assessment is essential to identify and prioritize the issues most important to a particular business and its stakeholders, and to make sure that efforts and resources are allocated in a manner that will produce the best results.*

For many of the world's leading companies, sustainability is at the heart of their business. The decisions and actions they take, and the way they run their operations revolve around the understanding that companies can no longer afford to achieve long-term growth and profitability at the expense of society and the environment. Idealistic though it may seem now, sustainability integration is fundamental to future business success. And it all starts with a well-planned, visionary sustainability strategy.

A strategy can very well define the course of action and priorities a company takes on environmental, social, and governance issues, and allows for better resource allocation for long-term value creation. It must be anchored by strong leadership and active engagement with all stakeholders – from the business owner to the board of directors, as well as the employees working in operations and the surrounding communities.

An integrated mindset across the company is essential. Hundreds of sustainability or corporate social responsibility (CSR) initiatives will not do justice to the impact of having a strong organizational culture driving sustainability forward. That, coupled with awareness on the part of employees and top-level management, can truly help a company recognize the risks and opportunities that will shape its future.

In Thailand, sustainability is increasingly accepted as the way forward for business. Its premises seamlessly intertwine with King Bhumibol Adulyadej's Sufficiency Economy Philosophy (SEP). Drawn from decades of His Majesty's development work as well as the ethical tenets of Buddhism, SEP has provided a foundation for sustainable growth applicable to enterprises big and small. During his annual birthday speech in 1998, His Majesty said:

"Sufficiency means to lead a reasonably comfortable life, without excess and over-indulgence in luxury, but enough. Some things may seem to be extravagant, but if it brings happiness, it is permissible, as long as it is within the means of the individual. Some translate 'sufficiency' from English as: to stand on one's own feet. This means standing on our own two legs planted on the ground, so we can remain without falling over, and without asking others to lend us their legs to stand on."

Interest in sustainability continues to be healthy, but the prevailing opinion among business executives is that adoption is rather slow. "What we don't often see in Thailand is companies using this mindset, SEP or sustainability, to lead their business," says Nat Vanitchyangkul, partner, ASEAN Corporates at Environmental Resources Management (ERM). "Sustainability is still being adopted as a framework to manage environmental and social issues, but not as a philosophy or concept to manage business," he explains. "There is not enough effort being put into it, so this results in significant differences between the mindset of the Thai business community and that of global sustainability leaders."

Rather than being a driver of value, innovation, or better returns on capital, sustainability is usually limited to risk and reputational management purposes – siloed to the periphery of a company's activities. This translates to heavy emphasis on CSR activities, awards, sustainability reports, and aspirations for Dow Jones Sustainability Indices listings. With some exceptions, sustainability among smaller businesses is typically an afterthought, or is not on the radar at all. Businesses today are nevertheless gradually responding to pressure from the public and civil society sectors, striving to achieve the United Nations' Sustainable Development Goals (SDGs), and embracing what some call 'CSR in-process' instead of 'CSR after-process.' Views on stakeholder engagement are slowly shifting as well, as companies realize they are more exposed to reputational risks from increased public participation on social media platforms such as Line, Twitter, and Facebook.

The starting point

Creating a sustainable company does not mean starting over from scratch. It involves playing to one's existing strengths and unique characteristics to develop an approach that is compatible with, and builds upon, core business objectives. Most importantly, you have to begin with a clear sustainability vision.

"Once you have a vision supported by tangible plans and a long-term commitment, that is a 50-percent enabler," says Sangob Auloong,

The corporate headquarters of SCG, Thailand's long-time sustainability pioneer. Pictured here is the company's certified LEED Platinum 100th Year Building and solar rooftop panels.

vice president of operations at Interface, a global carpet manufacturing company with operations in Thailand. Once this is achieved it becomes far easier to generate 'buy-in' across the organization, secure financing and resources, and ensure that sustainability is as valued by top management as any other business imperative.

"Sustainability is still being adopted as a framework to manage environmental and social issues, but not as a philosophy or concept to manage business."

SCG, Thailand's long-time sustainability pioneer, aspires to become "a regional market leader, contributing to the sustainable progress of ASEAN and local communities" where it operates; to be recognized as "an innovative workplace of choice, and a role model in corporate governance and sustainability." Examples of SCG's strategies to reach those ambitions include the company's successful SCG Eco Value and SCG Eldercare Solutions product lines (see *Products and Services*, page 112). In addition, a 2017 survey by Work Venture found that SCG was the top

STAGES OF SUSTAINABILITY INTEGRATION

The United Nations Global Compact (UNGC), a voluntary initiative of the UN designed to encourage global businesses to implement universal sustainability principles and take steps to support UN goals, has put forward the Sustainability Stages model representing a company's typical journey to sustainability integration.

Sustainability Stages Model

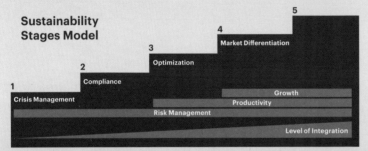

Stage 1
Crisis Management
A reactive approach to sustainability, focusing on short-term problem-solving, minimizing legal liability and protecting the brand.

Stage 2
Compliance
A focus on compliance with the law, and all labor, environmental, health, and safety regulations. Initiatives to improve environmental and social performance are managed as costs with little perceived additional value. Corporate sustainability is given "lip-service."

Stage 3
Optimization
Potential gains from sustainability beyond compliance and risk management are realized. A focus on reducing costs, increasing productivity, and reducing negative social impacts, with small-scale but highly visible projects. However, initiatives are marginalized from leadership and strategy, and implemented by specialized functions within the company.

Stage 4
Market Differentiation
Sustainability is viewed as investments and opportunities. An emphasis on sustainability-driven innovation, differentiation, and growth. Partnerships with diverse stakeholders and public policy advocacy are sources of innovation and market creation.

Stage 5
Purpose Driven
Sustainability is inseparable from a company's core vision, mission, and brand. Companies are driven by values-based commitments, and are more likely to seize new opportunities for shared value without being distracted by short-term gains from unsustainable business practices and products.

employer of choice among Gen Y employees and graduates.

Once a well-articulated vision is developed, goals and plans should organically follow. Companies must first take an introspective look at their strengths, weaknesses, and impacts across the value chain, then outline what is required to reach those objectives. A materiality exercise to determine which issues should be the company's top priorities is a practical next step to consolidating efforts, and will be discussed later on.

It is likely that sustainable practices already exist within most organizations, albeit in a piecemeal fashion. This was the case at Minor International, one of the largest hospitality and leisure companies in the Asia-Pacific region. Chompan Kulnides, vice president of investment and sustainability at Minor explains, "We looked at the inventory list of what we had done so far, and found that in pockets of places we had actually integrated sustainability into our operations without knowing it." The company's self-analysis concluded that sustainability is "not something new, but just about linking it back a bit more to the business and understanding the win-win implications of sustainability."

The same goes for small- to medium-sized enterprises (SMEs). Though the sentiment is often that sustainability is out of their reach, demanding time and resources they don't have, Sangob points out that "sustainability is much more tangible once you break it down into components." In his view, SMEs wanting to adopt sustainability just need "a model sustainable SME" to look to for guidance on strategy and best practices. In fact, there is no shortage of examples – Dhanabadee Ceramic and PlanToys are two (see *Human Resources and Organizational Culture*, page 72 and *Manufacturing*, page 212).

While sustainability is more accessible these days given the large quantity of available tools, resources, and best practices, its uptake in Thailand remains slow due to several factors.

Externally, operational context, competition, and market forces in each industry sector play varying roles in incentivizing or discouraging companies. Regulations for listed companies on the Stock Exchange of Thailand (SET) are progressively tackling these issues, but even so, the danger is that companies will resort to acting out of compliance rather than a genuine belief in the benefits of sustainability.

Internally, achieving buy-in continues to be difficult given limited collaboration between departments and the barriers imposed by organizational structure and corporate culture (or a lack thereof). What's common among Thai companies is that a sustainability team assumes responsibility for sustainability integration and strategy-setting without the active participation of other critical departments like corporate strategy, risk management (see *Risk Management*, page 62), finance, and human resources. The opposite approach would be to have no sustainability

Former Thai prime minister Anand Panyarachun (right) with UN secretary-general Kofi Annan and former prime minister of Norway Gro Harlem Brundtland in New York in 2004. Each leader has helped push the global sustainability movement forward.

department at all, which is the ultimate goal for the furniture giant IKEA. In their view, sustainability should be the shared responsibility of everyone in the organization.

The role of leaders

Successful sustainability integration and implementation stems from the combined commitments of the CEO and management, who should inspire others with their vision and purpose. Think of Paul Polman of Unilever and Elon Musk of Tesla. Having the buy-in of visionary, risk-taking leaders guarantees that sustainability is embedded in corporate culture and day-to-day work – a difficult feat to accomplish.

Whether a company is an SME, a state-owned enterprise, or family-owned business influences how sustainability can be incorporated into the organization. Likewise, organizational structure itself is a factor. At Minor International, senior executives and the board of directors annually review the company's five-year sustainability strategy. The Chief People Officer, Minor's highest level sustainability executive, has a key performance indicator (KPI) linked to the strategy that is deployed to each department. "With the very top executives and C-levels on board, the next challenge is to bring it down [to other levels]," says Chompan.

KRIP ROJANASTIEN, *CEO of Chiva-Som International Health Resorts, discusses how sustainability defines Chiva-Som and what it takes to make it work.*

How does sustainability guide your decision-making at Chiva-Som?

Sustainability to us means sustainable business practices: how you develop your business going forward, on what principles, what guidelines. We're not talking just environmental preservation, clean air and energy efficiency, waste minimization – all of those, to us, are regular practices that we have done since the beginning. What we operate on is called the 'quadruple bottom line.' Number one, naturally, is the business bottom line – the profits to make the business sustainable. Without it you can't have a business.

We are in the wellness business, so we think that it should be 'wellness for all stakeholders' – not just the clients who are our focus – but our staff, business partners, and the community around us. You can't be promoting personal wellness without the wellness of everyone around you and the environment. Because of that, we believe in environmental stewardship.

Business impacts resources. When you're building something on an empty piece of land, you're creating environmental impact, whether you like it or not. So, how do we minimize that? The fabric of the community and society around us need to be continually strengthened because of the impact of development and urbanization. It causes a breakdown of the traditional social structure, community life, and social fabrics. We need to help them sustain the unique features that they have, the traditions they've embraced over generations: things that make us unique as Thais. So that's our other bottom line: sociocultural development.

Whatever we do in planning for the future has to satisfy all of these bottom lines. Every year, as you know, businesses look for growth – how much bigger of a bottom line can you get, how much more profitable and efficient, and so on. But if you keep growing, and we only have so many resources on the planet, what is the point? The point should be how to best maintain what we have and how to maximize what we have – which is not always about outright growth or driving GDP.

What key pieces of advice would you give to other business leaders on embedding sustainability into their DNA?

When we talk wellness, we have to live it. Who's going to believe you when you say you should eat this, do that? You build credibility from leading by example.

Vanus Taepaisitphongse, CEO of Betagro Group, an integrated agro-industrial and food producer, acknowledges the difficulty of convincing employees about Betagro's holistic approach to sustainable development. "I use my power as the CEO [to move it forward]," he says, reflecting a lead-by-example mentality.

Smaller companies, by contrast, may have it easier. According to Nat of ERM, "SMEs can move faster than larger corporations because they are generally owned by individuals, so their decision-making processes aren't as hindered by complex hierarchical structures, pressures to meet KPIs, and the differing opinions of members on a board of directors."

Top-level management do not always get involved, however, and this is a major impediment for companies, regardless of size.

Employees understandably have a far harder time getting management on board than the other way around. And so, sustainability integration needs to happen both ways, from the top-down and the ground-up.

Power of the people

"You have to have confidence in the value of people," says Numpol Limprasert, sustainable development director at SCG. "The leader is very important, but what makes sustainability successful is the involvement of all."

Not everyone within a company has the same degree of influence on decisions, nor do they have the same level of sustainability knowledge. This means that at the minimum there should be active efforts towards employee development and knowledge-sharing on these issues.

TOOLBOX ENGAGING WITH STAKEHOLDERS

Stakeholders can exert substantial influence on a company, positively and negatively. Effective stakeholder engagement needs to be proactive, strategic, and focused on the issues that matter. The following points can serve as a guide when designing your company's engagement approach.

Define the purpose of engagement. Be clear in what you want out of your engagment and ensure that this purpose is strategic. Engagement should not be done only in the aftermath of a crisis, or used as a PR tool. Consider a holistic and methodological approach instead of an ad hoc style. In this way, efforts are linked to strategic goals and material issues.

Identify key stakeholder groups. Carry out stakeholder mapping and prioritize the most important groups. If some stakeholders are not engaged, why is that the case? What are the specific needs and interests of each

group? It is especially important to empower the marginalized and vulnerable to participate on issues that matter to them.

Determine the format, frequency, and level of engagement. There cannot be a one-size-fits-all approach to engagement, so companies should instead adopt a multi-pronged approach tailored to each group. What should be the frequency of engagement? Consider applying systems thinking and promote two-way communication.

Outline issues for engagement. Engagement is more impactful when it is issue-based, particularly if tied to material issues.

Delegate roles and responsibilities. This process heavily involves soft skills, which are not frequently learned in a classroom. Assigning the right people can make all the

difference. Don't delegate tasks to those on the ground in operations without equipping them with the right and necessary skills. If there is a gap in the availability of individuals who can carry out such tasks, be sure to invest in human capital development, as well as in training.

Assess results. Continuously monitor and assess effectiveness, and identify gaps. Determine suitable measurement indicators that align with the company's strategic priorities and internal targets. Refrain from developing superficial indicators for one-time events that don't reflect the bigger picture.

Report and disclose. Be transparent about engagement results and the issues that matter to stakeholders, which is a sure-fire way to earn trust. Share lessons learned and openly address how the company is taking steps to respond to concerns.

In 2015, PTT, Thailand's multinational energy company, introduced a company-wide sustainability training program for all of its staff, from top-level management to employees working in operations and subsidiaries. The course is now included as part of mandatory annual training at the PTT Leadership and Learning Institute.

To move from learning to application, it is crucial to tap into the distinct capabilities of each department and put the right person in place to handle the right job. For example, if human rights is a key concern in a company's supply chain, having a risk officer handle these issues could be less effective than appointing those with long-standing knowledge of working in supply chain management.

Here, an intimate understanding of a company and its employees will help in figuring out what works, and where skills or knowledge gaps remain. And given the boundary-less nature of modern-day businesses, all stakeholders – not just employees – should be involved in the setting of a sustainability strategy (to the extent that each group is relevant).

A stakeholder can refer to any individual or group that is impacted by, and has an impact on, a business. Consider for example the influence of local communities on a company's license to operate, or customer boycotts on reputation. Regardless of whether a company procures products from Chonburi, extracts natural gas from Myanmar, or harvests fish from the Indian Ocean, its relationships with

STAKEHOLDER ENGAGEMENT: TRENDS TO WATCH

Communication, Connectivity, and Hyper Transparency	**Individual Empowerment and the Rise of the Middle Class**	**The Demographic Shift and Automation of Work**	**Climate Change and Water Resources**	**Supply Chain Oversight Ramps Up**
• Transparency, timeliness, and accountability will be key operating principles for companies. • Focus on real-time and simultaneous management of global and local stakeholders. • Companies operate with the belief that everything they say and do could become public.	• Growth in demand for fulfillment of individual human rights. • Civil society circling in on concepts of human rights, environmental justice and transparency. • Call for business involvement in promoting inclusive economic growth and reducing inequalities.	• The threat of automation pressures jobs and wages. • Reevaluation of how companies can drive equitable shared value creation as job opportunities decline. • Business support for community resilience will be scrutinized and its impact measured.	• Convergence of human rights and climate justice challenges corporate environmental practices. • Pressing need for community water partnerships and better water resources management. • Investments in ecosystems become a priority.	• Expanded regulations on supply chain management and increased scrutiny of poor governance practices. • Call for balance in supply chain oversight and capacity-building. • Companies with proactive and transparent supply chains will dominate.

Source: BSR – The Future of Stakeholder Engagement (2016)

CASE STUDY	Interface's 'Mission Zero' Strategy Gains Traction

THE CHALLENGE: Interface, one of the world's largest modular carpet manufacturers, embarked in 1994 on 'Mission Zero,' an ambitious journey to become the world's first environmentally sustainable and restorative company. Spearheaded by visionary leader Ray Anderson, Mission Zero was the company's promise to eliminate any negative impacts on the environment by 2020.

That mission – well on track to fulfillment – has been carried out across operations in over 110 countries, including the company's Chonburi plant. Now called the "Climate Take Back" mission, Interface's aspirations are focused on reversing the negative impacts of climate change through four principles: Live Zero, Love Carbon, Let Nature Cool, and Lead Industrial Re-revolution. As with Mission Zero, all operations work toward this end goal of minimizing climate change. The challenge is how a plant in Thailand can match the far-reaching expectations of a global company while working within its own local context.

THE SOLUTION: According to Interface, the way forward is a matter of starting with what you have and systematically addressing gaps toward your vision. Interface Thailand grapples with everything from traditional sustainability activities, like planting trees and managing water treatments, to more progressive initiatives, like becoming Thailand's first LEED accredited manufacturing plant and constructing rooftop solar panels. The company has even bought green energy credits from a solar farm in Kanchanaburi province to offset electricity use in their quest to generate 100 percent of energy from renewable sources. Currently Interface is also looking to partner with local Thai energy companies to offset their LPG use. This, along with all other initiatives, will be captured in their 'Gap to Zero' metric that is used to monitor

Interface's Chonburi plant works to eliminate negative impacts on the environment.

progress towards Mission Zero. When it comes to sharing this mission with others, overcoming the barrier of budget-conscious Asian customers remains a challenge, explains Sangob Auloong, vice president of operations. "You must take a leadership position," he says, "getting out there and spreading awareness on the benefits of sustainable products, even if it sometimes means creating the market demand yourself." Though that admittedly translates to Interface absorbing some of the initial costs and finding ways to offset them, this approach delivers long-term results.

THE BENEFITS: The most tangible benefit that these sustainability efforts offer is the opportunity to access new markets and customers: Interface is always among the top contenders in a bidding process. Because their pioneering efforts have made them the standard to which other companies can aspire, they can differentiate themselves by providing another sustainability dimension to purchasing decisions beyond cost. For instance, their designs for the Urban Retreat line – a collection of tile designs inspired by nature – are embedded with a sustainability story, building on biomimicry and biophilia concepts to make the indoor environment a more welcoming place.

"Interface's success comes from its success in sustainability," says Sangob. So, it comes as no surprise that the company was recognized for the 20th consecutive year in GlobeScan and SustainAbility's annual Sustainability Leaders survey.

The late Ray Anderson set Interface on the transformative path towards sustainability.

stakeholders extend past physical boundaries. That's why securing the trust and backing of key stakeholder groups is an impactful way to drive the sustainability agenda, manage risks, and create shared value through partnerships (see *Collaboration*, page 134).

Securing the trust and backing of key stakeholder groups is an impactful way to drive the sustainability agenda.

Thai Summit Automotive Group, for instance, works with both its big-name customers and SME suppliers to uphold an exemplary safety standard throughout its supply chain. "The consequences of poor safety can be extremely costly," says Dr Chatkaew Hart-rawung, managing director. He notes that customers like Toyota will not buy from suppliers with a poor safety record or inadequate safety measures.

With so many courses of action available for different sustainability issues and countless stakeholders with whom to engage, companies can turn to materiality as the solution to prioritize one's most urgent concerns in a strategic and systematic way.

Focusing on the material

A materiality assessment is a strategic exercise designed to identify and prioritize the set of issues most important, or 'material,' to a company and its stakeholders. Once an issue is classified as material, it should be managed, measured, and reported on.

While traditionally confined to the financial and regulatory reporting arena, global sustainability authorities have concurred via the International Integrated Reporting Council's Corporate Reporting Dialogue that on sustainability matters, "material information is any information which is reasonably capable of making a difference to the conclusions stakeholders may draw when reviewing related information."

Using material issues as the basis for a strategy ensures that a company's efforts and resources are being directed to the right places. A 2017 report by MIT and Boston Consulting Group stated: "Companies that focus on material issues report up to 50% more profits from sustainability activities than those that do not. Those that don't...struggle to add value from their sustainability activities."

Determining if an issue is material or not depends on how a company evaluates its risks

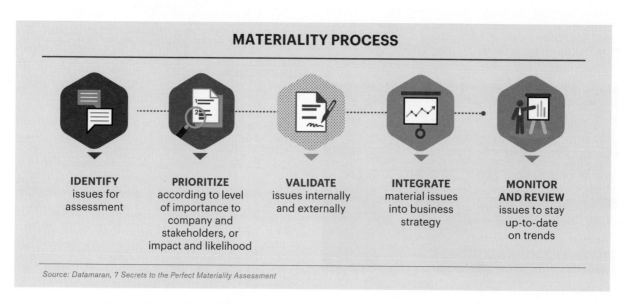

MATERIALITY PROCESS

IDENTIFY
issues for
assessment

PRIORITIZE
according to level
of importance to
company and
stakeholders, or
impact and likelihood

VALIDATE
issues internally
and externally

INTEGRATE
material issues
into business
strategy

**MONITOR
AND REVIEW**
issues to stay
up-to-date
on trends

Source: Datamaran, 7 Secrets to the Perfect Materiality Assessment

CASE STUDY | Chiva-Som's 'Quadruple Bottom Line' and Responsible Expansion

THE CHALLENGE: The success of world-renowned health and wellness resort and spa, Chiva-Som, rests not only on the top-quality service it provides, but also its long-term commitment to sustainability. Since its establishment in 1995, Chiva-Som has had every opportunity to expand its services worldwide. For CEO Krip Rojanastien, however, it was more prudent to avoid the strategy of unrelenting growth that currently defines so many hospitality industry players.

"Our long-term target is not to grow beyond six Chiva-Som properties around the world," says Krip. "We don't want to grow to 60. We'd rather have this brand and impact the world in a different way. I'd rather have it impact people for what it stands for, not what it is earning." Part of what the brand stands for is sustainability, and so the question remains: how can Chiva-Som manage that growth without risking the responsible leadership from which the resort made its name?

Chiva-Som's organic farm supplies healthy ingredients to its kitchens.

THE SOLUTION: When the company eventually made the decision to expand, first to Bintan Island, Indonesia, it did so upon the defining principles of their sustainability commitment – the 'quadruple bottom line' of CSR. Comprising integrated stakeholder wellness, environmental stewardship, sociocultural development, and economic sustainability, this holistic approach guides Chiva-Som in all of its decisions on expansion.

"We insist on this with our partners as necessary, and they very much share this view," Krip explains. "We have to agree with all the decisions they make – that's the condition. The suppliers, the designers, consultants, and material selection, we are involved in all of that."

The new facilities in Indonesia – which are planned to be ten times the size of Chiva-Som in Prachuap Khiri Khan province – will be designed to the LEED Gold Green Building standard, complete with solar power, water recycling, and comprehensive waste reduction initiatives. The goal is to minimize the resort's environmental impacts. A pristine 40-acre mangrove forest next to the resort will be preserved, and protected against becoming a multi-use complex. The partners must adhere to Chiva-Som's sustainability policy and budget at least US$2,500 per room, per year for sustainability purposes.

As a testament to the company's sociocultural sensitivities, Krip is also strongly in favor of helping Indonesian partners establish their own brand personality: "We're working very hard to integrate the Indonesian wellness practices, *jamu*, into our menu if the principles don't conflict, and we've found that they do not," he says. "Wellness is the same everywhere. It crosses boundaries, because who doesn't want to be well?"

Chiva-Som is restoring mangroves in Hua Hin with the support of the local community.

THE BENEFITS: Adopting a strong sustainability mindset from the very beginning helps the company compete in an ever-growing wellness industry, which expanded at the rate of ten percent from 2013 to 2015 and was valued globally at an estimated US$3.7 trillion dollars. On a more general level, Krip adds, "Benefits come in the form of the visitors that we have – they are high-value and low-impact." By integrating local cultural elements, working closely with partners, and committing to environmental preservation, Chiva-Som offers a truly holistic definition of wellness.

DR DONATO CALACE, *director of innovation at Datamaran, a London-based business intelligence provider, talks about the present and future of materiality and how Datamaran's cutting-edge work with data is redefining this field.*

What is your opinion of current companies' approaches to materiality assessments?
Current materiality assessments need to be more data driven and auditable to respond to the new challenges of integrated thinking. Until today, most companies had relied on surveys to do materiality assessments. They were sending questionnaires to their community stakeholders and assessing them with different methodologies.

It is an important way to keep you in touch with close stakeholders where you have the most impact. But the problem with this approach is in the scope of your analysis. If you only have a questionnaire with hundreds of stakeholders, you are living in a certain 'bubble vision' compared to the availability [of data] that you have today over the internet, public sources, and so on.

A challenge that often emerges is the different timeframes for material issues and their impacts. How would you address that?
It's all about data. The next trend in terms of analytical approach concerns ongoing or continuous materiality assessments. The traditional materiality assessment

allows you to do it once every year, in the best case, and in the worst case once every two years. But this gives you a pretty static definition of materiality and a static database as well. What we are adopting here is a continuous approach, in the sense that if you look at the different sources of materiality, all these change over a different timeframe.

Social media changes very quickly, for example, and it gives you an indication of what topics, at a certain moment, are linked to controversies or emerging risks. Other sources, like regulations, change less often, but they have a big impact.

How could a company move toward this approach?
Technology is the enabler. That's why our approach here is so different. We leverage data that is available out there, we use our artificial intelligence to analyze it because the information is raw, it is unstructured. But if you have a framework to analyze it and the tool to do so, then that information becomes usable. It's not about creating new sources of data, it's about analyzing them with the right tools.

How do you see materiality evolving over the long term?
My vision is that in the future, there won't be any more financial and non-financial issues. There will be only strategic or non-strategic issues. In this sense, materiality is a pivotal process in terms of strategy making and risk assessment, not only in the scope of reporting activities.

What are the benefits of using data for materiality assessments?
When you bring in data, which is auditable, is proven, then you can get buy-in and you are credible. This is essentially the big change in the ESG approach in sustainability. It's not a matter of ideology or PR anymore, it's all about data demonstrating the linkage between issues and impacts. And when you recognize the potential and impact of this data, and start integrating other departments in the exercise, you'll realize that you want more information and structure. This helps you become a better decision-maker.

TOOLBOX | **CONDUCTING A MATERIALITY ASSESSMENT**

A materiality assessment is essentially a management tool. It can help a company anticipate and manage emerging risks and opportunities, monitor social climates, changing regulations, and the like.

First, be clear about why you are undertaking a materiality assessment. The following steps can serve as a common baseline to move forward:

1. Identify issues for assessment. Data could be sourced from:

- Global and national trends (such as demographics, consumer preferences)

- Benchmarks against competitors and industry peers

- News, media sources, and social media (Facebook, Twitter, Line)

- Rules, regulations, and policies in countries of operation

- Stakeholder concerns (internal and external stakeholders such as NGOs, government, investors, employees, and communities)

- Existing selections of material issues and indicators from the SDGs, Global Reporting Initiative, Dow Jones Sustainability Indices, Sustainability Accounting Standards Board Materiality Map, Datamaran (eRevalue)'s emerging issues radar, and more.

Your issue universe should not be restricted to traditional ESG factors like health, safety, and biodiversity. Trends point to the greater inclusion of risk and financial indicators such as digitization and financial solvency – a telltale sign that materiality should not be the sole domain of sustainability departments.

2. Prioritize issues according to their level of importance to the company and stakeholders. Key internal and external stakeholder groups must be involved in this exercise, as well as top management.

Issues are typically presented in a materiality matrix, with significant impacts to business and strategic priorities indicated on the x-axis, and to stakeholders on the y-axis.

Given the subjectivity of the process, difficulties could arise when deciding which issue will affect the company, how, and when one will manifest in the form of financial impacts over the short, medium, and long term.

3. Validate selected issues internally and externally. Is the list of material issues representative of the company, its strategic priorities, and stakeholder interests or concerns? Have they received buy-in from senior management and relevant parties?

4. Integrate material issues into business strategy. To be impactful, a strong business case must be made for top issues and framed in a way that creates buy-in from leadership and key stakeholders.

5. Review and monitor issues regularly to remain abreast of evolving trends. Companies tend to revisit their material issues every one to two years, making materiality quite static. Instead, be proactive in anticipating changes over time by leveraging data and technology to capture emerging issues.

Sources: Datamaran (eRevalue) and Global Reporting Initiative

---

and opportunities, short- to long-term strategic objectives and business drivers, stakeholders, and so on. It also requires looking beyond obvious business-as-usual factors like gaining market share, revenue, and mergers and acquisitions.

The assessment outcome could reveal that a company's main focus should be water use, nutrition, innovation, or even responsible alcoholic consumption. Or it could point to weaknesses and risks in current supply chain management practices, and opportunities

for financial benefits from improved resource management efficiency.

The cross-cutting nature of material issues implies that multiple departments will often need to collaborate to manage those most relevant to them. An issue must therefore be framed in the language of those in the decision-making seats, and also upheld by a solid business rationale. For example, if an oil and gas company wishes to respond to climate change through a shift to energy storage and renewable energy technologies,

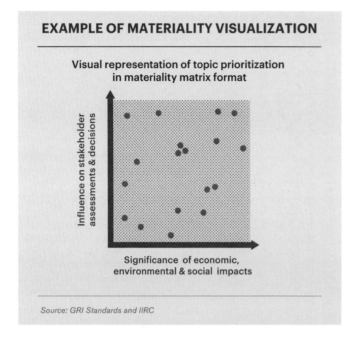

EXAMPLE OF MATERIALITY VISUALIZATION

Visual representation of topic prioritization
in materiality matrix format

Influence on stakeholder
assessments & decisions

Significance of economic,
environmental & social impacts

Source: GRI Standards and IIRC

arguing that it is good for society and complies with the Paris Agreement or SDGs will not suffice. The costs of this move would need to be calculated into potential scenarios, with accompanying risks and impacts on the business portfolio and bottom line defined.

SCG has recently taken the initiative to develop separate sets of material issues for all three of its business units: SCG Cement-Building Materials, SCG Chemicals, and SCG Packaging. In explaining the rationale behind this, Dr Patima Sinthupinyo, sustainable development consultant at the Center of Excellence and Sustainability of SCG, says, "It was essential that our [business units] understood how the material issues impacted them in their own contexts. That allows them to tailor responses specifically to their own business."

How each issue is managed in the company varies as well. "Some issues have targets and policies in place first, then a committee is established to support it. Others may already have a department, secretariat, or working team managing the issue before targets are established," says Numpol Limprasert, SCG's sustainable development director. An example

of the former is SCG's target to reduce GHG emissions per production unit by 10 percent from the base year 2007. Set back in 2008, the target precedes the formulation of SCG's Climate Change Policy and the SCG Climate Change Committee.

"Regular progress evaluations are needed to assess if a target is well on track," he adds. "If not, we need to seek additional support from executives, working teams, or committees." A reflection of this is the fact that the company's Sustainable Development Structure comprises 11 committees overseeing numerous issues.

For SMEs, a comprehensive materiality assessment may not be the best option due to resource constraints. They could instead begin by developing an awareness of the direct and indirect impacts of their activities. "The impacts of a single SME are not as relevant as those of multinationals," says Dr Donato Calace, director of innovation at Datamaran, a London-based business intelligence company. "They become relevant as a group – the aggregation of all SMEs."

"It would be important to have industry associations working with SMEs to provide them with guidance and standardized sector-based tools for understanding and reporting their impacts," Calace adds. Even so, he has yet to see an organization moving in that direction. "[At Datamaran] we are helping larger businesses remain on the right track. Businesses are exploring the strategic benefits they can get out of a data-driven materiality assessment."

The leap forward

Integrating sustainability is a work in progress for most companies in Thailand. But the business case exists for them to take the leap and grasp opportunities from sustainability, as well as to connect existing (yet sporadic) sustainability efforts in a more holistic manner. While this may still be about survival at the core, sustainability will be the new normal for business – a distinguishing feature that sets institutions apart from competitors. If companies do not move fast enough, those who are unsustainable may cease to exist.

TAKE ACTION

To integrate sustainability into your organization, bear in mind two essentials: (1) the sustainability priorities and objectives should align with your core business strategy, and (2) they should leverage your strengths.

The following recommendations should be adapted when appropriate.

1. Develop a sustainability vision that aligns with your long-term business objectives and strategies. Ensure it is practical and attainable.

2. Conduct a materiality assessment to determine the sustainability issues that make up your company's top priorities. When conducting the assessment, ask these important questions:

- Are all relevant parties or departments involved in the process? This could include business owners, senior management, as well as strategy, risk management, sustainability, and human resources departments.

- Did the board of directors or top decision-makers and investors have a say?

- Were relevant stakeholder groups consulted for their opinions on materiality?

3. Integrate material issues into your corporate strategy, or use it as the basis to form a sustainability strategy. Helpful questions to ask are:

- Would any issues conflict with existing business priorities or the organizational structure?

- What resources are required to manage the material issues? Examples include human resources, time, technology and know-how. If there are gaps in resource availability, how will they be filled?

- Set objectives and time-bound targets for your top material issues.

- Define measurement indicators and determine the frequency of performance monitoring to assess any gaps and improvement opportunities.

4. Develop a solid business case for sustainability and the selected material issues, framing them in a way that is easily understood by relevant parties and decision-makers.

5. Create buy-in among top-level management and decision-makers for the material sustainability issues and initiatives that you have identified with thorough assessments. Are there clearly designated roles and responsibilities for the issues?

6. Embed sustainability across all levels of the organization to build a strong culture. Consider using tools such as employee training courses, knowledge-sharing sessions, and tying sustainability to key performance indicators.

7. Foster innovation on multiple levels by clearly mapping your business model and sustainability impacts (or opportunities) across the value chain. Issues to consider include:

- The areas of weaknesses and strengths that could benefit from innovation.

- Context-specific issues and challenges that must be dealt with.

- Need for investment in R&D.

- Stakeholder groups that could be most negatively impacted by your activities, and ways to mitigate that impact.

8. Consistently monitor and report progress to stakeholders. Be transparent about the company's achievements and challenges. Be sure to identify gaps in sustainability strategy implementation and ways to remedy them.

9. Engage regularly with stakeholders to advance the sustainability agenda and encourage collaboration to create shared value. Greater engagement also leads to personal investment and buy-in.

Corporate Governance & Leadership for Sustainability

- *This chapter was prepared by Thai Institute of Directors (IOD) to express views and experiences in the field of corporate governance in Thailand.*

- *Bodies such as the Stock Exchange of Thailand, the Securities and Exchange Commission, and the Thai Institute of Directors have developed useful mechanisms and tools to promote good corporate governance in the kingdom.*

- *Many smaller and private companies wrongly view governance as a 'large company' issue while larger companies are still struggling to implement corporate governance in a way that truly impacts all stakeholders.*

Corporate governance is so important in today's business world that few companies can afford to ignore it. During workshops for top executives conducted by the Thai Institute of Directors (IOD), when participants were asked what came to mind when they heard the phrase "corporate governance," answers such as integrity, transparency, accountability, and compliance were some of the more popular responses. This is a good start. While most people know that corporate governance is about things that are good and worthwhile, few know how it is formally defined.

According to the Organization for Economic Co-operation and Development (OECD), corporate governance is about procedures and processes by which an organization is directed and controlled. A corporate governance structure specifies the distribution of rights and responsibilities among the different participants in the organization, such as the board of directors, shareholders, and other stakeholders, and it lays down the rules and procedures for decision-making. To put it simply, corporate governance is about how people work together for the greater benefit of the organization.

In the context of business, it is about how the three key participants in a business – the board, shareholders, and management – work together for the benefit of the company and its stakeholders.

The key word here is stakeholders. In any business, there are many disparate individuals or groups who are directly or indirectly affected by its decisions. These comprise shareholders, employees, customers, suppliers, creditors, investors, government, regulators, the local community, and even the environment. In short, the effects of the company's decisions spread well beyond the boardroom. If the business practices of the company are accepted and supported by all stakeholders, the company's business is likely to enjoy continued growth and success, making the business sustainable. This support can only come when the company has built sufficient trust and confidence among its many stakeholders. Such trust and confidence comes more easily if the company practices good corporate governance.

Although corporate governance is an important and powerful tool, its progress in the real business world still falls far short of expectations. This is evidenced by the many corporate governance failures and scandals – even by big and reputable global companies – some with serious consequences for stakeholders and society at large. If we look at these failures closely, we find that many have been the result of 'short-termism' – prioritizing short-term profit at all costs, with no regard for other goals. As a result, there have been calls from many quarters to aggressively raise corporate governance standards, and to take the interests of shareholders and other stakeholders more adequately into account. This outcry has been especially acute since the 2008 global financial crisis.

With concerns such as climate change and rapidly depleting global resources weighing heavily on the minds of consumers and policymakers alike, good corporate governance is more crucial now than ever before. As such, company directors must shift toward prioritizing sustainability and the long-term health of their business over short-term profits. Accordingly, the success of corporate governance in steering the company should not be measured only through the lens of financial assets and the company's share price, but also through the value of intangibles, including sustainability performance, value creation, visionary leadership, ethics, adequate and effective controls, trustworthiness, reputation, and legitimacy of company operations in the eyes of all stakeholders, including the community. While this kind of holistic approach to corporate governance is gaining traction, harnessing it as a means to drive the economy and society forward remains a challenge to overcome.

CG evolution in Thailand

In Thailand, corporate governance has become of paramount importance since the 1997 Asian Financial Crisis. It was this crisis that prompted the country's leaders and top executives to recognize the danger of excessive indebtedness and the need for more prudence. In addition to policy rigidity, serious structural problems in the financial sector, and weak prudential controls, failures in corporate governance were also a major contributor to the crisis. In fact, the majority of companies

Corporate directors attend courses provided by IOD to learn about corporate governance principles and implementation.

at the time had poor corporate governance standards at all levels. Corporate governance practices were characterized by weak internal controls, poor risk management, unreliable financial reporting, incomplete financial disclosure, inadequate protection of minority shareholder rights, and the lack of effective enforcement to ensure regulatory compliance.

There have been calls from many quarters to aggressively raise corporate standards, and to take the interests of other stakeholders into account.

Boards of directors were largely ineffective in their oversight roles, enabling the dominance of family or majority shareholder control over business operations. All of this gave way to corporate abuse, conflicts of interest, and excessive leverage and risk-taking.

For Thai entrepreneurs, the prevailing view equated majority shareholding to ownership. With ownership under a limited liability entity structure, the company became an instrument of wealth creation that sought to maximize short-term profits for these 'owners' through financial leveraging and risk-taking, with no

CORPORATE GOVERNANCE PROGRESS IN THAILAND

23 the number of Thai-listed companies that received

the ASEAN Corporate Governance award in 2015.

Thailand's 2015 Corporate Governance score of

87 ranks 1st among ASEAN nations.

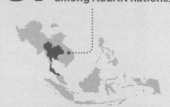

As of October 2017, **264 firms** have been certified for their implementation of effective anti-corruption policies by **Thailand's Private Sector Collective Action Coalition Against Corruption (CAC).**

855 companies have voluntarily declared to the CAC their intention to run **"clean" businesses**, as of October 2017.

Companies that participated in the 2017 Corporate Governance Report of Thai Listed Companies received an average score of

80%

at the "very good" level, marking the highest CG Score level since 2010 and up from 78% in 2016.

Sources: Asian Development Bank; Thailand's Private Sector Collective Action Coalition Against Corruption; Thai Institute of Directors

---

regard for the interests of minority shareholders and other stakeholders. Good corporate governance was not seen as a means to protect the company from failure. On the contrary, the primacy of the shareholder led to the perceived rights of the owners to intervene and influence the company's major corporate decisions according to their own wishes and financial interests. This weakened the checks and balances system inherent in a proper governance process and prevented major participants in the company from performing their roles and responsibilities in an appropriate manner.

The 1997 Asian Financial Crisis, it should be noted, also provided a strong reminder of the importance of King Bhumibol Adulyadej's Sufficiency Economy Philosophy (SEP), which called for more prudent and ethical practices as necessary for the country to truly prosper in

a more balanced way. The decision-making principles of SEP, which require honesty, careful risk management, and attention to stakeholder impacts, were consistent with the best practices of corporate governance. Its emphasis on moderation and restraint brilliantly captured the national mood of the time and further motivated the private sector to evaluate its weaknesses.

Following the Asian crisis, major reforms of corporate governance were implemented to support and ensure the robust and sustainable growth of Thailand's economy. To regulators, better corporate governance was the key to preserving the integrity of Thailand as a dynamic marketplace and a means to avoid systemic risk. For investors and the business community at large, poor governance was an investment risk and a threat to long-term business viability, performance, and returns.

Reforms centered on the efforts of the Stock Exchange of Thailand (SET) and the Securities and Exchange Commission (SEC) to improve the effectiveness of the legal and regulatory framework by introducing new laws and regulations, and to increase the efficiency of enforcement. These actions provided effective channels for protecting investor rights, such as enhanced requirements for disclosure, which created greater transparency.

In 1999, the SET issued a Code of Best Practice for Directors of Listed Companies that provides guidelines for board members regarding their roles and responsibilities. It also required listed companies to have an audit committee consisting only of independent directors. The importance of independent directors was further highlighted by subsequent regulations, which mandated that all listed companies have at least three independent directors on their boards to help reduce the risk of improper actions and strengthen checks and balances.

In 2002, fifteen corporate governance principles were developed and launched by the SET as sources of best practices in the design of listing rules, market regulations, and corporate codes for companies. The principles were subsequently revised in 2006 to bring them in line with the publication of the OECD's Principles of Corporate Governance. In 2012, a further revision was made by the SET to broaden the scope of corporate governance practices to bring them in line with international standards.

More recently the SEC, SET, and other key capital market participants, including the IOD, joined hands to develop a new Corporate Governance Code for listed companies. The new code, launched in March 2017, specifies the leadership role of the board in determining a company's strategic direction and in steering the company toward becoming a sustainable business.

Investors and other professional bodies in the private sector also played instrumental roles in enhancing overall corporate governance standards. Institutional and retail investors have been active in raising the importance of corporate governance in their investment

CORPORATE GOVERNANCE CODE 2017

1 Establish clear leadership role and responsibilities of the board

2 Define objectives that promote sustainable value creation

3 Strengthen board effectiveness

8 Ensure engagement and communication with shareholders

4 Ensure effective CEO and people management

7 Ensure disclosure and financial integrity

6 Strengthen effective risk management and internal control

5 Nurture innovation and responsible business

Source: The Securities and Exchange Commission, Thailand

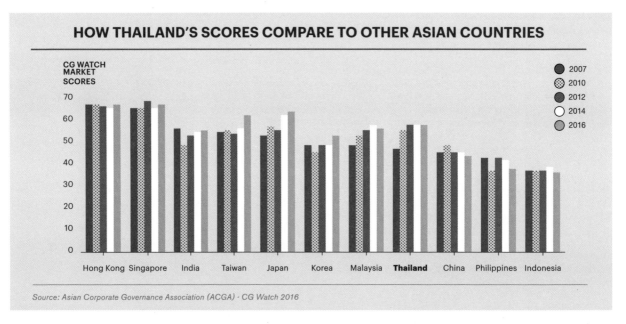

HOW THAILAND'S SCORES COMPARE TO OTHER ASIAN COUNTRIES

CG WATCH
MARKET
SCORES

- 2007
- 2010
- 2012
- 2014
- 2016

Source: Asian Corporate Governance Association (ACGA) · CG Watch 2016

decisions, and in protecting investor's rights and promoting financial literacy. In 2017, the SEC issued guidelines called the Institutional Investor Code (or I-Code) to promote corporate governance practices in the investment industry. Professional accounting and internal controls were also upgraded to international standards to create an environment suitable for effective implementation of corporate governance.

Founded in 1999, the Institute of Directors (IOD) was established to support company directors in the implementation of good corporate governance practices. It does so through a director education program, research and advocacy, knowledge building, networking, and fostering collective action against corruption. These efforts have contributed significantly to improvements in the corporate governance practices of Thai businesses. From 1999 to 2016, more than 20,000 directors from both listed and non-listed companies attended director classes at the IOD. Corporate governance scores of Thai-listed companies assessed annually by the IOD improved steadily, from a score of 50 out of 100 in 2001 to 80 in 2017. The network of companies voluntarily joining the Collective Action Coalition Against

Corruption (CAC) has rapidly expanded to reach 855 companies in October 2017 (about half are listed companies). This demonstrates the willingness of companies to commit publicly to tackling the country's most serious governance problem and shows how the business sector can be a driving force to improve corporate governance.

Thailand's progress on improving corporate governance is reflected in its performance in assessments against regional neighbors. The Corporate Governance Watch assessment by the Asian Corporate Governance Association – which covers rules and practices; enforcement; political and regulatory environment; adherence to International Generally Accepted Accounting Practices (IGAAP); and governance culture – has ranked Thailand in the top five countries in Asia since 2010. Similarly, the ASEAN CG Scorecard initiated by the ASEAN Capital Markets Forum in 2012 under the support of the Securities and Exchange Commission of ASEAN countries, found that Thai listed companies were outstanding in consistently applying corporate governance principles in line with ASEAN standards, especially the rights of shareholders and the equitable treatment of shareholders.

CASE STUDY   Businesses Tackle Corruption through Collective Action

Executives of Thai companies attend a CAC Certification Awarding Ceremony.

THE CHALLENGE: Thailand's private sector has long been aware of the negative impacts of corruption: flagging competitiveness, major investments derailed, and opportunities lost to other ASEAN countries. Globally, corruption contributes up to 25 percent to the cost of procurement contracts in developing countries. In 2016, Thailand ranked 101st in the Corruption Perceptions Index among 176 countries, according to an annual report published by Transparency International, which is based on the perceptions of foreign businesspeople.

Key conditions that have nurtured widespread corruption in Thailand include a deep-rooted patronage system, ineffective law enforcement, weak public governance and general acceptance of corruption as a necessary way of life. This cannot be overcome by the public sector alone. To successfully eradicate corruption, an orchestrated effort by all stakeholders to tackle the supply side of the corruption equation is required.

THE SOLUTION: Thailand's private sector Collective Action Coalition Against Corruption (CAC) was founded in 2010 as a platform for companies in Thailand to tackle corruption on a voluntary basis through collective action. This project has been run by the IOD, as a secretary to the CAC Council, which consists of a number of well-known business leaders and industrial experts. It aims to encourage implementation of effective anti-corruption policies and mechanisms in a bid to create a clean business environment, while it also takes an advocacy role in graft-fighting on behalf of the business sector.

Since its creation by an accord of eight influential business organizations in 2010, 855 companies have voluntarily joined

the CAC, and 244 have been certified. The CAC asks members to take three steps to address corruption: 1) implement a strong internal compliance program, 2) recruit more businesses to be part of the coalition, and 3) act as a change agent by advocating for public sector reforms.

"The reality is, if a company's budget is spent on things that don't create value, such as corruption, you are simply wasting that investment," says Vichien Phongsathorn, Chairman of Khon Thai Foundation. "The magnitude of this problem is huge. At the leadership level, CEOs need to act. They need to say that 'I will clean up'. Eventually if enough management jump on board, it will tip the scale and bring everyone in."

THE BENEFITS: By joining the CAC, companies are helping to establish a mechanism to prevent corruption, one that should substantially reduce the legal and reputational risks of members. Joining shows that a company adheres to clean and transparent business principles, which can make it more attractive to investors and other stakeholders, and give it a competitive edge over industry peers.

Many certified companies have undertaken substantial efforts to persuade their suppliers and other stakeholders to also adopt anti-corruption policies and install graft prevention mechanisms. Should all CAC members take similar steps, a clean business culture would soon prevail and become the norm in the Thai economic system.

Endemic corruption and cronyism are impediments to sustainable development.

Residents walk amid the towers of Bangkok's central business district, the nerve center of the corporate world.

Current weaknesses of CG in Thailand

Despite the progress made, many serious shortcomings remain. These are revealed by corporate governance assessment results and by the corporate governance scandals that continue to make headlines even among the country's largest and most established

The recurrence of scandals points to the dominance of self-interest and personal enrichment in the top echelon of business.

companies. Reported instances of bribery, insider trading, and administrative and criminal sanctions against wrongdoers involving Thailand's large private and state companies are a reminder of the true state of today's business world and of the important challenges that exist in moving Thai corporate governance forward.

First, the recurrence of scandals points to the dominance of self-interest and personal

enrichment in the top echelon of business, and highlights gaps between corporate governance policies and actual implementation of those policies. Many companies implement corporate governance mechanisms as required by regulators and utilize assessment criteria solely because of the regulatory or legal requirements of corporate reporting and compliance. This leads to the form of corporate governance practices taking precedence over the true substance of governance practices within a company. This gap reveals a weak corporate culture that allows actual corporate behavior to deviate from the expected norms of good governance. Weak culture is often the product of poor ethical leadership that occurs when people at the top fail to lead by example.

Second, governance assessment results have shown that equity for stakeholder issues remains a key weakness in implementing corporate governance practices. This includes a lack of policies on treatment of stakeholders such as business partners and creditors, a lack of effective anti-corruption policies, and the absence of established channels for stakeholders to communicate concerns or complaints regarding possible violations of their rights in company operations. Reflecting this, a rising number of governance failures have been linked to negligence in dealing with stakeholders on issues, including bribery and corruption. A greater focus on broad stakeholder interests in decision-making is vital to a company's long-term viability.

Another weakness revealed by ASEAN's and the IOD's corporate governance assessments relates to the roles and responsibilities of the

board. This includes company governance statements not having explicit policies dealing with the term limits of independent directors; on the number of board seats in listed companies that an individual director may hold; not implementing board and board committee evaluations; the lack of a CEO succession plan; and provisions for disclosing CEO remuneration and annual performance assessments. A comprehensive practice of the roles and responsibilities of the board is clearly crucial for further improvement in corporate

INSIGHTS

DR PORNCHAI CHUNHACHINDA, *the chairman of Phol Dhanya, a distributor of occupational safety products, discusses the role that corporate governance can and should play for small businesses.*

On the importance of corporate governance for a small company
Even though Phol Dhanya is a small listed company with registered capital of less than 300 million baht, its shareholders support a board nomination process that emphasizes diversity of qualifications and experience broadly in line with much larger listed companies. Prior to being a listed company, Phol Dhanya's board of directors emphasized the importance of corporate governance in the belief that it adds value to the company and helps to achieve business sustainability due to equitable treatment for all stakeholders. Eventually,

good corporate governance leads to strong business performance and sustainable growth.

On challenges for a small company
One important challenge for a small company is achieving an appropriate board structure. The structure largely reflects the controlling shareholder's perception of what share of board seats for independent directors is appropriate. For Phol Dhanya, its controlling shareholder was forward looking on this issue – requiring only a modest number of his directors on board. The remaining board positions are reserved for qualified independent, outside directors. As such, this board structure enables it to not only effectively monitor and guide the management, but also be alert to, and drive, relevant corporate governance issues through the board committees.

Final thought
For a small company, experience suggests that it should begin with a belief that business operations based on good corporate governance add value to the firm and lead to sustainable business development over time. Board diversity, with members having knowledge and experience fitting the business and an appropriate proportion of independent directors working in its committees, are important elements to insure that the company will operate according to sound corporate governance principles.

CORPORATE GOVERNANCE THROUGH THE FRAMEWORK OF SEP

The principles of the Sufficiency Economy Philosophy and Corporate Governance both came to prominence in the aftermath of the 1997 financial crisis. Indeed, they share many commonalities in the way they can be applied in business governance. Here's a look at how the SEP applies to CG, and how leaders can put these principles into practice:

KNOWLEDGE
- Building an understanding of market realities and stakeholders to make informed decisions.
- Adopting appropriate technologies and know-how in management.
- Continuously learning and sharing best practices.

VIRTUES
- Creating an ethical culture and promoting transparency.
- Leading by example and demonstrating integrity, ethics, honesty, and accountability at all times.
- Treating all stakeholders – not just shareholders – with respect.

MODERATION
- Shifting away from short-term profits and towards the company's long-term health.
- Not extending beyond one's means and optimizing available resources.

REASONABLENESS
- Communicating openly and regularly with management and employees to build trust.
- Developing an understanding of one's strengths, weaknesses, risks, and opportunities.

PRUDENCE
- Managing risks, including sustainability risks.
- Being vigilant about minimizing negative impacts.

governance standards and actual practices at Thai companies.

Third, many companies, especially smaller businesses, private companies, and non-profit organizations, still see governance as a 'large company' issue. They assume that corporate governance has no relevance for them, would be too costly to implement, and that governance structures need to only be adopted by larger companies that have more stakeholders. This is evidenced when one compares corporate governance scores of Market for Alternative Investment (MAI) companies against those of companies listed on the SET. In 2016, the IOD's assessment showed that 118 MAI-listed companies had an average corporate governance score three percentage points below that of the 483 SET companies. Despite the many examples showing how good corporate governance builds trust and improves reputation, a large share of Thai companies are yet to be convinced that it can bring benefits that far outweigh its costs.

Implementing CG

How does one put in place a successful corporate governance program? There are a number of practical steps that can guide a board of directors, starting with the proper understanding of the value of corporate governance and leadership commitment.

1. Establishing proper understanding and commitment

The first step to implementing a successful corporate governance program is to reach a common understanding and a commitment among the top leadership – namely the shareholders, the board, and senior management – that corporate governance is crucial and relevant to the organization. The leadership team should work together to build greater transparency and creditability with stakeholders – with the objective of enhancing value creation over the long term. Doing so requires changes in the way the board works and a greater commitment to the

CHOMPAN KULNIDES, *the vice president of Investment and Sustainability at Minor Holdings, talks about the pivotal role corporate governance plays in establishing, communicating, and meeting a company's sustainability targets.*

How can good corporate governance help support a company's sustainability goals?

Good corporate governance is a fundamental requirement for achieving a company's sustainability goals, which includes not only the sustainability of its organization, but also the long-term health and sustainability of our society and the environment. Good corporate governance ensures the company's transparency and accountability. It also encourages the company to take into consideration its multiple stakeholders' interests when making decisions, leading to mutual long-term positive benefits. Without good governance, the company could be exposed to many risks which could adversely affect the value and reputation of the business. Clearly, good corporate governance serves as the basis for a strong business foundation and underpins growth of the company.

How do you educate the board of directors on the importance of corporate sustainability?

Corporate sustainability at Minor International is a part of rolling five-year strategic plans, which are presented to the board and endorsed annually. This session includes discussion of current and forward-looking sustainability trends, relevant risks associated with sustainability, and the company's sustainability vision, framework, and five-year sustainability plans that are aligned to the company's business strategy. Sustainability is also included on the agenda in every quarterly board meeting. Moreover, the company publishes sustainability reports annually, which is another means of communicating the company's sustainability efforts to the board as well as stakeholders.

What are the best approaches for communicating to employees the need for corporate sustainability?

We employ multiple approaches to communicate the need for corporate sustainability to employees. All employees entering the workforce are required to read, understand, and sign an acknowledgement of the company's code of conduct and then re-sign this acknowledgment again on an annual basis. Presentations on the company's sustainability are part of the new employee orientation process. We have initiated many personnel development programs that include elements of sustainability – for example, many of our leadership development programs ask participants to come up with sustainability initiatives. In addition, we have senior management participate in the verification of stakeholders' interests, the identification of materiality issues, and the formulation of the direction of the company's sustainability framework as part of efforts to encourage management to integrate sustainability into their work.

In addition, as we are currently requested to participate in many sustainability assessment programs such as the Dow Jones Sustainability Indices and FTSE4Good, our sustainability team takes these opportunities to engage with the departments that are the "data owners" to explain to them why their initiatives and inputs are relevant and needed. In this way, we promote better understanding of sustainability and have greater reach to more people within the organization.

For all staff levels, we strive to foster social responsibility mindsets through their participation in corporate social responsibility activities. One example is the annual Founder's Day, when all employees are encouraged to do something good for society at least one day a year.

central idea of governance, putting in place a required system and processes to support it, and promoting corporate governance practices in the entire organization with the top leadership guiding the way. This process will change how the organization works, makes decisions, and communicates.

2. Assessing CG gaps and developing a plan

It is necessary to assess gaps in the current structure of corporate governance, identify additional processes that need to be put into place, and evaluate the capacity and readiness of the company's management and staff to adopt or implement the new system. This is the most crucial and most overlooked step in successful implementation of corporate governance. Initially, the company can make a self-assessment by benchmarking its existing practices against the best practices of other successful companies. After conducting such an analysis, the board can begin developing a detailed, multi-stage operational plan that fits the company's specific business strategy.

3. Setting policy

Policies related to corporate governance are implemented both at the board level – such

as those addressing conflicts of interest, use of material inside information, and related-party transactions – and at operational levels that address and engage everyone in the organization. The board must ensure that all necessary policies, codes, and guidelines are in place to support the company's corporate governance program. These include a corporate governance policy, ethics code, code of conduct, corporate responsibility policy, anti-corruption policy and, in some cases, a whistle-blowing policy.

4. Having a board structure that prioritizes governance

Directors who share a similar commitment to good governance are of great value to a board. Industry experience, the right skills, competency, and independence of mind are all key ingredients for the successful implementation of corporate governance policy by a board.

Another important aspect of board governance is independent chairmanship. Shareholders are better served when the board is led by an independent chairman who oversees the agenda of the company with the interests of the general body of shareholders and other stakeholders in mind. The right

---

THE DIRECTOR NOMINATION PROCESS

Different types of companies require a different mix of skills and experience that fit the unique needs of the company. For recruitment of new directors and re-election of directors it is crucial that the board develop a clear, formal process for making decisions. This is best done by using director qualification and skill set matrices that explicitly identify: (1) a desired skill set matrix, (2) the matrix of the prevailing skill set of current directors, and (3) a skill set gap matrix evident from discussions in analyzing the first two matrices.

The desirable skill matrix is usually identified upon the establishment of the company, but it certainly needs to be revised over time as the company's business grows and as new lines of activity are added to the original core businesses. The Nomination Committee should review and revise the three director qualification matrices described above as needed (at least once a year and before board elections). Having completed this review, the Nomination Committee will be able to identify missing skills and create appropriate director succession plans in the event of resignation, retirement, or end of tenure.

Source: Thai Institute of Directors Association (2017). Nomination Committee Best Practice Guideline

CASE STUDY | Siam Commercial Bank Brings Gender Equality to the Boardroom

The following case study was created through an interview conducted by the Institute of Directors (IOD) with Khunying Jada Wattanasiritham, who is an Independent Director of Siam Commercial Bank (SCB).

THE CHALLENGE: For a listed company with a controlling shareholder, a certain number of board seats must be allocated to the major shareholder. Thus, when a policy of gender diversity is applied, it must be communicated to and acknowledged by all parties involved if said diversity policy is to be effective in the director nomination process. Maintaining an appropriate balance between men and women on the board can be a challenge, but gender diversity at this high level is seen as important by a growing number of stakeholders.

THE SOLUTION: The policy of gender and skills diversification has long been discussed and agreed upon, and its importance has been a long-time preoccupation of SCB's chairman of the board. This has been well communicated to the Nomination & Corporate Governance Committee, which is entrusted with drawing up initial guidelines for the nomination of specific board candidates for final selection and the concurrence of the board. Moreover, in the nomination

Khunying Jada Wattanasiritham is an independent director of Siam Commercial Bank (SCB).

process each board member is invited to send nominations under agreed-upon guidelines.

The board has allocated four seats to the two major shareholders who each hold about 23 percent of total shares. Nominations from these major shareholders will therefore be according to their wishes, although the gender mix preference is communicated to them ahead of the nomination process.

THE BENEFITS: At SCB, gender diversity has not created any problems at the board level. The board has agreed that there should be a good balance between men and women directors, as a good mix allows directors to have greater understanding of how different people feel and react. Presently there are only three women on the board, despite the fact that it has been agreed that there should be no fewer than four. Currently, all three women directors are independent directors.

Board diversity in the view of SCB should cover not only the mix of men and women directors, but also must include different skills, experience, knowledge and age groups. As the needs and goals of the company evolve to meet modern challenges, board members with particular insight, experience, or skills may be more highly sought out for inclusion on the board. For example, if the role of international business is being emphasized, people with good knowledge of global practices will be prioritized. If digital technology is a focus, nominations of experts in this area will be preferred. Generally, however, SCB prefers to have a good mix of directors who are well versed in the fields of finance, law, business, public administration, technology, governance, knowledge management, marketing, public relations, and social and civil society issues. All this is to say that gender is not the predominant factor in decision-making.

Inside Siam Commercial Bank's Chaloem Nakhon branch.

INSIGHTS

BANCHONG CHITTCHANG, *independent director of Lam Soon (Thailand) and Thai Optical Group discusses the role of board leadership in today's changing business environment.*

On the challenges faced by boards today
In the present business environment, the board faces challenges from increased risks, slower growth rates, and volatile earnings; human resource shortages; disrupting technological changes, and growing environmental issues.

On how a board should responses to these challenges
To manage these challenges and efficiently facilitate the board's strategic oversight role, the board must:

• Clearly distinguish the roles and responsibilities of the board and those of management. The board is responsible for overall supervision and long-term performance of the corporation, while management is accountable for performance in the short run.

• Establish board committees such as audit, nomination, remuneration, and risk management to undertake specific tasks. This will enable the board and management to collaborate to implement agreed strategies smoothly.

• Oversee the arrangement of performance indicators to measure the effectiveness of strategic outcomes and the efficiency of work outputs.

• Regularly discuss strategic issues with management to monitor and respond to changes immediately. Meetings with management should occur at least once a year.

For a small company with limited resources, the board should focus on determining its major goals, providing for stringent risk management, maintaining a trustworthy financial position, and establishing communications and disclosures of information to stakeholders.

board structure and composition leads to a more proactive and effective board that adds value to the company's corporate governance.

5. Leading from the top

Specific to governance, the board will need to continually stress the importance of corporate governance within the organization, provide oversight on its implementation, and lead by example through the board's own behavior and practices. In addition, the setting of annual performance targets, executive remuneration, rewards, and bonuses will go a long way toward demonstrating the importance board gives to corporate governance.

6. The role of the CEO

For successful implementation of corporate governance within a company, the role of the CEO is crucial. The CEO is responsible for the execution of the company's strategy with full compliance to laws, rules, and regulations. The board, in its oversight role, can make the CEO responsible for the company's corporate governance performance and link it to the CEO's annual performance review and remuneration. The CEO is expected to oversee the implementation of, and compliance with, the company's corporate governance policies; develop and maintain a corporate culture that promotes integrity and ethical values; and ensure appropriate and timely disclosure of material information to stockholders and the public. For the CEO, the task of implementing corporate governance is never easy. It requires putting in place the necessary governance systems and processes, motivating employees to adopt corporate governance policies, monitoring and reviewing developments to ensure progress – all while

CHANIN VONGKUSOLKIT, *the chairman of mining and power company Banpu, highlights some ways to help good corporate governance take root.*

On implementing CG practice in an organization

The key step is for an organization to understand what CG is, and then see if their organization is in alignment with or different from best CG practices, and how needed changes in CG can be made doable if additional work is required. It is essential to understand how CG implementation would benefit the organization. For this step, top executives and senior management will have to reach an accord on key principles, such as the role of the board and conflicts of interest.

On the challenges of implementing good CG

First, the board and management need to understand and agree on all relevant CG issues. Next is how to promote CG understanding and guidelines to staff at various levels to ensure that they will comply accordingly. In fact, better CG may be just normal practices but with a slightly different process, and with clearer directions on what we should be doing and what we should refrain from doing. A final challenge is how to maintain CG guidelines and compliance as the organization grows amid a changing environment.

Final thought

CG is a way to adjust working, decision-making, and communication processes to make them clear, transparent, and credible to all stakeholders including the board, employees, shareholders, and the general public.

meeting the business objectives of the company. Ultimately, success in corporate governance rests on the ability of the CEO to integrate governance and ethical conduct into the existing work style and management style of all employees, while also championing high ethical conduct by leading by example.

7. Communicating, monitoring, and reviewing

One way to ensure successful implementation is to communicate to employees what is required of them. A well-designed communication effort helps ensure that employees 'buy in,' and promotes better understanding of corporate governance. It is also imperative to have a monitoring system that can assess whether the company is upholding or enhancing its corporate governance practices and standards, with a periodic review and report to the board.

8. Building an ethical culture

It is imperative to cultivate a strong ethical culture within the company. To make this happen, directors and CEOs must be role models of ethical leadership. They must be mindful that they are being watched by their employees, who are likely to follow their lead when it comes to ethical behavior and attitudes. Building an ethical culture begins with an expression of the desired norms, values, and behaviors that are to be upheld and observed by employees. These should be clearly articulated in writing in the form of a code of ethics or code of conduct, and become well-known guidelines to be used throughout the organization. Next, resources must be devoted to develop training programs

INSIGHTS

ANUWAT JONGYINDEE, *the internal audit director of SCG, talks about the importance of linking corporate governance with overall strategy.*

On implementing CG practice in an organization

Successful CG implementation begins with CG as an integral part of the strategic plan, agreed to by both the board of directors and management. Then, the management with CEO leadership initiates a CG agent team to communicate with and educate everyone in the organization on the company's CG principles. The team should follow up by making evaluations of actual practices and regularly reporting on developments to top management. The board of directors should monitor adherence to CG policies as a standard board agenda item, and take needed follow-up action to ensure compliance with the CG policy.

On the challenges of implementing CG

One challenge in CG implementation is to consider gaps and make everyone in an organization aware of, and adhere to, the CG principles so that they become rooted in the culture of the organization. Another issue is assessing the ability to forecast risk, which will help the board of directors to better determine the adequacy of the company's audit and internal control systems. Moreover, assessing the impact of company decisions on all of the company's stakeholders and their opinions is a challenge that should not be overlooked.

Final thought

Once CG is built into a strategic plan, the board of directors and management must provide a clear example by resolutely conforming to it. Continuing communication to aid understanding of CG principles to everyone in an organization motivates acceptance and thus turns CG into the organizational culture. Moreover, keeping an eye on CG trends, both internationally and domestically, helps develop company policies that are appropriate to changing circumstances and will facilitate sustainable business development.

Good corporate governance is the key to business sustainability and the long-term success of any company.

and tools that can teach employees how to handle themselves when faced with ethical dilemmas. Providing a channel or mechanism for employees to raise their concerns or report possible misconduct within the organization, such as a whistle-blowing system, can also help to foster a strong ethical culture. Lastly, systematic monitoring of whether the company is living up to its ethical values can help leaders see the progress of their efforts and provide them with knowledge of critical areas that need further improvement.

Good corporate governance is the key to business sustainability and the long-term success of any company. It is a process of value creation built on trustworthy relations between the company and its stakeholders. Successful implementation of corporate governance calls for an agreed understanding among the key participants of the business – the shareholders, the board of directors, and management – toward focusing on the long-term health of the company rather than just maximizing short-term profits. To this end, the duties of the company's board of directors are to focus on enhancing value creation in a sustainable manner through ethical leadership that creates trust and the legitimacy of the company in the eyes of all stakeholders. This is the crucial task that lies ahead for all Thai companies.

TAKE ACTION

Mindsets need to change in order to unlock the full potential of good corporate governance in Thai companies. Indeed, corporate governance should account for the interests of all stakeholders and focus on the long-term health of the organization.

To implement corporate governance, companies can start with the following:

1. Build a common understanding of corporate governance among top management and secure their commitment for its implementation.

2. Assess gaps in corporate governance and develop a plan of action to address them. This can be achieved by benchmarking existing practices against the country's best practices or those of leading companies. Some useful benchmarking and reference tools include:

- **Corporate Governance Report of Thai Listed Companies (CGR) prepared by the Thai Institute of Directors.**

- **Thailand IOD website (www.thai-iod.com), which provides a platform to access seminars, training courses, workshops, and best practice examples on various topics.**

- **Stock Exchange of Thailand (SET) website (www.set.or.th), which includes useful materials such as the Principles of Good Corporate Governance booklet (available at the CG Center), along with self-assessments and sample CEO evaluation forms.**

3. Establish policies on corporate governance and related issues, such as a code of conduct, transparency and anti-corruption policy, sustainability policy, and whistle-blowing policy.

4. Establish criteria for board composition and structure that prioritizes good governance and diversity, being sure to include stipulations for independent chairmanship and board diversity in terms of skills, competencies, and industry experience – and importantly, gender.

5. Determine clear roles and responsibilities for the board of directors and management to allow for close, productive cooperation between the two entities on strategic issues. The board and management can also assume leadership in driving sustainability in the organization by:

- **Clarifying roles for sustainability governance.**

- **Focusing on company-specific material sustainability issues in strategic oversight, namely those that will significantly impact revenues and operations of the company.**

- **Establishing stronger linkages between executive compensation and sustainability goals.**

- **Embedding sustainability into committee charters, and in discussions on strategy, risks, and incentives.**

- **Recruiting board candidates with expertise and backgrounds on sustainability issues.**

- **Undergoing regular sustainability training to stay abreast of emerging risks and trends.**

6. Ensure the CEO is responsible for overseeing the implementation of good corporate governance, complies with expectations, and promotes a culture of ethics and integrity across the organization through leading by example.

7. Communicate regularly with employees to secure their buy-in, participation, and compliance in corporate governance efforts. Mechanisms to do this include a signed acknowledgement of policies by employees, CG-related activities and events, and training.

8. Monitor and review corporate governance performance periodically to identify improvement opportunities and remaining gaps. Ensure this is carried out in a systematic way.

9. Promote an ethical culture to ensure that good governance practices are passed on across generations and becomes part of the organizational culture.

Risk Management

- *A sustainability lens in risk management offers businesses holistic ways to transform risks into opportunities, opening doors for competitiveness, new markets, reputational benefits, and stakeholder trust.*

- *Sustainability risks tend to emerge and manifest over longer periods of time.*

- *Thai companies predominantly focus on traditional risks – such as financial, operational, and market risks. Sustainability risks are still rather underappreciated.*

Companies managing risks today face these unfolding realities: operations traversing national and geographical boundaries, complex global supply chains, technologically enhanced connectivity, a climate crisis, and stakeholder pressures for greater transparency and accountability. This disruptive risk landscape is filled with uncertainty and unprecedented impacts to the triple bottom line. Running a business in this environment is a challenge, and business leaders must stand at the ready to adapt or transform to remain competitive.

> **"What is heavily underappreciated by Thai companies is the linkage between sustainability and strategic risk management."**

Risk management is a strategic business tool. It is essential in helping organizations reach their objectives and protect themselves against damages or undesired outcomes – fundamentally ensuring long-term sustainability. But certain events in Thailand have called its effectiveness into question,

among them the 2011 Thai floods; slavery allegations in the fishing and shrimp industries; the suspension of the Map Ta Phut Industrial Estate in 2009 following reports of pollution-related health incidents; the Rayong oil spill in 2013; and closures of popular island tourist attractions by the government in an attempt to reverse environmental degradation.

At each turning point, businesses learned the hard way about the consequences of overlooking (whether intentionally or not) social, environmental, and governance concerns in the pursuit of short-term benefits.

These incidents reveal a glaring weakness in Thailand's current risk management approaches that still narrowly focus on 'traditional' risks – namely financial, strategic, operational, and market risks. The intangible sustainability risks, also referred to as ESG risks, are yet to be fully captured in the spectrum of risk possibilities impacting business operations and value creation. According to Dr Veerathai Santiprabhob, Governor of the Bank of Thailand, "What is heavily underappreciated by Thai companies is the linkage between sustainability and strategic risk management."

Making this link will be vital as companies venture into a future far less forgiving of unsustainable businesses.

What sustainability offers businesses

A sustainability lens in risk management offers businesses a more holistic perspective of their exposure to risks and opportunities. This is invaluable to strategy and decision-making. Transforming risks into opportunities could open doors for competitiveness, new markets, reputational benefits, and stakeholder trust. It is a powerful driving force for innovation.

Bangchak Petroleum, confronting an unsteady revenue stream from its petroleum business, reduced their risk exposure to global oil prices by forming the subsidiary BCPG to oversee investments and operations of electricity generation and alternative energy. The company expanded their production of bio-based products and invested in Lithium Americas Corp (a company that produces batteries) to grow their alternative energy platform and prepare for a future less friendly to fossil fuel-based energy companies.

The global carpet manufacturer, Interface, in their newly launched Climate Take Back mission, declared: "We're adopting a fresh perspective – one that views the current crisis not as a problem but as an opportunity." Their commitment to 'Love Carbon' explores groundbreaking ways of making products with raw materials that use waste carbon or sequester carbon to reduce the total amount of carbon dioxide in the atmosphere. For example, a carbon-capturing carpet tile has now been prototyped.

Companies expanding their operations globally are susceptible to a wider array of sustainability risks. In the World Economic Forum's 2017 Global Risks Report, none of the top five risks listed were classified as economic, either in terms of likelihood or impact. Similarly, *The Economist*'s Economic Intelligence Unit reveals that political risks are at their highest level in years. Multinationals face a massive challenge to balance these risks across their supply chains.

Warehouses in Hat Yai in southern Thailand inundated by a flood, one of many environmental risks Thai companies face.

Take Charoen Pokphand Foods. The agro-industrial and food conglomerate has production and processing bases in 16 countries and products distributed to more than 30 countries on five continents. Their risks cover a broad range of issues but none seems to draw more public attention (or condemnation) than human rights. Since *The Guardian* exposé on slavery and trafficking in the Thai fishing industry, the company has been swift to clean up its act (see *Fisheries and Marine Resources*, page 186). CP Foods now regularly monitors the most salient human rights issues identified in their human rights risk assessment: forced and migrant labor in the supply chain, and the health and safety of their employees and contractors.

Sustainability risks, moreover, tend to emerge and manifest over longer time periods. Imagine issues like climate change, major demographic shifts, and disruptive technologies. These force companies to be more conscious of the long-term implications of their decisions, even across multiple generations. It is a perspective that sharply contrasts with the short-term thinking prevalent among business leaders today. Nevertheless, stakeholders certainly welcome this change.

"What helps with Thailand is that there is a sustainability philosophy and a Buddhist culture. I think this helps Thai businesses overall."

From an investment perspective, sustainability investing firm RobecoSAM explains that transparency about emerging risks can "improve investors' confidence in management's ability to plan effectively for long-term challenges and therefore may make the company a more attractive long-term investment."

The German reinsurance company Munich Re, whose business is risk itself, works with an emerging risk radar that divides risks into five main areas: Society, Technology and Science, Economy, Environment, and Politics/Regulation

(or "STEEP" analysis). A central think tank of more than 20 specialists, including underwriters, lawyers, geologists, mathematicians, and doctors regularly monitor the risk landscape. Their wide-ranging expertise gives Munich Re equally diverse perspectives on risk scenarios and mitigation measures and helps them stay one step ahead of customers' needs.

Finally, smaller companies and SMEs are just as vulnerable to ESG risks. True, big businesses have a higher risk exposure, but unlike them, the smaller players are less likely to have sufficient resources to independently manage risks or rebound from crises. Recall the aftermath of the 2011 floods, whose effects were felt on some 550,000 SMEs in the manufacturing, retail, wholesale, service, and construction sectors. Besides widespread production interruption and delays, SMEs suffered business closures and a slash in export growth projections from 23–25 percent to 12–16 percent that year.

Big and small companies therefore have vested interests in protecting their businesses from the most damaging impacts of ESG risks. Being proactive about sustainability risk management and creating a culture for it, rather than reacting only in times of crisis, is the solution.

The cultural foundation

King Bhumibol Adulyadej's Sufficiency Economy Philosophy (SEP) specially prepares Thai companies for this endeavor. Since the calamity of the 1997 Financial Crisis, SEP has served as a reminder to businesses about the costs of pursuing reckless and extravagant strategies in the name of economic growth. It was a hard-learned lesson, and a mistake no business wants to repeat.

SEP's emphasis on prudent management, gradual rather than overreaching expansion, and moderation in the name of long-term resilience has since guided some Thai businesses. It could therefore be said that SEP's most obvious link to the business community is in risk management – or prudence. "The prudence principle places a great deal of emphasis on being adaptive, assuming non-stationarity as the norm, regime change as an ever-present possibility,"

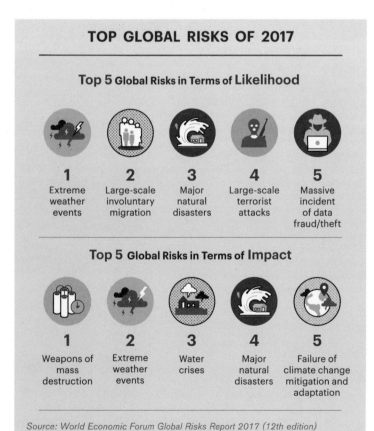

TOP GLOBAL RISKS OF 2017

Top 5 Global Risks in Terms of Likelihood

1	2	3	4	5
Extreme weather events	Large-scale involuntary migration	Major natural disasters	Large-scale terrorist attacks	Massive incident of data fraud/theft

Top 5 Global Risks in Terms of Impact

1	2	3	4	5
Weapons of mass destruction	Extreme weather events	Water crises	Major natural disasters	Failure of climate change mitigation and adaptation

Source: World Economic Forum Global Risks Report 2017 (12th edition)

TOOLBOX | WHAT IS A SUSTAINABILITY RISK?

Risk is everywhere, and has been defined in myriad ways. In the universe of business, it can largely refer to uncertainty. A risk is forward-looking and futuristic. A current risk is merely a problem to be solved. Risk does not only have negative connotations (downside risk) but offers opportunities for gain (upside risk). The ancient notion of risk – encapsulated in Greek mythology – is more heroic, something to be taken, a challenge to overcome. In ISO31000, risk is defined as "the effect of uncertainty on objectives" and is neutral.

A sustainability risk is an uncertain social or environmental event or condition that, if it occurs, can cause a negative impact on the company. This definition, provided by the World Business Council for Sustainable Development, also includes opportunities from changing social or environmental factors.

COSO ERM, the widely adopted risk management framework in Thailand, breaks risk down into four main categories: strategic, operational, compliance, and reporting. COSO has called for the systematic integration of sustainability into its risk management framework and provided examples of sustainability risks under each of its risk categories as follows:

- **Strategic risks** have a significant strategic impact on business. Sustainability risks include marketing positioning, changing consumer demand, strategic investments, stakeholder communications, and investor relations.

- **Operational risks** impact business operations. Sustainability aspects include changes in weather patterns, extreme weather events like earthquakes and hurricanes, escalating impacts of natural disasters, and value chain risks associated with suppliers.

- **Compliance risks** related to policy and regulations can directly and indirectly emerge from sustainability issues like health and safety, human rights and labor laws, bribery and corruption, environmental risks, and even policy uncertainty.

- **Reporting risks** emerge from the mounting pressure to be transparent and accountable for sustainability impacts – the reason why many companies are releasing sustainability reports. The failure to meet reporting requirements, such as from the Stock Exchange of Thailand, can also pose a risk to the credibility of the company.

- **Reputational risk** can originate from issues in strategic, operational, compliance, or reporting risk categories. When a sustainability crisis arises, reputation is often the hardest hit.

SMEs are not lost in this discussion. They too must manage their own risks, though usually without formal processes. In fact, SMEs could be more adaptable in the face of risk considering that they are not constrained by rigid organizational and decision-making structures.

ISO31000 has designed a risk management framework specifically for SMEs to counter the notion that SMEs are too small to warrant a formal risk management system, or are too busy running their company to see its value. ISO contends that SMEs implementing formal risk management are in a better position to survive and grow their businesses.

---

explains Dr Poomjai Nacaskul, first senior vice president of quantitative models and enterprise analytics at Siam Commercial Bank.

SEP adds a distinct Thai-ness to risk culture. According to Alan Laubsch, former risk analyst at JPMorgan, "What helps with Thailand is that there is a sustainability philosophy and a Buddhist culture where there are values [that are important to people], whether you are running a financial services or manufacturing company. I think this helps Thai businesses overall, that there is not just a sort of naked, spiritless profit at all costs. That culture matters."

Companies are working to make risk culture more apparent across all levels of their enterprise. Kasikornbank, for instance, launched the 'Honest K-Bank People' campaign under the K-Culture program to foster a culture of integrity. PTT Global Chemical established policies and objectives on risk management for the board of directors and executives, and promotes risk through their e-learning system, monthly newsletters, and employee training, among other measures. SCG appoints a 'risk champion' in each of its business unit's risk management committee.

Still, efforts generally fall short of cultivating a risk culture clearly attuned to sustainability. Some best practice examples for achieving that would be to tie sustainability risks to employees' financial compensation, developing sustainability metrics for supplier qualifications, and providing regular training on identifying sustainability risks. Culture is half the journey to integrating sustainability into risk management. The rest is technical.

Forming the link

According to Dr Narumon Saardchom, a professor at NIDA Business School, businesses in Thailand tend to be familiar with the two dominant risk frameworks, the COSO Enterprise Risk Management Framework and the International Organization for Standardization (ISO) 31000 Risk Management Standard.

Despite their widespread adoption, they have yet to offer direct guidelines on identifying and managing sustainability risks and opportunities – although COSO ERM has started to do so within their own risk categories (see *What Is Sustainability Risk?*, page 65).

Likewise, there is currently no universal standard for sustainability risk management. Companies have thus turned to their own methodologies for integrating sustainability risk into existing processes and systems. Using materiality assessment results to inform risk management is one method. However, several challenges remain.

First, companies may not have an adequate understanding of sustainability risks and their impacts on business operations, whether positive or negative. This makes them hard to identify. And because such risks are often emerging, they represent the unknown. Consequently, they may not be monetized or quantified in a manner that effectively informs decision-making and resource allocation.

What companies could do in this case is promote greater collaboration between their sustainability and risk management departments. To quantify or monetize sustainability risks, some companies turn to tools like carbon pricing, social return on investment measurements, and impact valuation. In addition, sustainability managers could sit on the risk management committee and assume a role in developing the risk register, a database containing all relevant information about a project's risks, their likelihood and severity, and possible responses.

Second, although the longer time horizons of sustainability risks encourage long-term thinking, this fact may well bar their inclusion in corporate risk assessments. A 2017 survey conducted by the World Business Council for Sustainable Development (WBCSD) of its members' practices reveals that most companies' risk assessments cover only a two- to five-year timeframe. The short-term bias could be linked to the time-bound tenures of employees and chief executives, strategic objectives, and even pressures to report quarterly earnings. In sectors with longer investment time periods, risk assessments

THE RISK PROCESS

▶ **Risk Identification:**
Scan environments for new and emerging risks and opportunities and maintain an understanding of existing risks.

▶ **Risk Assessment:**
Evaluate, quantify, and prioritize risks by considering impacts and likelihood of occurrence.

▶ **Risk Response:**
Determine and implement appropriate responses to identified risks. Mitigate or control based on risk appetite.

▶ **Communication and Disclosure:**
Disclose material risks to investors and other stakeholders, such as through sustainability reports and legal risk filings.

Source: World Business Council for Sustainable Development, 2017

RISK AND THE SUFFICIENCY ECONOMY PHILOSOPHY

A company applying an SEP-driven risk management approach can distinguish itself through the following features:

- An approach that centers on people as the company's most valuable assets. A robust human resources plan connected to business strategy is in place to reduce the risks of shortages of highly skilled employees.

- A systematic human capital development approach and knowledge-sharing platforms.

- A diversified market or diversified group of customers.

- A diverse product line that reflects the company's expertise.

- Cautious investments that factor in interest rates and

foreign exchange risks, with an emphasis on long-term growth over short-term gain.

- Regular monitoring of processes and product-and-service quality.

- Consideration of the health, safety, and working environments of all employees.

From a governance standpoint, an SEP approach aligns with contemporary risk management practices in stipulating the need for a centralized risk management committee. This committee would be responsible for managing and evaluating risks that are then reviewed by the Board of Directors. At the SME level, risk management could be governed with a decentralized approach through responsibilities delegated to unit managers. This will then drive accountability for risk at all levels of the company.

Source: College of Management of Mahidol University

---

may extend from five to 10 years. Materiality assessments for sustainability, on the other hand, could go as far as 10, 20, or 30 years.

If long-term risks are discounted due to the time horizon, companies could consider defining the risk or opportunity involved and formulating a response to be deployed in the future. Another option would be to leverage technology and big data to continuously monitor emerging issues, resources permitting, from potential sources of risk.

The third challenge is more structural. Sustainability and risk management functions are frequently siloed within their own domains and do not speak the same language. This is unfortunate given that they could be regarded as kindred spirits: "Both are dedicated to ensuring a kind of longevity to something we desire and pursue as an active enterprise," says Poomjai Nacaskul of Siam Commercial Bank.

Nat Vanitchyangkul, partner, ASEAN Corporates at Environmental Resources Management (ERM), explains further: "If you look at sustainability risks, opportunities, and emerging risks, risk management departments will not assume ownership over them. Their

There is no universal standard for sustainability risk management. Companies have thus turned to their own methodologies for integrating sustainability into processes.

position would be to see what it is that will stop a plan from being achieved. Their role is generally limited to protecting action plans and operational risks." Companies would thus benefit from helping risk management teams familiarize themselves with sustainability.

CASE STUDY | Sa Paper Preservation House Manages Risks through SEP

Sa Paper Preservation House focuses on moderate growth and product diversity.

THE CHALLENGE: The Thai sa paper industry is characterized by a high number of domestic and regional competitors, low barriers to entry, and an abundance of resource substitutes. It relies on the availability of a raw material, the paper mulberry tree (*por sa* in Thai), which, while easily accessible in the mountainous northern regions of Thailand, is steadily decreasing in supply. These conditions expose Sa Paper Preservation House, which has limited management tools at its disposal, to risks ranging from environmental to operational.

THE SOLUTION: Fongkam Lapinta, one of the company's founders, believes in letting the Sufficiency Economy Philosophy guide her business: "I follow His Majesty's teachings," she says. "We have to operate and grow within our means." And indeed, for over 55 years, her business has seen gradual and sustainable growth.

SEP guides the way she builds relationships with her stakeholders. For instance, this means that employees and suppliers must always be paid fairly and on-time, and that "you must learn to say no" if you cannot meet customers' demands. And because *por sa* is becoming harder to acquire, they reuse, recycle, and reformulate products where possible and innovate by diversifying into different products – from notebooks to bags and lamps to fans. Moreover, no chemicals are used in their manufacturing processes out of concern for long-term health risks.

THE BENEFITS: A mainstay of the Ton Pao community in Chiang Mai, this small family business serves a greater social good by being a reliable community partner and fair employer. To keep the business growing strongly, she advises, "Don't be careless and don't be greedy." Always share knowledge and give opportunities to others, because "kindness is not for sale."

CASE STUDY | Kasikornbank Addresses ESG Risks with Responsible Financing

Kasikornbank screens its investments and services for ESG impacts.

THE CHALLENGE: These days, banks are scrutinized for their every move – each loan, transaction, and project financed. This stems in part from a public more educated on sustainability issues and impacts, due to the lessons learned from financial crises in the past. Stakeholders like customers, civil society, and regulators hold banks to account for the direct and indirect impacts of their credit decisions. The moment banks are targeted with claims of unsustainable practices, they risk being saddled with stranded assets as well as a tarnished reputation.

THE SOLUTION: Kasikornbank integrates ESG considerations into all their credit underwriting of financial products, services, and investments. The Bank's ESG Credit Assessment Process screens project finance applications for ESG impacts using a preliminary Environmental and Social Impact Assessment (ESIA). One example is Kasikornbank's lending to conventional power plants, waste-to-energy plants, and wind power projects. Environmental and social considerations on these types of projects include compliance with laws and industrial standards; siting with minimum impacts to surrounding communities; evidence of local participation; no forced or child labor; health and safety standards; and pollutant levels kept below legal thresholds.

THE BENEFITS: Kasikornbank's responsible lending reduces two types of ESG risk: first, the reputational risk of being associated with projects with negative ESG impacts, and second, the indirect risks of communities and environments being inadvertently impacted by the projects they finance.

In 2016, 50 out of 66 projects requesting credit were approved, six were approved with conditions, and ten were rejected.

ALAN LAUBSCH, *Lykke natural capital markets director and a former risk analyst at JPMorgan, talks risk culture and sustainability.*

What is a risk culture and why is it essential?
A risk culture is a holistic way of thinking that looks at the entire system and doesn't just consider a short-term perspective. It is something that is so essential to risk management. You can put in the best systems in the world, and have all the best practices. You can hire consultants to tell you how to have the enterprise risk systems, statistics, and reports, and have the right organizational structure with the chief risk officer and all that. You can follow everything to a T, and yet if the culture isn't there, if there isn't a genuine interest in risk and understanding of uncertainty, it will not be as effective.

How can businesses build a risk culture?
Culture starts with leadership and vision. It's about the people. The good thing is that a lot of people are receptive to social influence, so what's important is this dynamic of leadership – the leaders must 'walk the walk.' A visionary is important. The mission of a company goes beyond just being a company. It's 'How do we actually change the world?'

Within the culture of a company, it's vital to have strong, open communication to build trust and to have high standards of ethics and integrity. Be relentless about enforcing this kind of quality control and messaging to people in and outside of the firm.

Cultures with strong risk management have a high tolerance for failure – as long as you can learn from that failure. Companies that are great at risk management are also very adaptive. They learn very quickly from small mistakes and failures as opposed to pushing projects through in a rigid way, not admitting that things aren't going in the right direction and then over-investing in something that's not working and having a dramatic failure.

It's kind of a paradox. If you want to reduce your risk, the best way to do that is by increasing your tolerance for uncertainty, volatility, and failure in the short-term. It's important to have this culture that's a bit more like Silicon Valley – that if you're aiming to do something great, then for sure you're not going to do it right the first time. It's building this resilience, designing a process with failure in mind. Managing risk doesn't mean you don't tolerate failure. If you look at organizations that have had the best cultures, they're ones that are not blinded by ideology.

How can risk managers start making the sustainability link?
The idea is that we need to start looking at scenarios. If you just look at your short-term data points, and if you monitor your KPIs too closely and that's all there is, then you get this sort of blindness where you don't see the big picture.

Your enterprise risk management systems are doing the easy stuff. They're looking at the risks that you should be monitoring. But your job as a risk manager is not to be a risk report producer. You're freed up to think of scenarios that are not captured by the models – really considering the full range of scenarios and sustainability; people's attitudes toward sustainability. The whole risk community is very quantitative. What I find so important is to emphasize that at the core, there is a philosophy to risk, and a qualitative dimension.

A burst pipeline managed by a major Thai energy company doused the popular tourist island Koh Samed with oil in 2013.

> *Once identified, sustainability risks should be treated no differently than traditional risks. They should be measured, mitigated, and reported.*

Similarly, sustainability professionals should receive training on risk management tools, techniques, and the language of risk management to allow for better informed cross-departmental dialogues.

The important thing to remember is that sustainability is not a standalone risk management tool. Once identified, sustainability risks should be treated no differently than traditional risks. They should be measured, mitigated, and reported on in annual reports and financial filings.

The WBCSD states that a balance of "art and science" inputs is required to capture and mitigate risks. Art refers to the qualitative dimension, such as intuitive understandings of risk, strategy, human behavior, and industry experience – or so-called 'gut feelings.' Science refers to formal tools and techniques used to monitor risks. Examples include decision trees, the Monte Carlo simulation, stress testing, scenario analysis, and forecasting.

In the absence of universal tools to assess sustainability risks, leveraging a mixture of art and science can help businesses better link their risks to sustainability objectives and vice versa. Along the way, companies should encourage internal collaboration and focus on existing risk systems to figure out what works.

A future of opportunity

Plenty of risks will, in the years to come, challenge how companies conduct business, but the additional opportunities could far outweigh the costs of inaction.

TAKE ACTION

Companies can start embedding sustainability in risk management by following these common steps in a risk process:

1. Identify the sustainability risks and opportunities that will impact your business over the short- to long-term. This could be achieved by:

- Mapping out your value chain to survey the landscape for hidden risks, and specifying areas of direct and indirect impacts. Consider key stakeholder groups impacted by your organization, from suppliers and communities to regulators.

- Making use of sources like stakeholder interests and concerns, global megatrends, regulations, social media, and business sector trends.

- Considering risks identified from existing enterprise risk management frameworks like COSO and ISO 31000 and tools. Use a mixture of 'art' and 'science' techniques. Are current frameworks adequately capturing sustainability risks and opportunities?

- Getting risk experts and sustainability experts at the same table. Ensure sustainability issues are presented in the language of risk to facilitate communication.

2. Assess risks for likelihood and impact, and prioritize areas of action and critical damage points.

- Decide on an assessment time frame that corresponds with business strategies and objectives. Is it two, 10, or 20 years?

- If a materiality assessment process exists, use the results to inform your company's risk management strategies. If it does not, engage both risk and sustainability functions in the materiality assessment process to provide input. Evaluate whether the output of risk assessment and materiality are aligned.

- Categorize risk issues. Are they latent, emerging, exploding, or regulated?

3. Develop risk response strategies to appropriately manage risks. Consider common responses like avoidance, transference, and tolerance. Be sure to include sustainability risks in the organization's 'risk appetite,' or the amount of risk the organization is willing to accept in pursuit of value.

4. Communicate and report risks to stakeholders such as regulators, investors, and communities to demonstrate your company's active stance in managing sustainability.

5. Monitor risks regularly within your organization and keep a lookout for emerging risk issues. Consider looking to sources of risks such as stakeholders, online and social media, and risks faced by competitors.

The United Nations Global Compact's Global Opportunity Report in 2017 stated: "Opportunities are avenues of action for systemic change that stakeholders in business, politics, finance, and civil society can choose to pursue when addressing global risks. They create value for societies and the planet, not just for individuals or businesses. An opportunity is different from a single business solution, because it creates systemic change via multi-stakeholder collaboration."

UNGC's analysis revealed five global risks with new sustainable market opportunities: unstable markets, soil depletion, rising inequality,

"An opportunity is different from a single business solution, because it creates systemic change via multi-stakeholder collaboration."

cities disrupted by climate change, and cyber threats. Representing more than just risks, these issues present opportunities that could allow businesses to create ways of contributing to society that go beyond pure survival. In the quest for sustainability, that is the vision to which businesses should aspire.

Human Resources and Organizational Culture

- *Investing in continuous employee development is vital for keeping up with today's fast-changing business environment and emerging risks and opportunities.*

- *Companies must empower their employees to be creative and innovative, finding ways to break through rigid organizational hierarchies and cultural barriers to pioneer radical and incremental innovations.*

- *HR should have a more strategic role in creating long-term value for a company through its talent decisions and in building a workforce that has a transformative impact on the wider sustainability agenda.*

People are often an organization's most valuable asset. A strong and capable workforce can determine whether a company is competitive and succeeds in reaching its sustainability objectives, or if it fails. Human resources can also be a pillar of resilience in times of crisis, or a force for innovation and growth during this period of unrelenting change. On many levels, human resources can create value for companies if managed effectively.

In Thailand, people management has always been a challenge for corporate leaders. Among the key challenges are how to recruit the right employees, how to develop them so that they have the specific knowledge and skills required to make the business more competitive, and, perhaps most importantly, how to retain them – particularly the talented ones. These questions are always on the minds of executives.

How would a sustainable approach to human resources help address these pervasive challenges and also help a company achieve its larger sustainability objectives? To begin with, from recruitment to retirement companies today must proactively engage and manage their people in a multi-dimensional manner. Because human resources are directly impacted by a company's actions and decisions, employees must be treated as key stakeholders (as opposed to easily replaceable labor) in the organization.

Thus, at the absolute minimum, sustainable human resources practices require a respect for human and labor rights. That means adhering to relevant laws and regulations concerning forced and child labor, safety, and providing work benefits – as well as ensuring that no one is subject to unfair treatment or discrimination of any kind. While such attention to ethical practices may seem obvious or be natural for some companies, Thailand has seen its fair share of human rights and labor scandals. These violations may not be a reflection of the corporate headquarters itself, but the existence of human rights and labor abuses among company subsidiaries, partners, or within the supply chain have created serious reputational harm and revenue losses for Thai corporations in recent years. And such abuses, even if largely out of sight, are now seen as the responsibility of the corporate headquarters (see *Human Rights and the Workplace*, page 76).

Engaging your employees

Beyond a basic respect for human and labor rights, conscientious Thai companies view their people as a prime asset that can always be developed. They try to create an engaged workforce, knowing that when employees are engaged in corporate activities, they work harder, which ultimately benefits the company. Studies show that Thai enterprises with engaged employees have higher shareholder returns, profitability, productivity, rates of retention, and customer satisfaction.

Similarly, beyond Thailand, employee engagement has been linked to organizational-level outcomes. Employee engagement was related to business-unit outcomes (productivity, customer satisfaction, profitability, turnover, and safety) in a large sample of business units. In a sample of 65 firms from different industries, the top 25 percent on an engagement index had greater returns on assets and profitability, and more than double the shareholder value compared to the bottom 25 percent. "An inspired employee is more than twice as productive as a satisfied employee and more than three times as productive as a dissatisfied employee," writes Eric Garton of Bain & Company in the *Harvard Business Review*.

Creating an environment that unleashes inspiration and engages employees is both a challenge and a worthwhile investment for employers. Well-recognized enablers for engagement include financial and non-financial incentives such as learning opportunities, stock options, bonus payments, and recognitions spanning the short- to long-term. And while financial compensation is still a significant motivator for most, this must be accompanied by opportunities for career advancement and challenging, continuous development. Particularly for millennials, a sense of purpose, the ability to have an impact on society, and work-life balance are important criteria during job assessments.

Communications conglomerate True Corporation employs a multi-faceted employee engagement framework grounded in six drivers:

PlanToys encourages innovation and nurtures a sustainability mindset among employees.

leadership, brand, company practices, the basics (i.e., safety, work-life balance), work, and performance. Through its annual employee engagement survey – of which the results have increased gradually year after year – True has identified its engagement gaps as rewards and recognition, enabling infrastructure, and career opportunities for its employees.

Moving beyond engagement at the work-place, proactive employers recognize employees as individuals with their own personal challenges, needs, and potential

Creating an environment that unleashes inspiration and engages employees is both a challenge and a worthwhile investment for employers.

for growth, and also engage them on issues impacting them outside of the workplace. At Nithi Foods, for example, employee benefits and training are designed around real needs and issues. Whether it involves debt, drugs, family problems, or educational opportunities, "it is important for employees to be satisfied with their home lives first," explains managing director Smith Taweelerdniti. Having that stability allows them to fully engage at work.

Indeed, Thai companies often go above and beyond purely legal or financial obligations to care for their employees like family members. In equipping employees with life skills, companies are also supporting the society in which they operate. Personal financial management and financial literacy training are especially common – and necessary – given Thailand's high ratio of household debt to GDP of 78.4 percent at the end of the second

Gone are the days of once-learned lifelong skill sets. Tomorrow's business environment calls for more agile and adaptable skills.

quarter of 2017. For some companies, such initiatives are specially informed by the Sufficiency Economy Philosophy (SEP), which emphasizes values such as prudence and moderation, and the benefits of foregoing unnecessary extravagances in one's life.

One of the hallmarks of sustainable human resource management in Thailand is the way in which some companies have maintained their commitments to people in times of adversity. This was true even during the devastating 1997 Asian Financial Crisis. Instead of laying off employees to reduce cost burdens, companies continued investing in their growth and development. This sends a message from executives to their employees that the company will weather all crises collectively.

SCG, for instance, which was drastically affected by the crisis and had to downsize its core businesses, did not lay off employees or freeze hiring. Management communicated regularly with employees so that they were aware of the company's financial situation and any related decisions. Employees could opt for a Mutual Separation Plan or early retirement. When a large number accepted the offer, this allowed lower-level managers to succeed them and advance in their careers. Policies such as these allowed SCG's business

to continue uninterrupted, and in the words of then-president Chompol NaLamlieng, "emerge stronger."

This focus on retention runs counter somewhat to Western views on human resource productivity. Indeed, just within four months of the 2008 financial crisis, 524,000 jobs were lost in the United States. However, with the forces of globalization influencing Thai businesses and even management styles, in the future this no layoff policy could be up for debate in favor of efficiency gains.

Unleashing potential

A 2016 World Bank Enterprise Survey of 1,000 Thai firms of various sizes and industries across the country reveals that only 18 percent of those surveyed offered formal training to their employees. This suggests that the issue of development must be tackled with greater urgency across the board in Thailand.

Gone are the days of once-learned lifelong skill sets. Tomorrow's business environment calls for more agile and adaptable skills, driven by technological know-how, critical thinking and complex problem-solving, creativity and entrepreneurship, emotional intelligence, and people management, among others. As the renowned evolutionary biologist E.O. Wilson famously stated, "We are drowning in information, while starving for wisdom. The world henceforth will be run by synthesizers, people able to put together the right information at the right time, think critically about it, and make important choices wisely." The earlier companies invest in preparing their people for a future of lifelong learning, the better they can future-proof the sustainability of their businesses.

If the kingdom is to achieve its Thailand 4.0 aspirations, having a highly skilled workforce is imperative. However, an analysis of employment trends for 2015 to 2019 by the Department of Employment reveals that skilled labor accounts for a mere eight percent of Thailand's labor force, though it is estimated to increase to nine percent by the end of that period. What's more, there is an imbalance in the supply and demand of skilled labor and

WORKPLACE TRENDS TO WATCH

Thailand's transition to an innovation-driven economy under the umbrella of 'Thailand 4.0' will transform the workplace – and the role of human resources in it. Adaptability and creativity will be the baseline for competitiveness and sustainable success. Here are the top trends to watch:

Ageing Society
Retiring employees signify loss of knowledge, skills and experiences of those individuals. HR must ensure knowledge is passed on to the new generation and reconsider the definition of retirement at 60 (or perhaps older), where appropriate.

Changing Economic Model
The shift towards an economic model based on knowledge, creativity, innovation and technology requires HR to strengthen the capacity of its workforce accordingly – building employees as creative 'thinkers' and innovators.

Digital Workplace
The Internet of Things (IoT) and move towards 'Thailand Digital Economy' means that HR must ready individuals for the digital world, consider management approaches via online systems, and leverage digital content for the benefit of the organization.

A Culture of Connectivity
The phenomenon of 'hyper-connected' individuals, able to communicate at all times and locations, will shift the meaning of work-life balance. The boundaries of work and leisure overlap such that HR will need to engage with employees in both worlds, and in different ways.

'Social' Learning
Social media, social networking, or social learning – the new generation of employees could be self-learning through various social platforms. HR roles could shift from 'trainers' to 'facilitators,' helping employees develop themselves.

Millennials in the Workplace
Millennials/Gen Y will become the dominant group in the workforce. HR must be prepared to adjust to the new generation's expectations for greater flexibility, and potentially devise tailor-made approaches for training and management.

Intensified Globalization
Global connectivity comes with the risk that situations and crises occurring all over the world could have rippling effects on Thailand's businesses. HR should stay abreast of current events and always be prepared for change.

Mobile Technology
Increased use of mobile technology, whether smartphones or other equipment, suggests that in the future HR employee training and management could be accomplished through mobile technology.

Sharing Society
Increased engagement of stakeholders like customers on a company's products/services will nurture an environment of continuous knowledge-sharing and creativity. HR should foster internal engagement and provide opportunities for employees to share ideas.

Increased Social Responsibility
The move away from corporate social responsibility to creating shared value will see companies placing sustainability at the core of their business. HR must assume a very active role in shifting employee mindsets and organizational culture towards sustainability.

Source: HR Society Magazine, August 2016

HUMAN RIGHTS AND THE WORKPLACE

In May 2017, a group of human rights defenders, NGOs, and advocacy groups released a joint statement calling on the Thai government and businesses to uphold the UN Guiding Principles on Business and Human Rights. They argued that while efforts to address human rights issues were commendable, violations and abuses committed by businesses and in government investment projects continued unchecked.

The sort of damages transpiring in businesses with poor human rights records are well documented: business interruptions, reputational costs, loss of social license to operate and trust among peers and stakeholders. Public scrutiny will only intensify with global interconnectivity, 24/7 news coverage, and rapid-fire digital communications.

Businesses must undergo a dramatic shift in how they manage human rights: being more proactive, transparent, and diligent about mitigating risks and violations. Besides complying with human rights laws and regulations, they should create better awareness about human rights within their own organizations. And in countries with weaker human rights law enforcement, they should strive to

operate higher than the minimum standard. As of this writing, Thailand is also developing its National Action Plan (NAP) on Business and Human Rights.

Companies can easily develop a baseline understanding of their human rights risks and issues through a human rights risk assessment. Some questions to consider are:

- Where are the human rights risks located across your value chain? Identify people and processes.

- How susceptible is your company to human rights risks or being complicit in abuses? Consider the context of operations, certain groups of employees, local cultures, political and social climate, and the presence of marginalized groups and minorities.

- Who is responsible for managing human rights issues?

- What is the level of human rights awareness?

- Does your company report on human rights risks and mitigation measures?

HUMAN RIGHTS IMPACT RISK ASSESSMENT

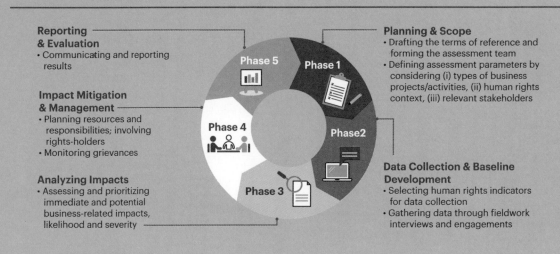

Reporting & Evaluation
- Communicating and reporting results

Impact Mitigation & Management
- Planning resources and responsibilities; involving rights-holders
- Monitoring grievances

Analyzing Impacts
- Assessing and prioritizing immediate and potential business-related impacts, likelihood and severity

Phase 5

Phase 1

Phase 4

Phase2

Phase 3

Planning & Scope
- Drafting the terms of reference and forming the assessment team
- Defining assessment parameters by considering (i) types of business projects/activities, (ii) human rights context, (iii) relevant stakeholders

Data Collection & Baseline Development
- Selecting human rights indicators for data collection
- Gathering data through fieldwork interviews and engagements

Source: The Danish Institute for Human Rights

a skills mismatch between students and the job market, the latter requiring skills related to engineering, vocational training, computer sciences, and finance.

All employees should have equal opportunity to access and personalize their own career development, be it through on-the-job training, coaching and mentorship, or external programs. Needs will vary depending on demographics and the individual, so companies must be proactive in anticipating emerging demands and skills shortages. This could involve partnering with academic institutions or NGOs to directly address skills gaps. For example, USAID has run a program for several years that communicates with Thailand's top employers and universities to develop curricula, internships, and workshops that will equip students with the hybrid, 21st-century skills required by companies today.

Companies outside Thailand, such as Gore & Associates, have invested heavily in employee training. Although it may seem counterintuitive, they avoid the kind of training that corrects a person's weakness, as this only leads to average performance. Instead, the focus of their management development program is to amplify existing strengths. Weaknesses are only addressed if they seriously impede personal growth or interaction with others. With extensive training, employees learn to govern themselves and their operations to achieve their shared goals.

Companies can easily make the case for employee development by demonstrating its material benefits on business performance. Measurements can help in this regard. Aside from high-level measures normally collected like revenue per full-time equivalent (FTE), training costs, costs per hire, and turnover rates, companies can turn to metrics that show value and returns. These include human capital return on investments, human capital value added (which measures average profitability per FTE), human capital market value, and myriad others. Importantly, chosen metrics should align to overarching business strategies.

Development must, moreover, be bolstered by a supportive work environment and efficient internal management processes. For instance,

regular performance reviews, channels for innovation, opportunities for knowledge-sharing and collaboration amongst peers, and notably, internal promotions and successions.

Besides preserving organizational culture, the argument for internal promotions is that it preserves firm-specific knowledge and skills. Insiders are already equipped with an acute understanding of a company's culture and dynamics, and have existing relationships with stakeholders. Mindflash, a learning management solutions company, reports that unsuccessful outside hires could cost a company as much as 25 to 200 percent of the salary allocated to that position.

Companies can easily make the case for employee development by demonstrating its material benefits on business performance.

At the CEO level, hiring outsiders has both benefits and risks. Though they may bring in objectivity and fresh perspectives on a company's challenges, once on-board, they could still face enormous obstacles in rallying forces for aggressive change. The 2015 global Strategy& 'CEO Success Study' by PricewaterhouseCoopers showed that bringing in outsiders more strategically and through planned successions could improve companies' chances of success. Comparing the periods of 2004 to 2007 and 2012 to 2015, the number of outgoing outsider CEOs who were dismissed decreased from 44 percent to 25 percent, respectively. Ultimately, of course, this is an issue to be determined at the discretion of each company.

Finally, if all employees are to develop to the extent that they can substantively participate – and make a difference – in business decisions, they must be empowered to do so. Companies should therefore provide opportunities and incentives for employees at all levels to be innovative and share ideas. According to the Director of Corporate Human Resources at SCG, "It's people at the bottom who come up with new ideas. They are very creative and are

CASE STUDY | Ticketmelon's Culture Drives Competitive Advantage

THE CHALLENGE: When Ticketmelon – a startup digital e-ticketing platform – launched in 2015, CEO Panupong Tejapaibul set out to build two things: an iconic organization and an iconic product. In his view, to achieve these goals a strong organizational culture could be the pillar of differentiation and offer Ticketmelon a competitive advantage over its competitors. Having an attractive organizational culture would enable the company to attract the best talent. The question is, how could this vision be put into practice?

THE SOLUTION: Culture begins at talent recruitment. During the interview process, Ticketmelon conducts two interviews, one technical and one cultural. This is to ensure that new recruits share in Ticketmelon's values and beliefs. "We have a duty to disclose what they are signing up for well in advance," says Tejapaibul.

While Ticketmelon initially had a set of seven values, these were scrapped in mid-2017 due to the belief that culture

must first come from the people. What they've developed as a team is: committed, proactive, and ownership. Tejapaibul acknowledges that while these are all related to work ethics, they demonstrate what it takes to succeed at the company.

Every two weeks, the company holds Ticketmelon Tuesdays, a town-hall that offers all employees insights into the company's financial performance and more. "We treat our employees like business partners. They have a right to know what the impact will be if we don't hit certain goals," he says. This is meant to serve as an incentive for job engagement – to show that employees have a stake in the company's success. Moreover, a stock option is offered to employees after one year of work, with 25 percent immediately vested.

Management commitment is integral, underpinned by the belief that "management serves the people." Ticketmelon also operates on a "hierarchy by skill set," rather than a traditional seniority basis, to show that all contributions are valued and that all employees have equal opportunities to grow.

THE BENEFITS: Though a work in progress, Tejapaibul is optimistic about the long-term benefits of this journey. Even now, Ticketmelon has a Glassdoor rating of 4.3 out of 5, and an annual turnover rate of 6.3 percent.

Going forward, Ticketmelon's goal is to grow to the stage where pay is no longer the main motivator of engagement. And with ambitions to expand first to Southeast Asia and then the Asia-Pacific region, the scalability of the quality of culture will become a challenge. Dynamism is needed now to ensure that this competitive and driven culture expands alongside the company.

highly responsible. That's where innovation comes from."

Sustainable enterprises in Thailand have proven to be pioneers of both radical and incremental innovations. Radical innovation means significant shifts in product lines and processes or developing entirely new products. On the other hand, incremental innovation refers to continuous, small-scale improvements to processes and products to enhance quality, a key characteristic of sustainable enterprises.

Indeed, sustainable Thai enterprises excel in incremental innovation because they invest heavily in people, and provide a system for their workers to express ideas. By nurturing both incremental and radical innovations, companies can save costs and innovate their products, services, and processes.

The wooden toy manufacturer PlanToys, for example, promotes innovation and creativity by encouraging employees to showcase their original designs. Innovation for them is also about embedding a mindset that brings out employees' leadership and problem-solving abilities. Rather than saying something can't be done, employees are confident in saying, "it can be done, and this is how."

In Thailand, rigid organizational hierarchies, the culture of saving face and deference, and an emphasis on seniority can hamper the necessary open communication between employees and their managers and suppress creativity. Generational gaps undoubtedly exacerbate this. The good news is that companies and their human resources departments are gradually picking up on this fact and developing means to facilitate better dialogues.

Organizational culture

Defined broadly, organizational culture comprises the underlying assumptions and beliefs that influence an organization's work environment and employee behavior. Fundamentally, culture is why and how an organization does things. A strong culture can provide long-term benefits for a company. Shared virtues and values can form the heart of organizational culture, define its intangible spirit, fuel the productivity of the workforce, and give the entire enterprise a meaningful sense of purpose.

For Thai companies, however, culture can also present its own thorny issues, particularly when so-called "Thainess" is invoked or held up as being core to that culture. Cultural principles such as deference or confrontation avoidance, for example, can pose obstacles for management teams seeking to discover the leading variable for recommending how to solve a particular issue or looking to create a more productive workforce.

As a result, companies in general have yet to give enough attention to culture as a strategic tool that shapes the norms and behaviors of their people. Often culture is not questioned or is simply accepted as an inherent norm, or else it tends to remain words on a page or a whiteboard, unsupported by management processes. But culture does matter, both for the intangible outcomes it provides, like employee satisfaction, and tangible financial returns over the long-run.

Thai companies must create employment opportunities for members of marginalized groups.

A 2015 report released by Glassdoor, an employment ratings website, evaluating the linkage between company culture and stock performance from 2009 to 2014 found that companies listed on Fortune's 'Best Companies to Work For' and Glassdoor's 'Best Places to Work' significantly outperformed those on the S&P 500 Index by 84.2 percent and 115.6 percent, respectively.

To be sustainable, enterprises must live their core values. They should regard social and environmental responsibility as a given by investing in it, often beyond the legal or standard requirement. They should also take into consideration such virtues as generosity, perseverance, and social and environmental responsibility as part of employee performance evaluation.

"Culture shouldn't be cosmetic," says Panupong Tejapaibul, CEO of Ticketmelon, a digital e-ticketing platform. "As soon as management recognizes the importance of culture, they must spend extra time and focus translating this to people." Ways to achieve this include regular communication with employees, culture-building activities, stories, songs and company traditions, and visual elements.

It can start as early as recruitment, with values and expected behaviors integrated into the criteria for candidates and interviews. Internal promotions should also be prioritized to ensure the continuity of culture from one generation to the next.

At SCG, the core values of 'Adherence to Fairness,' 'Dedication to Excellence,' 'Belief in the Value of the Individual,' and 'Concern for Social Responsibility' have been practiced since the 1990s – before being formalized in writing to be passed on through generations. This runs counter to the traditional approach whereby values are written down first and then implemented (often with much more difficulty). Today, these values are still a formative part of SCG's employee recruitment and retention.

Most significantly, organizational culture tends to reflect the actions, values, and ethics of top management. From the viewpoint of employees, integrity is a critical and admirable characteristic among leaders. "The moment employees start doubting the seriousness of their managers towards their values, cynicism is invariably the consequence," says Dr Sooksan Kantabutra, associate professor at the Mahidol University College of Management.

Indeed, is individual profit (such as bonuses) or personal success the key driver for employees in an organization or are they motivated by the success of the entire business? Weak ethics and poorly respected values could translate into reputational risks and a loss of stakeholder (and employee) trust. Numerous corporate scandals in Thailand attest to this. In fact, researchers Chung Hee Kim and Hugh Scullion find that employees are more intrinsically

---

CASE STUDY   Steps with Theera Creates Jobs for People with Special Needs

People with special needs also deserve fair and gainful employment.

THE CHALLENGE: "I believe up to 67 percent of people with learning differences in Thailand don't have access to education," says Max Simpson, founder and vocational program coordinator of Steps with Theera, a training center for people with special education needs. A lack of awareness and understanding within communities leads to the perception that people who differ from the norm are incapable of participating in the workforce. And while Thai law requires companies to employ one person with a disability for every 100 workers, the measure isn't enforced and employers can opt to pay a fine instead.

THE SOLUTION: Steps with Theera is a unique vocational training center in Bangkok that aims to create sustainable employment pathways for trainees. The center is a functioning bakery and café that is open to the public and gives trainees the opportunity to develop and test their skills.

While Max and her co-founder Theeta Hotrakitya aim to prepare their trainees for employment in a range of industries beyond food, the café format offers a relaxed and informative public interface. The venture is barely a year old but profits from the café, and sales elsewhere offer a sustainable revenue model for the training center, complemented by its program fees. Steps with Theera has also developed an employer guide to build bridges to industry and create pathways for trainees. The Thai government has also recognized them as a non-formal education center with an accredited curriculum from the United Kingdom.

THE BENEFITS: The Sustainable Development Goals of Quality Education (Goal 4), Decent Work and Economic Growth (Goal 8) and Reducing Inequalities (Goal 10) are all relevant for companies that want to be truly sustainable. Moreover, employers of disabled workers consistently report that, as a group, they perform on par or better than their non-disabled peers on measures such as productivity, safety and attendance. They also increase workforce morale.

motivated when employers behave more ethically and are not driven by financial reward.

Research by Khondkar Karim, SangHyun Suh, and Jiali Tang into the 'World's Most Ethical Companies,' an annual ranking by the Ethisphere Institute, similarly finds that ethical firms create higher value for their shareholders by showing that short-term positive returns are associated with firms' ethical performance. Theptarin Hospital, a private healthcare provider in Thailand, operates under the umbrella of 'ETHICS: Excellence, Teamwork, Hospitality, Integrity, Continuous Improvement, and Social Responsibility.' Physicians and other medical professionals are prohibited from marketing themselves or referring patients to other Theptarin services like spas and massages, because engaging in sales is inconsistent with their professional standards.

If a positive organizational culture exists, it can function as an intangible asset. A negative culture, alternatively, can drag on performance and spur an organization's decline. Companies more successful at fostering a healthy, positive culture are typically those with clear statements of visions and values, actively engaged leaders, and longer-term perspectives – meaning those not pressured to deliver on short-term metrics. In companies with high turnover and poor alignment between individual and organizational values, culture-building is much harder.

HR and the sustainability agenda

Now we come to the role of human resources departments in all of this. Traditionally, HR's role has been confined to the operational day-to-day management of employees and responding to routine business needs. That is, recruiting, engaging with, and developing employees; resolving conflicts and grievances; managing benefits and compensation; and planning successions.

But today HR can and should take on a more strategic position to drive major human capital decisions within a company and create long-term value – especially in terms of sustainability. As more and more companies are adopting sustainability visions, strategies, and

commitments (plus the SDGs), HR must be pivotal in developing employees to match and deliver on these goals.

The concept of social responsibility – in the traditional sense of corporate social responsibility (CSR) – has long been ingrained in the core values of the Thai workforce. A reflection of the tenets of Buddhism in the

Today HR can and should take on a more strategic position to drive major human capital decisions within a company and create long-term value – especially in terms of sustainability.

corporate setting, employees are well-versed and open to the concept of karma, and are genuine in giving back and doing good for society. Bathroom Design, a Thai producer of sanitary ware products, regularly uses seven to ten percent of its net profit for CSR-related activities. Employees are encouraged to donate a part of their salary to social causes, which the company matches 100 percent.

As CSR evolves into CSV (or Creating Shared Value) and is integrated into the broader concept of corporate sustainability, employees, too, must expand their understanding of what it means to be socially responsible and sustainable. To facilitate this, HR can begin incorporating sustainability into its existing processes and practices. They can recruit employees whose values are aligned with a company's sustainability vision and objectives – in the same way they would with ethics and organizational culture. Employees can be regularly trained on concepts and opportunities related to sustainable development. Metrics related to sustainability could be incorporated into employee KPIs for performance appraisals and compensation as financial incentives.

Furthermore, HR can assume leadership on sustainability issues where it has substantial influence, such as supporting the employment of persons with disabilities and promoting gender diversity in the workplace. According to business advisory firm Grand Thornton's

CASE STUDY   Dhanabadee Ceramic Navigates a Changing Demographic

functions (although these options are not exclusive to any age group). Among the ageing demographic, Dhanabadee recently piloted the concept of automation in tandem with human skill. This was driven in part by the high turnover of younger employees who may not stick around to support labor-intensive tasks. Health check-ups and retirement planning are regular staples.

Cutting across all groups is the focus on happiness. Panasin's ambition is to create "24-hour happiness" for all. This means a balance between physical, mental, and financial wellbeing, and sharing this happiness with employees' families as well. Buddhist principles are central to this vision. From helping employees practice meditation, to fostering consciousness, Panasin firmly believes that positive thinking and "defragmentation" will generate business resilience in times of crisis and uncertainty.

THE BENEFITS: To Panasin, the benefits of their efforts cannot be encapsulated by numbers alone. Profit numbers are not their competitive point. Nevertheless, the company has seen lower rates of turnover over the past five years, reduced hiring costs, and a 27 percent increase in their mid-year net profit for 2017. A more telling number is the higher return-to-work rate – employees who have quit and returned. The common sentiment among them is, "Dhanabadee Ceramic is our family," he says. An important takeaway is that Dhanabadée has built itself a strong, tight-knit culture that genuinely responds to people's needs and wellbeing – something that is invaluable to the Lampang community.

THE CHALLENGE: Over the past five years, two parallel trends have been shaping the workforce of Dhanabadee Ceramic, a Lampang-based ceramic ware company. The first is a new generation of employees demanding greater flexibility on the job and higher pay. Common among this group is comfort with the world of technology, reduced willingness to perform labor-intensive tasks, and high turnover. The second is an ageing and soon-to-be retiring workforce with long tenures in the company.

Both groups are critical to the company's success: it is these Lampang artisans and designers that have carried the company to world renown. According to Panasin Dhanabadesakul, managing director, "I have the responsibility to create a future for the company." Considering the important role of employees in this future, management must find constructive ways to juggle these diverging needs.

THE SOLUTION: Dhanabadee Ceramic is looking at these shifts simultaneously and tailoring specific solutions.

For the younger generation, the company has offered more flexibility in working hours and location, namely the work-from-home option as some departments, like finance, can still work efficiently on the cloud. To respond to the demand for more diverse and less repetitive responsibilities, employees have the option to rotate across different work

Dhanabadee Ceramic aims to foster the wellbeing of its employees.

2017 'Women in Business' survey, Thailand ranked third in the Asia-Pacific region for the ratio of women in senior management positions (at 31 percent, behind Indonesia and the Philippines).

But that trend is decreasing. Noel Ashpole, partner at Grant Thornton Thailand, said at the time of the survey's release: "The balance between motherhood and career is one of the biggest challenges for Thai women, since having a family is often a significant priority. As a result, many have to choose between having a family and having a successful and fulfilling career due to the lack of supporting infrastructure." Here is one area where HR can have a transformative impact through its strategies.

The prevailing weakness, though, is that HR departments may not yet be well-versed on sustainability themselves to take the plunge. Generally, there is not much collaboration between a company's human resources and sustainability departments, if the latter even exists. Limited collaboration could have a knock-on effect, where rather than HR enabling employees to drive sustainable development, they become merely passive observers of the sustainability agenda.

INSIGHTS

DR SOOKSAN KANTABUTRA, *associate professor at the College of Management, Mahidol University, shares his views on sustainability in human resources management and the future role of HR.*

What advice would you give business leaders on sustainably managing their human resources?

They have to view their people as a prime asset that can be developed. Invest in developing and retaining them even in times of financial crisis, as the investment will certainly pay off – particularly after a crisis. Keep in mind it is unethical not to allow people to develop.

How do you see trends in human resources and culture shifting with the new generation?

The new generation prefers to own a business rather than to work for a big company. They also feel more comfortable changing jobs. Not many people of the new generation will work for a company for a lifetime anymore. Therefore, companies have to develop a new business model so that, even in a large company, employees will have a full sense of business ownership. Maybe even a model that gives opportunities for employees to start new businesses.

What should be the role of HR in preparing its employees for Thailand 4.0?

Thailand 4.0 requires creative people with skills to deal with complexity. With that in mind, companies must change the way they develop people. Self-leading, self-managing skills are needed. Functional skills are not enough. Employees must have multidisciplinary skills that lead to innovation. A strong, productive culture is also needed to act as a soft rule in a company, at the same time allowing enough room for self-leading, self-managing employees to implement their ideas. Most importantly, we have to keep in mind that only happy and secured employees will come to work every day and try to do better for you. And that leads to continuing innovation.

The future workplace

There's no question that HR has a significant and strategic role to play in preparing its people for emerging risks and opportunities. We are already witnessing some of these future changes taking shape. These range from structural shifts toward a more "agile" HR, the use of people analytics to single out difference-making talent, automation, a mobile workplace, and a more socially responsible workforce. It remains to be seen how HR itself will be impacted and how HR will respond to these changes over time.

Fast-forward to 2030, the workplace could be even more different. PwC's 'Workforce of the Future' study looks at four possible models, or 'Worlds of Work,' that could materialize in the coming generations, helping companies to anticipate and prepare for that change.

The first could be a world that is a perfect incubator for innovation, driven by ideas, leveraging digital platforms and technology. The second could be one in which capitalism dominates and corporations attain unrestrained influence, using that to protect their profit margins at all costs. Or third, it could be one

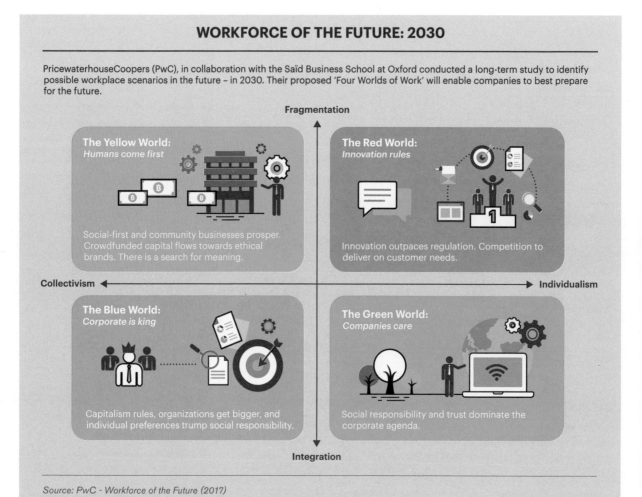

WORKFORCE OF THE FUTURE: 2030

PricewaterhouseCoopers (PwC), in collaboration with the Saïd Business School at Oxford conducted a long-term study to identify possible workplace scenarios in the future – in 2030. Their proposed 'Four Worlds of Work' will enable companies to best prepare for the future.

Fragmentation

The Yellow World:
Humans come first

Social-first and community businesses prosper. Crowdfunded capital flows towards ethical brands. There is a search for meaning.

The Red World:
Innovation rules

Innovation outpaces regulation. Competition to deliver on customer needs.

Collectivism ← → Individualism

The Blue World:
Corporate is king

Capitalism rules, organizations get bigger, and individual preferences trump social responsibility.

The Green World:
Companies care

Social responsibility and trust dominate the corporate agenda.

Integration

Source: PwC - Workforce of the Future (2017)

TAKE ACTION

Managing human resources sustainably requires looking both at how sustainability can improve HR practices and how HR can build employees that have a transformative impact on the wider sustainability agenda. Here are some recommendations to consider:

- **Recruit employees that share in your organization's values, culture, and sustainability vision** by integrating such criteria into recruitment and interview processes.

- **Identify engagement drivers for different groups of employees** in your organization and tailor engagement and management styles to specific needs, such as age group and gender.

- **Regularly engage employees on sustainability issues** to stimulate dialogue and ensure that employees know how they can contribute to the organization's sustainability objectives.

- **Continuously invest in employee development** to meet individual career objectives as well as business needs. Assess potential skills gaps and identify ways to address them, such as through partnerships, collaboration, and training.

- **Prioritize internal promotions and developing successors from within,** where applicable, to ensure the continuity of company skills, culture, and values, and to demonstrate to employees the potential for internal career advancements.

- **Empower employees to speak up and share ideas** to foster innovation and learning.

- **Measure the success of human capital development efforts** against your company's business objectives and make a business case for employee development.

- **Promote gender and cultural diversity in the workplace** by setting measurable targets for diversity and providing enabling infrastructure and measures for work-life balance and families. If possible, expand the geographic area of recruitment.

- **Foster a strong organizational culture and continuous innovation** through regular communication with employees, culture-building activities, and incentives geared towards innovation.

- **Regularly collaborate and communicate with the sustainability department** to build up knowledge on sustainability issues and identify gaps in improving human resources management.

- **Support the company's sustainability objectives** by determining the HR department's own commitments, resources, and responsibilities.

- **Leverage data and technology to engage with employees,** such as mobile and cloud technology, and apply data analytics to better identify talent to deliver business value.

where environmental and social responsibility reigns supreme, in which social purpose becomes the heart of corporate strategy and where rights, diversity, and justice are business imperatives. Finally, the workplace could be one in which "humanness" and ethics is valued above all else, and employees and companies seek greater purpose in what they do.

In Thailand and worldwide, we are already seeing variants of these possibilities emerging and even competing with each other. Which

model becomes most prevalent is certain to have significant impacts on Thai society.

Companies must act now to prepare themselves for these changes. And in a world increasingly driven by technology and innovation, it will be essential to make sure that people are not left behind. As Betsy Ziegler, chief innovation officer at the Kellogg School of Management expressed during a McKinsey roundtable session on the future of work, "There's a competitive advantage to being human."

Resource Management

- *As well as improving long-term resilience and driving returns, effective resource management can also reduce environmental impacts, and slow the depletion of finite natural resources.*

- *Companies that widen procurement parameters stand to achieve positive outcomes for the environment, society, and themselves.*

- *Through a life cycle mindset, new ways to ensure that all materials are used to their maximum potential can be found. Ways of transforming waste into valuable by-products can make extra income or generate energy.*

- *Employees are essential to practicing and establishing a sustainable resource management policy within a company. However, given their involvement in day-to-day operations, they can also help define it.*

It's no secret: we live in a world of depleting natural resources. Minerals, fossil fuels, land, timber, marine life, biodiversity – you name it, that resource has probably been on the decline since the Industrial Revolution. This is known as "resource scarcity," and it has huge implications for the private sector. To run its myriad processes, power its infrastructure, and produce its end products, the business world – especially large, multinational firms – consumes huge amounts of natural resources and raw materials. As a result, severe resource scarcity has the potential to profoundly disrupt the ways in which businesses function.

The bad news is that we are, in certain areas, rapidly approaching a level of severe resource scarcity. According to the UK-based Carbon Trust, an NGO focusing on carbon emissions and resource efficiency, continuing on an inefficient, wasteful, business-as-usual path could potentially lead to a 40 percent gap between water supply and water needs by 2030. In 2010, the EU published a list of 14 raw materials that were already considered "critical" due to lack of supply and high industrial demand. These included magnesium, tungsten, light and heavy Rare Earth Elements, coking oil, chromium, and graphite. Such challenges in material availability can lead to disruptions in product supply, range, and quality; global price fluctuations; and increased regulatory requirements and penalties – all of which end up threatening current economic models and the way we do business. In addition, companies are starting to recognize the negative externalities that resource use poses on society and the environment. When these externalities are factored into accounting costs, companies often find that their costs are much higher.

In Thailand specifically, an ageing population further complicates this landscape. Thailand's businesses are not only impacted by dwindling natural resources, but also by an ageing labor pool and limited human resources.

The good news is that it's not all doom and gloom. Resource efficiency is not just a reactionary measure against bleak forecasts; it is also an indispensable tool that provides business opportunities that can make companies more profitable, sustainable, and secure.

Managed effectively, resource management can translate into cost savings, increased competitiveness, improved agility, and reduced environmental impacts – all of which can be passed on to the consumer.

According to Thapana Sirivadhanabhakdi, the CEO of ThaiBev, resource efficiency has been key to the giant beverage company's success, and its ongoing attempts to be a more sustainability-focused business. "When we're facing a challenging time and talking about focusing on cost savings, we try to ensure that it's not about cost cutting," he says. "Cost saving for us means reengineering work processes, adapting yourself for better efficiencies, strengthening yourself for the better. Cutting costs to save, driving expenses to the bottom line – that's not the ideal."

Examples of efficient resource management include initiatives that help firms increase their internal production and reduce costs. Energy efficiency measures, for example, are widely recognized as a way to reduce waste while also contributing to the bottom line. The Carbon Trust found that shifts towards energy efficiency among 2,000 companies led to an average return on investment of over 40 percent, in comparison to 15 to 20 percent returns for typical business investments.

On an international level, resource management efficiency is seen as a pathway towards global sustainability, allowing firms to improve productivity, save costs, and increase profitability while simultaneously reducing impacts on natural resource consumption. Hence, resource management efficiency has become an important stepping-stone towards decoupling economic growth from unsustainable resource consumption.

While key findings from business executives and managers across the world vary, there are generally considered to be three areas for resource management efficiency intervention.

Procurement: Procurement management refers to the ways in which a firm tailors its input purchases to best fit their production processes. Any miscalculation of these input purchases – such as delivery of inventory, office supplies and equipment, building maintenance, outsourced services, or utilities – will translate to additional and unnecessary costs. If these

Coffee beans dry in the sun at Doi Chaang in Chiang Rai province.

key inputs and production costs can be more efficiently managed, firms can significantly reduce costs and gain a competitive edge.

Imagine a company that orders inputs that come in containers. In its current state, it must incur the costs for disposing of them. But what if that company arranged a procurement

Long-term sustainability relies on continuous assessments of, and improvements in, resource management.

system with the supplier that includes the collection of those empty containers on the next delivery? This arrangement would help the company save on container disposal costs and may also benefit the supplier, as they can reuse the returned containers as well. This is the kind of win-win solution that increases resource efficiency, eliminates waste, reduces input costs, and forges stronger ties with suppliers.

Procurement also holds far-reaching implications for the environment. In Thailand, leading companies have realized this and are

Used plastic bottles are turned into new polyester products at the Indorama Ventures factory in Nakon Pathom province.

making efforts to streamline their procurement practices to minimize consumption of such valuable resources as energy and water. ThaiBev, for example, is a massive consumer of water, as its products are primarily water-based. Recognizing that its procurement practices, consumption, and uses of water contribute to the depletion of this natural resource, ThaiBev has set a goal to reduce its overall specific water withdrawal by five percent by 2020, and to increase its use of reused or recycled water by 11 percent. The

> *Many firms find that what they once considered waste can be repurposed or transformed into valuable by-products.*

company continues to look for responsible ways to source and procure water, and ways to heighten efficiencies in the production process.

Procurement is also the key to IKEA's success in producing environmentally friendly furniture. IKEA does not just purchase inputs

from suppliers but also partners with them to ensure sustainability, efficiency, and quality (see *Case Study*, page 91).

The Life Cycle Mindset: Life cycle thinking is recognized across the globe as a way to significantly help firms save costs, minimize environmental impact, and stay competitive. At its core is a thorough analysis of the life cycle of material inputs and how these inputs can be fully utilized so as to create minimal waste. Such an approach cuts the costs associated with waste collection, processing, or disposal, while also potentially reducing forms of waste that pose health and environmental hazards – which often impose further costs. For these reasons, waste reduction is a common strategy that firms adopt in order to remain lean. Moreover, some types of waste can generate additional income. Many firms find that what they once considered waste can be repurposed or transformed into valuable by-products that can be sold to generate extra income. Examples include recycling wastewater to save on water bills, using biomass to generate electricity, gleaning additional energy from waste heat, and making fertilizers out of agricultural by-products.

HOW TO FAST-TRACK RESOURCE EFFICIENCY

• **ISO14000, ISO50001:** The International Organization of Standardization (ISO) offers guidelines for sustainability standards regarding almost every aspect of business, from forging equitable partnerships to managing health and safety. While ISO14000 covers environmental management systems, ISO50001 focuses on efficient energy use.

• **TBCSD's Green Label:** Seeking certification of Thailand's "Green Label" will ensure that a company's resource use meets national environmental standards. Launched in 1994 by the Thailand Environment Institute and the Thailand Industrial Standards Institute, the Green Label is awarded to products that can prove they have minimal negative impacts on the environment compared to similar products. The three key areas that determine label approval are resource conservation, pollution reduction, and waste management.

• **WRAP:** This nonprofit consultant is a global leader in helping organizations achieve optimal resource efficiency. In just England alone, WRAP initiatives helped companies and institutions reduce greenhouse gases by nearly 50 million tonnes between 2010 and 2015. WRAP's Business Resource Efficiency Hub provides tools, guides, and good practice case studies to help build resource management strategies.

• **Sustainability Reports:** There's much to learn from other industry leaders and players who have already implemented or are experimenting with innovative resource management systems. Thankfully, much of this information – including targets, goals, timelines, cost analysis, and action points – can be found in company sustainability reports. These are valuable resources for ideas and inspiration.

One impressive example is Wellman International, an Irish chemical company and subsidiary of Thailand-based Indorama Ventures, which has focused R&D on creating a closed-loop recycling process for polyester fibers. Their patented 'Eco-Core' system can recover up to 100 percent of polyester components from end-of-life products. Wellman Eco-Core fibers save 2.2 billion plastic bottles annually, which is equivalent to 200,000 barrels of oil. The process reduces harmful air emissions by roughly 300,000 tons and has a carbon footprint that is four times lower than the process of creating virgin PET fibers. The high-quality fiber is used for a diverse range of polyester products, such as insulation, automotive parts, plastic bottles, and the stuffing in duvets and couch cushions. If the ultimate goal of life cycle thinking is to make full use of material inputs without generating waste, Wellman International has proven that this is not only possible, but also profitable.

The concept of the life cycle also goes beyond the boundary of a business's normal operations and considerations. Companies must think about the resource's impact on the

Villagers in Pa Deng village, near the Thai-Myanmar border, make their own biofuel from cow dung.

RUNNING LOW: THAILAND'S ENVIRONMENTAL CHALLENGES

While the planet as a whole is suffering from resource scarcity – water shortages, loss of biodiversity, and depleted fossil fuels – the extent of that scarcity varies greatly at the country level. Natural resource availability in Thailand has, in many ways, governed how businesses have grown and evolved. The rich agricultural base in Thailand gave rise to agribusiness, the abundant marine resources provided raw materials for the frozen seafood exports, and the nation's diverse natural and cultural assets are vital to the tourism industry.

However, over time, the Thai natural resource base has deteriorated to the point where actions are urgently needed. The most alarming resource degradation is seen in forest destruction, severe droughts and floods, pervasive coastal erosion, marine resource depletion, and loss of soil fertility. While these resource issues have already generated negative impacts on Thailand as a whole, they seldom transmit impacts to private businesses and to urban areas. In the case of water shortages, Thai authorities tend to operate in such a manner where the urban population and the business sector are guaranteed sufficient water supplies. The deterioration of marine resources in the Gulf of Thailand has led Thai trawlers to expand their fleet into international waters to ensure the continued supply of marine products. As for forest destruction, the domestic demand has been met by timber imports from neighboring countries – some of it legal, some illegal.

Even though the Thai private sector and urban populations have not felt the full impact of natural resource scarcity, these shortages tend to generate negative consequences in rural communities that are less insulated from natural resource deterioration. A substantial impact of natural resource depletion will, undoubtedly, be passed on to future generations.

STEPS TO MANAGE WASTE

The Waste Hierarchy

- Prevention
- Prepare for re-use
- Recycle
- Recover other value
- Disposal

Source: WRAP UK

environment and society past the end user, or consumer. For instance, once the user of an early version of an iPhone upgrades to the latest model, where will the old phone go? If it goes straight to a landfill, what will be its environmental impacts? Does the phone hold materials that may, over time, pollute the land? Or does it hold materials that can be reused or recycled in some way? Could these reused materials save Apple costs on procuring virgin materials?

By asking these types of questions, a company can develop a life cycle mindset that contributes to a circular economy, which maximizes raw materials' function after the end of a product's service life. And, as the UK-based organization Environmental Services Association points out, all materials not reused to their maximum potential represent losses in revenue. In just the UK alone, an estimated 395 million tons of potentially recyclable materials will be disposed of from 2013 to 2020. Of those materials, only 65 percent will be reused, while 35 percent will not be recovered, representing roughly US$1.8 billion in potential lost revenues.

CASE STUDY	IKEA Puts Sustainability at the Heart of Procurement

IKEA plans to source 100 percent of its wood, paper, and cardboard from sustainable sources by 2020.

THE CHALLENGE: With the world facing natural resource scarcity, IKEA has been striving to turn these challenges into business opportunities. Trying to achieve sustainability by introducing efficiency in internal energy use or waste management, and to get customers and suppliers to join them in this sustainability journey, is no mean feat for any company – let alone one that has 500 stores worldwide and 1.5 billion annual customers.

THE SOLUTION: Giving sustainability top priority is essentially the IKEA business model. The key drivers of IKEA's business model are: 1) providing customers a sustainable livelihood, 2) use of renewable energy and energy efficiency, and 3) providing better lives for people and communities.

IKEA's products provide two solutions for customers: facing sustainability challenges and providing an improved standard of living. Thus, IKEA focuses on making environmentally friendly products at an affordable price. The company's interest in energy efficiency, water efficiency, waste recycling, compactly designed co-working and co-living spaces, storage management, and urban farming filter through to each and every IKEA product.

To foster this business model, IKEA has set – and in some cases, already met – the following targets: source 100 percent of its wood, paper, and cardboard from sustainable sources by August 2020; ensure all cotton is sourced from sustainable sources, such as Better Cotton, as of August 2015; have all home furnishing materials, including packaging, be made from renewable, recyclable, or recycled materials as of August 2015.

By August 2020, 90 percent of IKEA home furnishings will be more sustainable, with documented environmental improvements covering resource use and product functionality, according to IKEA's sustainability scorecard.

On the supply chain, IKEA has a sustainability code of conduct (known as IWAY), hence enabling both their customers and suppliers to become a part of their sustainability business. Materials supplied to IKEA need to conform to the Forest Stewardship Council (FSC), Agricultural Stewardship Council (ASC), Marine Stewardship Council (MSC), and Better Cotton Initiatives (BCI).

THE BENEFITS: IKEA's proven success demonstrates that sustainability can be built into the heart of a business without compromising it. The company's business practice rests very much on one Swedish Philosophy, Lagom, which simply means just the right amount. Lagom encompasses the concepts of simplicity, fairness, contentment, and consideration for others. This Swedish philosophy has much in common with Thailand's Sufficiency Economy Philosophy. The result of integrating this philosophy into the business model has been expansive growth. By 2020, IKEA estimates that its 500 stores around the world will generate 40 to 50 billion Euros per year.

CASE STUDY | Thai President Foods Smartly Cuts Costs

Sufficiency Economy Philosophy principles drive Thai President's business strategy.

THE CHALLENGE: Many Thais willingly admit that Mama Instant Noodles have, in some way, been a part of their youth. The success of Mama Instant Noodles is largely explained by their success in keeping prices low by maintaining resource management efficiency and running on a business model of moderation. So how does such a model work?

THE SOLUTION: Thai President Foods Public Company, creators of the Mama brand, began its instant noodle business in 1972. Since then, the price of oil has risen from three dollars per barrel to about 50 dollars per barrel in 2017, constituting a 17-fold price increase. However, the price of Mama Instant Noodles only rose from two baht per pack in 1972 to six baht per pack in 2017 – only a three-fold price increase. The key of being able to keep prices low compared to general inflation is cost efficiency through innovation.

Thai President Foods continuously introduced technological innovation into their production process. A notable example is the case of energy saving. Previously, instant noodles needed to be steamed by steamers, then fried in cooking oil that used burners. The company innovated a way to switch its energy source to biomass, which is used to heat up their steamer. Any leftover heat is indirectly used to heat cooking oil. An executive of Thai President Foods reveals that,

at present, the company can do away with all burners, and that the current production line releases zero waste water and zero oil discharge. This energy innovation led the company to realize substantial cost savings, enabling it to keep its prices competitive.

Another key success factor lies in a conservative business model – moderation. In the same way that many firms find the Sufficiency Economy Philosophy a key for sustainability, Thai President Foods has been guided by the concept of not leading in technology, but being up-to-date with technology. The company recognized the risk of advancing past its competitors technologically. Instead, the company employed technologies that kept it sufficiently competitive. In addition, Thai President Foods' business survival relies on many forms of moderation: moderate employee working hours, moderate capital utilization to prolong capital life span, and moderate investment to minimize under-utilization.

THE BENEFITS: Thai President Foods' cost saving via technological innovation and sufficiency thinking have helped sustain Mama Instant Noodles' popularity and place on supermarket shelves for around 45 years. In that period, the company has expanded production to Myanmar, Cambodia, and Europe.

Energy innovation has kept the price of the nation's favorite instant noodle snack down.

Employee Engagement: Effectively managing resource efficiency requires vast amounts of information on how an organization can reduce cost, save time, or save inputs. How, then, can a firm obtain the required information, knowledge, or innovations on how to best improve productivity? One common approach is through employee engagement. Although it is possible to hire an outside consultant to provide analysis and reports on efficiency, it is often more cost effective to make concerted and continuous efforts to engage with existing employees.

Because a firm generally involves thousands of procedures, ranging from product design, procurement, line production, and marketing to storage, waste treatment, security, sanitation, and even canteen management, it stands to reason that the people who might know best how that firm can become leaner are the employees themselves. In many cases, employee engagement can help firms identify cost-saving strategies that are tailored to the organization's unique conditions and specifications.

Getting the buy-in of employees also helps ensure that whatever methods are being institutionalized are actually adopted. Because corporate culture and employee engagement play a significant role in implementation, resource efficiency methods that are borne of concerted employee efforts are less likely to meet resistance and more likely to be implemented than recommendations put forward by external consultants.

Employee engagement entails involvement of personnel starting from shareholders, executives, directors, all the way down to security guards and building caretakers. All stakeholders have the potential to provide useful information as to how to save costs and improve productivity in their own realms of expertise. Therefore, regular employee meetings to discuss resource efficiency have been implemented in many organizations.

One way to make employee engagement more effective is through incentives. These can be financial or non-financial. While a bonus system that links firm profitability with an employee salary increase or bonuses is common, non-financial incentives – such as increased fringe benefits, better recreational facilities, or simply recognizing successful initiatives and employee contributions – have also proven successful in many instances.

Employee engagement can help firms identify cost-saving strategies that are tailored to the organization's unique conditions and specifications.

"It's important to keep communicating improvements to your staff and ideally to try to tie those improvements with more incentives or bonuses," says Benjamin Lephilibert of LightBlue Environmental Consulting, which works with hotels to

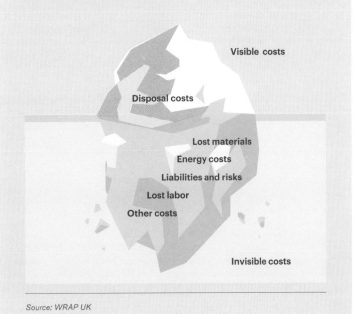

THE HIDDEN COSTS OF WASTE

The true costs of waste in an organization may not be what it seems. In fact, there are many invisible costs associated with waste disposal. According to WRAP UK, on average, the true cost of wasted materials is approximately 10 times the cost of disposal. This makes waste a key target area for efficiency initiatives.

Visible costs

Disposal costs

Lost materials

Energy costs

Liabilities and risks

Lost labor

Other costs

Invisible costs

Source: WRAP UK

LARS SVENSSON, *sustainability and communication director at IKEA Southeast Asia, shares his insights on the sustainability transformation and successful resource efficiency drive at IKEA.*

What is the heart of sustainability at IKEA?

We are aiming to make sustainability an integral driver of our business. We were sort of "green" before we even knew what green was. And we did it for the reason of being as cost-effective as possible. On the other hand, it was to provide decent, reasonable, well-defined, quality furniture for as many people as possible at affordable prices. To achieve that, you need to be cost-efficient in all levels. But we also said that we can't be low-priced at any price or at any cost. We recognized the fact that there are certain human rights and standards as well. The concept expanded to become an all-encompassing part of how we design the products and build the stores, how we work with people, how we source, and work with our suppliers. So that is the essence: having sustainability integrated into our everyday business.

What does IKEA do internally to increase efficiency and lower costs?

One of our core values is cost-consciousness, and cost-consciousness also translates into using less resources. [That can go] into transportation – the frequency of transportation; how well you can pack a container – and that's where the flat-pack furniture comes in, because it's much more cost-efficient to transport flat-pack furniture than assembled furniture. We work with renewable energy sources at our stores, either trying to buy them or install them for direct uses in our stores. We also build our structures so they're well insulated and we can achieve as much efficiency as possible for materials and for operating the stores effectively.

IKEA works a lot on procurement. How do you introduce certifications – such as the marine and forest stewardship councils – and get your suppliers to comply?

When you talk about buying standards and certain ethical procurement methods, there's a fear that costs will increase. But our experience over time is we managed to pair these standards with new ways of working, so we can also achieve efficiencies in the system. We managed to lower the cost and lower the prices over time…through increased productivity, through better efficiencies, or through volume – or in a combination. These may not be immediate results that happen the first year.

This is not only to fulfill certain environmental requirements or because it's good for Mother Earth over the next 30 or 40 years. But it actually makes good business sense. This helps us develop our business in a good way while being able to maintain integrity with the brand, and also run ahead of policy making. It's important that you find partnerships. You need to find individuals and companies and entrepreneurs that have the same mindset of wanting to develop their business efficiencies.

IKEA has a lot of targets – difficult ones too. How do you plan, monitor, set strategies, and put everything to practice?

Our work is trying to make sustainability an integrated part of everyone's department and everyone's area. The reason we want to do that is because the best decision-makers are the ones who have the responsibility for their respective area. We're trying to make the sustainability goals an integrated part of their KPIs. When it comes to energy, that's something we look at in our facilities department. When it comes to waste management, it's the store operations and the facilities again that take a look at it. The goals have been distributed out into the organization, so ownership is distributed.

STEPS TO SUSTAINABLE PROCUREMENT

The following diagram can help your business consider ways to integrate sustainability thinking into each step of the procurement process.

1 Understand the **business need** and make the case for sustainable options

2 Develop **category strategies** that incorporate sustainability opportunities

3 Identify potential **suppliers** that could meet sustainability requirements

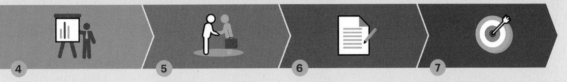

4 Create a sourcing **strategy** that includes specific sustainability requirements

5 **Negotiate** and select competitive suppliers that meet the sustainability requirements

6 Finalize **contract** with sustainability requirements and align on performance objectives

7 Manage supplier **performance** and develop collaborative efforts to increase sustainability impacts

Source: BSR Center for Sustainable Procurement

establish and fulfill resource efficiency needs and objectives. "It doesn't have to be financial. You should also celebrate their achievements. And put people that are proactive forward and shed a nice light on them."

Baselines and beyond

When adopting or prioritizing resource management strategies, businesses must be strategic, as implementation can be costly. To ensure that resource management practices are financially and strategically sound, managers or leaders should approach things analytically. Before doing anything, sufficient data and information must be collected to enable decision-making – namely, the quantity of inputs used and how much output is produced. This will provide the baseline information necessary for making comparisons between proposed scenarios, so enabling managers to calculate the unit cost of each resource management strategy available.

The manager will also need to evaluate the overall operations of the firm to identify which department or line of work should take priority.

Wellness resort and spa Chiva-Som engaged with the Clinton Climate Initiative's Energy Efficiency Building Retrofit Program in 2013 to improve energy efficiency and reduce their carbon emissions. The company replaced its lighting and air conditioning systems, which resulted in a 26 percent reduction in monthly electricity consumption and a related 20 percent reduction in carbon footprint.

Whether it's switching from fossil fuels to renewable energies or adopting the use of energy-saving light bulbs, the simple rule of thumb is to engage in activities that yield the highest value to your company and that are suited to your business model. Hence, continued data collection, employee engagement, analysis of unit costs and rates of return – and reviews of past achievements and obstacles – are key steps to adopt when moving towards efficient resource management. Companies should also not overlook the importance of partnerships and working with like-minded suppliers or business partners.

The final stage is to establish a set of resource management procedures that generate the highest profits. In other words, implementation is more likely when a strong business case is made for resource management efficiency.

Ultimately, resource management efficiency is a tangible way for the private sector to contribute to the national bottom line. While maximized

efficiencies and highly competitive companies will contribute to a robust economy, continued innovations in resource use will spur more sustainable development. According to the sustainable investment specialist RobecoSAM, "The quest for resource efficiency can stimulate technological innovation and create new markets, which are the engines for future economic growth." Such positive impacts can be felt globally, too. Resource efficiency, especially when adopted on a large, industrial scale, has the potential to further the UN's Sustainable Development Goals by leaps and bounds. Numerous goals – such as Goal 9: Industry, Innovation and Infrastructure; Goal

---

CASE STUDY | Mitr Phol Transforms Sugarcane Waste to Energy

Turning sugarcane into fuel reduces the CO_2 emissions traditionally released by burning.

THE CHALLENGE: On average, every ton of sugarcane processed results in 250 kgs of bagasse, 250 kg of cane waste (top and trash), and 43 kg of molasses. Both bagasse and cane waste can be converted to produce steam and electricity, and the molasses to ethanol, which leaves 6-10 liters of vinasses per liter of ethanol produced.

However, about 65 percent of cane harvesting involves cane burning before cutting – a major source of carbon dioxide and air pollutants, not to mention a lost opportunity for harnessing the latent energy potential of cane waste. The predicament: how to harness all the available resources and maximize their utility?

THE SOLUTION: Mitr Phol Group set up dedicated companies to run highly efficient bagasse- and molasses-ethanol-fired power plants, this with a view to producing steam and electricity for its own use and exporting the surplus to the grid. Mitr Phol has also pioneered the "modern farm" approach by managing groups of small- and medium-sized contract cane growers, enabling farm mechanization and better agriculture practices, such as irrigation, reduced tillage, and smart logistics.

THE BENEFITS: Today, Mitr Phol contributes 490 megawatts of power from bagasse, and 1.4 million liters per day of ethanol. The business generates 20,000 million baht annually (35 percent of total revenue) and 900 jobs, and benefits more than 30,000 contract farmers. The modern farm practice has doubled cane output per hectare and avoided cane burning, benefiting cane growers in income. It has also improved the environment, avoided 10 kilograms per ton of cane CO_2 emissions, and enabled recovery of cane waste. Options to convert vinasses into useful products are also being investigated.

Recent life cycle environmental footprint assessments show that Mitr Phol's cane-based bioenergy industry outperforms internationally accepted sustainability standards. "Our ultimate goal is a zero-waste, multi-generation biorefinery and realization of the bioeconomy vision," says Pravit Prakitsri, managing director at Mitr Phol Biofuel.

TAKE ACTION

To tackle resource challenges and improve efficiencies, consider the following steps:

- **Develop a baseline understanding of your resource use and existing (in)efficiencies** by gathering data on the quantity of inputs and outputs, analyzing cost information, and evaluating past resource management procedures. Identify gaps, obstacles, and improvement opportunities.

- **Establish a resource management program for the short-term and long-term**, which can be targeted to a specific resource, department, process, or all of the above (as an all-encompassing strategy). Consider the stakeholders affected and resources required to put the program/strategy into action. Initiatives could include:

  - Company-wide energy/water/waste efficiency management

  - Environmentally-friendly product and service design that applies life cycle thinking

  - Replacing chemical or toxic materials with organic inputs

  - Adopting certification requirements for procured materials and goods to ensure that suppliers use environmentally and socially safe inputs

  - Returning empty containers and boxes to reduce waste disposal costs and reap additional discounts on procurement

- **Adopt the 3Rs approach: Reduce, Reuse, and Recycle** as a way to secure business opportunities and savings for the bottom line. Examples include water-saving or recycling strategies, zero waste to landfill, transforming waste and by-products, and switching to supplies (office, raw materials, etc.) that are recyclable or reusable.

- **Regularly engage with employees to identify pathways for resource and productivity improvements.** Provide channels for employees to offer ideas in their respective areas of expertise such as meetings, internal company websites, events, site visits and knowledge-sharing sessions.

  - Consider integrating resource management and productivity criteria into employee performance evaluations to incentivize their involvement.

  - Establish financial and non-financial incentives that recognize employee contributions.

12: Responsible Consumption and Production; and Goal 13: Climate Action – will benefit from the private sector's conscientious use and reuse of resources. In other words, companies can not only reap bottom line benefits through better resource management, but they can also help shoulder mankind's obligation to nurture a more sustainable world for everyone.

Companies that earnestly pursue resource efficiency are finding that it offers numerous business opportunities. As the Carbon Trust puts it, "Businesses that adapt their business models through assessing their exposure to such resource constraints can identify how to manage these risks and exploit commercial opportunities. In turn this will improve efficiency, strengthen long-term resilience, and drive business returns." What's more, many organizations have found that prudent resource management results in long-term advantages that far outweigh the immediate costs. In fact, the long-term advantages are not limited to the company but extend far into the development and sustainability of the nation, communities, and the environment at large. At the heart of responsible resource procurement and consumption is innovation – trends that help companies rethink and re-engineer the way they consume, produce, and operate. Such initiatives will help companies improve productivity and save costs, while allowing them to stay competitive and absorb shocks.

Supply Chain Management

- *For businesses to remain competitive and to meet public demand, they must factor environmental, social, and governance concerns into their supply chain decisions.*

- *Increased supply chain efficiency offers ESG benefits as well as earning potential through reduced costs and improved reputation.*

- *Companies must embrace "resilience" and "responsibility" to meet the wide-ranging challenges of building a sustainable supply chain.*

- *Close collaboration with suppliers – including information and resource sharing, compliance assessments, and open communication – is essential to effective supply chain management.*

In the past, supply chains were simple. The hunter-gatherers were, effectively, their own self-contained supply chains: planners, suppliers, makers, and end consumers. Later, in the Neolithic, or Stone Age, the advent of pastoral and crop farming allowed people to produce more than they needed, and simple forms of exchange evolved. Even by the time of Europe's Industrial Revolution, a simple, if transcontinental, line – from, say, the tea plantations of Darjeeling to the drawing rooms of Victorian-era London – could still be drawn from source to customer.

But as the world has gotten flatter and smaller, supply chains – the networks of resources, activities, and labor involved in planning, sourcing, making, and delivering products and services – have gotten more complex. Successive and accelerating waves of globalization – especially the current one, with its free trade agreements, seamless transport connectivity, transnational outsourcing and offshoring, and component-based tech – have turned simple linear tracks into elaborate webs with vast magnitudes of scale. Raw materials and services now flow without regard for geography, distance, culture, or even language. A suit that purports to be "Made in Italy," for example, can consist of wool sourced from Mongolia, which is processed and woven into fabric in China, then finally sent to Italy for sewing and assembly.

What does the labyrinthine nature of contemporary supply chains mean for Thai businesses? In a nutshell: more risk and more responsibility. Until recently, a conscientious procurement officer or supply chain manager focused on removing the fat from every step: improving technical qualities, cost effectiveness, speed of delivery, and reliability. Today, however, there is much more at stake. Media exposé after media exposé – some pointing a finger at Thailand – has shown that merely streamlining your supply chain and trying to gain more output from less input is no longer enough, especially for those companies who procure, produce, or sell beyond the country's borders.

Exploitation, pollution, corruption – the supply chain issues that were once hidden from view, ignored, or blithely brushed under the carpet by businesses are increasingly their dirty laundry. Technology has gifted supply chains with enormous economic, sociocultural, and even geo-political power – but it has also exposed them to scrutiny. With much of the modern world now more cognizant of the impacts, or externalities, that the manufacture and distribution of a specific product or service can have, businesses must be more cognizant of them too. Being found complicit in environmental or social damage can make a huge dent in a company's brand, reputation, and shareholder value.

But it should also be pointed out that the reasoning behind the rise of sustainable supply chains is not just risk-driven. The need to comply with growing regulatory requirements is also a factor, and, as we shall see, there are also strategic opportunities and benefits to be gained and leveraged from them too.

What is a sustainable supply chain?

The UN Global Compact – a resource offering concrete steps and practical resources to help businesses achieve corporate sustainability –

defines supply chain sustainability as "the management of environmental, social and economic impacts, and the encouragement of good governance practices, throughout the life cycles of goods and services." It also delineates three areas that companies sincere about adopting good corporate sustainability practices and spreading them throughout the wider business community should engage with their upstream suppliers on.

Merely streamlining your supply chain and trying to gain more output from less input is no longer enough.

Human Rights and Labor: Supply chains are now inextricably linked to human rights and labor issues. Often migrants, day laborers, and other vulnerable people are involved in the producing, growing, gathering, processing, and distributing of commodities and goods – and due to the sheer number and various

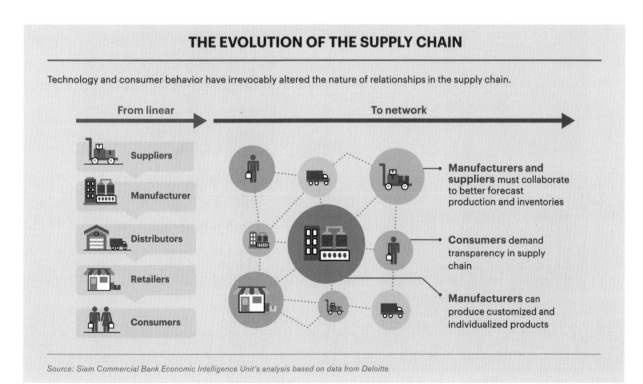

THE EVOLUTION OF THE SUPPLY CHAIN

Technology and consumer behavior have irrevocably altered the nature of relationships in the supply chain.

From linear → To network →

Suppliers
Manufacturer
Distributors
Retailers
Consumers

Manufacturers and suppliers must collaborate to better forecast production and inventories

Consumers demand transparency in supply chain

Manufacturers can produce customized and individualized products

Source: Siam Commercial Bank Economic Intelligence Unit's analysis based on data from Deloitte

tiers of suppliers and subcontractors involved, keeping track of how they are paid and treated can be tricky.

Unscrupulous labor practices and human rights abuses can, it has been proven, damage the reputation, operations, and bottom line of businesses. Recently, Thai fisheries came under fire for failing to stop human trafficking and forced labor in the wild seafood trade. In 2014, the US State Department's Trafficking in Persons (TIP) Report downgraded Thailand to tier three, the lowest level, before upgrading it to tier two ('watch list') in 2016. In April 2014, the EU issued Thailand a 'yellow card,' threatening to ban seafood imports from the region unless the country cleared up illegal fishing and labor abuses.

The current Thai government's new policy to create more systematic and efficient management of migrant workers will hopefully solve such human rights and labor issues. The Royal Decree on Managing the Work of Aliens, which came into effect in June 2017, aims to root out illegal, unreported, and unregulated (IUU) fishing in Thailand. Furthermore, it should also address the human trafficking problem and ensure the protection of rights of migrant workers who are often marginalized and exploited.

However, even as the government and the private sector try to address such issues according to international standards, small- and medium-sized firms will continue to struggle to implement sustainability practices without proper resources and education. This remains a risk for the Thai fishery industry as a whole – and for any industry that operates without sustainable supply chain management.

The Environment: For most manufacturing companies, supply chains account for

THE BUSINESS CASE FOR SUPPLY CHAIN SUSTAINABILITY

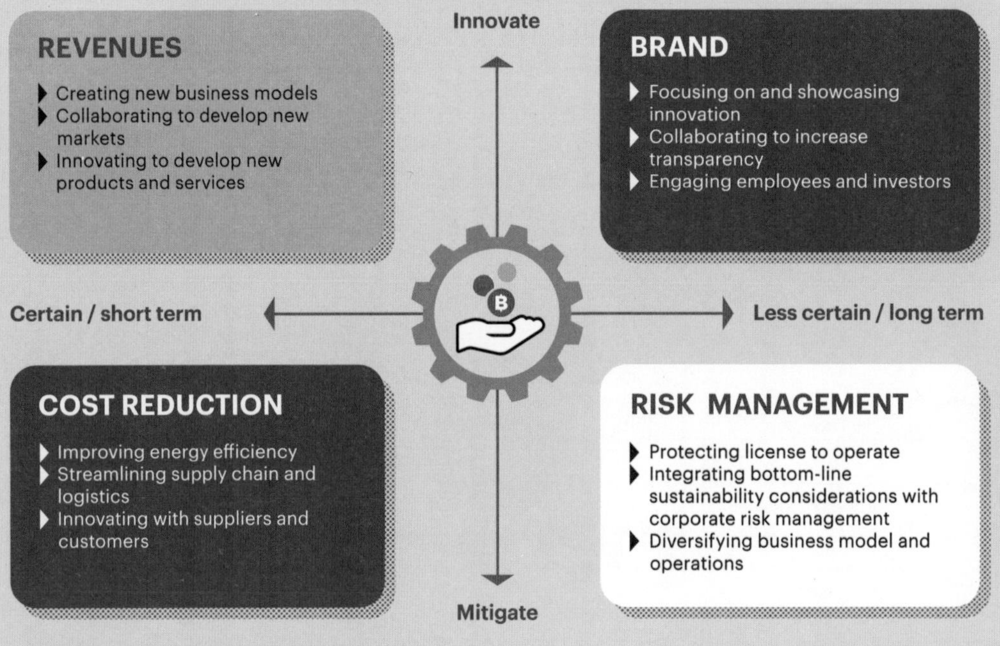

Innovate

REVENUES

▶ Creating new business models
▶ Collaborating to develop new markets
▶ Innovating to develop new products and services

BRAND

▶ Focusing on and showcasing innovation
▶ Collaborating to increase transparency
▶ Engaging employees and investors

Certain / short term ← → Less certain / long term

COST REDUCTION

▶ Improving energy efficiency
▶ Streamlining supply chain and logistics
▶ Innovating with suppliers and customers

RISK MANAGEMENT

▶ Protecting license to operate
▶ Integrating bottom-line sustainability considerations with corporate risk management
▶ Diversifying business model and operations

Mitigate

Source: Accenture analysis

between 50 and 70 percent of total expenses and greenhouse gas emissions. As a result, forward-thinking firms are taking steps to 'green' both their direct operations and indirect supply chains – pursuing measures that cut pollution, minimize waste, and boost energy efficiency, and encouraging their suppliers to do the same.

One high-profile success story is that of Zara, a global clothing manufacturer and retailer that boasts more than 2,000 stores in 88 countries – and practices a form of supply chain sustainability that's built on local sourcing. Rather than procuring and manufacturing textiles in Asia, as many garment manufacturers do, Zara has created a centralized supply chain in and around Europe. Over 50 percent of Zara's products are produced in Spain, Turkey, and North Africa, enabling the company to cut down on emissions, save on transport costs, and distribute goods to any one of its global stores in just 48 hours.

Another important supply chain issue relating to the environment is food miles: the long distances that food travels to reach our plates is having serious consequences on the climate, as well as health. A UK study of food miles has determined that the globalization of the food industry has led to a concentration of the food supply base into fewer, larger suppliers, partly to meet demand for bulk year-round supply of uniform produce. It has also resulted in major changes in delivery patterns; a rise in use of larger heavy goods vehicles; and a switch by consumers from frequent trips on foot to small local shops to weekly supermarket shops using cars. This rise in food miles has led to increases in CO_2 emissions, air pollution, traffic congestion, accidents, and noise.

One ray of hope is that people all over the world are discovering the broad benefits of buying locally produced goods. A Thai example would be the success of organic and natural food supermarket and e-store Lemon Farm. In pursuit of chemical-free produce that consumers can trust, it works closely with Thai farmers and nurtures short, transparent supply chains that begin and end in Thailand. Another would be Central Group's attempts to create shared value with Thai SMEs and farmers

Thailand's seafood industry has come under fire for labor abuses hidden deep in the supply chain.

through a range of different approaches, including farmer's markets, product development, and knowledge sharing. While farmers and businesses benefit directly from these kinds of local supplier relationships, there is a knock-on effect for the environment too: buying local means that products don't travel long distances, which dramatically reduces energy consumption as well as the pollution that contributes to global warming.

For most manufacturing companies, supply chains account for between 50 and 70 percent of total expenses.

Anti-corruption: Corruption makes business more costly by imposing extraordinary obstacles to growth. In Thailand, the corruption situation is alarming. According to Transparency International, Thailand ranked 101st in the 2016 Corruption Perception Index, dropping from 76th place a year earlier. This directly impacts the supply chain of many sectors for many reasons, not least of which is the high correlation between public sector corruption and trafficking for labor exploitation, according to the international labor watchdog Verité. Corruption can also impose significant reputational, operational,

CASE STUDY   Tesco Lotus's Sustainable Supply Chain Distribution System

THE CHALLENGE: The distribution system of the modern trade retailer requires constant transportation of goods from suppliers to Distribution Centers (DCs), and then from their DCs to various retails stores and shops. Inefficient logistics are not only unsustainable in terms of energy consumption, but also in the availability and competitiveness of the business's inventory in stores.

Tesco Lotus is a hypermarket chain in Thailand operated by Ek-Chai Distribution System Co., Ltd. On busy days, such as over holiday periods, the company's transported distances in one day are approximately equal to the distance between the earth and the moon. This creates challenges in managing the distribution system efficiently.

THE SOLUTION: Distribution solutions involve many elements in the supply chain process, ranging from inventory reduction strategies to packaging and distribution, as well as transport operating optimization. All elements relate to sustainability.

An efficient distribution system will reduce inventory cost. In the past, Tesco Lotus used only one big distribution center located in Wang-Noi, Ayutthaya Province. As the number of stores upcountry increased, a central distribution center posed serious issues on delivery lead time and volume of delivered merchandise to optimize transportation costs. It was also vulnerable to transport network disruptions, such as the flooding of 2011, which blocked routes to the DC. Thus, Tesco Lotus opened two new DCs, one in the northeast's Khon Kaen province, and one in the south's Surat Thani province.

Packaging also came under scrutiny. Tesco Lotus operates three sizes of stores, from super stores (Tesco Lotus Department Stores) to small stores (Tesco Lotus Express). Package sizes delivered from suppliers are often standardized to 12 or 24 items per package. However, some small stores may not require a whole package to restock. This creates inventory burdens and packaging waste. Currently, Tesco Lotus recycles and compresses around 650 tons of package waste per week to resell to SCG. Thus, a new initiative with supplier collaboration was created to increase case sizes as much as possible. This way, the distribution center can use a single picking operation to reduce both unnecessary inventory and package waste simultaneously. Tesco Lotus also reduced CO_2 emissions by innovating its cold chain systems. Normally, a refrigerated truck will only begin cooling compartment temperatures once the engine is started. This created a lot of emissions. Instead, Tesco Lotus modified the truck to be able to plug-in the refrigerated system with the starting of the vehicle engine, which can reduce a significant amount of CO_2 created.

THE BENEFITS: Since the opening of new DCs in Khon Kaen and Surat Thani, inventory costs were reduced, transportation distances and costs were optimized, and the supply chain network became more resilient to network disruption. Reduced transportation distances in turn reduced the amount of CO_2 emissions. In addition, the arrangement with suppliers to change their case sizes has reduced inventory costs significantly over the past couple of years, says Tesco Lotus Supply Chain Director Dr Apiruk Detwarasiti. This also reduced packaging waste. These efforts show that smart design and management of the supply chain can lead to both business gains and sustainable benefits.

Tesco Lotus built distribution centers in Northeast and South Thailand in an effort to improve supply chain efficiency and reduce inventory costs.

| CASE STUDY | SCG Logistics Suppliers Collaborate to Improve Road Safety |

SCG Logistics trains and tests truck drivers in an effort to reduce road accidents.

THE CHALLENGE: According to a report published by the World Health Organization in 2015, Thailand reported a higher road death rate than any other country apart from war-ravaged Libya. In terms of business operations, traffic accidents during the delivery of merchandise create disruptions in the supply chain and also affects society negatively.

Third-party logistics providers often contract out transport activities to subcontractors, but managing and supervising these subcontractors in terms of safety standards is difficult.

SCG Logistics Management, a subsidiary of SCG Cement–Building Materials, is a third-party logistics provider (3PL), offering total logistical support and transportation of products, ranging from raw materials to finished goods, both locally and internationally.

SCG Logistics manages around 200 carriers (subcontractors) with more than 7,500 vehicles in total. Due to the large scale of these operations, steps must be taken to increase service reliability and road safety.

THE SOLUTION: SCG Logistics' safety initiatives include stringent maintenance of transport vehicles as well as the development of drivers. GPS technology is used to monitor driver behavior in all vehicles in operation.

However, simply using technology is not enough – the key issues are the safety training, skills, and behavior of the driver. Because the current driver's license application system does not guarantee the quality of the driver, SCG Logistics has

established the Skill Development School to design and develop several levels of training for drivers. The carrier's drivers are required to attend this driver training program before they can work. Furthermore, all drivers are retrained at least once a year. The driver-centric safety management system covers all logistics stages and aspects that correspond to a safety-security procedure.

Moreover, truck stopping points present high risks because they create roadside hazards that can cause accidents with motorcyclists. Thus, SCG Logistics also built public truck stations in many regions of Thailand so drivers can rest on long-distance hauls. This ensures that they can drive safely, and that communities along driving routes are also kept safe.

THE BENEFITS: Reducing road traffic accidents throughout the supply chain can reduce the level of inventory waste. In addition, SCG Logistics' customers can reduce their inventory burden with Just-In-Time inventory delivery. The Skill Development School for drivers and other staff proves how important human resource development is, as it promotes and develops staff at various levels and fosters a safety-first mindset.

Syamrath Suthanakul, managing director of SCG Logistics, emphasizes, "We are in the logistics service business, not a killing business." Although it may seem like the private sector's efforts to improve road safety is a small step, this attempt should be seen as an encouraging example of supply chain sustainability and should be promoted as a good practice in this field.

ORGANIZATIONAL SUPPLY CHAIN MODELS FOR INTEGRATIING SUSTAINABILITY

Siloed	Hybrid	Integrated
▶ Supply chain sustainability responsibility is segregated from core supply chain management. ▶ Sustainability criteria are developed and managed separately. ▶ In some cases, limited dialogue among functions occurs, but this is not formalized and often occurs on an ad hoc basis.	▶ Sustainability function collaborates with procurement or supply chain to provide input in supply chain management process. ▶ Typically, sustainability function will establish strategy, governance, and process. ▶ In many cases, a cross-functional working group will facilitate the collaboration.	▶ Sustainability is embedded in procurement, category management, and sourcing processes. ▶ Sustainability is weighted and considered along with traditional supply chain factors (price, quality). ▶ Programmatic integration of sustainability issues goes across business units (training, measurement, standards).

Source: EY: The State of Sustainable Supply Chains (2016)

financial, and legal risks along the supply chain through bribery, fraud, nepotism, and extortion. Companies that address corruption improve product quality, reduce legal and fraud costs, enhance reputations, and build a solid foundation for sustainable business growth.

In Thailand, steps are being taken to root out corruption in public procurement. The government's piloting of the Construction Sector Transparency Initiative (CoST) – a global initiative to increase the levels of disclosure and accountability in public construction projects – is one promising recent example.

However, as a country that ranks high in corruption, Thailand still has a long way to go in instilling and ensuring transparency. However, the private sector can contribute to making anti-corruption a top priority by establishing supplier compliance standards, conducting annual inspections or audits, and nurturing a corporate culture of good governance.

Tailoring a sustainable supply chain vision

While these kinds of potential impacts are becoming increasingly visible to stakeholders of all stripes, keeping accurate tabs on them

in today's world of deep, twisting, multi-tier supply chains is not easy – for Thai companies, or for any company.

A 2010 *Harvard Business Review* survey revealed that while 50 percent of respondents were confident in the sustainability performance of their internal suppliers, that figure reduces considerably as supply chains become more convoluted: only 33 percent were confident in their first-tier suppliers' sustainability credentials, 16 percent in the second tier, and only 10 percent in the third tier.

Other research has shown that the deeper into the supply chain you delve, the more environmental and social risks you find. These risks tend to be more critical than the risks found on the first tier: Sedex, a nonprofit dedicated to improving ethical business practices in global supply chains, recently found that tier two on the supply chain poses around 18 percent more risk issues than the first tier; however, only a third of companies globally seek transparency below the first level.

So how should a company begin keeping tabs on them? The short answer: it depends on your company, and also the industry – and spirit – in which it operates. Defining what sustainability means to your company and its stakeholders is a key first step (see *Sustainability Strategy*, page 32), as is figuring out how your supply chain intersects with – and informs – that strategy. For some companies, a sustainable supply chain might mean empowering women or minorities; for others it could be managing conflict minerals, eliminating child labor, identifying opportunities for creating a circular economy – or all three. A supply chain risk assessment or a materiality assessment (see *Sustainability Strategy*, page 32) can help in identifying relevant supply chain priorities.

Figuring out who takes ownership of sustainability in the supply chain is also important. Typically for big businesses, accountability resides with the supply chain or procurement team, but EY's 2016 survey of 70 international companies revealed that it sometimes resides with the corporate sustainability team, or even the marketing, legal, risk, or operations departments. This same survey also showed how sustainability is being integrated into supply chains – another sticking point. Researchers found

INSIGHTS

KOSIT SUKSINGHA *is chief of supply chain management and executive vice president at ThaiBev, one of the largest food and beverage companies in Southeast Asia.*

What is ThaiBev's overarching vision for sustainability in its supply chain?
ThaiBev Group manages our supply chain by adopting sustainability practices to minimize our environmental and social impacts and by utilizing digital platforms to maximize the efficiency of our operations. Sustainability is integrated into our end-to-end supply chain from raw material acquisition to post-consumption.

How do you encourage your suppliers to adopt sustainability?
We have established the ThaiBev Supplier Code of Practice, a sustainability standard for suppliers to follow and to apply to their own business, and it is embedded throughout our procurement process. For our logistics, safe and on-time delivery is our priority. We strictly adhere to human rights and occupational health and safety standards to ensure the welfare of our employees and communities. In addition, we are concerned with the environmental impacts from our transportation, i.e.,

energy consumption and greenhouse gas emissions. To minimize such impacts, we regularly conduct route planning to optimize the transportation distance as well as improve the condition of our vehicles and keep track of the energy consumption from each journey. As for our post-consumption impact management, we strive to maximize the value of our operational waste and by-products and return it into our production to create a circular supply chain. Aside from our own operations, we also collaborate with our suppliers to optimize their resource consumption e.g. working with our packaging suppliers to constantly optimize our packaging while maintain the quality of the packaging for our consumers.

What is the role of technology in ThaiBev's supply chain management?
Digitalization is a key driver of our supply chain development. Technology adoption allows us to automate non-value added tasks in our supply chain, optimizes overall processes, and gives room for our supply chain to transform from operation-based to a strategic one. Online and real-time data give way to supply chain visibility and transparency. With this enabler, we are able to synergize across business functions, which helps us improve end-to-end collaboration. The goal is not solely creating and exploiting benefits but also sharing them with our business partners. For this reason, we emphasize capability development for our suppliers to foster a strong and sustainable business relationship.

that, while an 'Integrated' approach – whereby sustainability is fully embedded in procurement and sourcing processes, and weighted equally alongside traditional supply chain factors – is most desirable, a 'Hybrid' one is the more common (see chart, page 104). As things stand, this organizational model, along with the more segregated 'Siloed' approach, is currently prevalent in Thailand.

In broad terms, the end goal should be a sustainable supply chain that is, to paraphrase EY, both resilient and responsible: *resilient* because it is adaptable to external factors that may impact a company's ability to produce a product or service; and *responsible* because it is as benign as possible, and is structured and monitored to produce minimal impacts on communities, the environment, and across the value chain. Why is supply chain resilience and responsibility so important? Just look around you. Recent events in Thailand have proven that companies that lack resilience or take a narrow view of their responsibilities – from manufacturers ill-prepared for severe floods to the aforementioned fishing companies – expose themselves to risks that may jeopardize their reputation, sales, social license, or longevity.

Implementing a sustainable supply chain

A 2013 PricewaterhouseCoopers (PwC) survey of 211 companies in five major ASEAN economies (Indonesia, Malaysia, the

---

CASE STUDY | Anek Farm Becomes a Sustainability-conscious Supplier

THE CHALLENGE: Back in the 1990s, Anek Farm – a producer of raw and boiled quail eggs in Angthong province – was already well-established as a supplier for both the wholesale and consumer markets. But when its client base grew, so did the need to scale up and to meet the standards that the big players enforce these days.

THE SOLUTION: Anek Farm's production facilities used to be primitive: there was a basic boiler, there were facilities for the manual cleaning and peeling of the eggs, and that's it. But when a friend brought a big new client into the fold – Minor Food Group, a Thailand-based food services giant in need of a steady and safe supply of quail eggs for its Sizzler restaurant concessions – things began to change.

"Minor has introduced a standard of quality and sustainability through our supply chain," says Anek Seekiawsod, the farm's owner. According to Sarnsakul Wongtiraporn, Minor Food's vice president of Global Supply Management, the conglomerate has had input on Anek Farm's facility design, filling accuracy, and quality monitoring and inspection process. It has helped introduce production process improvements, including the design of a production room that eliminates cross contamination. As Minor Group implements a strict chemical-free policy, Anek Farm, like all suppliers, has also had to follow suit.

THE BENEFITS: Initially, some staff were not happy with some of the changes, says Anek. But working closely with Minor, in tandem with Anek Farm's continuous investments in technology, has helped it achieve higher food safety standards and productivity. It has also improved the product overall and helped bring new clients into the fold. Anek's outlook has also changed. "I believe in sustainable practices and the wellbeing of those who buy my products," he says.

"Anek Farm is one of our success stories," adds Sarnsakul. "This success would never have happened if the passion, attitude, and business alignment was not genuinely connected along the value chain to strengthen the level of partnership and, in turn, the contribution to the society."

SHAKING UP THE SUPPLY CHAIN

In a SGM World Future survey of 1,415 senior supply chain practitioners, the following technologies emerged as the most disruptive and important.

Big Data Analytics

Machine Learning

Cloud Computing

3D Printing

The Sharing Economy

Digital Supply chain

Advanced Robotics

Internet of Things

Drone / Self-guided Vehicles

Source: SCM World Future of Supply Chain Survey 2016

Philippines, Thailand, and Vietnam) found that, although almost 80 percent of them feel the need to operate their businesses in a sustainable way, fewer than half had committed the resources necessary to implement a sustainability strategy. Furthermore, 80 percent of ASEAN companies were not managing sustainability in their supply chains.

Since that survey was conducted, however, that percentage has fallen markedly. Things have changed – and fast. Whereas suppliers were once left out of sustainability considerations, they are now increasingly being factored in and even helping shape them. Several overarching trends are helping to fast-track this welcome paradigm shift. Examples of them are already peppered, albeit sparingly, throughout Thailand's private sector.

Shared commitments with suppliers: In Thailand, as elsewhere, many big players with high brand recognition and a heavy dependence on many suppliers are now using assessment criteria to help them select, monitor and incentivize them. In their quest for stable suppliers and longer, larger contracts, some are also moving beyond merely defining

and enforcing expectations to establishing closer, more mutually beneficial relationships.

To single out one example, PTT Global Chemical (PTTGC) – a leading chemicals producer – has a strict supplier compliance code. All through the supply chain, from raw materials producers to machinery sellers and logistics companies, PTTGC's Supplier Code of Conduct requires adherence to rules regarding occupational health and safety, contribution to society, environment, and good governance. Even after an initial assessment ensures supplier compliance, PTTGC steadfastly conducts annual performance evaluations and capacity-building projects to guarantee continued compliance and even improvement.

Minor Group also uses codes of conduct and supplier engagement in an attempt to build supplier capacity and integrate sustainable procurement with broad operational risk management. Its relationships with suppliers go beyond mere policing of minimum standards (see *Case Study*, page 106); it also stages an annual vendor conference at which its suppliers share experiences, disseminate best practices, and address sustainability issues.

TOOLBOX | HOW TO CREATE A SUPPLIER CODE OF CONDUCT

A supplier code of conduct is used to establish and manage the expectations of a company's suppliers and subcontractors. It typically stipulates requirements concerning fair labor practices, environmental impacts, ethics, and monitoring of suppliers' practices. This ensures that suppliers implement safe working conditions, treat their employees with respect, and operate in compliance with laws and regulations.

When a company's supply chain is complex and multi-layered, a code of conduct can minimize risks to their business operations and reputation. This is essential if raw materials and products are sourced from politically volatile areas, or those with weak enforcement of labor and environmental laws.

After securing commitments from highest-level executives, companies can begin developing and implementing their own codes of conduct as follows:

Development:
- Collaborate across functions to develop the code. Involve key personnel such as supply chain professionals, quality assurance, legal and HR, risk, strategy, and sustainability. If necessary, create procurement policies and formalize existing practices in tandem.

- Conduct multi-stakeholder consultations with suppliers, industry peers, and external experts to identify supply chain risks and issues for inclusion.

- Turn to existing resources and standards for guidance rather than develop new standards of practices. For example, the UN

Global Compact, the International Labor Organization, UN Guiding Principles on Business and Human Rights, ISO14001 Environmental management, and SA8000 social certification standards.

- Ensure that the code of conduct addresses high-risk groups and processes, namely vulnerable groups such as women and children, minorities and indigenous workers, and outlines grievance mechanisms and penalties for non-compliance.

- Consider developing joint codes of conduct with industry peers, if applicable, or a group-wide code to reduce the compliance burden on suppliers.

- Consider having suppliers apply the code within their own supply base as a requirement, so that it is cascaded to lower tiers of the supply chain.

Implementation:
- Establish internal processes, policies, and accountability systems to implement the code of conduct, if required.

- Disseminate the code of conduct to suppliers through supplier seminars, training, internal websites and procurement portals, requests for proposals and contracts.

- Monitor compliance through mechanisms like audits and leverage technologies. Incentivize supplier compliance using financial and non-financial rewards. Integrate their performance into procurement and relationship decisions.

- Ensure that suppliers formally acknowledge the code and are regularly updated on any changes, such as through annual supplier conferences and web portals.

SHARED COMMITMENT MODELS

Basic	Improving	Established	Mature	Leading
▶ Minimum standards or guidelines ▶ Poor understanding of supplier risks	▶ Focus on risk and compliance ▶ Assess against supplier code of conduct or contractual terms and conditions ▶ Focus on audit approach for high risk areas ▶ Transactional relationships with suppliers	▶ Understand the significant issues to prioritize suppliers based on risk ▶ Optional or mandatory processes in place to screen, select and manage suppliers based on sustainability criteria ▶ Focus on short-term risks ▶ Include site visits of suppliers in monitoring ▶ Reporting KPIs on sustainable supply chains	▶ Sustainability requirements globally aligned, adopting the highest standard ▶ Apply leading standards and certification programs ▶ Monitoring and visibility beyond Tier 1 ▶ Process to screen, select and manage suppliers based on sustainability criteria integrated with other processes ▶ Suppliers segregated based on performance impacting spend ▶ Conduct training ▶ KPIs for measuring supply chain sustainability performance integrated scorecard ▶ Work with suppliers to identify areas for improvement ▶ Engaged with government to develop regulation ▶ Rely on suppliers to cascade sustainability requirements on to their own suppliers	▶ Sustainability part of the company's culture and DNA ▶ Suppliers considered an extension of the business ▶ Engaged more in asking and less in telling ▶ Make sustainability part of the upstream design or purchasing decisions ▶ Work with suppliers to build capacity and embed a culture of sustainability ▶ Selecting suppliers based on sustainability criteria (even where cost is higher) ▶ Focus on long-term risk and opportunity ▶ Prominent lead in industry initiatives and working groups ▶ Ahead of emerging regulation ▶ Transparency about performance reporting metrics beyond number of audits to include outcomes

Source: EY: The State of Sustainable Supply Chains (2016)

Both of these examples can loosely be considered a 'Mature' approach to supplier commitment sharing (see chart above). However, the agribusiness Betagro is striving to go one further. Community projects started near its factory and farm suppliers about ten years ago have evolved into what CEO Vanus Taepaisitphongse calls "Holistic Area-Based Community Development." Inspired by SEP and the Japanese concept of *kaizen*, or continuous improvement, this supply-chain management-meets-social-enterprise hybrid looks beyond bottom lines and processes to other concerns, such as the health and solvency of workers, and nurtures contractor-supplier relationships based more on

sharing than telling. In other words, Betagro's knowledge, including its deep-rooted sustainability ethos, is its suppliers' knowledge. "We apply what we have learned to help our contract farmers," he says.

Similarly, IKEA fosters relationships that are teamwork-based, not merely transactional. The Southeast Asian wing of the famous Scandinavian furniture brand is upfront with potential suppliers: explains its stringent standards and expectations, as articulated in its IWAY code of conduct, from the get-go. Sometimes this results in suppliers deciding not to work with them, "because it's easier for them to do what they've always done," explains sustainability and communication director Lars Svensson; but often it results in just the kind of long-lasting, dialogue-driven partnerships they're looking to nurture. "Others say, 'We think this is good and we want to invest ourselves in IKEA values, as we see this as a way of improving our own efficiencies and also becoming more marketable.'"

Technology & Transparency: Advanced sensors, mapping tools, mobile technology, data analytics, and other forms of technology are opening up new frontiers in supply chain transparency. Whether they deal in cars or clothes or cod, companies are using the myriad forms of new tech to help them see deeper into the supply chain – especially beyond the first tier – and protect their brands.

There is no more salient a Thai example of this trend than the wild sea fishing industry. A range of technology is now helping to ensure that the scandals that erupted around illegal, unreported, and unregulated fishing and labor exploitation don't erupt again.

Vessel monitoring systems, which allow companies and other stakeholders to track fishing vessels, as well as fish DNA testing are finally shedding light on a perilously murky supply chain (see *Fisheries*, page 186).

Digitally-driven supply chains look set to become more common. The explosion in mobile technology and cloud-based software systems is helping companies improve the efficiency and integrity of supply chain data. As the years march on, and progress with it, so too will the ways in which companies harness tech to connect with suppliers, conduct audits, interface with existing enterprise resource planning systems, and monitor and manage supply chain risk on a day-to-day basis.

These and other technological developments will, in effect, allow sustainability and supply chains to become more tightly integrated. They may also compel proactive companies to move beyond compliance and share their supply chain successes (and shortcomings) with stakeholders.

Workers in Thailand load a ship bound for Africa with 1,000 tons of rice.

TAKE ACTION

The following recommendations can be applied across supply chains of all sizes and complexity:

- **Map out your supply chain to identify the most pressing issues to be managed.**

  - Consider using a materiality assessment and supply chain risk assessment to flesh out top risks, impacts, and issues.

  - Engage with key stakeholders to gather input.

- **Embed supply chain sustainability into the structures, policies, and processes of your organization.** This can be achieved by:

  - Inserting sustainability criteria into your procurement process and supplier qualifications;

  - Announcing a sustainable supply chain or procurement policy and developing a supplier code of conduct;

  - Assigning responsibilities to a specific department;

  - Incentivizing staff to apply sustainable supply chain practices through KPIs and financial rewards;

- Setting long-term targets that dovetail with your sustainability strategy.

- **Engage internally with management and relevant staff**, to build their knowledge and capabilities on supply chain sustainability.

- **Engage regularly with suppliers, subcontractors, and partners** to build the business case for supply chain sustainability.

  - Build partnerships, collaborate with suppliers and industry peers to extend sustainability objectives beyond the first supply chain tier.

  - Consider leveraging tools and platforms such as supplier management seminars, training, and supplier codes of conduct in the process.

- **Deploy technologies to support supply chain sustainability initiatives** and increase accountability, traceability, and efficiency.

- **Invest in a diverse and inclusive supply chain** by working with small and diverse businesses in areas of sourcing and operations.

- **Disclose supply chain sustainability performance** through websites or reporting channels. Be transparent about achievements and challenges.

Source: Adapted from EY: The State of Sustainable Supply Chains: Building Responsible and Resilient Supply Chains

Collaboration: Multi-stakeholder collaboration is playing a crucial role in the spread of sustainable supply chains. Leading companies are increasingly collaborating not only with suppliers, but also peers, industry associations, regulators, and even other companies from other sectors in an effort to achieve them.

One example of this trend in action is the Sampran Model, a grassroots initiative whereby organic rice farmers conduct direct, 'fair trade' sales with hotels and consumers. A runaway success, this supply chain ecosystem – which eliminates chemicals from rice and empowers debt-ridden farmers – began as a pilot project at Nakorn Pathom Province's Sampran Riverside hotel and has since been fine-tuned and expanded with the help of government bodies, NGOs, and universities. And, through more collaboration, it looks set to continue spreading: having proven that supply chains can dovetail with sustainability, its creator is now trying to cross-pollinate the model with big business. "Us working with Mitr Phol [the Thai sugar producer] is a test of its scalability," says managing director Arrut Navaraj.

Products and Services

- *There is growing consumer demand for sustainable products and services, yet most Thai businesses continue to underinvest in sustainability-focused R&D and ignore what is a burgeoning business opportunity.*

- *New revenue opportunities can be revealed when companies make a sincere commitment to sustainable production and adopt the life cycle approach.*

- *Engaging consumers directly on topics such as food quality and raw material sourcing can help win loyalty and bring future customers into the fold.*

- *Thai companies that fail to embrace the concept of sustainable consumption and production risk becoming obsolete in the mid- to long-term.*

Production processes, and the way that products and services are consumed, are key contributors to the environmental and social problems we face, both domestically and globally.

To address these concerns, concepts such as Sustainable Consumption and Production (SCP) and Sustainable Product and Service Development (SPSD) are being widely promoted by sustainable development advocates, both in and outside businesses.

As defined by the 1994 Oslo Symposium, SCP refers to "the use of services and related products, which respond to basic needs and bring a better quality of life while minimizing the use of natural resources and toxic materials, as well as the emissions of waste and pollutants, over the life cycle of the service or product so as not to jeopardize the needs of further generations."

For SCP to be realized, it requires a systematic approach and cooperation among all actors operating in the supply chain, from producer to final consumer. The ultimate aim is to create wider markets for sustainable offerings, improve consumption habits, and formulate new business models that help us address the challenges we face.

In addition to reducing negative impacts, studies have indicated that products and services conceived and produced with sustainable development in mind can leverage both financial and non-financial benefits. Some of these include:

- **Increased innovation driven by sustainability goals that go well beyond conventional business objectives**

- **Differentiation and competitive advantage based on environmental and social benefits**

- **Promotion of brand equity from sustainability values**

- **Cost reduction resulting from a more deliberate use of resources**

- **Value-added pricing rather than price wars**

- **Access to global markets with wider regulatory compliance**

A handful of leading Thai firms have made notable efforts to incorporate the principles of sustainable development into their production processes. As a result, sustainable new products and services are being introduced to the market all the time. This is reflected in the growth of the voluntary Green Label Scheme, which was founded in 1993 by the Thailand Business Council for Sustainable Development (TBCSD), and highlights products and services that cause minimum environmental impacts in their sectors. As of July 2017, the list includes 645 items across 26 product categories from 61 companies. Another example is the Thailand Greenhouse Gas Management Organization's Carbon Footprint label, which can be found on around 1,800 low-emission products from 400 companies. Some companies, meanwhile, such as state-owned oil and gas giant PTT and cement and building material conglomerate SCG, have devised their own sustainable product labels ('Green for Life' and 'SCG Eco Value,' respectively).

Eco-labeling has its flaws – some, especially the self-declared ones, are arguably not challenging or credible enough – but is still a promising development. Together, they are helping raise the standards of sustainability practices in the Thai market, encouraging higher expectations from consumers who want high-quality products with better environmental and social performance, and compelling more businesses to hop on the sustainable product and services bandwagon.

On the government policy side, the National Economic and Social Development Plan has taken into consideration the impact of Thai industries on the environment since 2002. More recently, the Green Growth Policy Toward Sustainable Development (2014–2018) incorporates sustainable consumption and production, sustainable infrastructure, investment in natural capital, green business and markets, green tax, and eco-efficiency indicators.

Other initiatives to promote sustainable development in products and services include the Department of International Trade Promotion's Design Excellence Award (DEmark), which was established in 2008 to

Many companies are finding that they can charge a premium for sustainably produced goods.

promote outstanding Thai-designed products in international markets. In 2017, "social and environmental impacts" became one of the five criteria by which DEmark winners are judged.

Guidelines to practice

Before venturing into the realm of sustainable products and services, a company should clearly define its corporate vision, as well as make a strategic commitment to integrate sustainability into its core business model. This can enhance continuity in a firm's operations, as the development of sustainable products and services will be a crucial aspect of the firm's strategic vision, rather than a series of special projects separate from primary business operations.

Before venturing into sustainable products and services, a company should clearly define its corporate vision.

In addition, a committed business should incorporate the life cycle approach that takes into account the six major product "life stages": planning, development, production, launching to market, usage, and end of life.

THE LIFE CYCLE APPROACH TO SUSTAINABILITY

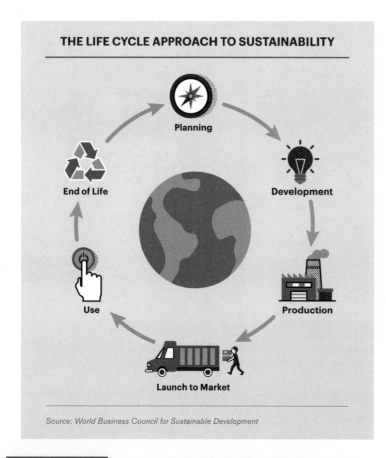

Planning

Development

Production

Launch to Market

Use

End of Life

Source: World Business Council for Sustainable Development

This method, which is increasingly being adopted by top global firms, is forward-looking, encourages long-term decision-making, and creates synergy of practices within and across businesses.

1. Planning

There are two mutually compatible objectives that any business looking to create sustainable products and services should strive to meet: (1) minimize negative impacts through all stages of the life cycle, and (2) maximize environmental and social performance while still achieving economic benefits. For example, a food manufacturing company can apply the life cycle approach in their supply chain to promote efficient use of resources, both in production and consumption. At the same time, it can try to maximize the benefits of delivering safe and nutritious food to people for consumption while also striking an ecological balance.

A good example of both these approaches is offered by Betagro Group, which started out in 1967 as a producer of animal feed, but has since evolved to become a leading food and agribusiness conglomerate with a strong focus on sustainability. Today the company strives to achieve a triple bottom line by developing

TOOLBOX   LIFE CYCLE ASSESSMENTS

A Life Cycle Assessment (LCA) can be an invaluable means of assessing the full range of potential impacts associated with each stage of a product or service's life cycle. As LCAs can potentially be time-consuming and costly, be explicit in your reasons for conducting one.

Prasit Vaiyavatjamai, a partner at Environmental Resources Management, says that the key benefit for a company is that it receives "hot spot analysis for process improvements." He elaborates: "For example, a factory

can identify which part of its production line uses the highest amount of raw materials, consumes the most water, requires the highest man-power for production, and so on. The analysis of these results can help the company with cost savings. Moreover, it can help support market entry, such as to European countries which have an Environmental Product Declaration (EPD) certification system. Compliance with such regulations can greatly help with risk management from liability, impact to reputation, and license to operate."

Most LCA methodologies build upon the ISO14040 and ISO14044 standards. Typical assessments consider the environmental impacts of products from "cradle-to-grave" (resource extraction to disposal), "gate-to-gate" (gate through which materials enter a production process to exit), or even "cradle-to-cradle" (resource extraction to recycling). The main phases of an LCA are: (1) goal and scope definition, (2) inventory analysis of extractions and emissions, (3) impact assessment, and (4) interpretation.

JOHN THØGERSEN *is a professor of economic psychology at Aarhus University, Denmark. He is also the former chairman of the steering committee of the Global Virtual Community on Sustainability and Consumption, which initiates, develops, and organizes research on the tension between sustainability and consumption.*

What are some global developments regarding sustainable products and services?
The most fundamental development is the attempt to get out of fossil fuels and into renewable energy, because the basic ways our products are produced and the type of energy we use is the most fundamental determinant of how sustainable products and services will be. Another development in the same sort of direction is the electrification of transportation. If you look at Norway, in the first quarter of 2017 nearly one-third of the new cars registered were electric.

Another positive development is that a lot of material things that we had before, like cameras, stereo players, and other gadgets, are now digital applications on our phones. That's helping to dematerialize production.

What do you see as the future trends for sustainable products and services?
I believe that we will see a rise in trends with regard to sustainable products and services in the future, spurred, among other things, by the UN sustainability goals. The SDGs are splendid because they create a common language that is global and that everybody can refer to. I have the hope at least that this will spur a development whereby sustainability becomes even more of a focus point for competition in the future.

What are some of the exciting shifts or developments in the life cycle approach?
The aspect of this that I personally have worked on the most is eco-labeling, which is labeling of products based on a life cycle approach. I'm convinced that eco-labeling is an extremely effective tool for consumers that are already aware of environmental problems and consider environmental goals important in their consumption pattern. For them, a well-designed and reliable eco-label on the product is extremely helpful when making a purchase.

How do you view the development of sustainable products and services within Thailand?
I definitely see some focus among Thai consumers on sustainable consumption and production. But I believe it will be too little as long as the government hesitates in creating credible institutions that could facilitate this development, and removing some of the many impediments. Some of these impediments are quite natural. For instance, I'm thinking about corruption. Institutions that further sustainable development are very much based on credibility, trust, and also credible governmental controls. So, there is a need for general trust in the population that these goals are actually implemented and controlled and that companies that commit violations of the principles are being caught, brought to justice, and punished for it.

How can Thai businesses become more sustainable?
Big businesses in Thailand should press the government to fight corruption and create more credible institutions for regulating economic life and sustainability. The second thing is to use the official eco-labels when they are there. That means, for instance, using the Thai organic label rather than just the loose claim "organic." The Thai organic label right now has a low level of trust in the population, but trust needs to be built. If the reliable companies don't use the label it will be very difficult to build trust. So, they should help build the institutions and use these official labels. The third would be to look at the transportation of goods and people. Right now, traffic is a major problem and a major polluter in Thailand and there are definitely gains to be reaped by implementing best practices in terms of low-emission transportation of both people and goods.

Andaman Discoveries Impacts Local Communities Positively

Andaman Discoveries gives tourists a hands-on chance to understand community culture.

THE CHALLENGE: For Thailand, tourism is a key sector that has strongly driven economic expansion and countrywide development. Yet it is widely recognized that tourism can create a host of challenges in the destination area and surrounding community.

This dynamic was keenly felt In the aftermath of the 2004 tsunami. Coastal villages in Southern Thailand recognized the potential for tourism to help get them back on their feet. However, many villagers were skeptical, believing that tourism would create a host of new challenges: environmental degradation, resource damage, and a loss of cultural identity.

THE SOLUTION: Having initially offered relief to villagers, the social enterprise Andaman Discoveries now works closely with them so that they can strike a balance between taking advantage of tourism opportunities and preserving local culture and natural resources. Following the tenets of community-based tourism, the company targets a niche – conscientious travelers looking to have meaningful village experiences. All products and services are crafted in close collaboration with the community according to their local traditions and way of life.

Tour packages include village tours, eco tours and homestays — all with the goal of promoting responsible travel with minimal negative impacts on the environment and community. Andaman Discoveries has also created a Visitor's Guidebook and Thai Phrasebook to facilitate cross-cultural exchanges. With a focus on sustainability, written codes of conduct, pre-departure guides, and briefings are used to communicate and ensure that visitors respect local communities' expectations about how their culture and environmental concerns will be treated. Andaman Discoveries has also created a "Sense of Place" book that encourages villagers to explore, acknowledge, and value their own cultural identities and the surrounding environment.

THE BENEFITS: The community-based tourism project has received support from donors and volunteers who collaborate on community development as well as business-related activities, such as providing skill training to locals, assisting local guides to explain points of interest, and helping guests fully engage with villagers. The collaborative networks share common interests in working to promote community wellbeing. The success of Andaman Discoveries is demonstrated by its many awards (it was the winner of the SKAL sustainable tourism award in 2016). In terms of business performance, the Ban Talae Nok village has seen a 35 percent increase in income. Besides allocating fair revenues to the guides, host families and handicraft cooperatives, Andaman Discoveries has also given 20 percent of guests' in-village costs to the village community fund to support development programs such as scholarships, youth activities, and other initiatives.

More and more tourists are looking to engage with local traditions and ways of life.

and producing high-quality, safe, and nutritious food products. To overcome the hard-to-control nature of food supply chains in Thailand, the company has adopted a life cycle approach that enables it to manage quality control all the way from livestock farming to animal breeding, to manufacturing and distribution. All of Betagro's processes and products are free from chemical residues, contamination, and harmful microorganisms. The company is also forging ahead with resource-efficiency initiatives – chicken fat waste is used to produce biodiesel, animal waste is used to produce biogas, and solid waste such as manure, bones, and residues is used to produce organic fertilizer for farmers in nearby communities.

To maximize the market opportunities of its sustainably produced foods and to further promote healthy consumption, Betagro has grown its business to include ready-to-cook and ready-to-eat foods, and branched out into service businesses including Betagro Shop wholesalers, Betagro Deli, and several restaurants. The success of these initiatives is seen in annual revenue figures, which have climbed from 59 billion baht in 2011 to 96 billion baht in 2015. To a certain degree, Betagro's 12 to 14 percent annual growth (compared to three to four percent industry

R&D spending in Thailand has been woefully low for decades and this is, in part, because many Thai firms lack knowledge about core product development principles and processes.

growth) also demonstrates how an emphasis on sustainable products and services offers better revenue-making opportunities than the business-as-usual approach.

2. Development

The development stage is highly important yet remains one of the weakest areas for most Thai companies. Research and development (R&D) spending in Thailand has been woefully low for decades and this is, in part, because many Thai firms lack knowledge about core product development principles and processes such as

---

GROWING MARKET FOR SUSTAINABLE PRODUCTS & SERVICES

The market for sustainable products and services has been continuously expanding worldwide with increasing support from consumers.

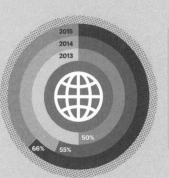

66% of global respondents are willing to pay more for sustainable goods, up from 55% in 2014 (and 50% in 2013).

Sales of consumer goods from brands with a demonstrated commitment to sustainability have grown more than 4% globally while those without such a commitment grew less than 1%.

It is estimated that the global sustainable packaging market alone will be worth US$244 billion by 2018 and US$440.3 billion by 2025.

Sources: The Nielsen Global Survey (2015); The Sustainability Imperative: New Insights on Consumer Expectations; Smithers Pira; "Global Sustainable Packaging Market Analysis & Trends - Industry Forecast to 2025"

THAI PRODUCTS GO GREEN

Green Label Thailand uses **123 criteria** to distinguish the products that cause the lowest environmental impacts in their sectors.

As of July 2017, it included **645 products** in **26 categories from 61 companies**.

Source: Green Label Thailand

needs analysis, ideation, concept sketching, prototyping, and testing.

Needs analysis is often seen as the fuzzy front end of R&D because it requires gathering relevant information to help identify areas of opportunity, either from an existing gap in the current market or from unmet needs. To be sustainability-minded, that analysis must

Thailand is the only country in ASEAN that complies with the international GHG reduction certifying process.

exhibit an understanding of human, societal and environmental needs. An example of this would be SCG conducting an in-depth study of the specific needs and behaviors of the elderly, as it did when it began work on SCG Eldercare Solutions – its consultation-based service for Thailand's rapidly ageing population.

Next, an ideation process is required to find a systematic solution to the identified needs based on holistic thinking. This solution should

go so far as to encompass the perspectives of direct and indirect stakeholders (including society and the environment). Ideation then leads to concept formulation and design development. This process should take into account the need to incorporate sustainable practices throughout the stages of production, distribution, use, and end of life. These practices may include, for example, using environmentally friendly materials, reducing weight or volume to support efficient logistics, and increasing the duration of time that products and services can be used.

After a design is properly sketched out, prototypes are then developed and tested until they demonstrate a high level of feasibility. This process is not only used to confirm the potential of products and services, but also to carefully identify and address unforeseen problems. This effort is crucial to mitigate risk.

3. Production

Sustainable production begins with sourcing raw materials that deliver low environmental impacts (e.g. renewable or recycled materials). Sustainable sourcing also takes into account social issues such as equitable trading and fair allocation of economic and social benefits, particularly of resources obtained from local communities. These represent important concerns for Thailand, both as a country in possession of significant natural resources and as a transit hub for resources from neighboring countries.

Sustainable production also aims to reduce the impact of extraction and processing techniques, to cut emissions, and to improve waste management. According to a report by the Thailand Greenhouse Gas Management Organization, Thailand is the only country in ASEAN that complies with the international greenhouse gas reduction certifying process. As of September 2016, a total of 648 products have been included in the carbon emission reduction scheme (resulting in 1.3 million fewer tons of GHGs being released into the air). However, more concerted efforts are needed to achieve greater benefits.

NXP (Thailand), a semiconductor manufacturer with operations in more than 25 countries, has demonstrated how a proactive approach on this front can achieve positive results. The company mainly produces integrated circuit (IC) devices, generally in wafer form, which are electrically connected to substrates with precious metals such as gold, silver, or copper, and encapsulated by plastic. Unfortunately, the manufacturing process produces a significant amount of waste, which the company has smartly sought to leverage to create other business opportunities.

According to NXP's global innovation director Bodin Kasemset, the leftover waste contains precious materials that are "post-treated to turn them into pure precious material again for further use." Plastic waste, meanwhile, is offered to external company partners. "They use it as fuel for their incinerator, which generates heat for their production processes of other products such as cement," he says. This initiative goes well beyond compliance with international laws and regulations and demonstrates how innovation can generate significant revenue: in this case, more than 100 million baht annually. The initiative also results in an average waste reduction of ten percent and a five percent reduction in energy consumption.

4. Launch to market

More efficient and less resource-heavy logistics and transport are a key strategic area for Thai businesses looking to capitalize on the opportunity of expanding markets in ASEAN. The agreed ASEAN Connectivity 2025 master plan includes integrated, safe, and environmentally sustainable transport linking all ASEAN member states and neighboring countries. As a result, Thai businesses need to carefully consider these developments and adjust their procedures accordingly.

The launch-to-market process also includes marketing aimed at consumers interested in sustainable consumption and lifestyles. Furthermore, this marketing strategy should attempt to educate and motivate consumers who are yet to support sustainable products and services with the aim of growing the market. This practice should not overlook inherent consumer values such as quality performance, cost effectiveness, and

convenience – otherwise it can result in so-called sustainability marketing myopia. The focus should be on delivering information in a truthful and transparent manner; for example, introducing labeling initiatives and traceability systems.

In terms of pricing, sustainable marketing does not focus on cutting prices to gain market share. Instead, it offers quality products at reasonable prices and guarantees that all stakeholders in the value chain have been compensated and treated fairly. Channel-wise, these products and services should be easily accessible by the market so that sustainable consumption can be widely adopted.

During the launch-to-market stage, it is wise to consider engaging local channels and traders, specifically in developing countries. For example, the Siam Hands company, which produces the t-shirt brand Tangmo, has carved out a niche by committing to sell through

SCG packaging paper is certified by the Forest Stewardship Council.

CASE STUDY	SCG Creates Home Solutions for the Elderly

A bathroom designed to minimize caregiver dependency and maximize mobility.

THE CHALLENGE: In 2015, the number of Thais aged over 60 was 15.3 percent of the total population (about 9.9 million people). This number is expected to grow to 20 percent by 2021 and 28 percent by 2031. As people live longer, their vision, hearing, and mobility deteriorate and hence they need extra care to continue healthy living and prevent potential accidents. Research shows that 40 percent of injuries among the elderly are from falling. Given these new realities, Thailand's leading cement and construction material manufacturer, SCG, tackled the issue of building better, more functional homes for an aging population.

THE SOLUTION: Spurred on by the belief that a home can be comfortable for all, yet customized to the specific needs of seniors, SCG commenced an in-depth study of how old age impacts physical competency, behavior, psychology, and wider society back in 2013. The study was a multi-disciplinary collaboration between experts in fields as diverse as behavioral science, biomedical engineering, gerontology, ergonomics, and architecture.

This research led SCG to classify the elderly into three different segments: green for those in full health, yellow for those with few or minor health problems, and orange for those who require mobility assistance equipment and care. These and other findings helped the company come up with a range of design products that meet the physical and psychological needs of all the different segments. Prototypes of these products were made and tested before launching.

SCG Eldercare Solution begins with a consultation service. A consultant explains to the customer the options available for customizing their home, be it a new or existing one, and making it as elderly-friendly as possible with a view to reducing the risk of injury. The next step is proposing a design plan featuring a range of specially-designed products such as bathroom accessories, intelligent night lights, shock absorption floors, stairlifts, and interior sliding doors. Once a plan is agreed upon, an SCG installation team then makes it a reality.

THE BENEFITS: Having developed and honed SCG Eldercare Solution gradually since 2013, SCG launched a communications campaign in 2015–2016. This has not only promoted wider awareness of innovative new SCG products and services, but it has also brought wider attention to the issue of caring for the elderly – a step forward that is in line with the Sustainable Development Goals and the quest for a more inclusive society.

Beyond dovetailing with the SCG marketing tag line "Building Trusted Innovation," SCG Eldercare Solution products and consultation services answer the specific needs of the elderly while showing the company to be proactively engaged in the sociocultural challenges of our times.

SCG Eldercare Solutions aims to meet the physical needs of an ageing populace.

HOW TO FOSTER SUSTAINABLE CONSUMPTION

Business approaches to sustainable consumption can be grouped into three broad categories:

INNOVATION	CHOICE INFLUENCING	CHOICE EDITING

Business processes for the development of new and improved products, services, and business models are shifting to incorporate provisions for delivering maximum societal value at minimum environmental cost.	The use of marketing communications and awareness-raising campaigns to enable and encourage consumers to choose and use products more efficiently and sustainably.	The removal of "unsustainable" products, product components, and services from the market-place in partnership with other actors in society.

Source: World Business Council for Sustainable Development

long-term, local partners. The brand is now sold at more than 2,200 local shops, local fairs, and events. This model has managed to prove its worth, leading to revenue growth of around ten percent per year in a sluggish economy. Lastly, another key strategy is customer relationship management (CRM), which is aimed at building long-term brand loyalty, and, most importantly, trust.

5. Use

In the usage phase, a sustainable product is one that offers longer-lasting functionality, reduced energy consumption, and easy and effective maintenance. An example of this thinking in action is Thailand's Label No.5, a labeling scheme that allows consumers to easily assess which household appliances are the most energy efficient. Since its launch by the Electricity Generating Authority of Thailand (EGAT) in 1994, it has expanded to cover an ever-wider array of applications. According to EGAT, the project provided 1,400,000 labels between 2012 and 2015.

In May 2017, a collaboration between Label No.5 and the National Housing Authority led to the building of 115,000 electricity-saving houses that will save 128 million units of energy per year. Collectively, they will result in an estimated savings of 512 million baht, and 67,000 tons of CO_2 emissions per year.

A sustainable product is one that offers longer-lasting functionality, reduced energy consumption, and easy and effective maintenance.

Models of ownership that are finding favor among sustainable development advocates, such as sharing, pooling, or pay-per-use, also fall within this phase. Organic forms of the shared economy have, in fact, already been present in Thailand for generations – think of how new inventions such as the telephone and television have, historically, often been shared by rural communities. However, globally the

Thai companies are still struggling to incorporate recycling into the end-of-life phase of their products.

emergence of modern technology is creating new models and new opportunities.

Take Indonesian startup Go-Jek. What began as a motorbike taxi on-demand service has now expanded to services such as food delivery, cleaning, and beauty, among others.

Models of ownership that are finding favor with sustainability advocates include sharing, pooling, and pay-per-use.

Valued in excess of US$1 billion, Go-Jek is one of the only startup success stories in the ASEAN region. In Thailand, meanwhile, the sharing economy has long been promoted by advocates of community-based tourism; homestays where visitors pay local residents to let them stay in their homes for a night or two are common.

6. End of Life

Reuse, recycling, recovery, repair, or refurbishment are still not widely practiced in Thailand. However, the global trend is towards innovative "take-back solutions" whereby businesses play an active role in the disposal of their products and consider their life cycles from cradle to grave.

With the problem of e-waste growing with each passing day, Thailand is in dire need of sustainable disposal solutions. The improper disposal of old computer hardware and electronic goods has resulted in toxic substances leaking into the environment and causing health problems. In a 2013 report, the Institute for Global Environmental Strategies estimated that Thailand generates 1.15 kilograms of solid waste per capita per day, while the recycling rate was only 19 percent and the proper disposal rate only 27 percent.

TAKE ACTION

Integrating a life cycle approach to products and services development is one of the most important steps in making sustainability a reality. These steps can be applied to new developments or improvements of existing product/service offerings.

Planning:

- Set objectives for sustainable product and service development that focus on minimizing negative impacts on society and the environment and/or maximizing environmental and social performance.

Development:

- Conduct a needs analysis to identify product and service needs of consumers, society and the environment, as well as opportunities from existing gaps in current market or unmet needs.

- Brainstorm solutions to address identified needs. Make sure that solutions consider the perspectives of direct and indirect stakeholders, and incorporate sustainable practices throughout, such as the use of environmentally-friendly materials and energy efficient technology.

- During prototyping and testing, carefully ensure consistent quality and keep an eye out for potential risks and impacts over the short- to long-term.

- Ethically source raw materials (or work towards ethical sourcing) and prioritize materials that have low environmental impacts. Be aware of potential resource conflicts and issues related to equitable trading, fair allocation of economic benefits, and impacts on local communities.

- Identify and act on opportunities for improvements in resource management processes and work to reduce any harmful impacts of extraction and processing techniques.

Launch to market:

- Work on creating a safe, environmentally sustainable logistics and transport network that is more efficient and less resource-intensive. Consider partnerships across the supply chain.

- Fashion marketing and communications that help cultivate wider and larger markets for sustainable products and services.

Use:

- Innovate ways of extending the lifespan of products and services. Consider new models of ownership that leverage trends in the sharing economy, pooling, or pay-per-use.

End of life:

- Reuse, recycle, recover, repair, or refurbish – to extend the life cycle and relieve the pressure on landfills.

The number of Thai businesses attempting to manage the end of life of their products is growing, but even for the majority of them it remains a separate, fragmented add-on service rather than part of the core business model. However, more integrated solutions are slowly taking hold in Thailand.

For example, the multinational carpet manufacturer Interface, which has a facility in Chonburi province, is successfully recycling post-consumer materials into new products with minimal contamination. It has devised "ReEntry 2.0," a process whereby used nylon fiber is, in combination with new materials, made into new nylon. Backing material is also transformed into new backing with 98 percent recycled content. The statistics are impressive. In its 2016 report, Interface claims to have saved 4.5 million kilograms of post-consumer carpet from landfills, and, in tandem with its other sustainability initiatives, reduced the average product carbon footprint by 35 percent since 2008. Furthermore, Interface's Mission Zero commitment aims to eliminate negative impact on the environment by 2020.

Technology

- *To escape the middle-income trap, Thailand's weak performance on the technological world stage must improve.*

- *In tandem with the government, Thai businesses should help foster a healthy R&D ecosystem and improve worker skills.*

- *Tech can be a sustainability enabler – many of the world's most promising technologies are tied to clear environmental and social outcomes.*

- *Efficiently implementing and scaling up the latest technology may prove more crucial than having the wherewithal to invent it.*

We are living in an exciting age: one in which technology evolves faster than ever before. Be it in manufacturing, energy, or agriculture, technological innovation is leading to a boom in sustainable solutions. These innovations have the capability to solve many of the critical challenges of our time, such as climate change, food security, and social inequality. They are also key drivers in the new era of growth we are experiencing.

But many countries, including Thailand, have yet to experience the full developmental benefits of such technology. Given the massive shift in competitive advantage that technology and innovation can offer, the risks of slow or poor adoption could, as things stand, have dire consequences for industries, the government, and the nation as a whole. It is inevitable, for instance, that emerging technology will have a disruptive effect on existing business models. Many business practices may soon become obsolete due to changes in the technology landscape or a shift in customers' preferences.

Around the world, companies are wrestling with these challenges – and discovering that digital transformation is not a technological

fix, or a one-size-fits-all strategy. Rather, it is a learning process sustained over time and involving diverse stakeholders. The ultimate objective is to harness the power of the global digital revolution with a view to meeting a country's specific socioeconomic priorities. It needs to be driven by vision, leadership, innovation, learning, as well as partnerships among government, business, and civil society.

Thailand has a lot of work to do in this regard, especially in the areas of technology adoption and innovation. In the 2017 Bloomberg Innovation Index, Thailand did rank within the top 50 innovative economies, but only just. Holding it back were poor ratings for R&D spending, patent activity, and productivity, among other factors. These shortcomings are also confirmed by the 2016 Global Innovation Index – where Thailand ranked 55 out of 128 economies – and the World Economic Forum's 2016 Networked Readiness Index (62 out of 139 economies). The latter assesses a country's ability to fully leverage Information and Communication Technologies (ICTs) by examining key factors such as the political and regulatory environment, infrastructure and digital content, business and innovation environment, social and economic impacts, etc. In all of these areas, Thailand posts rather modest scores. It should be noted, however, that Thailand fares well among emerging and developing Asian economies in ICT readiness, ranking 5th after China, Malaysia, Mongolia, and Sri Lanka.

Finally, on the education front, Thai students continue to perform poorly in comparison to their international counterparts. In the latest study from the Organization for Economic Co-operation and Development's (OECD) Programme for International Student Assessment (PISA), Thailand placed 54th (out of 72 nations) on the performance of 15-year-olds in reading, mathematics, and science.

Challenges ahead

The downward trend for manufacturing in Thailand, including the decline of its once-booming electronics industry, is indicative of the country's struggle to gain a foothold in the global supply chain for modern

technology. The country is mired in the so-called 'middle-income trap,' where it can no longer compete against less expensive neighboring countries in less skill-intensive economic activities, and still lacks the technological know-how, innovation capabilities, and human resources needed to compete with countries that dominate sophisticated industries.

Thailand needs to become an innovator – to redefine economic models and to embrace new technology to keep pace with quickly evolving Digital Age trends.

As the world enters the Fourth Industrial Revolution, where the full impacts of new technologies are unfolding, Thailand needs to become an innovator – to redefine economic models and to embrace new technology to

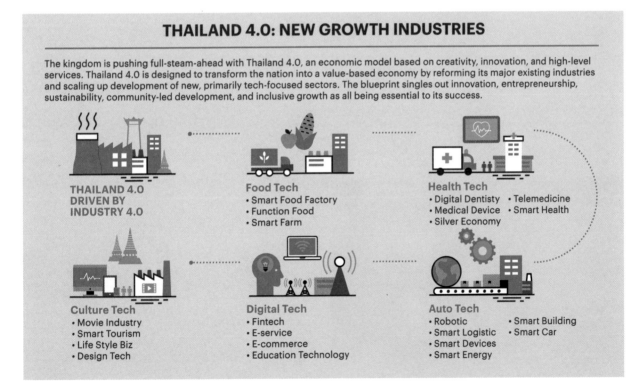

THAILAND 4.0: NEW GROWTH INDUSTRIES

The kingdom is pushing full-steam-ahead with Thailand 4.0, an economic model based on creativity, innovation, and high-level services. Thailand 4.0 is designed to transform the nation into a value-based economy by reforming its major existing industries and scaling up development of new, primarily tech-focused sectors. The blueprint singles out innovation, entrepreneurship, sustainability, community-led development, and inclusive growth as all being essential to its success.

THAILAND 4.0 DRIVEN BY INDUSTRY 4.0

Food Tech
• Smart Food Factory
• Function Food
• Smart Farm

Health Tech
• Digital Dentisty • Telemedicine
• Medical Device • Smart Health
• Silver Economy

Culture Tech
• Movie Industry
• Smart Tourism
• Life Style Biz
• Design Tech

Digital Tech
• Fintech
• E-service
• E-commerce
• Education Technology

Auto Tech
• Robotic • Smart Building
• Smart Logistic • Smart Car
• Smart Devices
• Smart Energy

CASE STUDY | TechFarm Puts Soil and Water Management in Farmers' Hands

THE CHALLENGE: Agricultural commodities and aquaculture products represent high volumes for Thai exports and employ millions of people across the country. Thai farmers are facing more pressure from consumers, both domestic and abroad, regarding food quality and safety. In many instances, small producers cannot access global markets due to an inability to meet international food safety requirements. Locally, the excessive use of chemicals has also produced damaging consequences such as ecological degradation and health afflictions.

THE SOLUTION: TechFarm started their work in 2014 after traveling extensively throughout Thailand with agriculture and aquaculture experts. Despite increasing demand, many smallholders in the aquaculture industry have given up their farms due to worrisome financial risks or because their plots have become too polluted for cultivation. Meanwhile, the soil quality in many regions of the country is actually quite poor and often there is a mismatch between the soil and the type of crops being grown. This leads to poor cultivation and low productivity. Due to a lack of knowledge, Thai farmers often try to compensate by overusing pesticides and fertilizers on their crops. This not only makes environmental matters worse, but in many cases also drives the farmers deeper into debt as such chemicals are costly.

TechFarm determined that tools to analyze the soil and water could have a significant impact on productivity and quality. Existing tools and mechanisms are not necessarily expensive but can be quite cumbersome or time consuming, as farmers would need to take soil samples to a local agriculture laboratory before planning their harvest. In the aquaculture industry, almost none of the tools available could provide real-time reporting, which is crucial to the survival rate of shrimp and other aquaculture livestock.

TechFarm's LenDin app and hardware offers real-time reporting of soil quality.

To bridge this gap, apps dubbed 'LenDin' and 'LenNam,' or literally 'Play With Soil' and 'Play With Water,' were developed. LenDin helps farmers reduce the usage of fertilizers and pesticides through smarter planting techniques and management of soil. Len Nam allows aquaculture farmers to increase the efficiency of water-quality measurement and sustain the quality of natural resources, which significantly reduces the risk of diseases. TechFarm is also working to change mindsets through market incentives, convincing farmers to comply with recognized standards through easy-to-use technology, and matching them with buyers whose priority is food safety. The apps increase farmers' capacity through gamification, knowledge-sharing via social media and chat platforms, and advice on market conditions and trends. Because both apps capture related data on a regular basis and store it in the cloud, customers can also track product details by using a TechFarm app developed for the buyer side, enabling more transparency and traceability in the value chain.

THE BENEFITS: To date, TechFarm has worked with more than 400 farms in Thailand, in collaboration with many private sector companies and the government. Through TechFarm, participating farmers and farm owners have embraced innovation and shifted their focus to quality products which have added value, bring in sizable profits and answer to the modern demands of customers. With plans to expand operations to Vietnam in 2018, TechFarm is positioning itself to improve the livelihoods of millions of farmers in Southeast Asia and increase food quality and safety for consumers.

Due to industrial farming, soil quality is an issue across much of the kingdom.

respond to digital disruption and to keep pace with quickly evolving Digital Age trends. Recent efforts by the government to spur collaboration with the private sector through "Thailand 4.0," an economic model that outlines ten high-tech 'S-Curve' target industries, show that the government finally recognizes the urgent importance of transitioning the country's economic model to meet the demands of a rapidly changing world.

There are a number of significant challenges Thailand must overcome to succeed in its next economic transformation. For starters, the majority of Thai companies have not invested sincerely in human resource development. Moreover, statistics show that for decades research and development (R&D) spending in Thailand has been stagnant at just 0.2-0.3 percent of GDP (Vietnam, by comparison, has set a target of two percent R&D spending by 2020). Typically, only the biggest players in Thai industry have taken on the financial risk of investing in R&D to accelerate innovation. Thailand's scarcity of advanced researchers further hinders the ability of Thai companies to pursue R&D projects.

Perhaps most notably, Thailand needs to upgrade its human resources by drastically reforming and improving the education system. Doing so is imperative if the country is to increase the number of Thai graduates with the ability and know-how to thrive in high-tech

industries and multinational working environments. The fact that Thai students continue to underperform in mathematics and science tests shows just how far the country

Blockchain, big data, cloud-based computing – these are a few of the new technologies that will help businesses improve performance while acting as drivers to support sustainability.

must improve to effectively compete at both the regional and global levels. This holds particular importance given that the high-tech, 'S-Curve' industries Thailand has placed at the heart of its future economic model will require a growing workforce of scientists, engineers, IT personnel, cloud services specialists, software developers, big data architects, and system integrators.

How technology shapes businesses

Blockchain, big data, cloud-based computing – these are just a few of the new technologies that will help businesses improve performance while acting as drivers to support sustainability. Imagine a tracking system that verifies sources of products as they move across a supply

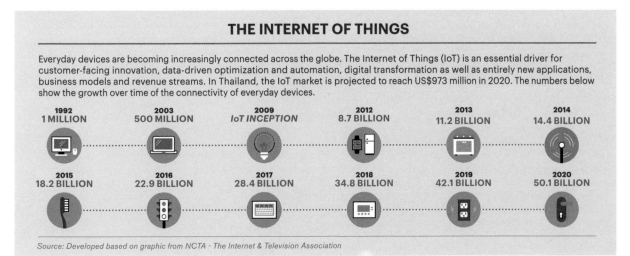

THE INTERNET OF THINGS

Everyday devices are becoming increasingly connected across the globe. The Internet of Things (IoT) is an essential driver for customer-facing innovation, data-driven optimization and automation, digital transformation as well as entirely new applications, business models and revenue streams. In Thailand, the IoT market is projected to reach US$973 million in 2020. The numbers below show the growth over time of the connectivity of everyday devices.

| 1992 | 2003 | 2009 | 2012 | 2013 | 2014 |
| 1 MILLION | 500 MILLION | IoT INCEPTION | 8.7 BILLION | 11.2 BILLION | 14.4 BILLION |

| 2015 | 2016 | 2017 | 2018 | 2019 | 2020 |
| 18.2 BILLION | 22.9 BILLION | 28.4 BILLION | 34.8 BILLION | 42.1 BILLION | 50.1 BILLION |

Source: Developed based on graphic from NCTA - The Internet & Television Association

chain, enhancing traceability and making it easier to automate processes. Or think about advanced materials such as plant-based plastics and materials generated from recovered waste. Not only is technological innovation booming, but it is rapidly shifting toward more sustainable solutions. When you take a look at some of the World Economic Forum's top 10 most promising technologies, they tend to have a clear environmental and social focus, such as energy-efficient water purification, enhanced nutrition to drive health at the molecular level, precise drug delivery

Around the world, governments and companies are launching initiatives and startups in industrial automation and other digital technologies.

through nanoscale engineering, or organic electronics and photovoltaics. Technology offers great opportunities for the private sector not only in cutting costs, but also in critically redefining business models and integrating sustainability into business strategies and operations.

The United Nations' 2017 Global Opportunity Report highlights the fact that every business, regardless of the sector, must invest in cutting edge digitization to stay relevant in the global economy. Around the world, governments and private companies are launching initiatives and funding startups in industrial automation and other digital technologies that can transform future manufacturing. In Germany, the government is sponsoring 'Industrie 4.0,' a multi-year initiative that brings together key players from the public, private, and academic sectors to develop a comprehensive vision and action plan for the application of digital technologies in the industrial sector. Closer to home, China has also recently proposed a 'Made in China 2025' strategy to promote domestic integration of digital technologies and industrialization.

Despite Thai industry's modest progress on adopting new technology, the country has recently upped its game. The ICT and Finance Ministries of Thailand announced a US$570 million venture fund in 2016 for the establishment of a startup ecosystem, with tech-related startups accounting for half of all funding recipients. Thailand 4.0 is also intended to help the country transition to a

GLOBAL RANKINGS

Thailand ranked

62nd
out of 139 countries
in the 2016 Network Readiness Index, which evaluates the impact of ICT on the competitiveness of nations.

Among the top five emerging and developing Asian economies,

Thailand ranks
4th
in terms of ICT readiness
(after Malaysia, Mongolia, China, and before Sri Lanka)

Thailand scores poorly in global innovation rankings, placing

44th
out of 78 economies
in the 2017 Bloomberg Innovation Index and 51st out of 127 countries on the 2017 Global Innovation Index.

Sources: World Economic Forum Global Information Technology Report 2016, 2017 Bloomberg Innovation Index, 2017 Global Innovation Index.

CASE STUDY | BBOXX Brings Clean Energy to Off-grid Communities

THE CHALLENGE: Greenhouse gas emissions from energy production are unarguably an environmental problem that pose a considerable threat to mankind. On the other side of the coin, an estimated 1.3 billion people go without reliable electricity each day. This shortage has a serious negative impact on health, education, productivity, and the general quality of life across large parts of Africa and Asia. Often, these off-grid communities tend to be rural and hard to reach, which makes on-grid solutions costly and unlikely. Rapid electrification, likely using fossil fuels, may seem like the cheapest way to bring power to everyone, but the environmental damage from such a solution is too severe. Even the most impoverished countries are increasingly aware that more sustainable answers are needed. How we expand energy infrastructure to deliver clean, reliable, and renewable power to this unserved market is of the utmost importance.

THE SOLUTION: Low-carbon renewable energy is emerging as a new green growth and poverty reduction strategy. Nonetheless, most governments and utilities in poor countries are often too cash-strapped to revamp their grids. A handful of tech-savvy entrepreneurs are seeking to bridge this gap by providing access to clean, cheap energy with local systems, metered and paid for by mobile phone.

Founded in 2010, BBOXX made its humble start delivering electricity to a village in Rwanda, but has quickly turned into a serious global business proposition. Each BBOXX solar generator is capable of being managed centrally. Customers can buy the solar unit on credit, repaying the loan via a fixed monthly fee, or in certain countries through a pay-as-you-go system. Remote monitoring allows BBOXX to check for faults, install firmware updates and, as a result, also increase operational efficiency due to lower maintenance costs and fewer unnecessary service trips. Units can be up and running almost as soon as they come out of the box. Activation normally takes less than five minutes. BBOXX manages the units from London, making the product extremely scalable. To date, more than 40,000 tons of CO_2 have been offset, and over 1.4 million customers now have access to clean, reliable energy.

THE BENEFITS: Apart from being greener and safer than fossil fuel alternatives, BBOXX is also now able to construct a detailed picture of consumers' energy consumption patterns, mapped geographically and socio-economically. This level of detail regarding off-grid energy use, payment data, location, and behavior has never been collected before and offers investors fresh insight into this untapped market. Sold in more than 35 countries around the globe, BBOXX's financial structure has brought off-grid solar into the world's financial markets. By 2020, the firm aims to expand its operations to meet the needs of 20 million rural people in developing countries.

An employee of BBOXX installs a solar panel on the roof of a house in Rwanda.

THE SIX TECH MEGATRENDS SHAPING THE WORLD

People and the Internet

How people connect with others, information and the world around them is being transformed rapidly through wearable and implantable technologies.

Computing, communications, storage everywhere

As computing and connectivity technologies are declining in both size and cost, access to the Internet is growing exponentially.

The Internet of Things

Smaller, cheaper, and smarter sensors are being introduced in homes, cities, transportation, and energy networks.

Artificial intelligence (AI) and big data

The rise of big data for decision-making is inevitable, along with AI and robotics' influence on decision-making and jobs. In Thailand, jobs will be both lost and created as a result of this emerging technology.

The sharing economy and distributed trust

Emerging blockchain technology will create whole new business models and opportunities, along with new ways of contracting, voting, and more.

The digitization of matter

3D printing will allow for the printing of products at home, as well as create a whole set of human health management opportunities.

Source: World Economic Forum, 2016

THE TOP 10 EMERGING TECHNOLOGIES

1. Nanosensors
Tiny sensors capable of circulating in the human body or being embedded in construction materials.

2. Next generation batteries
Batteries that are capable of providing clean, renewable and reliable energy sources to entire villages.

3. The Blockchain
Blockchain is expected to become a decentralized trust system that will revolutionize the way markets work.

4. Two-dimensional materials
Mixing and matching ultra-thin compounds to produce tailored materials for a wide range of functions: from water filters to wearables.

5. Autonomous vehicles
Self-driving cars boast the potential for saving lives, cutting pollution, improving quality of life for the elderly and other segments of society.

6. Organs-on-chip
Miniature models of human organs allow scientists to study physiological mechanisms and behaviors in ways never before possible.

7. Perovskite solar cells
This new generation of solar cell is easier to make, can be used virtually anywhere and keeps on generating power more efficiently.

8. Open AI ecosystem
Artificial intelligence could unlock higher productivity and better health and happiness for millions of people.

9. Optogenetics
Enhanced by emerging wireless microchips, this technique could offer new routes to treatment for conditions like Parkinson's and depression.

10. Systems metabolic engineering
Unlike fossil fuels, chemicals made from microorganisms are indefinitely renewable and emit relatively little greenhouse gas.

digital economy and promote inclusive growth and sustainability.

Some Thai banks are also engaging in partnerships with fintech startups and investing in the potential of digital currencies running on blockchain technology. Siam Commercial Bank was the first Thai bank to make a move on this front, launching its venture capital arm, Digital Ventures, in 2016 with more than US$50 million in fintech funding allocated for the first year alone. Kasikornbank and Krungsri followed suit, each setting up their own US$30-million fintech venture capital funds. Kasikornbank also established KBTG which, among other things, will partner with fintech firms and tech startups to explore financial innovations and develop new information technologies to fill the gap between traditional banking options and evolving customer preferences.

Leveraging value from technology

Technology is enabling radical new levels of efficiency in materials, energy, water,

and other resources – as well as enhancing transparency in corporate ethical practices. For instance, the Internet of Things (IoT) – the interconnected world of billions of objects with tiny sensors that can communicate to one another and to us, and make real time optimization decisions – is enabling factories, power grids, buildings and even cities to do much more with fewer resources.

Smart chief executives know that without adaptation their companies run the risk of becoming obsolete.

As part of the Chiang Mai Smart City initiative, Maejo University is developing wireless sensor systems for farmland irrigation techniques that minimize the use of water and increase productivity in Chiang Mai province, where 80 percent of people are small-scale farmers. PTT, one of the biggest companies in Thailand, is utilizing big data technology for its operations to uncover customer insights and improve efficiency across its operations.

KRATING POONPOL *is the venture partner behind 500 TukTuks, a micro-fund focused on nurturing promising Thai startups.*

"If we are serious about our vision of Thailand 4.0, we urgently need to modernize our entire regulatory framework – which should answer to rapid changes in the world and embrace technology and innovation. Certainly, education plays a major role. The crisis in the education system in Thailand is not a matter of rankings on world performance scales. The heart of the crisis is that our young people are learning within a system designed for a world that increasingly does not exist. The future is to be 'rediscovered' – be it medicine, finance, agriculture, or just about anything one can imagine. Thais need to learn how to rediscover. Many countries have had progress by redefining learning to be an 'original and personal process of discovery aided by technology and innovation.' And Thailand needs to start with the same concept as of today."

DR ANTHONY WATANABE *is a well-respected leader in water and energy innovation. In 2013 he was awarded the prestigious Clean50 award for individuals who are driving clean capitalism. Founded in 2014, his latest business venture, Asia Clean Innovations (ACI) is at the vanguard of cleantech adoption in the ASEAN region.*

Should businesses consider adopting technologies to improve their sustainability performance?
Without a doubt, yes. Thai businesses could benefit by looking at smart, clean solutions for energy, water, waste, and mobility. And while many larger Thai organizations are on the path of either delivering such solutions or taking advantage of them as customers, many of these innovations are not on the radar of most SMEs.

What are the main drivers and benefits for the business sector to consider such a move?
For businesses both large and small, there are at least two separate motivations. First, there's the opportunity for efficiency in operations, saving time and money through automation, reduced energy demand, reducing input costs of virgin materials through reuse, etc. Second, there's the lure of new products and services in an ever-changing market of opportunities.

What roles can businesses take in furthering the objectives of Thailand 4.0?
The push for Thailand 4.0 holds great promise in

forward-thinking domains like energy storage and smart cities. It even goes beyond sustainable business, extending into areas like strategies for an ageing society. A practical example is the Eastern Economic Corridor where priority areas include advanced bioenergy, medical tourism, robotics, and more. The government decided to build on the industrial foundation of the Eastern Seaboard in order to seek solutions for the decline in Thailand's exports and promote a new vision of technological development. With good infrastructure already in place such as highways, ports, and an airport, the region is ripe to realize some of the Thailand 4.0 aspirations to move up the innovation value chain.

Are there certain sectors that could be particularly suited for technology applications?
There are several existing areas where Thai policy and practice are headed in the right direction. One example is Energy Storage Thailand, which is managed by the National Science and Technology Development Agency. It is a government-sponsored project to develop next generation storage techniques and technologies in security and disaster preparedness, renewable energy, offshore and automotive estates and more. With a hefty budget of 765 million baht, Thailand is aiming to get ahead of the competition in developing, then using, and then exporting storage – the linchpin, according to experts like Elon Musk, for scaling renewable energy into mainstream adoption.

What would help accelerate technology adoption in the business sector?
A cursory analysis of the sustainable business landscape in Thailand shows that more companies are producing sustainable technologies than using them, when in fact the reverse is a much easier transition to accomplish.

More could be done to encourage both private sector and public sector adoption of new technologies, Thai or otherwise. Policy is one of the key ways for de-risking the use of new technologies. On the one hand, through subsidies and incentives, tax or otherwise, policy can encourage private enterprise to adopt sustainable technologies. Look at the success of the feed-in-tariff and adder program for solar farms that have made Thailand the ASEAN leader for installed capacity at nearly 3GW.

TAKE ACTION

Opportunities from technology abound for companies of all sizes. But it is not a matter of obtaining the most cutting edge technology to create value for your business. Rather, your company should take strategic steps, such as:

- **Identify your technological needs**, keeping in mind current and long-term business objectives. Will it improve efficiencies, facilitate internal processes, or create more burden?

- **Assess the value of technologies in meeting those needs**, from the perspective of costs, know-how, and available infrastructure.

- **Invest in employee training and development** to improve their skills and industrial relevance, to meet the needs of a digital and creative economy.

- **Increase investments in R&D** to attract talent in the field of research.

- **Step up partnerships and cooperation** between the academic and government sectors, as well as industry peers and leaders to enable learning and technology transfers.

The government has selected Phuket to be the country's first 'Smart City,' which will cater to digital industry, integrate ICT and modern technology to help local businesses, and enhance energy efficiency with the use of a smart grid.

Technology can make sustainability goals attainable without sacrificing company profits. One reason is that while the implementation of new technology can involve significant initial costs, on the flip side, early and strategic adoption can help reduce longer-term costs, helping companies to recoup their initial outlay. Leading companies, both domestic and international, are embracing such net-positive strategies where buildings, factories and supply chains generate more beneficial impacts than negative ones.

The revolution is here

The world is entering the Fourth Industrial Revolution. We are at the beginning of a worldwide transformation that is being driven by the convergence of digital, physical, and biological technologies. The speed of developments, and the disruption across major industries differentiates these developments from previous industrial revolutions. Naturally, despite the exponential opportunities this revolution offers, the fundamental change also poses new threats related to the disruptions it may cause in, for instance, labor markets, income inequality, or social value systems. Both the private sector and governments need to step up their efforts to drive positive social impacts and manage technology so that they can encourage long-term growth and increase ecological, economic, and social sustainability – and make sure these innovations place people at their core.

It is imperative that the country focuses on following through on implementation, removing unnecessary bureaucratic barriers, and transferring and scaling existing sustainable technologies.

For Thailand, it is important to bear in mind that the challenge of making society more sustainable may not be about discovering a miraculous new technology. Rather, it is imperative that the country focuses first on the sharing of information, following through on implementation, removing unnecessary legal and bureaucratic barriers, and the transferring and scaling of existing sustainable technologies.

Collaboration

- *For sustainable development to prosper, collaborative initiatives must be inclusive, clearly defined, and place people at the heart of the matter.*

- *The needs of companies often overlap with public sector interests. Firms can benefit by addressing common goals and creating long-term shared value.*

- *One-off, unilateral philanthropic endeavors such as donating to charities or planting trees are no longer adequate to improve brand reputation.*

- *By investing in sustainability-minded partnerships now, businesses can benefit by winning market share and wooing future customers.*

- *Public-private partnerships are poised to play an increasingly important role in helping Thailand overcome economic and development challenges.*

Collaboration is one of the keys to unlocking sustainability. The challenges we now face – be it food security, water scarcity, or clean energy – are so immense and the targets so daunting that we cannot overcome them alone. No individual company, institution, or government has enough resources or knowledge to single-handedly provide every solution. Leaders from all sectors of society agree that solving the challenges of sustainability requires unparalleled cooperation and the building of partnership models that are long-lasting, scalable, transformative, and create shared value.

Partnerships come in many forms. They can involve direct alliances between private firms and the government, between a company and a civil society organization, or a group of companies joined together in an industry-level body designed as a substitute for government oversight, such as a business association. Organizations understandably also have different motives for linking with others. In the private sector, it could be the desire to enhance the reputation of a company and brand it as socially or environmentally responsible. For civil society organizations,

the focus may be on resource sharing, whether it be funding, knowledge, or training. On the other hand, for the government, partnerships allow public service and infrastructure improvements to be made in an innovative and cost-efficient way.

Unfortunately, partnerships are not Thailand's strong point, as is evidenced by its score of just 29 out of 100 for Goal 17 (Partnerships for the Goals) on the Sustainable Development Goals (SDG) Index. Among other things, Goal 17 – which aims to enhance North-South and South-South cooperation by supporting national plans to achieve all the targets – highlights the fundamental role of the private sector in advancing the sustainable development agenda. While a diverse range of factors have contributed to Thailand's poor showing in this area, a lack of interest from the private sector remains the principal one.

The business case

Investing in sustainable development is not only about building goodwill with key stakeholders but also about mitigating business risks, be it from the disruption of operations or supplies, or from potential reputational damage. Furthermore, given that many customers nowadays have expectations regarding sustainability, businesses can win higher market share and dominate future markets by establishing relationships with these customers now. This is even more crucial in the developing world, including Thailand, where a great deal of market growth potential resides.

A report by risk management firm DNV GL highlighted actions from companies on specific SDGs and concluded that leading businesses are ready to take "extraordinary action" to achieve the goals. These firms include global brands such as Unilever, Siemens, Marks & Spencer, Danone, and more. These firms are characterized by their ability to see the potential of combining growth and sustainability, form collaborations, and view the SDGs as a tool to achieve competitive advantage.

Take, for example, Coca-Cola. The company's income depends heavily on emerging markets and its operations leave a giant environmental footprint. Due to this, Coca-Cola has joined forces with the World Wildlife Fund (WWF) on its Beyond Water Partnership to maintain resilient freshwater systems in 50 countries. It also partnered with the Bill & Melinda Gates Foundation on Project Nurture to help small-scale farmers in its supply chain identify new market opportunities, improve productivity, and develop strong agribusiness groups.

Businesses can also harness their existing resources and experiences to create a greater impact with partners. Bupa, a global healthcare group with more than 32 million customers in 190 countries, teamed up with the International Telecommunication Union (ITU) and World Health Organization (WHO) to tackle non-communicable diseases (NCDs) in low- and middle-income countries. Their "Be He@lthy, Be Mobile" initiative uses mobile technology in its implementation, taking advantage of the fact that 96 percent of the world has access to mobile phone networks. NCDs, such as cancer and heart disease, cause 68 percent of global deaths and the estimated cumulative loss of economic output due to NCDs in developing countries alone was estimated at US$7 trillion during 2011–2025, according to a Harvard University

A gathering of the Anti-Corruption Organization of Thailand.

study. This is a smart partnership from which Bupa benefits directly by building up its brand reputation and attracting future customers. It also benefits indirectly, as current and future customers are able to live healthier lifestyles.

No individual company, institution, or government has enough resources or knowledge to provide every solution.

Apart from these two examples, there is a direct motivation for businesses to get involved in achieving the SDGs – even on issues they had not previously considered. For example, the World Bank found that investing in gender equality can have a direct impact on economic growth. Investing in girls with a view to closing the education gap between genders can lead to lifetime earnings increases equivalent to an increase in annual GDP growth rates of about 1.5 percent.

Creating value from partnerships

The way companies incorporate sustainable development into their business strategies has evolved over the years. Many companies started from a purely philanthropic standpoint whereby they committed a certain amount of donations or undertook volunteering activities to improve trust and reputation.

Businesses are creating shared value by developing profitable business strategies that also deliver positive social benefits.

This Corporate Social Responsibility (CSR) strategy then moved on to risk mitigation in which businesses tried to minimize the negative impacts from their value chain: an example can be seen in organizations that are trying to reduce their energy use. The latest strategy, however, is Creating Shared Value (CSV), which came to the fore during the last decade. CSV embraces CSR as an "investment," not as an expense, and focuses on social issues that affect the drivers of company competitiveness.

Today, businesses are increasingly creating shared value by developing profitable business strategies that also deliver positive social benefits – even those that are known for their tough-minded approach to business, such as GE, IBM, Nestle, and Unilever have started putting a lot of effort into CSV. The underlying notion is that the value created by an organization's activities should not only benefit shareholders, but also the society and the environment which enable these activities to occur in the first place. While measuring and valuing impacts is still a work-in-progress for most companies, the model provides major new opportunities for profit and competitive advantage because society's unmet needs are huge. Nevertheless, it is important to recognize that creating shared value is not just social responsibility or philanthropy, but a more

SHARED VALUE PARTNERSHIPS

Through creating shared value partnerships, businesses can develop business models that contribute to social and environmental needs. Conceptualizing business models around such needs can increase company productivity, respond to a large untapped or underserved market, and improve the environment and relationships with communities in areas where the company operates. Partnerships can be built with various entities, as follows:

Who	Traditional Relationship with Business	Pathways to Partnerships
NGOs	- Recipient of business donations - Holds businesses accountable for their actions and are potential sources of conflict with businesses due to their advocacy efforts	- Mutually implement and scale shared value solutions for social and environmental needs
Government	- Regulator of business operations - Taxes businesses to pay for social services	- Provide incentives to businesses to jumpstart market solutions - Invest in infrastructure to facilitate business delivery of products and service solutions
Foundations	- Independently donate to charitable causes	- Partner with companies, NGOs, and government to deliver solutions for social needs
Business Competitors	- Implement CSR activities for their own purposes, typically for branding and marketing	- Partner with other businesses to improve the overall operating environment

Source: Professor Michael E. Porter (2014), Harvard Business School

CASE STUDY | DoiTung and IKEA Give Local Products a Global Platform

DoiTung and IKEA have been co-creating handicraft collections since 2012.

THE CHALLENGE: Founded in 1988 by Her Royal Highness Princess Srinagarindra, the Doi Tung Development Project (DTDP) is one of Thailand's oldest and best-known social enterprises. Within Thailand it is widely credited with having helped to economically and socially transform a large swath of Northern Thailand's once-notorious Golden Triangle region. Today, hundreds of ethnic inhabitants of the mountainous Doi Tung region – an area previously renowned for opium cultivation – earn a licit and steady income by producing high-quality macadamia nuts, Arabica coffee, and handicrafts, all of them sold under the DoiTung brand.

Since its inception, the DTDP has always strived to meet international standards in order to expand the market for DoiTung products and ensure the sustainability of the business. Part of this approach includes an openness to global partnerships, if the right one presents itself.

THE SOLUTION: An equal partnership with IKEA with mutual learning at its core was forged. The partnership began after an informal meeting where the two organizations discussed common grounds, values, the mutual interests that would drive such a collaboration, and their shared long-term vision. In conjunction with the opening of the first IKEA store in Thailand in 2011, IKEA invited DTDP to work on a special collection with their Swedish designer. Also, DTDP designer Jackrayu "Jim" Kongurai was admitted in IKEA's Design Apprentice Program at the IKEA Global Range and Development Centre in Sweden to understand the design work of IKEA.

In 2006, IKEA set up a CSR program called The Next Generation Initiatives, working with different self-help groups in India and Sweden. They approached DTDP to join the program. This was an opportunity for a cottage industry like DTDP to learn from a global conglomerate like IKEA, whose standards and production control process is applicable worldwide. At the same time, IKEA will be able to understand another type of supplier and the social benefits it can generate. Since 2012, IKEA designers have worked with DTDP ceramic and fabric designers to produce exclusive collections for IKEA stores in Europe.

THE BENEFITS: When the program started with IKEA, the number of workers in the handicrafts section stood at nearly 300. Up until that point they had been producing complicated high-value products, but only small amounts. However, IKEA has brought a high number of orders, and so productivity has had to increase. From designers to weavers, potters to logistics support, the team has learned to work efficiently and control quality, time, and costs. DTDP has to strictly follow the IKEA supplier code of conduct, IWAY, which covers labor, safety, and environmental procedures, and is also audited.

DTDP's relationship with IKEA has introduced the DoiTung brand to another commercial platform. Through the arrangement, a truly sustainable partnership – long-term, equitable, and commercially successful – has been realized.

Shared interests and knowledge sharing are at the heart of the DoiTung-IKEA relationship.

VICHIEN PHONGSATHORN *is one of Thailand's most socially active corporate leaders, having dedicated much of his time over the past two decades to serving social causes. Apart from being the chairman of Premier Group of Companies and Khon Thai Foundation, he is also Vice Chairperson of the Anti-Corruption Organization Thailand and a key advisor behind the creation of BKIND Fund, Thailand's first socially responsible investment mutual fund.*

BKIND fund, the capital market and social sector then joined forces to establish the Thailand CG Fund, which promotes good corporate governance and combats corruption. This second fund is supported by a network of 11 asset management companies, along with other players, which means much larger access to investment. They work within their expertise as investment banks, still getting their fees, and play a role in sustainability – a profitable business that positively contributes to society.

What is your biggest concern for Thailand in terms of sustainability?

I think inequality poses one of the greatest risks for Thailand. In this regard, there is a huge opportunity lost for businesses in Thailand. When a large number of the population is poor, there is less productivity and less consumption. Businesses have a role to play in tackling inequality through "fair sharing." They need to recognize that there are gaps and use their capacity to overcome these. The private sector can do this smartly and align their efforts with their first bottom line, which is of course financial.

For instance, while the unemployment rate is low, this does not mean people are getting paid well. Companies are fighting to get qualified people. So, fair sharing in this case can mean training, or improvement of skills in the workforce. Things can change for the better without firms sacrificing their financial benefits. Actually, such initiatives benefit them.

What is crucial to a successful partnership?

A good collaboration should be designed with incentives in mind, and not only goodwill. You need to think about creating shared value (CSV). Ask yourself: "How best can we utilize our existing businesses and engage other stakeholders to improve on something?" Eventually, "doing what we can" won't be enough – we need to shift to "doing the most with what we've got."

A good example from our previous work is a partnership that originally started with BBL Asset Management on BKIND Fund. The fund was used to support practitioners on various social projects and had a portfolio of almost two billion baht. Building on the success of the first

Is there a way to ensure success in collaboration?

I think the private sector is more willing to take action in a group, and not alone, as seen in the Collective Action Coalition Against Corruption. Although corruption is a heavy topic, the willingness to act increases significantly when companies work collectively.

Thailand is not stingy in terms of support. A lot of companies donate a lot of money or commit staff time for volunteering. However, the mindset is, once a donation is done, the project is satisfied. There is not so much focus on impact and outcome – we need to encourage people to put more emphasis on that, not only the act of giving.

holistic, collaborative means of achieving economic success.

Thai examples of CSV abound, but one of the most illustrative is offered by Thai energy company Bangchak and its cooperative gas stations. These came about when the company began bartering fuel for rice with the Si Prachan Agricultural Cooperative in Suphanburi province, then donating the rice to student lunch programs at nearby schools located around its refinery. The trust fostered with the community then developed into an

arrangement whereby service stations could belong to cooperatives.

By 2014, 626 community service stations were owned by community members. In addition to generating income from fuel sales, community members also receive dividends at the end of the year. The initiative benefits local communities economically and also strengthens the communities' self-reliance. The total sales turnover by the service stations is more than 62 million liters a month, or about 28 percent of the company's nationwide sales.

TOOLBOX | PARTNERSHIP PLATFORMS

Numerous collaborative platforms for sustainable development have materialized in recent years. Some of the most notable include:

The United Nations Global Compact helps businesses create partnerships across sectors through networking, collaboration with local networks, resource development, and online partnership matchmaking. UN Global Compact works with more than 9,000 companies and 4,000 non-business partners worldwide. Thailand currently has 35 active private sector and non-business partners participating.

World Business Council for Sustainable Development (WBCSD) is a CEO-led organization of more than 200 leading businesses worldwide. These businesses work together to accelerate the private sector's transition to a more sustainable and just world. WBCSD assists their member institutions on maximizing positive impact for shareholders, the environment, and societies by providing a one-stop shop for tools, guidance, and expertise.

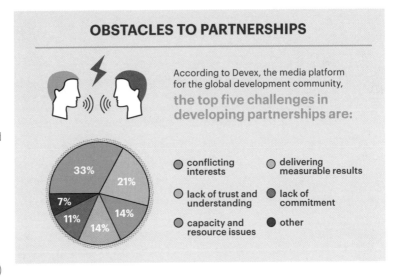

OBSTACLES TO PARTNERSHIPS

According to Devex, the media platform for the global development community, the top five challenges in developing partnerships are:

- conflicting interests
- lack of trust and understanding
- capacity and resource issues
- delivering measurable results
- lack of commitment
- other

33% / 21% / 14% / 14% / 11% / 7%

The Sustainable Stock Exchange Initiative (SSE) is a peer-to-peer learning platform for exploring how exchanges and listed companies – in collaboration with investors, regulators, and companies – can enhance corporate transparency and, ultimately, improve performance on environmental, social, and corporate governance issues and indicators.

The Sustainable Stock Exchange now has more than 60 partner exchanges from both the developed and developing worlds, including the Stock Exchange of Thailand (SET), which assesses the sustainability of listed companies and publishes the Thailand Sustainability Investment (THSI) list each year, with top performers in the ESG dimensions.

Businesses located in the vicinity of the capital's river have been creating shared value with Creative District, a community initiative that brings local artisans and businesses together and fosters collaboration with local architects, professors of urban planning, the Thailand Creative and Design Center (TCDC), and the Bangkok Metropolitan Administration (BMA). Founded in 2012 by Bangkok River Partners, a group of riverside hotels that aim to promote leisure and tourism, the initiative's main goal is to support local communities through trade and tourism, as well as to preserve the authentic character of Bangkok's riverside areas. Organically, and without direct government support, it seems to be working – shophouses and buildings that once stood empty are now home to small creative businesses, while the project itself has gained domestic and international media coverage, and helped maintain good relationships between hotels and communities along the riverside.

Measuring shared value

Better understanding of the direct and indirect impacts and value creation stemming from business activities is crucial to collaborative decision-making. But while there has been significant progress in terms of environmental impact measurement, there is still much that

can be done to better assess the social and socioeconomic impacts of business activities, such as in improvements in livelihoods.

There are different guidelines and tools for measuring impact but the principle remains largely the same and can be summarized in the following four steps:

Identify the social issues to target: The starting point is identifying specific issues that represent opportunities to increase revenue or reduce costs. A systemic analysis of unmet social needs and gaps that overlap with your business is the key.

Make the business case: Develop a solid business case based on how social improvement will directly improve business performance. Be specific, outlining the activities and costs involved.

Track progress: Track inputs, business activities, outputs, and financial performance (revenue and costs) relative to projections.

Measure results and use insights to unlock new value: Focus on validating the anticipated link between social and business results; evaluate whether it produced a good joint return; take note of lessons learned and improve.

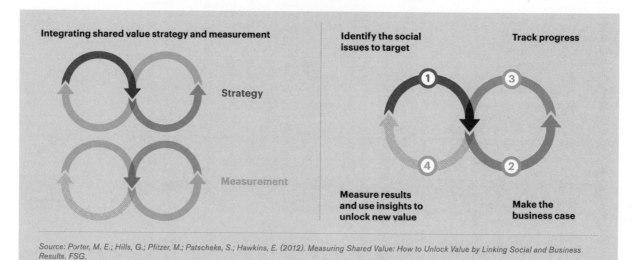

Source: Porter, M. E.; Hills, G.; Pfitzer, M.; Patscheke, S.; Hawkins, E. (2012). Measuring Shared Value: How to Unlock Value by Linking Social and Business Results. FSG.

CASE STUDY Pracharat Strives to Boost Incomes in Grassroots Communities

The farmers of Baan Pak Duk, in Petchabun province, are among Pracharat's participants.

THE CHALLENGE: Thailand is one of the world's great development success stories. The country has made remarkable progress over the last four decades, officially becoming an upper-middle income economy in 2011 and moving from low-income status to an upper-income status in less than a generation. Nonetheless, growth has slowed and rising inequalities present a significant challenge. Growing disparities in income and consumption can be seen across regions of Thailand, particularly in rural areas. Moving forward, the transition from middle- to high-income status cannot be achieved without addressing this problem. So, how does the nation pursue inclusive economic growth while also enhancing Thailand's competitiveness?

THE SOLUTION: The Pracharat, or "people's state," policy was unveiled by the government in December 2015. The model aims to strengthen Thailand's economy at the grass-roots level and empower local communities and enterprises.

To do so, it envisions a public-private-civil society nexus acting in the interests of sustainable development through the execution of four major strategies, which are good governance, innovation and productivity, the upgrading of human capital quality, and participation in bringing about national prosperity. It includes tax breaks and economic stimulus packages, such as US$2.6 billion in state loans for the rural sector and a 100-billion baht (approximately US$2.8 billion) credit guarantee to encourage banks to lend to SMEs.

One of the pressing issues involves empowering rural communities, where there is a need to increase income, build up new entrepreneurs, and promote social enterprises. The aim is for participating firms to conduct a broad range of activities with the populace in these areas, from marketing local signature products to improving vocational education. "We will educate people on transforming produce from agriculture into a community product and how to develop the area into a community-based tourism community. We will also help them find markets for their products and assist in making people understand other aspects such as capital, investment, management," explains Thapana Sirivadhanabhakdi, CEO of ThaiBev, who leads one of Pracharat's 12 public-private steering committees.

THE BENEFITS: Some have criticized Pracharat as the rebranding of "Pracha Niyom," or populist policies. However, while populism generally refers to pouring money into rural communities, the newer policy positions itself as an integrated approach among different sectors. Whether or not this is true will largely depend on the sustainability and success of the new enterprises that have popped up across the country as a result of Pracharat. It is expected that the results of this ambitious policy – and the private sector's role in it – will be seen clearly in the next four to five years.

For Thapana, enabling the sharing of knowledge between stakeholders is one of Pracharat's clear strengths. "This is already creating so much value for our society," he says.

ThaiBev CEO Thapana Sirivadhanabhakdi leads a Pracharat meeting.

PUBLIC-PRIVATE PARTNERSHIPS: THE POWER AND THE PITFALLS

Public-private partnerships (PPPs) are critically important in meeting the challenges of sustainable development. There are billions of people in the world without access to roads, safe drinking water, sanitation, or modern communication technologies. The reason PPPs are so important is that they can weigh in when traditional financing from governments fails to meet needs. The World Bank estimates that Asia will need to invest US$1.7 trillion per year in infrastructure until 2030 to maintain growth, tackle poverty, and respond to climate change.

There is no single model or definition of PPPs. However, the World Bank's Knowledge Lab defines them as "a long-term contract between a private party and a government entity for providing a public asset or service, in which the private party bears significant risk and responsibility, and remuneration is linked to performance."

Thailand has undertaken a number of PPPs since the 1990s in the energy sector and transport sector. In an effort to speed up economic growth while anticipating the opportunities and challenges of the country's transition into the ASEAN Economic Community (AEC), the Thai government intends to use public-private partnerships to drastically expand infrastructure development such as the building of high-speed railways, metros, highways, and other core projects in the coming years.

These plans promise substantial benefits to both government and private investors. For the government, it allows infrastructure development and other public service improvements to be made with off-balance-sheet financing and introduces private sector technology and innovation in the process. For the private sector, it allows access to secure, long-term investments and presents a substantial economic opportunity.

All this said, Thailand has had mixed experiences with public-private partnerships due to a complicated bureaucracy and a lack of transparency. However, the development of a more conducive environment for PPPs is picking up due to the latest Private Investment in State Undertaking Act 2013 (PISU), the growing network of Thailand 4.0 provisions, and the upcoming Eastern Economic Corridor Development plan.

Simply having the public sector and private partners collaborate does not guarantee success. A partnership's strength lies in input from diverse stakeholders who leverage leading practices from their fields of expertise. Nonetheless, many public-private partnerships fail due to an inability to align on targeted outcomes, an unclear understanding of implementation risks, overly ambitious goals by some of those involved, weak organizational structure, or a lack of engagement from key players. There are some building blocks that businesses should ensure are in place before embarking on any PPP.

The public-private partnership checklist:

Identify the right project(s). They must be demand-driven and highly responsive to the specific needs of industry and/or society.

Set realistic and measurable common goals. Think long-term, establish metrics for success, and track them.

Clearly define a business plan and detailed contract from an early stage.

Take into account cultural complexities. Understand the ways of thinking and working of the different actors that may have different organizational backgrounds.

Actively engage all stakeholders and partners (including people who will be affected by the partnership) and have recognized public figures as advocates or spokespersons for the project.

Create sustainable and diversified revenue streams. Seek revenue streams beyond government or public funding and continually drive innovation, efficiency, and return on investment.

Display core structural integrity. Leading organizations have a reputation for being trustworthy, on budget, innovative, productive, reliable, and resourceful.

Put people first by defining public interest, consulting with stakeholders, and involving independent auditors.

TAKE ACTION

A partnership is likely to be ineffective if partners do not share the same values, interests, risks, responsibilities, and benefits. With this in mind, companies embarking on collaborations should take a strategic rather than an ad hoc approach.

HOW TO COLLABORATE SUCCESSFULLY:

- **Identify clear reasons to collaborate.** The collaboration needs to help each partner organization achieve something significant. Vague incentives such as "good publicity" or "doing good things" are not sufficient. Without identifying strong incentives for all partners, commitment and accountability from each player may be weak.

- **Align the expected outcome with your company's core strategy.** Project sustainability relies on business operations. To make a partnership more than a one-time thing, you need to revisit the core corporate strategy. If it is cost-cutting, then an energy-saving mechanism or waste-recycling initiative may be areas to look into. If it is product quality, then ensuring that goods and materials are sourced in a sustainable and responsible manner may serve as priority.

- **Have a core of totally committed and knowledgeable people.** Coordinated action can be difficult since the first movers take the biggest risks. Choose a person with suitable qualifications and commitment to be the lead, and clearly define the person's role. Also give career recognition for a job well done.

- **Set simple but credible goals for collaboration.** Partnerships will stall unless everyone agrees on the same goal. Businesses, government, and civil society may have different motives, but if they share the same objective, collaboration can work more sustainably. Roles and responsibilities should also be clearly defined so that the private sector does not get tangled up in the realm of the government's responsibility, for instance.

- **Build trust.** In general, companies worry about their sensitive and proprietary information when interacting with an external party, but in practice this is not the information people are after. A successful partnership requires that each party makes efforts to keep the others informed and is willing to share information when called upon. Transparency goes a long way.

Ideally, this process should not be a one-time effort, separate from measuring business performance, but an on-going feedback loop that provides a roadmap for understanding and unlocking shared value creation.

Growing together

A successful sustainable development agenda requires partnerships between the private sector, government, and civil society. In fact, 85 percent of CEOs surveyed by the UN Global Compact and Accenture see cross-sector coalitions and partnerships as essential to accelerating transformation.

Businesses do not exist in a vacuum: their own success is tied to good governance, energy security, and sustainable economic development, among other factors. These needs often overlap with the public sector's interests in sustaining peace and security, and reducing poverty. Companies therefore can benefit greatly by helping to address these common goals and creating long-term value.

Much progress has already been made. In the last decade, Thai business leaders have embraced cross-sector partnerships like never before. And in the decades to come, new and more efficient forms of collaboration founded on shared values – not philanthropic or classic business-as-usual ideals – will no doubt emerge. In light of these developments, the business that moves beyond being a responsible corporate citizen from day-to-day towards becoming a responsible corporate partner for the future stands to gain the most.

Reporting and Disclosure

- *Reporting is valuable as both a communication tool for a company and its stakeholders, and as a benchmark for sustainability improvements.*

- *Disclosures of ESG-related information is quickly becoming a regulatory requirement across the world, including for companies listed on SET.*

- *The reporting process is an incremental one, often hindered by a lack of leadership support, resources, and unavailability of data.*

- *The field of reporting is evolving fast. Advances in technology and data analytics are redefining information disclosures, and a more informed public means that companies must be transparent about a wider range of issues.*

Reporting is an important tool of communication for a company and its stakeholders. Its output exists in many forms: a sustainability or CSR report, financial statement, annual report, or the Form 56-1 Annual Registration Statement submitted by listed companies on the Stock Exchange of Thailand (SET). No matter the intended audience or purpose, these reports serve as critical platforms for disclosing a company's financial, economic, social, and environmental performance resulting from its business activities.

The drive for these disclosures in Thailand stems from various factors, among them stakeholder expectations for transparency, government policies in support of sustainable development, and business leadership. Regulatory requirements from the Securities and Exchange Commission of Thailand (SEC) and the Stock Exchange of Thailand (SET) also play an increasingly central role.

Likewise, heightened investor interest and the popularity of sustainability investing are strong incentives for companies to be more transparent about their non-financial performance. Mechanisms like the Thailand Sustainable Investment List (THSI) developed by SET, the ESG100 Index of the Thaipat Institute, and the Corporate Governance Report of Listed Companies by the Thai Institute of Directors, which reward companies for their sustainability and governance performances, rely heavily on publicly available information in their assessments. From the perspective of recognition and reputational gains, disclosure is becoming a necessity.

The Global Reporting Initiative's (GRI) Sustainability Disclosure Database reveals that 107 Thai organizations released sustainability reports in 2016. The vast majority of these were published by large organizations, with a smaller percentage attributed to multinational enterprises and SMEs. This finding supports the GRI's analysis that sustainability reporting is used mainly by large companies with international operations and far-reaching supply chains. Similarly, in 2015 the GRI noted that 72 percent of global companies that produced such reports were publicly listed.

With reporting playing a valuable part in corporate sustainability efforts, the number of Thai companies producing them is growing. New names and smaller players are entering the fray. Reporting frameworks and disclosure guidelines such as the GRI, the Dow Jones Sustainability Indices (DJSI), the Integrated Reporting Framework, and CDP are no longer unfamiliar concepts. For companies, such guidelines make non-financial disclosure easier than ever, enabling them to understand what to report, how to report, and where they stand on these global benchmarks of sustainability excellence.

Why report?

Broadly speaking, sustainability reporting serves a twofold purpose for an organization: internal management and process improvements, and external engagement with stakeholders. The former leads to a better understanding of a company's risks and opportunities over the short- to long-term. The latter supports external stakeholder engagement and reputational benefits.

When reporting is viewed as a driver for internal value creation, it has the potential to improve cross-departmental collaboration through data and resource sharing; enable more informed decision making owing to better awareness of financial and non-financial linkages; and promote accountability for a company's performance against its sustainability goals. Charoen Pokphand Foods (CPF), for example, credits the creation of its supply chain sustainability improvement strategy to the gaps identified from its annual reporting. Reporting is also consistent with the Sufficiency Economy Philosophy (SEP) principle of prudence, as it supports risk management through strategic stakeholder communication. The list goes on.

Nevertheless, in many organizations such benefits may not be fully realized. Limited leadership support, resource constraints, and a lack of data are major impediments to extensive reporting. In cases where companies achieve the bare minimum, reporting is often reduced to mere compliance or a box-ticking exercise. And while this is an achievement in itself – particularly for first-time reporters – critics of a compliance-driven approach argue that it remains ineffective for informing the public of progress in a timely and accessible manner.

Regulatory pressures have intensified on companies to disclose their sustainability performance.

Even among companies applying the Integrated Reporting Framework (IR), an approach that promotes 'integrated thinking' and clearer connections between business and value creation, pushing beyond compliance is a challenge. A 2014 study by Pricewaterhouse-Coopers on early adopters of IR revealed that

"The value of the sustainability reporting process is that it ensures organizations consider their impacts on these sustainability issues, and enables them to be transparent about the risks and opportunities they face."
– The Global Reporting Initiative

too often a compliance mindset and spin on messages prevents authenticity in reporting. Focusing too much on using reporting terminologies and meeting requirements for content results in a less compelling story

REPORTING BY THE NUMBERS

107
Thai companies released sustainability reports in 2016

188
Thai companies have released a total of **442 sustainability reports** since 2007, ranging from small-medium sized enterprises to large multi-national companies

21%
of publicly listed companies in Thailand have adopted third-party verification for their reports

SET The 1st ASEAN stock market
to commit to promoting long-term sustainability by enhancing corporate transparency and ESG integration

Sources: Stock Exchange of Thailand, Global Reporting Initiative's Sustainability Disclosure Database, Lloyd's Register Quality Assurance

The importance of materiality

Key to successful reporting is the concept of materiality. An integral component of a sustainability strategy (see *Sustainability Strategy,* page 32), materiality is likewise central to the reporting universe – the 'essential filter' by which companies sift and sort through sustainability-related information and identify the core ESG issues that warrant disclosure. Everything that is disclosed hinges upon how a company defines materiality for the purpose of reporting.

Selecting the right approach to materiality is a vital first step. The different reporting frameworks available offer varying definitions of materiality depending on their intended audience. For instance, GRI defines a material topic as one that "reflects a reporting organization's significant economic, environmental and social impacts; or that substantively influences the assessments and decisions of stakeholders." Materiality for GRI is rooted in their emphasis on multi-stakeholder engagement, which in practice means that a GRI-led materiality assessment must include real engagement sessions on report content.

Meanwhile, organizations like the Sustainability Accounting Standards Board (SASB) in the United States, and RobecoSAM's Corporate Sustainability Assessment for the DJSI have a more investor-centric notion of materiality. In these two cases, guidance is framed within the scope of financial materiality, which relates more closely to the financial origins of the concept, defined as any information that could influence the economic decisions of users of financial statements. Climate-related financial disclosure is one example. Poorly informed decisions on climate change risks and opportunities can have destabilizing impacts on an unsuspecting company. This is particularly true for financial institutions handling investment and lending solutions, which rely on the financial costs of climate change being accurately priced in their decision-making.

To avoid unknowingly creating an information gap in their sustainability reports, a company

that misses the opportunity to tell the most relevant information in a way that reflects the uniqueness of the organization.

The risk is that the amount of resources invested in collecting these large quantities of information spanning all ESG dimensions culminates in a lengthy, insipid, and ultimately minimally-read report. The GRI alone provides over 400 potentially relevant metrics that an organization can report on. For stakeholders, this implies sifting through an often unnecessary abundance of information to get to the substance most material to them. While one upside of reporting is that it shows an organization to be more seriously committed to transparency, stakeholders face the challenge of how to make use of what is presented to them in an informed and impactful way.

should report on the same material ESG issues as those that drive its sustainability and/or corporate strategy. Aligning separate sets of material issues – one for reporting and one for strategic decision-making – can guarantee that a company discloses 'decision-relevant' ESG information to its wide-ranging stakeholder groups (the assumption being that this is an objective). Even so, reaching this end remains a work in progress for many, as it demands smoother integration between a company's core business strategy and its sustainability priorities.

Once materiality – and therefore content – is confirmed, the next step involves drawing the boundaries and responsibilities for data and information collection.

The (un)availability of information

For companies new to reporting, the process of gathering the necessary data and information may be daunting at first. It requires a concerted effort by all relevant parties, a platform for data consolidation – whether through means as basic as Microsoft Excel or advanced database systems like SAP – and knowledge of what data to collect, and how. But investing the time to do this well will pay off in the long-run, because a solid data platform can help a company understand its impacts and value creation potential across its supply chain and beyond.

Reporting guidelines are extremely helpful starting points in this endeavor (for details, see *Reporting and Disclosure*, page 144). To begin with, most offer explanations of the requested data indicators, suggest boundaries for collection, and provide support through designated representatives. Indicators selected for disclosure should be narrowed down to those that represent a material issue for a company.

Fundamentally, this is an incremental process, often hindered by a lack of data. At other times it is available but not in the format required. For Bangchak Corporation, a petroleum refining company, "getting environmental

accounting right" was critical in their early reporting efforts – to the extent that this postponed reporting by a year. "If the data was not accurate, it was not getting published," says Dr Chongprode Kochaphum, vice president for sustainability management at Bangchak.

A company should report on the same material ESG issues as those that drive its strategy.

Herein lies another significant test of reporting: disclosing accurate and reliable information. Failing to do so could reflect poorly on stakeholder trust. The GRI itself emphasizes these aspects as part of its Principles for Defining Report Quality, which state that a report should be balanced, comparable, accurate, timely, clear, and reliable. To respond to this need, most companies turn to sustainability assurance and verification.

Collecting relevant, sustainability-related data is vital to accurate reporting.

TOOLBOX | **REPORTING GUIDELINES & DISCLOSURE STANDARDS**

Given the abundance of national and international reporting guidelines, it can be hard for a first-time reporting company to determine which is the most suitable. Harnessing the full benefit of these guidelines involves going beyond compliance to using them as performance benchmarks across all dimensions of sustainability. Their evolving nature means companies can rest assured that the contents are regularly updated to reflect the most up-to-date trends. Here are some of the most common:

Annual Registration Statement (Form 56-1)
Stock exchanges demonstrate leadership

All listed companies on the Stock Exchange of Thailand (SET) are mandated by the Securities and Exchange Commission (SEC) to annually disclose ESG-related information through the 56-1 Form, or Annual Registration Statement. SET's leadership here is also part of the larger trend of increased regulatory pressures on ESG reporting worldwide.

In addition, SET regularly offers guidance and training on ESG reporting to listed companies through its SR Center, and communicates with its stakeholders on sustainability trends. A 2016 analysis by the UN-led Sustainable Stock Exchange Initiative comparing ESG-related initiatives of 82 stock exchanges around the world concluded that the only area in which SET was lacking on sustainability promotion was in offering green bonds.

GRI Standards
The first global standard for sustainability reporting

Released in October 2016, the GRI Standards is a successor to the widely embraced GRI G4 Standards developed by the Global Reporting Initiative, an international independent standards organization. With 74 percent of the world's largest 250 corporations using GRI's Standards to report, it is arguably the most internationally popular standard.

Here in Thailand, 188 companies have, as of November 2017, submitted a total of 443 sustainability reports to the organization's Sustainability Disclosure Database. An explanation for GRI's monumental success could be in its pioneering ability to create a "common language" for quality sustainability reporting between organizations and their stakeholders.

INTEGRATED REPORTING ⟨IR⟩

Integrated Reporting Framework
The perspective of value creation

The Integrated Reporting Framework (IR), developed by the International Integrated Reporting Council (IIRC), cultivates a more holistic approach to reporting. Companies are encouraged to transition to an "integrated thinking" mindset that views business functions and operations as connected to its use of "capitals": financial, intellectual, manufacturing, human, social, and natural. By understanding these relationships, companies can better

grasp how these capitals create value over the short, medium and long terms.

Proclaimed as a game changer by many, the IIRC envisioned IR as the new reporting norm. For Professor Robert Eccles at the Harvard Business School, the move to integrated reporting from current approaches closely resembles that of the move from CSR to CSV. However, IR adoption in Thailand remains slow.

CDP
Environmental disclosure makes sound business sense

CDP, formerly the Carbon Disclosure Project, has for the past 15 years built an extensive global disclosure system of environmental data under its three areas of focus: Climate, Water and Forests. Data is self-reported by participating cities, companies, states and regions through CDP's annual questionnaire, and is subsequently transformed into detailed analyses of critical environmental risks, opportunities and impacts for use by decision-makers.

Separate scoring methodologies are applied in all three questionnaires, but all participants are assessed for their overall progress toward environmental stewardship in four levels: Disclosure, Awareness, Management, and Leadership. CDP states that these methodologies are "designed to incentivize" companies to improve their environmental performance.

CASE STUDY Bangchak's Strategic Use of Reporting

THE CHALLENGE: Extensive amounts of information go into a sustainability report. Collecting and consolidating all the relevant data spanning from a company's headquarters to its operations calls for significant internal coordination.

For Bangchak Corporation, information had to be compiled from all of its business groups in Thailand, and, for certain reporting indicators, from subsidiaries in which it holds over 20 percent in equity. These business groups range from refining to marketing, to petroleum exploration and production. Their distinct natures already suggest different starting points on sustainability awareness. Thus arose the challenge for Bangchak: to report information from different sources to the same level of quality and detail – and in a way that still complies with reporting requirements and communicates the identity of the company.

THE SOLUTION: Successful reporting on these wide-ranging issues is achieved by clearly "designating responsible functions for each," explains Dr Chongprode Kochaphum, vice president for sustainability management at Bangchak. "For example, we have individuals responsible for collecting data on energy use in the refinery and office, water consumption, results on employee engagement and training KPIs."

Each department receives internal and external training on what information is expected, why, and how it fits into the company's sustainability strategy. Reporting is about much more than merely generating numbers for compliance. "We use GRI as a baseline to determine what is expected at the international level on sustainability," says Dr Chongprode.

In turn, they can "identify sustainability gaps, opportunities, and delegate appropriate individuals and resources to push improvements forward."

To be effective in this endeavor, she continues, "[The Sustainability Development Function] must strengthen our own knowledge of the issues first before we inform other departments what is expected of them. You could hardly expect them to do as you suggest without sufficient buy-in of the rationale behind it."

THE BENEFITS: Bangchak's multi-faceted formula combining reporting with capacity-building, benchmarking, and knowledge-sharing is an effective way to drive sustainability improvements across the organization. This collaborative nature creates value by shifting away from the isolated efforts that marked their earlier reporting attempts. "As the reporting scope expanded and became more challenging," explains Dr Chongprode, "it became necessary to involve different functions in the process."

Bangchak's 12th Sustainability Report was published in accordance with the GRI G4 Standards Core Level, the GRI Oil and Gas Sector Supplement, and the UN Global Compact Advanced Level. It has now integrated its 4 Green Sustainability Strategy as part of its corporate business strategy. What started in 2002 as an internal process confined to a few departments measuring internal progress on environmental indicators has transformed into a powerful communication and benchmarking tool that helps move the company forward, always keeping pace with change.

The value of having a report independently verified is, at the very core, "for the prevention of risk," says Pornphan Sirisomrithikul, chief representative of Lloyd's Register Quality Assurance (LRQA) Thailand. That is, to protect against risks ensuing from the disclosure of inaccurate information which could be misconstrued by decision-makers. Not only that, third-party verification enhances a company's credibility and strengthens internal reporting processes. "By drilling down into both the process and people involved in data collection, auditors work to eliminate any misunderstanding of reporting requirements, help companies identify the right sources of

data from their operations to be included, and make sure the information responds externally to public interest and market demand," explains Pornphan.

Naturally, this process takes time and money. Its difficulty varies according to the level of assurance sought – typically reasonable or limited – and could be taxing on companies that are unprepared for audits. But as Pornphan says, "Data that passes through the audit process means it is accurate and ready to be disclosed to the public." Indeed, in a 2015 global survey on the assurance practices of members of the World Business Council for

THE ESG 100

Thailand's first sustainability index, ESG 100, lists the top 100 companies that demonstrate "outstanding" ESG performance. Launched by the Thaipat Institute, in 2017, 656 publicly traded companies listed on the Stock Exchange of Thailand (SET) and the Market for Alternative Investment (MAI) were evaluated on their sustainability performance.

▶ Companies listed on the ESG100 have a combined market capitalization of **6.2 trillion baht**.

▶ ESG100 firms account for **40.6%** of SET's total market capitalization of **15.3 trillion baht**.

▶ The 2017 ESG100 recognizes **10 companies** from the MAI.

▶ Rankings are determined using **12,148 data points** taken from six public data sources.

NUMBER OF ESG 100 COMPANIES BY INDUSTRY

 Services: 18

 Agro & Food: 11

 Resources: 10

 Property & Construction: 14

 Technology: 13

 Financials: 12

 Industrials: 16

 Consumer Products: 6

Source: Thaipat Institute

Sustainable Development, 76 percent of responders reported adopting external assurance. In Thailand, at least 21 percent of publicly listed companies have done so – with that number certain to increase.

Expanding boundaries

As things stand, reporting metrics are more output-focused: number of training hours, number of female employees, volume of water withdrawn, and so on. While these are indeed solid indicators of performance, current measurement trends are challenging companies to reconsider if the methods of sustainability and financial reporting used today paint a complete enough picture of their real impact and value.

Today a company would typically measure and report on the inputs and activities needed to generate their products and services, plus their outputs and by-products. Such metrics

are limited, however, as they do not factor in the impacts of these outputs on the wider society and environment – the positive and negative externalities that occur beyond the immediate boundaries of their operations, or even the impacts of their subsidiaries or joint venture companies.

The future of reporting looks set to find companies providing a more complete picture and assuming greater accountability for their impacts, both direct and indirect. According to RobecoSAM, which introduced this criterion in its annual DJSI assessment, "giving visibility to the significance of impacts enables a company to take better decisions to minimize negative impacts and maximize its positive impacts." To reach that point, a company must first identify where the social and environmental values and impacts occur in its value chain, and translate these into financial terms to enable comparability.

"Monetizing impacts translates sustainability into the language of business," stresses

RobecoSAM. Consequently, this gives investors and other stakeholders better information for decision-making and strengthens the value of reporting beyond mere compliance purposes. Over the long term, such impact visualizations will facilitate the seamless integration of sustainability into business strategy.

Although this is a new and emerging trend, companies beginning to grapple with impact measurement and valuation can look to existing methodologies for guidance, such as calculations of social and environmental Profits & Losses (SE P&L), and applying the Natural Capital Protocol and Social Capital Protocol. Examples of recognized global best practices include Akzo Nobel's 4D Profit & Loss Methodology, Kering Group EP&L (see *Kering Identifies Its Environmental Impacts*, page 152), Disney and Google's use of shadow pricing to account for the indirect impacts of their greenhouse gas emissions, and Natura's valuation of its suppliers' environmental impacts.

The future of reporting

It is possible to envision a time in the not-so-distant future when sustainability reporting embraces the beauty of virtual reality. Analysts at GreenBiz, for instance, propose a scenario in which distribution center workers use Augmented Reality (AR) glasses to "look" at a product on a warehouse shelf and identify its origins and components. Drawn from a real-life partnership between SAP and Vuzix Corporation, this example reveals that companies are already pushing the technological boundaries of sustainability applications. Now, imagine if such technologies were to allow individuals to immerse themselves in a company's operations, and to see for themselves what is real, and what is not? Reporting would take on a whole new level of significance – essentially shifting what it means to communicate transparently with one's stakeholders.

Beyond technology and digitization, here are several important global trends poised to influence the future of reporting in Thailand.

ANATOMY OF A SUSTAINABILITY REPORT

 Sustainability reports are a unique representation of a company. As such, there is no one-size-fits-all approach to reporting. They could be presented in print and digital form, on a website, or both. Here are some of the most common elements found in reports:

- Statements from top executives

- Materiality assessments, issues, and results (typically presented in the form of a materiality matrix)

- An overview of business operations, corporate and/or sustainability strategy

- Management approach and performance highlights of each top material issue (commonly found in a GRI report)

- Explanations of risks and opportunities impacting the business over the short- to long-term

- Case studies on projects or initiatives

- Stakeholder engagement approach and dialogues

- External assurance statement

- A description about the report and contact information

An informed reader would expect a company to be transparent in disclosing what they have or have not achieved, and why. It would be unrealistic that a company's performance was only positive. It is better to see a goal in place and explanations for why it wasn't achieved, rather than no goals set at all. This honesty and balance is what helps a report translate over well with its stakeholders.

CASE STUDY   Kering Identifies Its Environmental Impacts

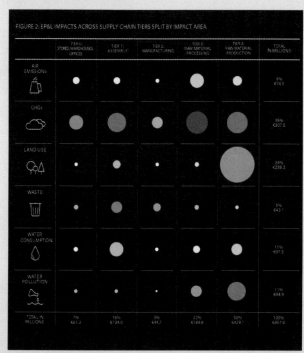

FIGURE 2: EP&L IMPACTS ACROSS SUPPLY CHAIN TIERS SPLIT BY IMPACT AREA

Kering's publicly-disclosed 2016 EP&L Statement reveals where most of its impacts lie.

THE CHALLENGE: Growing consumer awareness of sustainability impacts, tighter regulations, and resource competition is prompting many luxury brands to review their use of critical – yet diminishing – natural capital. For companies like Kering, a global luxury goods group whose operating environment is shifting due to megatrends such as resource scarcity and climate change, it became necessary to find a better way to factor the externalities of their impacts into their business model.

THE SOLUTION: The Kering Environmental Profit & Loss (EP&L) Statement was developed as an innovative, first-of-its-kind tool to measure business impacts and dependencies on the environment in monetary terms. Working with one of its major luxury brands and PwC, Kering unveiled its natural accounting tool to identify environmental impacts across six major categories throughout its global supply chain, spanning from Tier 0: Operations and Stores, to Tier 4: Raw Material Manufacturing.

The EP&L is determined through a seven-step methodology that begins by quantifying the company's environmental footprint, estimating the likely environmental change resulting from the impact (factoring in the local context of operations), and valuing the consequences of environmental change on human wellbeing.

For Kering, this tool is not intended to monetize the intrinsic value of natural capital, but is a 'human-centric' approach that attempts to express the important benefits people gain from the environment. As one of the pioneers in the larger movement of impact measurement, Kering has open-sourced its methodology to encourage companies to collaborate.

THE BENEFITS: First published at group-level in 2013, the EP&L has evolved from a natural accounting tool into a powerful integrated and automated resource for strategic decision-making – becoming "first and foremost a business management tool." By monetizing environmental impact into business language, it provides 'decision-ready' information to decision-makers, offering them the flexibility to explore the implications of different choices in real time. Moreover, it allows the company to measure the progress of their sustainability targets under the 2025 Sustainability Strategy.

Results from Kering's latest 2016 EP&L revealed that 72 percent of their most significant environmental impacts were generated from the raw materials production and processing stages of their supply chain. Of the raw materials, leather is the primary impact driver. Looking only at Thailand, which is considered one of the key sourcing locations in Asia for cotton and other textiles, water pollution and GHG emissions are the primary impacts.

This understanding has had significant business implications in showing that material choice generates the biggest sources of impacts for the group. In response, Kering took proactive steps to increase transparency in their supply chains to avoid high-impact sourcing locations, and implemented changes in product mix and design, as well as material use.

The company has reported multiple positive benefits since the launch of its EP&L, with revenue growth outstripping that of its impacts. The 2016 EP&L intensity was €69 for every €1000 of revenue, steadily declining from €77 in 2012. While Kering does not yet internalize these externalities into their financial accounting, they continue to add to and adjust their methodology. A key lesson from the nearly year-long process, in which the group surveyed over 1,000 of its key suppliers spanning five continents, was that collecting and maintaining a consistent level of detail in data and calculation is not easy, but vitally important.

TOOLBOX — THE DOW JONES SUSTAINABILITY INDICES (DJSI)

The Dow Jones Sustainability Indices, commonly known as the DJSI, refer to a family of indices comprising global sustainability leaders identified by sustainable investment firm RobecoSAM. Over 3,400 publicly traded companies are invited each year to participate in RobecoSAM's Corporate Sustainability Assessment.

In 2017, 33 Thai companies from wide-ranging industry groups were invited as part of the DJSI World, DJSI World Enlarged, and DJSI Emerging Markets Family of Indices. The results of the 2017 assessment saw 18 Thai firms in the DJSI (including one not listed on SET), five of which were included in the DJSI World Index.

The assessment is based on RobecoSAM's 'Financial Materiality' methodology, whereby they consider "any intangible factor that can have an impact on a company's core business value – namely growth, profitability, capital efficiency and risk exposure – to be financially material." Focusing on the intersection between business performance and sustainability, this approach serves the key stakeholder group for which it was designed: investors.

The inherent weakness of the DJSI disclosures lies in its reliance on responses and supporting documents submitted by companies. While these are verified through the 'Media & Stakeholder Analysis' component, which examines media coverage and other publicly available information from consumer organizations, NGOs or governments, it remains the responsibility of companies to provide the most relevant, accurate information on their performance.

In the same way that reporting supports value creation – so too does DJSI. Its value extends beyond reputation building and granting bragging rights to a company. Instead of striving for score improvements through any means, the DJSI should be viewed as a global benchmarking tool for companies in their respective industries, helping them to recognize what more needs to be accomplished to achieve sustainability leadership and attain – or maintain – competitive advantage.

Companies on the 2017 DJSI are:

1. Airports of Thailand
2. Banpu
3. Charoen Pokphand Foods
4. Central Pattana
5. CP All
6. Home Pro
7. Indorama Ventures
8. IRPC
9. Kasikornbank
10. Minor International
11. PTT
12. PTTEP
13. PTT Global Chemical
14. SCG
15. Thai Beverage
16. Thaioil
17. Thai Union Group
18. True Corporation

Data & Metrics

Globally, the volume of sustainability data being collected is unprecedented. The strategic and sustainability implications of this development are endless, but what is needed is the technological sophistication necessary to perform better data analytics and to generate data for more informed use.

Similarly, better metrics are called for to measure business progress on the SDGs. With companies adopting SDGs left and right, metrics should be comparable and attuned to the local context in which they are being implemented. Taking it a step further, long-term sustainability metrics tied to executive compensation are also touted as a way of building leadership accountability on the sustainable development agenda.

Increased harmonization

The push for improved alignment between financial and ESG issues in reporting and management processes is being felt through trends in impact measurement and integrated reporting. However, their growth remains slow in Thailand.

Only a small number of companies have published self-declared integrated reports as of 2017. Pornphan of LRQA Thailand explains that widespread adoption may take at least a

THE ROBECOSAM CORPORATE SUSTAINABILITY ASSESSMENT IN BRIEF

 59 RobecoSAM industries from the GICS Industry Classification System are assessed.

 3 Dimensions: Economic, Social, and Environmental.

 6–10 criteria in each dimension.

 80–120 questions in total. Each company receives a Total Sustainability Score of **up to 100 points**

Source: RobecoSAM

few years: "To make IR happen, the different streams of work in a company focusing on finance and sustainability, such as the Safety, Health and Environment (SHE) department, would need to work closely to streamline their reporting and accounting models to deliver the intended integration." Doing so requires "more understanding of reporting outside of the sustainability function alone," she says.

On a related note, given that the many available reporting guidelines have raised the problems of overlaps and contradiction for companies, prominent organizations in the field are actively working to harmonize them. One example is the IIRC-led Corporate Reporting Dialogue initiative, which has included the issue of materiality into its discussion.

Issue-specific Disclosures

The momentum generated by the Paris Agreement has propelled climate change to the forefront of corporate disclosure efforts. Businesses must effectively demonstrate their long-term commitment to forestalling the two degrees Celsius warming threshold and link these efforts to Thailand's intended nationally determined contribution to greenhouse gas emission cuts.

The tangible connection between climate change and a company's financial bottom-line

implies that companies would benefit from publicly disclosing the relevant information (whether it is mandated by regulations or not). Not only will public commitments create more accountability for climate change, as Matthew Kahn of the Harvard Business Review argues, a better understanding of climate risks will also create a net effect being that firms would invest in resilience to limit their climate risk exposure.

Human rights is another issue demanding specific attention in Thailand. Following international exposure of Thailand's human rights record and the accompanying scrutiny of corporate practices, Thai companies are now ostensibly more open about the human rights challenges they encounter and how they are managing them. Besides the guidance provided by the UN Guiding Principles on Business and Human Rights (see *Human Resources and Organizational Culture*, page 72), reporting frameworks have now integrated human rights into their disclosure requirements as well.

A public commitment to human rights principles is no longer sufficient. The expected minimum is that a company conducts human rights due diligence and reports on its results, addressing questions such as: Where are the human rights risks in your operations? What mitigation plans have been developed? What groups of people are specifically at risk? Aside from the obvious reputational benefits awarded by greater transparency, public reporting and monitoring of human rights can support corporate risk management efforts, too.

Though these issue-specific disclosures may add to the burden of additional reporting (be it through separate channels or existing platforms), disclosing such detailed information may also prove useful to specialist readers. Some of them may leverage it for substantial change, such as in policy circles. Moreover, it reveals commitment to issues that are uniquely material to a company's industry group, which, besides human rights and climate change, could include conflict minerals, political donations, supply chain impacts, and tax payments in extractive industries, among others. Keeping abreast of these trends will ultimately benefit companies by preparing them for changing expectations on disclosures.

TAKE ACTION

To obtain the most value from reporting, your company should first establish the objective for doing so. A clear vision for reporting will help in allocating appropriate resources, determining a timeframe, and planning for improvements and milestones over the mid- to long-term.

Before you start:

- Identify the primary reason for reporting. Is it to monitor internal progress against targets? Meet investor demands for disclosure and stock exchange listing requirements?

- Determine the reporting framework that best suits your business needs and objectives, and responds appropriately to stakeholder interests. Consider:

  - What benefit will this framework provide my company? Is it worth the investment of time and resources?

  - Does my organization have the resources and readiness to meet the requirements of the framework? Factor in aspects like time, human resources, knowledge and expertise, technology, and data consolidation platforms.

During the reporting process:

- Conduct a materiality assessment to identify material issues for reporting. Work with relevant entities in your organization, such as the sustainability department, corporate strategy, risk management, and finance. If your company already has a set of material issues in place for a sustainability strategy, the same issues should be used.

- Collect and consolidate information to be included in the report by designating responsibilities in the organization for data collection, and a tool or platform for data.

- Verify the accuracy of data and information reported, including figures, graphs, and performance tables through internal or external verification processes.

After publication:

- Evaluate the successes, difficulties, and failures of the reporting process.

- Assess emerging trends in disclosure against your report. Are there areas for improvements that could be addressed in the next reporting cycle?

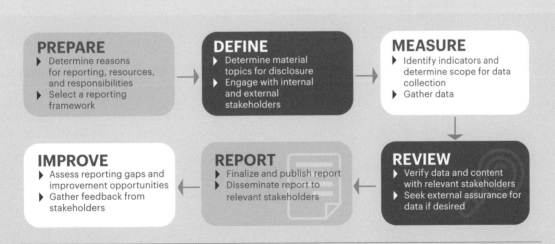

PREPARE
- Determine reasons for reporting, resources, and responsibilities
- Select a reporting framework

DEFINE
- Determine material topics for disclosure
- Engage with internal and external stakeholders

MEASURE
- Identify indicators and determine scope for data collection
- Gather data

IMPROVE
- Assess reporting gaps and improvement opportunities
- Gather feedback from stakeholders

REPORT
- Finalize and publish report
- Disseminate report to relevant stakeholders

REVIEW
- Verify data and content with relevant stakeholders
- Seek external assurance for data if desired

Source: Adapted from GRI and SustainableBusiness.com

PART 3

How to Solve Industry Challenges

Sustainability integration is possible for all businesses in all industry sectors. And in Thailand's diverse economy, there are equally diverse opportunities to do just that.

In this section, we present the critical challenges and explore the ways in which companies across various sectors are acting on sustainability – in their own ways, and within their own contexts. Whether it is through **innovations** that respond to social and environmental needs, partnerships, or managing sustainability risks in their supply chains, our **case studies** show that Thai companies are taking confident strides to address the issues material to their business.

With **insights** from top business executives across wide-ranging sectors like agribusiness, healthcare, energy, fisheries, manufacturing, real estate, tourism, and more, readers can catch a glimpse into the minds of those working to make their businesses more sustainable. For businesses in each sector, it is also a chance to see how peers are responding to commonly shared risks and opportunities, inspiring them to **take action** in concrete ways on the most pressing issues of our time.

Agribusiness

- *Agriculture and food production remain two of the biggest emitters of greenhouse gases and contributors to a warming planet.*
- *Due to high external-input agriculture and lack of know-how, many Thai farmers are trapped in a debt cycle of high production costs and minimal negotiating power.*
- *A paradigm shift in the way Thailand produces food will necessarily involve integrating environmental stewardship into the corporate missions of agribusinesses and building the capacity and resilience of individual farmers.*
- *Increased utilization of smart farming technology and greater access to farm machinery could help Thailand address issues such as the growing labor shortage and overuse of harmful chemicals.*

Despite being one of the world's major exporters of food, Thailand is facing mounting problems concerning unsustainable agriculture practices. While individual farmers struggle with the daily challenge of earning a living, the nation's large agribusinesses are facing future threats from a shrinking labor pool, climate-related disasters, and an increasingly infertile landscape.

The nation's small-scale farmers are vulnerable to a host of risks, such as extreme weather events, global price fluctuations, and the demands of middlemen. Many are also deeply indebted to banks and agribusinesses for the chemicals and equipment they employ to increase production and guarantee yields. The prevalence of high-external-input agriculture arose with the so-called Green Revolution of the 1960s and 1970s, a form of industrialized farming that addressed issues of food security but also led to unsustainable and unhealthy agricultural practices, trapping farmers in a debt cycle of high production costs and minimal negotiating power. According to 2015 government figures, 1.6 million Thai farmers held a combined debt of roughly 388 billion baht, averaging more than twice their annual income per household.

The relationship between farmers and agribusinesses is becoming more complex as large corporations provide employment through contract farming. While farmers may be grateful for the job opportunities, this practice has its downsides. Many are increasingly opting to grow corn, cassava, and other monoculture crops used for animal feed instead of rice, which once helped to feed the farmers' families. Moreover, corn requires more water than regions such as the arid Northeast are able to provide, leading to poor yields, depleted water sources, and soil erosion.

Then there's the climate change conundrum. While agriculture remains one of the biggest contributors to a warming planet, climate change and the havoc it wreaks threatens to damage global crop yields. According to UN Environment, Thailand is one of the countries most at risk when it comes to climate change's impacts on agricultural production, with possible losses of between 15 and 55 percent by 2080. Severe droughts and floods are likely to be the catalysts for these losses.

This negative feedback loop can only be stopped by a paradigm shift in how we produce food. Part of the answer lies in integrating sustainability and environmental stewardship into the corporate missions of agribusinesses, while another lies in strengthening the capacity, resilience and knowledge of individual farmers. For example, the livelihoods of smallholder farmers could be improved by applying the principles of King Bhumibol Adulyadej's New Theory and Sufficiency Economy Philosophy (SEP). When Wiboon Khemchalerm, the late headman of Baan Huay Hin in Chachoengsao province, switched his cassava plantation to an integrated farm of diverse crops, he was acting largely on SEP principles. He was able to cultivate roughly 700 species on his 10 rai of land, and although his family was never rich, they became debt-free and reclaimed the ability to sustain themselves. Many other Baan Huay Hin farmers also adopted the same methods.

Another potential solution is innovation. Smart farming and chemical-free farming both have huge yet largely untapped potential in Thailand, and some experts believe the country can become a regional leader in the emerging bio-economy, which is seeing rising demand for biomass (organic matter that can be converted into alternative energy sources). Dr Pruk Aggarangsi, director of the Energy Research and Development Institute of Nakornping, believes that Thailand is well suited for the development of biofuels due to its high level of agricultural activity. By slashing and burning agricultural waste rather than repurposing it, "we're burning away money," he points out.

While the government has tried for decades to ensure the longevity of agribusiness, the primary agent of change will continue to be the private sector. When major agribusinesses take on a more sustainable mindset and step up to serve as environmental stewards, the whole nation stands to gain. Not only will the sector repair its impact on the environment and its contribution to climate change, but it will also lift a significant chunk of society out of poverty, ensure food security, and safeguard the role of agriculture as a robust, highly functioning sector of the economy for the long term. In particular, human capital and natural resources – two of the country's greatest assets – stand to benefit from a more sustainable approach to how food is produced in the kingdom.

Charoen Pokphand Foods is one of the kingdom's largest producers of eggs.

Environmental issues

Globally, agriculture is one of the biggest emitters of greenhouse gases (GHG), and Thailand is no exception. According to the Thailand Greenhouse Gas Management Organization, almost 25 percent of Thailand's GHG emissions come from the agricultural sector. Rice farming is thought to release half of Thailand's methane emissions, which are a major climate threat, as methane can trap 72 times more heat than CO_2 over a 20-year period.

When agribusinesses take on a more sustainable mindset and step up to serve as environmental stewards, the whole nation stands to gain.

Meanwhile, the prevalence of monoculture in Thailand has not only led to razed forests, decreased biodiversity, and depleted freshwater sources, but has also nurtured an overreliance on harmful pesticides, herbicides, and fertilizers. Many chemicals like DDT, long-banned in Western countries, are still used heavily in Thailand. The overuse of such chemicals can give rise to a laundry list of social, environmental, and economic ills, including poor health among farmers, mounting debt, infertile soil, and increased vulnerability to blights and extreme weather. Until such issues are addressed, the agriculture sector will never be sustainable.

However, organic farming could help to address many of these ills. Organic practices are proven to improve soil fertility, foster biodiversity, and in many cases, increase

Organic practices are proven to improve soil fertility, foster biodiversity, and in many cases, increase yields.

yields. In 2011, UN Special Rapporteur Olivier De Schutter conducted a study in Africa and Southeast Asia that showed how organic-based farming yielded an average crop increase of 80 percent. He concluded that agroecological approaches (the application of natural, ecological processes to agriculture) could double food production in ten years. Such findings have been confirmed time and again: one University of Essex study covering nearly 300 projects across 57 developing countries found that agroecological methods

saw a more than 40 percent yield increase over high chemical-input monocropping, as well as improved nutrition, health, and water usage efficiency.

In Nakhon Pathom province, the Sampran Model project offers one successful case study on organic farming. The project incentivizes organic farming by connecting organic farmers directly to consumers through online and physical outlets, including major hotels and weekend farmers' markets. New farmers are encouraged to join existing organic groups to learn from role models and to benefit from a support network. Collaborations with public sector players – such as Kasetsart University, the Ministry of Commerce, and the Tourism Authority of Thailand – provide a two-way dialogue about best practices, marketing strategies, and market access. The model has not only improved the fertility of the land, but also the health and socioeconomic state of participating smallholders. "For farmers, it is about changing their mindset," says Arrut Navaraj, who created the Sampran Model. "If they see there are better opportunities, such as higher prices to be fetched, lower production costs, and better health for them, they will change their practices. We need to develop positive examples like this to show it's possible to succeed with organic crops."

INNOVATION   BIOMASS GIVES BIG PLAYERS A BOOST

A whole new industry based on agricultural by-products is on the rise. For those at the vanguard, it is opening up new opportunities for processing waste and reducing fossil fuel dependence while generating income. At the Beijing Deqingyuan Chicken Farm, for example, a previously untapped source of energy – manure produced by three million chickens – is providing significant amounts of heat energy and electricity. The 220 tons of manure produced per day now yields 14,600 megawatt-hours of energy per year.

Similarly, in Thailand, Betagro's R&D department is teaming up with the National Nanotechnology Center and the National Science and Technology Development Agency to turn chicken fat into biodiesel. The project has also led to the development of prototype machines for fuel processing and distribution within Betagro's manufacturing facilities. This initiative is building on the company's earlier efforts to turn factory wastewater into biogas, and animal bone, manure, and other solid waste into organic fertilizer.

INDUSTRY SNAPSHOT

IMPACTS OF THE AGRICULTURE SECTOR

43%
of Thailand's total
land area is farmland.

Agriculture contributes
11 to 13% of Thailand's GDP.

Agriculture releases roughly
25% of the nation's GHG
emissions.

Just
45,587
hectares of land
were being used for organic
cultivation as of 2015.

In 2016 alone, the BOI
approved more than **320
agricultural projects**
valued over **US$4.8
billion**.

AGE AND DEMOGRAPHICS OF FARMERS

Registered
farming
households
nationwide:

6,482,650

85%
of farmers are aged 41
years or older, while less
than 3% are under age 30.

WEALTH AND LAND HOLDINGS OF FARMERS

The average Thai farming household
holds **18 rai of farmland**.

80% of Thai farmers own 10 rai or less.

100,061 baht: the average annual
income per farming household.

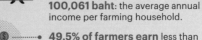

49.5% of farmers earn less than
60,000 baht per year.

Only 15.3% of farmers make more
than 180,000 baht per year.

1.6 million Thai farmers held a
combined debt of roughly **388 billion
baht** in 2015.

TECHNOLOGY IN AGRICULTURE

Only 11% of Thai farmers own tractors, and less **than
1%** own a harvesting machine.

The remainder rent or borrow
such machines, use other
equipment, or **hire labor**
to do **the work of a tractor**
or **harvester**.

Government spending on
agriculture research amounts
to just **0.2% of GDP**.

ONE OF THE WORLD'S TOP EXPORTERS

Thailand is the world's

#1

exporter of
cassava, shipping
10.6 million tons in
2016

2ⁿᵈ

largest exporter of
rice, exporting 10
million tons in
2016

2ⁿᵈ

largest exporter of
sugar, exporting
7.1 million tons in
2015/2016

*Sources: World Economic Forum; World Bank; The Age of Sustainable Development, by Jeffrey D. Sachs; UNFCCC; BIO; Farmers' Registration Data,
2016. Ministry of Agriculture and Cooperatives. Accessed July 27th, 2017; Reuters; Thai Tapioca Trade Association*

Precedents for Thai agribusinesses that have benefited from the switch to organics exist. For example, Dairy Home, Thailand's first organic dairy producer, found a way to successfully market organic dairy as a premium product, applying strict international dairy standards in its supply chain. The company produces a value-added product that is better for both people and the environment. As such, its products have gained fierce customer loyalty despite higher-than-average costs.

In spite of such evidence, the adoption of organic farming on an industry-wide level remains a daunting challenge. There are several reasons for this. First, it's a hard sell to agricultural conglomerates that reap enormous profits from chemical sales, seed sales, contract farming, and other monoculture

practices. Second, in terms of agribusiness profits, if market demand for organic products is weak (as it currently is in Thailand), then companies are not able to fetch the prices that would validate their production. Thus, major inhibitors to the adoption of organic or agroecological production could be put down to a matter of perspective. Until consumer awareness and market demand shift toward organics and chemical-free produce, such production will not expand to a large scale. Similarly, until companies begin to see the long-term benefits of more ecologically sound practices over the short-term gains of monoculture, sustainability in food production will remain stagnant, if not decline over time.

Smallholder suppliers, however, can be more flexible in adopting sustainable practices, such

INNOVATION   PEER REVIEW MAKES ORGANIC FARMING ACCESSIBLE

A farm audit is conducted by participants in the Sampran Model.

Transitioning to organics requires not only courage and diligence but also adherence to strict standards. As an alternative to expensive third-party certification, some farmers are turning to Participatory Guarantee Systems (PGS), a community-based quality assurance system whereby actors in the local value chain – farmers, buyers, rural advisors, and local authorities – visit farms to inspect crops and verify

that they qualify as organic. Suitable for smallholder farms, these close-knit networks are built on a mutually beneficial foundation of trust and knowledge exchange.

With the support of governments and nonprofits, PGS is rapidly being adopted in the Greater Mekong Subregion, allowing farmers to transition to organic farming without

having to take on the cost burdens of certification, and within the supportive structure of a peer network. According to a 2017 UN report, there are 16 Thai agricultural groups using PGS, among them Lemon Farm and the Sampran Model – both successful organic groups that have found markets in Bangkok stores, farmers' markets, and eco-tourism hotels.

Already recognized by Tops Supermarket, giving it mainstream credibility and access, peer reviews foster capacity building and prepare smallholder farmers for IFOAM certification. As the use of PGS spreads, an argument could be made for harmonizing standards, monitoring bodies, logos, and structures to facilitate regional trade and stronger consumer education. For now, however, the system is a valuable first step in making organic farming a feasible practice among farmers who seek to add value at little cost.

ISARA VONGKUSOLKIT *is the chairman of Mitr Phol, Thailand's largest sugar producer, and a keen proponent of by-product innovation.*

What can the private and public sectors do to help support farmers?

We have too many rice fields that are unproductive, especially in the Northeast and in the highlands. The national average of rice growing in Thailand per rai is about 440 or 450 kilograms. The central area yields about 800 or 1,000 kilograms. In the dry area, in the Northeast, they only get 200 or 250 kilograms – a very low yield. If they're growing for their own consumption, it's fine. But if they want to sell for export, there's no way. The cost of producing is much more than that. So it's about yield and know-how – how to improve land fertility, methods for growing rice, harvesting, etc.

Among farmers, is there resistance to switching from rice to other crops?

Historically, rice is very important because it provides the farmers their food security. But now that they grow for export, it's different. If they own land, they will not change right away. If they want to see whether they can grow something else, the most they will change is half of their land. That's the normal practice I've seen.

How do you enable farmers who work for you to share knowledge?

We organize meetings and forums during the off-season, but when it's us telling them they don't believe it, or they don't trust us. Our people have no farms; we just have experimental farms. So we have extension services and

R&D, which we use to do knowledge transfer. These departments are now trying to promote the New Theory of agriculture. This is the philosophy of the late king. This is very successful because for the small farmers, it can help them to live well. With sugarcane, you can get money annually, and New Theory allows you to allocate a small portion of your farm. Let's say you have 20 rai, you can allocate two rai to grow your own vegetation and dig a pond to breed fish, and you can use that water to irrigate the vegetation. Or maybe you could breed chickens. So the farmers have food all year. Every day they can consume their own food. If they have better quality produce, they can also sell to the nearby market.

What is your take on organics?

Organics will be suitable for smaller crops. There is no denying that organic foods fetch higher prices, which is beneficial for the farmers. However, the economies of scale will continue to reduce costs of production and will be beneficial to the farmers using industrial fertilizers together with organics in the long run. Pure, organic food needs care and attention and has to follow international practices. What worries me more is the use of chemical pesticides and their runoffs into organic farms, which will pollute and create more problems for farmers and consumers in the short term.

What are the best practices, in your mind, of sustainable agriculture?

When I was the chairman of the Thai Chamber of Commerce, we initiated Thailand's Good Agricultural Practice, called ThaiGAP. ThaiGAP is a private, voluntary food safety standard for sustainable farm management to support small farmers and SMEs. Good Agricultural Practice complies with international food safety requirements. GAP is an international food safety protocol endorsed by international food organizations, such as CODEX. The EU practices GlobalGAP, and Switzerland has SwissGAP, for instance. The original ThaiGAP has 234 protocols or control points, which have proven to be too cumbersome for some Thai farmers. We at the Thai Chamber of Commerce then created the PrimaryGAP as an alternative. It has only 24 protocols or control points. For this PrimaryGAP, we worked with the Ministry of Agriculture to allow us to audit farms and certify their products, which enabled them to export to other countries.

CASE STUDY   Baan Thung-Kaam Swine Farm Learns How to Fatten Profits

The farmers of Thung-Kaam village have learnt to turn pork into value-added products.

THE CHALLENGE: Due to a lack of basic marketing know-how, a group of swine farmers in Thung-Kaam village in Nan province faced a daily oversupply of fresh pork, causing price-cutting by middlemen. In general, farmers' lack of negotiating clout, marketing skills, and access to markets make price gouging a common problem among smallholder farmers, especially in remote areas. Like most Thai smallholders, this group of swine producers was never equipped with skills such as the ability to assess input costs and supply, or to process products to add value.

THE SOLUTION: The Chulalongkorn University School of Agricultural Resources stepped in to find ways for these swine producers to earn higher incomes, improve the quality of their products, create additional marketing channels, and implement better accounting systems.

As the farmers were already experts at breeding and raising pigs, the improvement efforts were mostly directed at downstream activities in the value chain, such as making pork products, marketing, and selling directly to customers. Farmers were advised and trained how to turn fresh pork meat into high-quality, value-added products such as crispy pork skin and deep-fried dried pork.

THE BENEFITS: With improvements in product quality, hygiene, and processing, the swine farmers were able to

secure steady consumption of their products from a new group of customers, including those working in nearby government offices, and a contract with the local hospital. The farmers earned more profits, and eventually organized into a small community enterprise. Thanks to this value chain improvement, the group of farmers managed to increase its daily profit from about 200 baht to 1,500–2,000 baht. They also learned to improve their management skills by reviewing their business accounts as well as their household expense reports to keep track of revenue and to better manage debt.

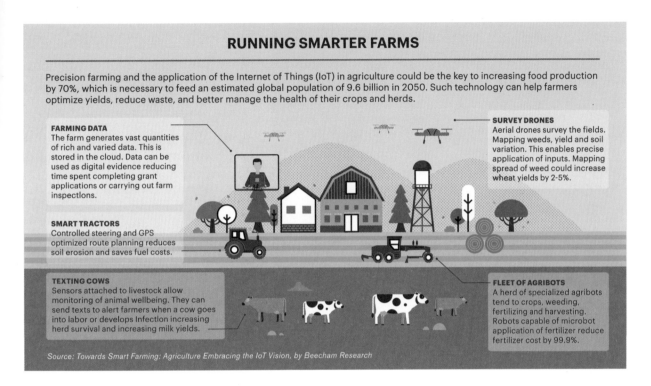

RUNNING SMARTER FARMS

Precision farming and the application of the Internet of Things (IoT) in agriculture could be the key to increasing food production by 70%, which is necessary to feed an estimated global population of 9.6 billion in 2050. Such technology can help farmers optimize yields, reduce waste, and better manage the health of their crops and herds.

FARMING DATA
The farm generates vast quantities of rich and varied data. This is stored in the cloud. Data can be used as digital evidence reducing time spent completing grant applications or carrying out farm inspections.

SURVEY DRONES
Aerial drones survey the fields. Mapping weeds, yield and soil variation. This enables precise application of inputs. Mapping spread of weed could increase wheat yields by 2-5%.

SMART TRACTORS
Controlled steering and GPS optimized route planning reduces soil erosion and saves fuel costs.

TEXTING COWS
Sensors attached to livestock allow monitoring of animal wellbeing. They can send texts to alert farmers when a cow goes into labor or develops infection increasing herd survival and increasing milk yields.

FLEET OF AGRIBOTS
A herd of specialized agribots tend to crops, weeding, fertilizing and harvesting. Robots capable of microbot application of fertilizer reduce fertilizer cost by 99.9%.

Source: Towards Smart Farming: Agriculture Embracing the IoT Vision, by Beecham Research

as organic or integrated farming, to improve environmental impact and to ensure subsistence while selling surplus to conglomerates. To some, this may seem idealistic, or even counterproductive. As integrated farms allot less land to a single crop, it may be more difficult for individual farmers to meet contract quotas. But in such cases, community enterprises and collaborations have been successful in pooling resources and efforts to meet contract agreements or to launch cottage industries to market directly to consumers (See *Case Study*, page 168).

Social issues

Every spring, the air over Chiang Mai province hangs heavy with ash, a repercussion of slash-and-burn agriculture in the surrounding region. The resulting poor air quality causes a number of deaths annually and has become a point of social concern, as it affects the health, productivity, and wellbeing of locals. Food insecurity also remains a prevalent issue among Northeastern farmers, as does the migration of rural, working-age people to

cities, a practice that weakens family and social structures. According to the National Statistical Office, around 21 percent of the nation's children do not live with either of their parents due to internal migration. Meanwhile, the elderly and children make up the majority of Thailand's rural population, with the corresponding lack of working-age adults depriving these communities of potential strong leaders. Many of these social issues

Food insecurity remains a prevalent issue among Northeastern farmers, as does the migration of rural, working-age people to cities.

stem from unsustainable agricultural practices that disregard human externalities and view the work of individual farmers as cheap and easily replaceable.

King Bhumibol Adulyadej was keenly aware of such issues and developed SEP specifically to help empower the rural poor. While individual

A worker harvests corn outside Kanchanaburi province.

200 percent more per kilogram than conventionally grown rice and requires farmers to keep 25 percent of the harvest for personal consumption. Having started with just 25 farming families, the Siam Organic cooperative has now grown to encompass 1,100 households. What's more, Siam Organic's social return on investment is 4.3, meaning that for every US$1 invested in the company, $4.30 is generated for the farmers.

Economic issues

Unsustainable farming hurts the national economy over the long term because of its personal financial impact, namely the continued poverty of farmers caused by high household debt. Globally, the poverty and debt cycle of smallholder farmers has led to a shocking prevalence of suicides, and many have been traced back to the unsustainable practices of monoculture giants. Not only is such loss of life tragic: economically it also spells disaster. For Thailand's agricultural sector, which already has a shrinking and ageing labor pool, impoverished conditions among farmers will only propagate problems such as low productivity, low health, low education, and low opportunities for growth and scalability.

Farmers have rarely been educated to consider market needs, financial management, and production sustainability. To help address these gaps, the School of Agricultural Resources at Chulalongkorn University created an academic program that incorporates holistic agriculture approaches and is training a new generation of farmers to run their farms as sustainable businesses.

When farmers gain a better understanding of accounting, marketing and business management, the progression from survival to self-reliance and, finally, sustainability can be remarkable. The Royal Initiative Discovery Foundation has seen previously impoverished and unorganized farmers in Nan province – one of the poorest regions of Thailand – come together to form a community enterprise and succeed not only in paying back debts, but also in reforesting their land, increasing biodiversity, building the capacity to subsist

farmers who adopt SEP principles can benefit by improving their health, self-reliance, food security, and quality of life, agribusinesses also stand to gain by integrating SEP principles into their operations. For one, SEP approaches business from a long-term sustainability standpoint and can be effective in reducing inefficiencies while improving risk

> **When farmers gain a better understanding of accounting, marketing and business management, the progression from survival to self-reliance and, finally, sustainability can be remarkable.**

management. An ethical approach to labor management also results in happier, healthier workers, lower turnover, increased engagement, and higher productivity – all of which are proven to improve the bottom line.

Siam Organic, for example, is a social enterprise that places the needs of rice farmers first, generating substantial income by marketing organic products to the global market. Their trademark Jasberry rice is grown by small-scale farmers who are trained to international organic farming standards. Siam Organic pays

Betagro Group CEO VANUS TAEPAISITPHONGSE champions an holistic approach to agricultural and food supply chain management that includes social development as well as knowledge sharing.

What do you think of precision agriculture?

Of course, it's the way to go. The shift is toward Thailand 4.0 and everything, but I do worry about the people who are between steps. How to help them? There should be a group of people who try to chase those dreams [of implementing precision agriculture], but still, the majority should take care of the people who will fall through the cracks.

How is Betagro using precision agriculture? Would you say you're an early adopter?

I cannot say we are an early adopter. Every time we try to study those new systems, it's always too expensive. It sounds good. So yes, it's on our radar. However, we have to do more studies. It will come for sure but I don't know when.

Is there more of a move toward organic? The demand seems to be growing.

Organic is something romantic in my opinion. It sounds good. We like to promote it. But I think there needs to be a system to try to promote it – a strong system. You have to know who the farmer is, you have to have a traceability system, you have to know how to take care

of the people around you, and then you have to go step by step. That's why when I talk to farmers I always say why don't you start with GAP first – with good agricultural practices?

Where do you see Betagro growing into the future? What is your vision?

R&D is very crucial for our business. We believe that through R&D, we will be able to provide better food solutions for consumers in the future. Currently, we have a lot of projects in the pipeline, and R&D will probably lead business direction in the future too. However, the work on R&D always takes a long time. So, in parallel, we also focus on services we provide to our trade partners in order to improve their capability, knowledge and skills. Our aim is to raise the level of quality throughout the whole supply chain.

In the traditional world, business organizations exist to make profit first, and I believe in making profit. However, I have a different approach on 'how' we make profit. I personally believe in 'give' first. So, my principle is to give and to help our business partners, and at the end of the day, the business will grow.

CASE STUDY — Nan Province's Honey Farmers Combine Forces

Better collaboration and improved marketing skills have helped the honey farmers of Nan province slash costs and boost income.

THE CHALLENGE: The honeybee farmers of Baan Pa-Sak, in Nan province, knew how to breed and raise honeybees, but their product commanded relatively low prices when sold to middlemen. They also had problems with high production costs, chemical contamination, and lack of collaboration among farmers.

THE SOLUTION: Under the guidance of the Chulalongkorn University School of Agricultural Resources, improvements were introduced throughout the entire value chain of honey production. Sugar is one of the key inputs in raising honeybees, so the farmers developed a working cooperative to purchase sugar, rather than each farmer making purchases individually. This led to huge cost savings, as well as the improved production and processing of honey.

Production was also upgraded to meet the standards of Good Agricultural Practices (GAP). The farmers learned to use natural synthesis products instead of chemicals during honey production to eliminate chemical contamination. To increase the marketability of the products, branding, container design, sizing, and packaging were enhanced. To sustain the operation, a farmers' group was formally established under an agreed risk, cost, and profit allocation formula. The farmers began to foster better collaboration, and a stronger community enterprise emerged with increased market penetration.

THE BENEFITS: The honeybee farmers reduced their input costs for sugar by 30 percent per year as a result of group purchasing. Their branding and redesigning of product packages, as well as improved marketing capability, contributed to a 26-percent increase in their total profit when compared to the old packaging and brand. They also gained a better understanding of how to improve the quality of their products as well as more effective marketing skills to enhance competitiveness. And they discovered that pooling resources to invest in innovation and technology – even at a small scale – provides far better competitive advantages.

CASE STUDY Betagro Sows the Seeds of Community-Based Sustainability

Farmers in Lopburi province follow Good Agricultural Practices.

THE CHALLENGE: Established in 1967 as an animal feed producer, Betagro has grown to become a vertically integrated agricultural giant and an "A" rated business by the Thai Rating and Information Services. Today, it is one of Thailand's largest producers and distributors of chicken, pork, and eggs. However, the massive scale at which Betagro operates necessitates monoculture and the use of contract farmers. In such a system, how does it ensure environmental, social, and financial sustainability?

THE SOLUTION: Betagro CEO Vanus Taepaisitphongse believes the biggest potential to do good comes from a holistic approach encompassing the pillars of good occupation, good health, good environment and good society. Based on this belief, the company began its efforts at community-based sustainable development ten years ago in Chong Sarika district in Lopburi province, near one of the company's largest manufacturing facilities. The project set an ambitious target that strives to achieve positive change among 80 percent of all stakeholders.

The impetus for the project came from the desire to improve the lives of the nearly 30,000 people involved in Betagro's farming and factory operations. But rather than focus specifically on work-related issues, the company took an interest in the personal lives of workers in these communities. "I realized that if I don't understand their life outside the factory or the farm, I cannot see the whole picture," Vanus says.

For its pilot program, in 2007, Betagro partnered with the Population and Community Development Association (PDA) to set up an outreach office in Chong Sarika district. The company invited experts and specialists to share knowledge with villagers, established village banks, and began promoting

public health, supporting education, and entrenching shared values within the community. Four years later, the program expanded to include agricultural and vocational training, not only to supplement staff incomes, but also to create additional primary occupations outside the Betagro supply chain. At this point, Betagro began to manage the program entirely on its own, without the help of PDA.

THE BENEFITS: The program has given rise to higher awareness about Good Agricultural Practices among villagers, increased incomes and yields, and led to the establishment of SEP schools and the Betagro Group's Learning Center for the Sufficiency Economy in Lopburi. The center offers training modules in agroecology such as composting, egg production, food processing, biodiesel, and waste management.

Over the long term, the effects of this commitment have rippled out to benefit company operations as well. Stakeholder satisfaction breeds better relations with the company, and Betagro's reputation and support network grows with each new project. As of January 1, 2017, Betagro's area-based development projects have expanded to 16 locations – 15 in Thailand and one in Cambodia. Just as importantly, the skills and knowledge gleaned from helping communities has provided the company with valuable lessons on better agriculture, efficiency, management, and human resources. For example, improving vocational skills and productivity management among its Yakitori factory workers has led to annual savings of 12.2 million baht due to higher productivity.

Public health is one of the many social aspects that Betagro addresses.

Better technologies and tools could pave the way for more sustainable agriculture.

on their own means, and scaling up their efforts into more profitable businesses. The power of community enterprise has been proven by villages that have received an injection of knowledge and matched it with

Resource- and knowledge-sharing reaps a return on investment through higher yields, and improved productivity and competitiveness.

the initiative to learn and grow. The very active Alternative Agriculture Network of Isaan, comprising more than 3,000 farming households devoted to small-scale sustainable agriculture, offers a network of successful community enterprises and smallholder cooperatives that share knowledge.

R&D for sustainability

Region-specific technologies, practices, and innovations also offer a way forward. Machinery could play a significant role in reducing the use of herbicides and making up for the labor shortage. But at present, most smallholders do not have access to farming machinery and still rely on human labor for most cultivation. Currently, without the support of labor-saving tools and techniques,

a sudden crisis or labor shortage could have a detrimental impact on agricultural production.

Major conglomerates are proving to be early adapters of efficient technologies. To try to transition away from slash-and-burn practices and deal with refuse, Mitr Phol has invented a machine that breaks down unwanted sugarcane material while mixing it back into the soil. It is also currently planning to invest in cutting-edge John Deere and Case sugarcane harvesters that reduce soil loss and improve energy efficiency. Betagro's chicken farms use a form of high-tech livestock rearing that combines an automatic feeding system with precisely controlled lighting, temperature, and moisture in a closed environment. Such innovations reduce inefficiencies and help mitigate the industry's labor issues.

Developing effective technologies and tools requires the collaboration of scientists, academics, individual farmers, the public sector, and the private sector. Part of the task is to make technology simple and affordable, since a large percentage of farmers are smallholders. Providing good agricultural extension services can ensure effective and proper technology and knowledge transfer to farmers. Key public sector players, including the Thai government (especially the Department of Agricultural Extension) and the Royal Initiative Discovery Foundation, are already playing significant roles in transferring knowledge and technology to farmers. The private sector can and should follow suit, training contract farmers and suppliers in best practices, international quality and sustainability standards, and the latest innovations. This kind of resource- and knowledge-sharing reaps a return on investment through higher yields, and improved productivity and competitiveness.

The roots of change

Agriculture is a vast and complex industry spanning many geographical regions, each with its own unique challenges and interdependent players. This means there is no simple path to a more sustainable sector. Indeed, while organics and SEP offer some solutions, a successful, industry-wide shift toward sustainability will likely involve a

TAKE ACTION

- **Transition to ecologically friendly food production.** Agribusinesses and farmers can test the benefits and pitfalls of organic production by first converting a reasonable percentage of their land. For example, a farmer with ten hectares might try organic farming on one hectare to begin with. Agribusinesses can make use of biowaste, manage water use, invest in labor-saving technologies, train suppliers in best practices, and use local or regional resources to the industry's advantage.

- **Create an area-based social enterprise.** Rather than traditional CSR, companies would be better off partnering with local farmers and communities to form a social enterprise. The company can provide marketing know-how and distribution channels for a longer-lasting and more impactful community project. Key to the project is finding a local partner such as a local NGO or university with regional knowledge to help facilitate it. Stronger community relations will also benefit the company in other ways such as the sharing of knowledge, better mutual understanding, and reputational benefits.

- **Precision agriculture** can be practiced on a small plot of farmland as much as on a vast plantation. Several experts in the field, such as Dr Prateep Verapattananirund and the Royal Development Study Centers, offer hands-on training and multi-day workshops for individual farmers on precision agriculture, New Theory farming, and agroecological methods.

- **Network, cooperate and set up small-scale agribusiness and community enterprises.** Cooperation will facilitate a flow of information, shared resources, higher yields, and fairer trade among smallholders. When small-scale farmers unite, local businesses and economies improve, promoting income distribution within communities.

- **Improve marketing and value chain management.** All levels of industry players will benefit from enhancing interaction with consumers and adding value to products by following international standards, moving toward organics, and improving packaging. Look to sources such as the Department of Agricultural Extension, Chulalongkorn University School of Agricultural Resources, GreenNet, and Raitong Organics Farm for training.

- **Support the creation of technology and innovation, especially from local sources.** Innovations can provide agribusinesses with more sustainable competitive advantages, such as cost reduction, energy savings, precise production, and better marketing opportunities.

combination of stronger consumer demand; better agricultural knowledge, land management, and business skills among farmers; better use of innovation and technology among larger players; and an across-the-board reduction of chemical usage.

GlobalGAP or ThaiGAP – international and Thai standards for "Good Agricultural Practices," respectively – are a good place to start. Both provide clear checklists for ensuring food safety, environmental protection, worker health, animal welfare, reduced waste, and reduced chemical usage. GlobalGAP standards and consultation are accessible through its website, www.globalgap.org, and ThaiGAP assistance is made available through the Department of Agriculture and the Thai Chamber of Commerce, both of which have developed their own sets of standards.

Notably, there is beginning to be more buy-in on sustainability from large agribusinesses, especially where sustainable farming methods intersect with efficiency. CP Group, for example, became one of 25 leading global companies in 2017 to launch Food Reform for Sustainability and Health (FReSH), a global research initiative led by the World Business Council for Sustainable Development to transform global food systems into more sustainable ventures. Vanus Taepaisitphongse, CEO of Betagro Group, says that it falls upon conglomerates to come up with these sorts of ambitious projects and to help smaller farmers. "It's very simple," he says. "When you're strong, you just help people."

Food and Beverage

- *Sustainability is still a sideline issue within the sector. A true understanding of the high-stakes issues at play is necessary before a sustainable culture shift can happen.*

- *Rising consumption of products high in sodium, fat, and sugar is impacting the national waistline as well as the prevalence of non-communicable diseases like heart disease, hypertension, and Type 2 diabetes.*

- *Lack of accurate labeling, reliable certification, and lenient standards contribute to a disparity in the quality of domestically available produce versus exported produce.*

Thailand is often billed as the "Kitchen of the World," and a sense of plenty is certainly visible in its markets and at street level. Economic figures further reveal the true scale of the country's food and beverage sector, which accounted for 23 percent of GDP in 2015 and generated US$26 billion in exports in 2016.

Thai companies accordingly play a significant role in global food supply chains and will be increasingly called upon to address key sustainability issues like food safety, traceability, labor conditions, and the environment. "Global brands are now being held to account for social and environmental impacts in their supply chains," says Alyson Slater, director of the Regional Network and Sustainable Development at the Global Reporting Initiative (GRI), an independent sustainability reporting and standards organization. "They are putting pressure on their suppliers to raise their standards and behavior to global norms."

A revealing indicator of the state of sustainability culture within the food and beverage sector in Thailand was the difficulty that researchers for this chapter faced in obtaining access to relevant information within certain privately held Thai companies. Even when external reporting regulations are not applicable, transparency is essential as a lack of disclosure can hide vulnerabilities in the complex interconnectivity of modern supply chains. Sustainability is an essential business practice that no executive can afford to ignore. The stakes are far too high as the consequences of food scandals can be costly, both in terms of reputation and a company's bottom line.

The 2008 melamine baby formula scandal in China was the catalyst for leading food manufacturers to form Food Industry Asia (FIA), an association that works to improve food safety and nutrition amongst its member companies and ultimately the public, even in the absence of mandatory regulations. The Singapore-based FIA also takes a proactive approach to advocate for harmonization of standards across Southeast Asian markets. "This enables our members to plan for and implement incremental changes rather than be forced to comply with sudden and potentially severe government policies," says Steven Bartholomeusz, FIA's communications director. Pending sugar taxes are a case in point for

Thai beverage companies where advance planning could have meant gradual and voluntary formulation changes instead of potential price hikes.

As for the general public's sustainability concerns, Prae Piromya, vice president of sustainability at Pace Development, notes that Thais are more concerned with taste than with issues like food safety. "Thais are not afraid of diarrhea," she says. On the topic of provenance and traceability, she points to the case of salmon, an essential component of the ever-popular Japanese cuisine. "Ninety-nine percent of people don't know where or how salmon is raised, let alone the issues surrounding it."

Ninety-nine percent of people don't know where or how salmon is raised, let alone the issues surrounding it.

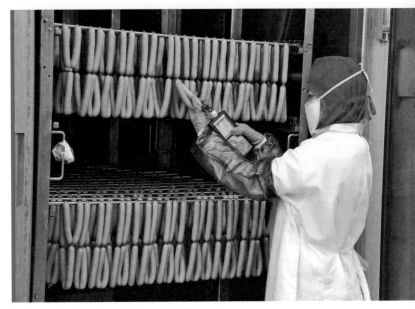

A Betagro worker checks on the company's sausage products.

Changing demographics are manifested in the evolving food habits of Thai consumers. An increasingly urban population is living in smaller family units with more time constraints and therefore seeks convenient, often instant, food solutions. This, coupled with increased purchasing power, can be seen as fueling the number of convenience stores opening nationwide with a 12 percent compound annual growth rate from 2014 to 2020. The associated rise in processed food consumption is also negatively impacting the national waistline and health indices (see *Sweet Dilemma*, page 180).

Meanwhile, the organic and naturally healthy food segment is expected to grow at a rate of six to seven percent between 2014 and 2019. The rising demand for clean food can be attributed to an increasingly health-conscious upper class as well as the country's ageing population. Both of these important demographic segments are looking to prevent or combat diet-related diseases. To capitalize on this demand, companies would do well to make their product portfolios healthier.

Beyond consumer health, the Thai food and beverage sector also needs to address sustainability issues with social and environmental impacts. Domestically, the opportunity is to lead and educate the market by implementing initiatives like food rescue, waste reduction, and related community projects. The increased value to be had for multiple stakeholders at different steps of the supply chain can lead to improved quality for consumers, fairer conditions for growers, and improved results internally.

Transparent supply chains

Transparency has never been more vital for businesses looking to deliver on food safety requirements. A complete overview of an organization's supply chain can prevent contamination or quickly identify where an issue has arisen and the response required. A transparent supply chain that delivers information to the consumer can also build brand loyalty. This is especially important as more cases of fake food make headlines like

QR codes provide customers with details about products, as well as traceability.

the discovery of fake orange juice (tap water, coloring and a sweetener) on sale in Ayutthaya province in 2016. Such incidents tend to weaken consumer confidence in the entire food system regardless of the company or individuals involved.

Consumer awareness in Thailand is low regarding toxic residues in food, and agricultural regulations are not as stringent as in some export markets.

Tesco Lotus has bypassed wholesalers to go directly to farmers to improve food safety and productivity. Cabbage is the retailer's highest volume product and its cool chain now begins at the source instead of the pack house. Refrigerated trucks collect produce at the farm soon after picking and it is kept cool right through to the store. "This has increased the yield from 30 to 70 percent, and shelf life has been extended from five to nine days," says Pornpen Nartpiriyarat, head of Tesco Lotus' quality control team. The reduced wastage, and the value and volume increase, are better for farmers, customers, and Tesco Lotus alike.

Tesco Lotus is also connecting consumers with suppliers. In 2014 it introduced a QR software

system for food traceability, the first retailer in Thailand to do so. Initially it was just for meat, but it has now been expanded to include seafood, fresh produce, and eggs. "In 2016 about 1.2 million consumers countrywide accessed QR codes," says Pornpen. She points out that the initiative was driven internally, rather than by external forces like legislation or consumer demands. Benefits for Tesco Lotus include improved food safety and inventory management, while consumers have better product knowledge, including nutritional information.

In 2015, Central Food Retail Group also implemented a QR code traceability initiative, providing shoppers details on approximately 20,000 products from up to 2,000 suppliers. Like at Tesco Lotus, the drive for traceability came from within the organization, says Gerald Lim, assistant vice president of digital & innovation for Central Food Retail Group. Consumer uptake has, however, been slow. "Only about 30 people a day scan the codes," says Lim, referring to the Central Chidlom pilot site. Educating consumers to "demand and access the information will take five to eight years," he predicts. Regardless, it has been a valuable internal tool. "The content helps staff to appreciate the whole supply chain. They can then share this knowledge with consumers."

Food safety

In 2012, Thailand became the first country to accept peach imports from Fukushima, a famed peach-growing region of Japan. This was 18 months after the 2011 tsunami and nuclear disaster. 2017 marks the fifth anniversary of this trade, the details of which are openly available on the Internet. However, the lack of public concern and healthy sales figures indicate that consumers often take food at face value and accept product claims or trust retailers to only sell quality food.

In general, consumer awareness in Thailand is low regarding toxic residues in food, and agricultural regulations are not as stringent as in some export markets. Produce labeled "export quality" can be found in Bangkok supermarkets. Does this imply different standards for domestic consumption? Yes, according to Watcharaphol Daengsubha,

INDUSTRY SNAPSHOT

Thailand's food and beverage sector

accounted for
23% of GDP in 2015,

generated US$
26 billion in exports in 2016,

and includes **10,000 food-processing companies** that **employ 800,000 people**.

4 **The number of Thai food and beverage companies** in the 2017 DJSI Emerging Markets Index (3) and DJSI World Index (1).

ORGANIC TRENDS

The global organic food and beverage market is expected to be worth

$320.5 billion by 2025.

The organic and naturally healthy food segment in Thailand has grown at a rate of **6-7% since 2014**.

58% **of organic food** sold in retail outlets in Thailand is **imported**.

Just **0.3%** of Thailand's agricultural land is **certified as organic**.

CONSUMER TRENDS

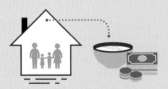

Thais spend more than
30% of their household income on food for meals at home.

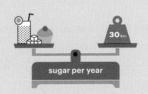

sugar per year

The average Thai person consumes **30 kilograms of sugar per year**, which is more than three times the maximum recommended intake of **25,000 milligrams per day**.

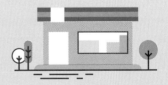

Consumption of so-called convenience foods is on the rise in Thailand, where the number of **7-Eleven stores alone reached more than 10,000 in mid-2017**.

Sources: Thailand Board of Investment; Thai-Pesticide Alert Network; Grand View Research, Inc.; DJSI; World Economic Forum; Ministry of Public Health; Bangkok Post; SCB Economic Intelligence Unit

A vendor sells fruit juice at Bangkok's sprawling Chatuchak Market.

aware of how often certifying bodies carry out inspections. Sometimes it's only annually. Watcharaphol advocates a peer-to-peer review system like that used by Lemon Farm and the Sampran Model. "It's not internationally recognized but it's better than an annual visit," he points out.

Similarly, Bryan Hugill of Raitong Organics Farm in Sisaket province believes that transparent peer-to-peer auditing – or Participatory Guarantee Systems (PGS), as they are called by the organic farming sector – is ideal. "However, whether this is readily achievable on a large scale in Thailand at the moment is debatable, due to the propensity for corruption, not wanting to cause inconvenience to others, and general consumer apathy," says Hugill. Prioritizing the common good over self-interest, as well as technology and innovation, is needed for such a system to prove itself over current third-party auditing services, he adds.

a former Greenpeace campaigner and mangosteen farmer in Trat province. "The worst [quality] goes to Cambodia, the second worst stays in Thailand, and the best is exported." Improved domestic standards and better enforcement are needed to avoid the country being a dumping ground due to lower relative standards versus other countries.

Formal certification can be costly, so some producers don't apply for it even if their products satisfy the criteria. It's helpful to know what the certification covers and to be

For the past seven years the Thai-Pesticide Alert Network (Thai-PAN), a collective of activists, academics, and farming interest groups, has conducted an annual survey of random samples of fruits and vegetables from supermarkets, fresh markets and mobile vendors around Bangkok. Independent laboratory testing of the produce in the United Kingdom has revealed chemical residues that are banned in the European Union. According to Kingkorn Narintarakul Na Ayutthaya, deputy director of the BioThai Foundation (the Thai-PAN secretariat), supermarkets have responded positively by investigating their supply chains and implementing changes. "Their reputations are at risk," she says. "It isn't an individual problem, though. Structural change is needed."

Cost constraints limit Thai-PAN to an annual survey. The group's work raises public awareness about the issue of food safety, and the ultimate goal is for a rapid alert system with both government and private sector cooperation for ongoing monitoring. In the meantime, Kingkorn says consumers need to scrutinize their food: "Question how it is produced, distributed, the fairness of the supply chain, and social justice issues. It's their role to put pressure on supermarkets."

PESTICIDES IN THAI FRUIT AND VEGETABLES

35 chemicals
31 chemicals
30 chemicals
22 chemicals
22 chemicals
18 chemicals

A 2016 laboratory testing of randomly selected Thai fruit and vegetables revealed that oranges, Chinese broccoli, red chilli peppers, long beans, holy basil, and dragon fruit contained the highest number of chemicals.

Of these fruit and vegetables, the majority of samples tested contained pesticide residues above the Maximum Residue Limits (MRLs), making them a concern to human health.

Source: Thailand Pesticide Alert Network (Thai-Pan)'s 2016 report on pesticide contamination. 158 samples were collected between 23–29 August 2016, sent to a ISO/IEC 17025: 2005 standard certified laboratory, then tested for over 450 chemicals using the MRL standards of the Thai Ministry of Public Health and CODEX.

INSIGHTS

PHAIROJ PINYOSAKUL *is the CEO of Rimping Supermarket, which runs nine stores in Chiang Mai province and is well known for its sustainability-centered ethos, especially its in-house testing, grading, and color-labeling of fruit and vegetables.*

Of Rimping's many initiatives, which are you most proud of and why?

We have launched a number of projects designed to benefit the community as a whole. Environmental concerns are also vitally important to us. We encourage customers to eschew the use of plastic bags, and we make a charitable donation of 0.5 baht each time they do. Even so, our plastic bags and containers for seafood and meat products are all 100-percent biodegradable. Lastly, our five-color coded vegetable selection offers customers the choice of produce from known sources ranging from pure organic down to general market items. As a further control, each color-coded category is tested in the same way as other incoming products. Realizing these initiatives gives a huge sense of achievement, of doing what is right, and what is worthwhile.

How did you develop your in-house testing systems of products?

We have our own laboratory where representative samples are tested for pesticides, formalin, toxic residues, and other chemicals. We also monitor the quality of cooking oils, the cleanliness of containers, and swab surfaces of products such as meat and fish to check for possible contamination by hands not wearing protective gloves. We also check the quality of soil, water, and crops on farms and other growing areas. This is followed up by additional testing when items from these sources are delivered to us.

What was the catalyst for adopting sustainable business practices?

Years ago, any supermarket could sell fresh products from any source. Not today. Well-informed consumers know what can be sprayed on, added to, or injected into foodstuffs. The lifelong consequences of today's children consuming even trace amounts of pesticides cannot be foreseen. In this respect, fundamental business ethics should oblige all supermarkets to verify the integrity of their suppliers, and their products. Rimping is committed to doing this. We test and we reject any contaminated

produce. We terminate agreements with offenders. If only all supermarkets did this, controls would tighten, standards would improve, and we would all be able to live in a safer and more sustainable world.

Do your customers know what sustainability means?

The late King of Thailand, Bhumibol Adulyadej, tirelessly championed the concept of sustainable development, and people listened. His legacy lives on. And to every thinking person anywhere, it becomes increasingly obvious that sustainability is quintessential to human survival.

What benefits have you seen from your approach to doing business?

I believe that increasing customer awareness, coupled with the resulting pressure on consumer protection agencies, will eventually bring about legislation to make testing obligatory. This is likely to take time, but if further evidence appears, such as falling sperm counts, or other abnormalities possibly linked to pesticides or additives, it may happen much sooner. Meantime, those of us aware of the danger should constantly make our collective voices heard, and continue setting an example for others to follow.

GIVING FOOD PACKAGING A BETTER WRAP

Disposable polystyrene foam containers are a staple at street stalls and in restaurants around Thailand. Some vendors line the containers with plastic film to prevent the foam from melting when it comes into contact with heated food. Others place hot food in plastic bags and then in foam containers. "People are aware of the foam melting but not the health implications," says Jantima Pipitsoontorn, co-founder of Be Greening biodegradable food ware. The real danger is that styrene, a potentially carcinogenic toxin, is ingested by leaching into hot, oily, or acidic food. Additionally, polystyrene foam isn't biodegradable and can cause harm to wildlife when ingested as well as ongoing leaching into the environment.

A number of biodegradable packaging alternatives made from readily available raw materials are available in Thailand. Be Greening sources the Areca palm leaf sheath from southern Thailand and uses heat to mold it into containers that can hold liquids for up to three hours. While villagers used to dispose of the leaves by burning them, now the leaves provide a new income stream.

Gracz packaging is made from bagasse (pulp residue following juice extraction from sugarcane) and offers another viable alternative to polystyrene. It can hold hot and cold liquids without losing shape or leaking, and it decomposes within six weeks. A Gracz container costs approximately 1.3 baht while the equivalent polystyrene foam unit is about 0.5 baht. But the company estimates that the ultimate cost of foam can be up to 328 baht per

Many street vendors in Thailand use non-biodegradable packaging.

container if the associated healthcare costs of treating cancer, which is linked to using foam containers, are factored in.

The KU-Green line of biodegradable food ware developed by Kasetsart University is made from cassava starch. The product has inherent insulation properties for both hot and cold items, and will dissolve within seven days in room temperature water. It takes just a few months to decompose when composted. In 2010, Universal Biopack took over the patent and commercialized the product under the UBPack brand.

A number of biodegradable packaging options are available in Thailand.

Higher unit costs and low awareness about the risks of eating from foam containers are key barriers preventing the widespread usage of biodegradable containers by restaurants and street vendors. Solutions could include government and city council subsidies and working with manufacturers to lower costs through increased orders. Another idea is to create access to raw materials and processes that spark cottage industry production.

FOOD WASTE

1.3 billion tons of food

worth **more than US$1 trillion** is lost during production, harvest, handling, transportation, distribution, and storage – or is discarded at the consumer, retail, or food services level worldwide.

30-50% of fruits and vegetables

in Asia-Pacific are ruined during transportation and handling,

while **12-37% of rice** produced in Southeast Asia is lost during harvest, processing, transportation, and storage.

Feeding the projected global population of **9 billion people in 2050** will require increasing overall food production **by at least 70%.**

Today
75% of the world's food is generated from just **12 plants and 5 animal species.**

Sources: Food and Agriculture Organization of the United Nations

---

One company that is helping consumers navigate the confusing provenance maze is family-owned Rimping Supermarkets. Rimping, which has several outlets in Chiang Mai province and one in Laos, developed its own five-color coding system for produce. This enables consumers to make informed purchases. The spectrum ranges from green for 100 percent organic through to red for items where details aren't known, but the items are randomly tested. The system educates consumers about different cultivation methods and where pesticides have and haven't been used. Rimping's in-house testing covers a number of contaminants including pesticides, salicylic acid, which may be illicitly used as a food preservative, and E. Coli bacteria.

Beyond chemical safety, better labeling of food products is needed for consumers to make informed dietary choices about what they eat. Products high in sodium, fat, and sugar can impact the long-term health of consumers by causing heart disease, hypertension, and Type 2 diabetes. Improved labeling design should take into account font sizes and colors as well as the presentation of nutritional information like sugar content, which could be presented graphically with teaspoon icons.

Food wastage

Food wastage can be deceptive. Balance sheets may still show a healthy profit despite food wastage occurring. There may also be denial that there is a problem in the first place. However, the scale of food wastage globally is enormous. A 2014 FAO report estimated that "each year, approximately one-third of all food produced for human consumption in the world is lost or wasted." And the true cost of food wastage includes the energy required to produce, transport, and dispose of it in addition to the social and environmental costs.

Independent laboratory testing of Thai produce in the United Kingdom has revealed chemical residues that are banned in the European Union.

A key barrier to solving the problem is the perception gap about the scale of wastage according to Benjamin Lephilibert, founder of Bangkok-based LightBlue Environmental Consulting, specialists in sustainability for the hospitality industry. "A chef in a major Bangkok hotel estimated that 20 kg was wasted a day. The true figure was 200 kg a day of edible food

SWEET DILEMMA: CURBING THE NATIONAL SUGAR ADDICTION

A girl holds chocolate in front of her face in Harrod's Cafe in Emquartier mall in Bangkok.

The World Health Organization (WHO) recommends that both adults and children should limit their daily consumption of free sugars to less than ten percent of their daily energy intake. But the surprising amount of sugar in sugar-sweetened beverages (there are almost 35 grams in a 330ml can of Coca-Cola, and 22 grams in a 380ml bottle of Oishi Honey Lemon Green Tea), combined with those found in snacks and white rice, means that many Thais are consuming more than is good for them. Globally, in fact, Thailand ranks ninth for sugar consumption.

With experts worried about the rising rates of obesity and Type 2 diabetes, the Thai government approved a sugar tax in May 2016. Beginning implementation in 2017, this new tax will see the cost of beverages with more than six grams of sugar per 100ml rise by at least 20 percent. The taxes could mean the loss of market share as consumers switch to cheaper options that are tax exempt. In other words, reducing sugar content may soon be in the best interest of profits as well as health.

Manufacturers of high sugar content beverages would be wise to reduce the sugar in their products and innovate low- or zero-sugar options with new ingredients. In other markets some companies have replaced sugar with artificial sweeteners that aren't included in the tax regulations, or used natural sweeteners like stevia, which is reported to be 30 times sweeter than sugar. Another natural alternative is monk fruit extract. It contains no calories and is 150–200 times sweeter than sugar.

ThaiBev has a stated goal of increasing the volume of healthy non-alcoholic drinks in their portfolio from 61 to 67 percent by 2020. For CEO Thapana Sirivadhanabhakdi, it's all about giving consumers choice and education on the matter. "We need to offer healthier product choices and let the consumer know what is in them so they can decide."

Brands can take a proactive stance to raise awareness of diabetes and the need to reduce sugar intake, while also communicating their own efforts to reduce sugar content. They could also increase the availability of smaller pack sizes, and reformulate products that target children. Eliminating added sugar from drinks that target babies and small children could be a critical first step toward weaning the population off sugar. At present, some plain milk products in Thailand even contain added sugar.

Super foods with powerful nutritional profiles offer product innovation opportunities. Whapow is a frozen super food snack that is both nutritious and pleasantly sweet due to the addition of blended fruit. The all-natural products contain 10–15 percent Spirulina, an easily digested micro-algae, as well as over 100 types of vitamins and minerals.

High blood sugar levels and Type 2 diabetes are not just a sugar consumption issue. Dr Kongkiat Kespechara, the director of Bangkok Hospital Phuket, points to white rice consumption as another major dietary factor that causes blood sugar levels to rise significantly. He has researched heirloom rice varieties that keep blood sugar levels relatively low and has worked with farmers to organically cultivate healthier crops and create value-added rice products under the Pensook brand. This solution allows both farmers and consumers to benefit, and creates greater awareness of health.

waste," Lephilibert says, referring to a case study. His firm conducts seven-day food waste audits for clients investigating every stage of the value chain from purchasing, storage, preparation, and cooking through to the table.

For effective food waste management, a complete picture of the entire value chain is needed with standardized key performance indicators (KPIs) across all departments, instead of one measuring waste by cost and another by weight. Additionally, all staff need to be involved and educated about the issue. Lephilibert holds up the Sampran Riverside (see *Tourism*, page 250) as a gold standard case where sustainability is embedded in corporate culture. "Prior to our audit they were already separating waste in six categories and had good employee engagement through ongoing training," he says.

Two Bangkok hotels, The Anantara Riverside and AVANI Riverside, began a food wastage program in September 2016 in collaboration with ThaiHarvest|SOS, a non-profit dedicated to rescuing edible food for redistribution to those in need and collecting non-edible waste for composting projects. So far the hotels have donated over 38,000 kg of non-edible food for composting and, in a nine-week trial period that began in early October 2016, over 1,000 kg of edible food was donated.

A by-product of this food wastage program has been discovering an untapped CSR opportunity as well as new internal efficiencies. "We are highly encouraged to know that our waste and surplus go to good use and benefit those that are in dire need of healthy nutritious food," says Elizabeth Dass-Brown, director of marketing communications for both hotels. "We also see a great reduction in food waste, having instilled the importance of controlling wastage throughout food production at every stage."

Enterprises large and small can find value in effective food waste management. Starbucks' "Grounds for your Garden" program began in North America in 1995 and some of its Thai outlets offer used grounds for customers to take home. Coffee grounds are ideal for composting as they slowly release nitrogen into the mix. It's a win-win for both the customer and the cafe's reduced trash volume.

Creating value from waste

Harnessing waste materials and transforming them into useful by-products can unlock new revenue streams and previously untapped value. It can also reduce disposal costs and lower environmental impacts.

Very little is wasted on the Harmony Life organic farm in Pak Chong, northeast of Bangkok. An impressive array of biodynamic laundry and dishwashing detergents, household cleaners and liquid soaps – all made from fermented fruit and vegetable waste or enzymes – is sold in the farm's Bangkok store Sustaina. The process involves placing the organic matter in water with brown sugar and leaving it for up to a month to allow fermentation to take place. Enzyme drinks that aid digestion are another by-product of this process.

ThaiBev is a far larger operation, which includes 18 distilleries, three breweries, and 11 non-alcoholic beverage production facilities in

Harnessing waste materials and transforming them into useful by-products can unlock new revenue streams and previously untapped value.

Fermented fruit and vegetable waste can be turned into detergents and soaps.

CASE STUDY | Brands and Restaurateurs Make Insects More Palatable

Grubs are processed into high-protein snacks.

THE CHALLENGE: Eating insects is nothing new in Thailand, but it is a predominantly rural habit. They have long been served as crispy treats in the northeastern provinces and can be found on street carts in the capital, but not often on menus in air-conditioned venues.

"It's harder to convince urban Thais to eat insects than people in the EU [European Union] due to their environmental awareness," says Nathan Preteseille, Coordinator of the ASEAN Food and Feed Insect Association (AFFIA), a newly formed advocacy body seeking government regulation for the industry.

Challenging consumer perceptions in markets remains an issue. Another issue is scale. While there are reported to be over 20,000 cricket producers in Thailand, they are mostly small scale with low production output due to the low demand for processed insect products.

THE SOLUTION: Three brands have taken different gastronomic approaches to consumerizing insects. Bugsolutely has used cricket flour – roasted crickets in a powder form – to create a fortified pasta. Cricket flour has a slightly nutty taste but the resulting pasta product is like any other pasta. When covered in tomato sauce consumers find it familiar, delicious and completely hygienic.

Hi-So Snack brand is serving up insects in their original form. They come in handy snack packs with cute bug motifs on the outside for shelf appeal. The company claims that their product is healthier than the street version as it is baked, not deep-fried in oil. Deep-fried products can be of dubious quality due to repeated use of oil. The cricket and silkworm

snacks come in flavors such as salted, cheese, and BBQ.

Restaurateurs, low-carbon event organizers, and sustainability advocates Joke and Regan Pairojmahakij don't shy away from putting insects on the menu. They even emphasize the word 'cricket' when describing Bugsolutely pasta at their Seven Spoons restaurant in Bangkok's old town. The couple went all out when conceptualizing Insects in the Backyard, Thailand's first fine dining insect restaurant. "Affecting change is about exciting the right people at the right time and place," says Regan of her desire for a tipping point in the consumption of sustainable foods like insects.

THE BENEFITS: The cultivation of insects is in line with Sustainable Development Goal 12 of ensuring Responsible Consumption and Production. Insects are rich in protein and offer a highly sustainable food source. They require less food and space to cultivate than traditional protein sources, yet have a high yield and are often referred to as "the protein of the future." Crickets, for example, contain up to 70 percent protein and are favored in the body building community.

Supply is also plentiful in Thailand, which is the world's largest producer of human-consumption-grade crickets. There are also more than 200 edible insect species in the country, according to a 2013 study by the United Nations Food and Agriculture Organization.

Bugs are the go-to ingredient at Bangkok's Insects in the Backyard restaurant.

THAPANA SIRIVADHANABHAKDI, *CEO of leading international drinks company ThaiBev, addresses the issue of industrial waste and the ongoing debate surrounding sugary drinks and consumer choice.*

How is ThaiBev addressing waste in the food and beverage industry?

The aim for any industry is zero waste. For us, the distillation process gives us waste that we can work with. Before we invested in biogas. Then we had the part of energy – the evaporation of all the O_2 liquid – that we call vinasse. That's the leftover from the concentration. But those leftovers are used as fertilizer. Apart from that, we're now looking to extract parts of it from the brewery to the distillery.

Polyethylene terephthalate (PET) bottles are also a huge issue. The consumers don't take care of this waste, so it costs the city, the country, and the overall environment to take care of them. That's why we work on recycling, collecting glass, and PET bottles.

As for the plastic waste from old crates, we're working with our suppliers to recycle the plastic we use to create pallets for logistics. This is already valuable to PET plastic collectors. But I'm also talking about the crates we use for beer bottles and EST Cola. When they've been out in the sun for over eight years, they're not going to come back fresh in terms of the look or color, so we turn them into pallets.

Diabetes and sugar content in drinks is a global health issue. How does ThaiBev promote health among consumers?

We see how we can provide a better choice of product for consumers. Sometimes we even look to ourselves to see how we can play a role to shape the market for the benefit of consumers. If we're not looking out for the best interests of our users that basically means that we will have less users and less consumers in the end.

That's why we focus more on other categories, such as drinking water, healthier choices of carbonated soft drinks (CSD), like 100PLUS for the Thai market. In Malaysia and Singapore, isotonic drinks are being consumed as a healthier substitute to CSDs.

When you're talking about how you directly link all of this with your consumers, sometimes it's difficult because we want to share with them – I'm not using the word 'educate' – and make them think how they should choose certain products. That's the difficult part because you're changing someone's mindset. That's why when we're doing all the marketing and positioning, it's about slowly engaging them with the key positive elements we'd like them to understand and about why we're focusing on such products.

So educating consumers is tricky?

People are people. It's how we'll be able to let them know what is good or bad for them, but definitely it's the consumers' choice to make their own judgment call.

We'd like to educate them, but still provide these products. Prohibition in many places in the world doesn't work. Basically, you stop letting people have certain things. If they still need it, they'll find ways to get it. So it's not ideal for any government or regulators to actually shape change.

Generally speaking, we cannot stop the behavior of any individual. What we can do is provide sufficient information for them to understand and to choose for themselves. I think it's our responsibility to play a part in better educating consumers about how they choose the products that they consume.

NUNTIVAT THAMHATAI, *public affairs and communications director for Coca-Cola Thailand and Laos, explains what the outcome of the soft drink company's stewardship approach to resource management has been for the kingdom and world at large.*

Coca-Cola has a stated goal of being a global water steward. What does this involve?
Communities here in Thailand and across the world rely on a sufficient quantity of safe, accessible water from sustainable ecosystems for their continued prosperity. For our company and our bottling partners, water is equally important. It is the primary ingredient in our range of beverage products and it also enables our manufacturing processes. In June 2007, The Coca-Cola Company announced our aspirational goal of replenishing – or balancing – all the water we use. This involves working through community water programs to safely return to communities and nature an amount of water equal to what we use in our finished beverages as well as improving water efficiency in our manufacturing operations.

Coca-Cola announced last year that it had met its 2020 goal of water replenishment five years early. How was this achieved?
In August 2016, we were proud to announce during Stockholm World Water Week that the Coca-Cola system (the Company and our bottling partners) had achieved our goal to replenish all of the water we use in our global sales volume back to communities and

nature, five years ahead of our original target. Today, we are returning to communities and nature more water than we use in our global sales volume. We're doing this through hundreds of community water programs in dozens of countries around the world. Here in ASEAN, we have community water programs up and running in eight countries in collaboration with government and NGO partners.

A local Thai Coca-Cola initiative of note is the RAKNAM ('Love Water') partnership program that commenced in 2007 and will shortly be rolled out in other ASEAN countries. What was the inspiration for the project, what does it involve, and what have the key sustainability impacts been?
RAKNAM originated from our commitment to water stewardship and sustainability. It is a partnership started a decade ago with government and civil society to drive public awareness, education, and collective action on water resource management, especially in water stressed areas in six provinces: Lampang, Nakornsawan, Khon Kaen, Pathumthani, Burirum, and Surat Thani. RAKNAM has reached more than one million Thais to date.

This includes support toward a water retention and flood control Monkey Cheek project following the late King Bhumibol's initiatives toward sustainable development. In Buriram, northeastern Thailand, we've been working with the Utokapat Foundation under the Royal Patronage of H.M. the King and the Hydro and Agro Informatics Institute (HAII) under the Ministry of Science and Technology to bring Monkey Cheek water retention ponds, over 40km of water canals, and piping facilities to communities that historically suffered severe drought and water shortages. The network captures rainwater during the rainy season to increase crop production during periods of water scarcity, resulting in improved livelihoods. Agricultural revenues in the village have increased by approximately 2.8 times and, with enough water, villagers can generate an income all year round, improving their productivity and food security. The project has been expanded to 59 villages in Thailand, and we are also now working with our partners to export this successful initiative to other Lower Mekong countries that face similar issues, starting with Laos.

- **Address sustainability issues** like food safety, traceability, labor conditions, and environmental protection before external bodies mandate compliance. Set voluntary sustainability targets and engage with authorities to help shape change.

- **Invest in supply chain management for total food transparency** from suppliers through to consumers. It's good for health and good for business for everyone to know where his or her food comes from.

- **Innovate and implement healthier product portfolios** to combat the rise in non-communicable diseases locally. Look to smaller artisan brands for innovation and potential partnerships.

- **Educate consumers on food issues** and how to lead healthier lifestyles. The private sector should get ahead of the message and help educate the public while also offering improved, healthier options.

- **Educate staff on sustainability issues** so they can be advocates both within the company and wider communities.

- **Reduce packaging where possible,** invest in better waste management, and use sustainable packaging alternatives.

- **Monitor food wastage**. Put in place strategies to reuse or redistribute food; innovate new uses for by-products.

Thailand, as well as international operations as far away as Scotland. In line with the company's goal to be the "Stable and Sustainable ASEAN Leader in Total Beverages Business" by 2020, efficient waste management is a priority. The company transforms vinasse, the residue left over after the distillation process, into an alternative fuel to power its boiler systems and produce approximately 144,000 metric tons of steam per year.

ThaiBev is also looking for new applications for its food waste. Currently much of it is sold for animal feed (1,086 metric tons of bread and fish scrap in 2016). However, two new value-added products made from these scraps may soon be available as a result of a research collaboration between ThaiBev and the Faculty of Agro-Industry at Prince of Songkla University.

Finding the right recipe

Food is at the intersection of personal health as well as social and environmental issues. It has immediate and long-term impacts for individuals and the broader society that produces it. However, the base level of awareness on relevant sustainability issues needs to be raised among business leaders in Thailand's food and beverage sector in order to enact meaningful change. It has to be about more than fulfilling regulatory requirements.

In Thailand, there is growing interest in wellness products and services, but consumers are still very much taste-driven. Individual food education needs to be injected into the country's vibrant food culture of street stalls and restaurants. Greater public education about food provenance, nutrition, and healthy eating is needed. The private sector could get ahead of the message, and in doing so help educate the public while at the same time offering improved products. Sponsoring nutrition and gardening programs in schools is one way to reach youth, but adults also need to learn how to buy and cook better quality food.

Let's not forget that top business executives are consumers too. They, like everyone else, should know and care where their food comes from. When such leaders are on board with promoting sustainable choices and actions, it's easier for large-scale shifts in mindsets to occur, and for food transparency policies to be implemented. In short, inspired leadership can drive the innovation required to change the way a country produces and consumes food.

Fisheries and Marine Resources

- *Wild-caught seafood and aquaculture will play a vital role in feeding the world as the population rises to an estimated 9.6 billion by 2050.*

- *Since unethical and illegal fishing practices came to international attention, many big players in Thailand's fishing industry have reacted to limit the reputational and financial damage.*

- *Technology is enabling better fish traceability but is far from a cure-all.*

- *Supply chain transparency and ethical labor are stubborn but solvable problems.*

- *Commitment to new standards and practices – and consistent and collaborative enforcement of them – could make or break the industry.*

For centuries, people living along and around the 3,200 kilometers of coastline that shape modern-day Thailand have found a vital source of protein in the surrounding waters. After World War II, this primarily small-scale fishing sector grew into one of the largest fishing industries in the world, with the 1960s and 1970s seeing the introduction of trawling and an increase in the use of purse seining. Today, Thailand is the fourth-largest seafood exporter in the world.

With the global population expected to reach 9.6 billion people by 2050 (from 7.6 billion today), consumption of fish will be key for future generations. Not only is the number of people rising – so too is fish consumption, which rose to over 20 kilograms per capita for the first time in 2016. "Globally there's a protein challenge [and] wild caught seafood and aquaculture definitely have to be part of that solution," says Dr Darian McBain, director of Sustainable Development at Thai Union Group, one of Thailand's largest fishing companies.

But before it can capitalize on any new opportunities, the Thai fishing industry must first untangle a complex knot of challenges. First, the rapid growth of the industry has led to the overfishing of national waters and the depletion of stocks. Since catches peaked back in the 1980s, reaching 1.8 million tons, they have steadily decreased. As a result, the industry started to expand to waters outside of Thailand in the 1990s and 2000s, which in turn made it harder to trace the origin of ocean-caught fish due to the lack of control over distant water fleets.

As for social impacts, the Thai fishing industry relies on a migrant workforce, as most Thais are not willing to work in the sector. The vulnerable situation of these workers, many of them unskilled and undocumented, has led to dire labor conditions on many vessels and in many pre-processing factories. Some have been denounced in news reports and research studies from non-governmental organizations, such as Greenpeace or the Environmental Justice Foundation.

Because of these malpractices, the Thai fishing industry is now tainted with a reputation for using slave labor and illegal fishing. With consumers increasingly aware of the sustainability and traceability of what they buy, this reputation will be difficult to overcome.

Inaction from the industry could not only lead to a reduction in consumer demand from Western countries, but also to sanctions. In 2015 the European Union issued Thailand with a yellow card for illegal, unreported, and unregulated fishing (IUU). This was a shot across the bow of the Thai fishing industry, a warning measure that, if ignored, would have led to a full-scale ban on seafood imports from Thailand. On paper, the impact of a red card was estimated at around US$200–300 million by SCB's Economic Intelligence Unit, with the cost rising to US$500 million if, as its report stated, "shrimp farmers are unable to validate a products' legality because they use small fish in fishmeal to feed shrimp."

Improving seafood traceability

With a large portion of the supply chain located hundreds or even thousands of kilometers offshore, traceability – the capacity to follow a product back to its origin – is especially complicated in the case of seafood. As a result of this opaqueness, and also, arguably, a lack of foresight, the seafood sector has, as the United Nations Environment Programme writes, "taken longer than other sectors to react to social and environmental ethical concerns."

But a sea change is underway, much of it consumer driven. In a global survey conducted by the Marine Stewardship Council (MSC) in 2014, nine out of ten respondents said ocean sustainability is important to them. Moreover, consumers are demanding more supply chain accountability. The most pertinent transnational example is the lawsuit filed in California against US retail chain Costco for selling allegedly slavery-tainted shrimp farmed by Thai food group CP Foods. The lawsuit was finally dismissed, but it showed the level of engagement of many consumers, especially in Western countries. In this part of the world, fish consumers' interest in the traceability of seafood doesn't just involve the origin of the fish that they eat but also other factors: the species, whether the fish is wild or farmed, the method used to capture it, the date of that capture, whether the fish has been frozen, and labor conditions.

Thailand's seafood industry is struggling to introduce ethical labor practices.

For its part, the Thai government has amended its laws to improve the traceability of the supply chain. One major step was the approval of the Royal Ordinance on Fisheries in November 2015. This new regulatory framework is aimed mainly at combating IUU. Under the new legislation, vessels above 30 gross tonnage have to be equipped with a Vessel Monitoring System (VMS), a satellite-based monitoring tool that calculates the position of the craft using GPS. The government also implemented a Port In/Port Out system (PIPO), which entails inspecting every commercial vessel coming in or out of any Thai port.

Traceability – the capacity to follow a product back to its origin – is especially complicated in the case of seafood.

Partnerships between the private sector, NGOs, and the Thai government are also key to improving traceability. One of the first initiatives of this kind was the Shrimp Sustainable Supply Chain Task Force, which was initiated by CPF and Costco in July 2014. Others have followed, such as the Multi-stakeholder Initiative for Accountable Supply Chain of Thai Fisheries (MAST), which was established by the Labor Rights Promotion Network Foundation (LPN), one of the longest running organizations fighting against human trafficking and labor abuses in Thailand, and TLCS Legal Advocate Company. MAST's goals include the creation of a Thai fishermen's union; the establishment of port centers providing shelter, food, and first aid to fishermen; and strengthening public awareness about migrant worker living conditions.

Despite these moves, tracing seafood supply chains remains a big challenge, according to Thon Thamrongnawasawat, deputy dean of the Faculty of Fisheries at Kasetsart University. "Fishing in Thailand is different from Europe or America. It is a multi-species [model]. Local fishermen don't catch only one type of fish," says the scholar. He adds that many fishermen do not sell their catch on the open market,

Companies should try to diversify their offerings with new products made with less popular, but also less threatened, species.

and also have their own clients among restaurants or hotels. "It is more difficult to control here," he says. However, the information provided by the VMS system can help clarify the origins of the fish, as long as the product is not mislabeled and the data on the vessel that caught it is provided to the upper levels of the chain.

Knowing where wild fish is caught – and by whom exactly – remains a big issue.

The fight against illegal fishing

Improving traceability might be the first step in the fight against IUU, but it is far from being the last – further actions are required to ensure the sustainability of the industry. First, companies need to reconsider the origins of the fish they catch or use, even if caught legally. Fishing in areas with healthier stocks is prudent, as eventually the law will compel companies to do so; the Marine Fisheries Management Plan 2015–2019 (FMP) includes a significant reduction of fishing capacity in the Gulf of Thailand and the Andaman Sea to allow for the recovery of the fish stocks in the area. This means that Thai companies will have to either fish in distant waters, buy from other countries, or source more sustainably and try to gain a premium price for their catch.

Companies should also try to diversify their offerings with new products made with less popular, but also less threatened, species. Some companies, such as Thai Union, are already developing new products based on these varieties of fish. In the case of fresh fish consumption, the Thai certification standard Blue Brand (see *Case Study*, page 196) is guiding consumers toward seasonal and less popular species, leading the way in raising awareness so that buying preferences match the production capacity of the oceans.

There are still concerns, though, about the increasing demand of some of the most popular species, such as tuna. "Companies still try to expand, of course. For example, Thailand has never been a tuna consumer but companies are now trying to push the market," says Anchalee Pipattanawattanakul, oceans campaigner at Greenpeace. For instance, Sealect, one of the main brands of Thai Union, launched "Gin Pla Dai Boi, Aroi Dai Tookwan" (Enjoy your daily meal with tuna), a campaign promoting the daily consumption of tuna, in 2012. The campaign included road show activities, online media and a set of advertising commercials. "The latter was to convey the message that Sealect Tuna is a suitable ingredient for preparing different dishes, both Thai and international," says the Thai Union 2012 Annual Report. Some other

INDUSTRY SNAPSHOT

Thailand is consistently one of the world's four largest seafood exporters with a total export value of **US$7 billion in 2015.**

Thailand is the **#1** **producer of canned tuna.**

Thailand's **42,512 active**, registered fishing vessels caught **1.34 million tons of fish** in 2014.

Roughly **20,000 unlicensed vessels,** or "ghost boats," also ply international waters as part of the Thai fishing fleet.

The Thai fishing industry employs some **170,000 to 300,000 fishermen,** of which

82%
are migrants.

An additional **515,000 people work in support industries,** including fish processing, ship building, and factories

Some **17% of migrants** working on Thai fishing vessels can be classified as "forced labor."

ADDRESSING SUSTAINABILITY CONCERNS

Thailand launched a new regulatory framework in 2015 to combat **Illegal, Unreported and Unregulated fishing (IUU).** Some of the key stipulations include:

Vessels above 30 gross tonnage must be equipped with a Vessel Monitoring System (VMS), which can calculate the craft's location and movements through GPS.

A Port In/Port Out system (PIPO) that aims at **inspecting every commercial vessel** coming in or out of any Thai port.

A maximum fine of 30 million baht for "serious infringements" such as fishing without a valid license, or tampering with government issued identification markings.

Also in 2015, the Thai Frozen Foods Association **banned any kind of third-party pre-processing** as a measure to combat forced labor.

GLOBAL SIGNIFICANCE

Asia produces 90% of the world's aquaculture, 80% of which is produced on smallholder farms.

20%

Wild-caught shrimp accounts for **20% of internationally traded seafood products** in market value, with 1.3 million tons caught annually.

The tropical shrimp industry generates **income for 900,000 fishermen** worldwide with more than **400,000 trawlers** from 65 countries in operation.

By 2030 the world will need **75-85 million more tons of fish** to meet human consumption needs, an increase that cannot be met by fish from the oceans.

Sources: WWF; Food and Agriculture Organization of the United Nations; USAID; Thailand Department of Fisheries; International Organization for Migration; DJSI; International Labour Organization.

THON THAMRONGNAWASAWAT *is the deputy dean of the Faculty of Fisheries at Kasetsart University and one of Thailand's foremost marine conservationists. Recent years have seen him drumming up support for ambitious new mass tourism management policies at marine national parks, but he is also an outspoken authority on the fishing industry.*

What challenges stand in the way of a sustainable Thai fishing industry?

We have problems of overfishing. What we are trying to do right now is to regulate our fishing vessels. We've separated commercial fishing and local fishermen and we're trying to decrease the number of fishing boats that destroy our ecosystem by asking the fishermen to change their fishing gear. We are also trying to regulate tracking – commercial fishing vessels [now] need to have a GPS system. But we also have a problem with tracking local fishermen's boats because they are quite small, and if you [ask them] to invest, [they won't do it because] they don't have enough money. We also have a problem with overseas fishermen coming to our waters.

What are the main challenges related to management of sea fishing?

It is difficult to regulate local fishermen because impacts are different depending on the region. In some areas, the fishing techniques used impact the ecosystem but in other areas they don't. So if we use centralized regulations, with one law for the whole country, for some areas it can be good, but for other areas it can cause problems. Also

you have to understand that some local fishermen don't have a port of entry because, in areas where there is a lot of tourism, they go directly to the restaurant or the resort with their catch and they don't have to go to a port or market. So it's hard to regulate everything.

How do you foresee the Thai fishing industry evolving over the next decade or so?

I think there will be a shift to aquaculture. We cannot overfish again. If we want to supply seafood to the world, we must turn to aquaculture. At the moment, we are trying to concentrate on seafood that has a high price, like lobster or some kinds of grouper, which the Chinese are willing to pay a very high price for. We need to go to something like this – to identify very specific targets for export. But when it comes to fishing in the sea, it should only be for local fishermen or commercial fishing for the domestic market, for Thai people or tourists. So it should be like this: aquaculture for export, and local and commercial fishing to satisfy the country's needs.

What else will need to change?

We will have to improve our regulations from time to time, and also learn to compromise. Each group, commercial fishermen and local fishermen, must work together. Before they had conflicts. But now we ask them to talk – and many local fishermen have joined fishing committees in their areas. If they are willing to speak and to compromise, they can work together.

South Thailand's shrimp farms continue to leave a big environmental footprint.

companies, such as Roza Foods, have also been advertising tuna products with a view to increasing consumption.

Thai companies also need to drop some of the most controversial fishing methods from their supply chains, or at least minimize their impacts, if they want to regain consumer trust. Most notably, they will need to address problems surrounding transshipment, which is the transfer of fish from one vessel, normally the fishing vessel, to another, usually one that brings the catch to port. Transshipment boosts the productivity of fishing vessels since it allows them to stay in distant waters for months or even years, but it also hinders the control of port authorities on the activities of these vessels. Another big concern, especially for species such as tuna, is the use of Fish Aggregating Devices (FAD): permanent or temporary structures deployed at sea to attract fish. While FAD have boosted the productivity of the fishing fleet, they have also been key in the depletion of fish stocks.

Elsewhere in Thailand, fish farming is also having a big environmental impact. Farmed shrimp is especially culpable for unsustainable land conversion, notably the deforestation of mangrove areas. According to the Mangrove Action Project, Thailand has lost more than half of its mangrove forests since 1960, when the government started an active policy to promote semi-intensive and intensive

Intensive shrimp farms have been linked to the discharge of untreated water into natural streams.

shrimp production. Not only does this deforestation destroy a high value ecosystem, it also releases large amounts of greenhouse gases: converting one hectare of mangrove to shrimp farming in Thailand can release 330 metric tons of CO_2 per year. Meanwhile, intensive shrimp farms have also been linked to the discharge of untreated water into natural streams, releasing antibiotics, disinfectants, and pesticides into fragile ecosystems.

In terms of reputation, complying with new laws may not be enough. Some companies are taking full advantage of sustainability certification bodies such as the Marine Stewardship Council and Aquaculture Stewardship Council. For instance, Thai Union has committed to source at least 75 percent of its tuna supply chain from MSC-certified sources by 2020. With only 13 percent of their raw tuna currently certified, there is

The best way to avoid being linked to IUU and labor abuses going forward might be to simplify the supply chain and to eliminate subcontractors.

still a long way to go. Certifications can also fall short. "If tuna companies can get MSC certification, there would be a quick improvement in their management, but it won't mean that all problems are solved," says Amanda Nickson, director of Global Tuna Conservation at The Pew Charitable Trusts.

Thai companies must work to simplify and tighten their supply chains to root out labor abuses and eliminate IUU.

Avoiding labor abuses

While the focus of the government-led reforms of recent years has primarily been on IUU, new regulations and policies regarding labor issues and the recruitment policies of the crew quickly followed. The Thai government updated the Memorandum of Understanding (MoU) between Thailand and its neighboring countries and approved a new regulation on employing migrant workers in August 2016. Under this system, only agencies registered and approved by the governments in the countries of origin, namely Myanmar, Cambodia and Laos, can facilitate the employment of foreign workers with Thai companies. Recruitment can also be done directly by employers. Moreover, employers are also required to absorb all fees related to the process and workers are supposed to pay only for personal costs, such as passports, work permits, or visas.

For Thai companies, the best way to avoid being linked to IUU and labor abuses going forward might be to simplify the supply chain and to eliminate subcontractors, thereby gaining tighter control of their suppliers. Indeed, it is a route many big companies are already taking. For instance, there were, until recently, typically two processing steps in the export supply chain. During the first step, fish were cleaned and prepared in pre-processing plants. Then in the second step, fish were canned at big exporting companies. But since January 2016, when the Thai Frozen Foods Association (TFFA) banned any kind of third-party pre-processing and its members brought in-house all related operations, the first step has disappeared. Some companies are also turning to sustainability certifications that include social aspects, such as the International Fishmeal and Fish Oil Organization (IFFO), or other programs that aim to improve working conditions.

Activists recognize that the industry has made progress over the last few years, but many concerns remain. "A lot has been done on IUU and prevention of trafficking. But many labor abuses remain," says Daniel Murphy, an independent researcher on the fishing industry. He highlights flaws in the recruitment system, the abusive terms of most contracts, and the often appalling working conditions.

CASE STUDY | Thai Union Prioritizes Safe and Legal Labor

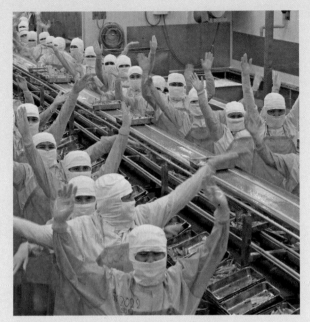

Workers no longer pay broker fees to gain employment at Thai Union.

THE CHALLENGE: Migrant workers in the seafood industry, most of them unskilled and undocumented, have experienced dire working conditions for decades. Having been exposed by an *Associated Press* investigation that documented slavery-like conditions at one of its suppliers, Thai Union, the largest canned tuna producer in the world, needed to confront the issue head-on.

THE SOLUTION: In 2015, Thai Union released a new business ethics and code of conduct. Both were part of a broader Sea Change strategy – a global policy that comprises programs on four topics: responsible sourcing, marine conservation, safe and legal labor, and caring for local communities.

One of the main improvements in working conditions at Thai Union has been their Zero Recruitment Fee Policy, through which the company wants to end the well-established practice in Thailand of migrant workers paying brokers to get jobs in factories. "One of the things that kept coming up [as a problem among workers] is that people were starting their work at your company with debts," says Dr Darian McBain, director of sustainable development at Thai Union Group. Thai Union now work with the recruitment agency International Focus in Myanmar, among others, in order to train them in their recruitment policies. "It's really been a long process because we had to move the capacity within the recruitment agents because their whole business model is based on charging workers," says McBain. "We are saying to them that we will pay those costs." One of the local organizations they partner with, the Migrant Worker Rights Network (MWRN), also verifies that workers do not pay fees to any brokers to get jobs at Thai Union.

THE BENEFITS: Recruitment fees, activists say, are still widespread in the seafood industry. By being the first to implement a policy to eliminate these fees, Thai Union has earned a leading position in the fight against slavery. "It is appalling that Thai Union has been the only company to implement a real zero fee policy," says Andy Hall, advisor to the MWRN.

Thai Union was nominated for the Thomson Reuters Foundation's inaugural 'Stop Slavery Award' in 2015, but recognition aside, it has gained tighter control on its supply chain and labor conditions at every step. It also brought all pre-processing tasks in-house a few weeks before the Thai Frozen Foods Association made it mandatory for all its members in January 2016. "We realized we couldn't manage the risk [of not being in control of pre-processing operations]," says McBain.

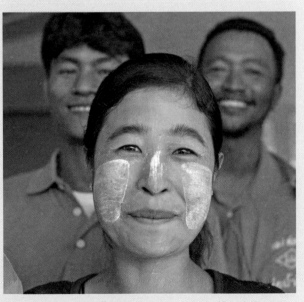

Thai Union now works with an official recruitment agency, International Focus, in Myanmar.

Frequent changes in regulations, though often well intentioned, are also not helping. For example, the government approved a new regulation in June 2017 that has raised concerned among activists, as it toughens punishments: high fines will be imposed on foreigners working without proper permits, and jail terms handed down to employers who illegally hire foreigners. The implementation of the most controversial provisions have been delayed until January 2018. And yet, as things stand, the system looks more, rather than less, confusing for migrants, and they still need to rely on abusive brokers to get their work permits and visas.

A future driven by technology?

New technologies are emerging as the key to improving traceability of raw materials and avoiding IUU and labor abuses in vessels and factories. Over the last few years, more precise technologies that are better at tracking boat movements, such as the Pelagic Data System, have been developed. "With this new technology we can see the behavior of the fishing vessel," says Dornnapha Sukkree, from the Multi-stakeholder Initiative for Accountable Supply Chain of Thai Fisheries (MAST). "In addition, it serves not

---

CASE STUDY Charoen Pokphand Foods Eliminates Untraceable Fishmeal

THE CHALLENGE: Fishmeal, an animal feed usually made with trash fish or leftovers from fish processing plants, is one of the most controversial products of the fishing industry due to the opaque origins of its raw materials. In June 2014, *The Guardian* published an article linking the fishmeal used by Charoen Pokphand Foods (CPF), one of the leading food groups in Thailand and Asia, to slave labor.

THE SOLUTION: When *The Guardian* story broke, CPF was already working on improving its fishmeal supply chain, but in the wake of it the company took drastic action: ceased buying fishmeal and started an investigation of the whole supply chain. "We cut a lot of fishing vessels in our supply chain, and a lot of fishmeal factories because they couldn't pass our standards. Now we don't use the fishmeal [coming from] by-catch, only by-product," says Pitipong Dejjarukul, vice president of CPF's quality control department. Now all fishmeal is 100-percent traceable and certified by the International Fishmeal and Fish Oil Organization (IFFO). Audits of fishmeal suppliers have also been prioritized.

THE BENEFITS: International markets and consumers are demanding greater traceability in every step of the supply chain and malpractice in this regard can lead to a loss of customers. CP Foods experienced this first hand when big retailers, such as Carrefour, temporarily stopped buying from the Thai company right after *The Guardian* exposé was published. Even though the company recovered its most

important clients, the challenge was to avoid any new scandals: "If [someone like Walmart] stops buying from us, we lose some of our profit but we can survive, but the reputation would be destroyed," says Pitipong.

By acting fast, CP Foods seems to have regained customers' trust. According to the company's annual report 2016, shrimp was one of the fastest growing areas for the company, also thanks to the recovery from the Early Mortality Syndrome (EMS), a disease that causes a high shrimp mortality rate, which had impacted the Thai industry since 2011.

CP Foods' fishmeal is now 100-percent traceable.

WHY INVEST IN THE TRANSITION TO SUSTAINABLE FISHERIES?

260 million people globally
are employed directly or indirectly in fishing, and 97% of these are in developing countries

75% of global fisheries
are underperforming

Fisheries could be worth an extra **US$50 billion** every year if managed sustainably

Fisheries contribute **US$274 billion** a year to global GDP

3 billion people
rely on fish as their primary source of protein

The global fish harvest could be **40% higher** if under sustainable management

Source: The Prince's Charities – Prince of Wales

only to avoid IUU, but also to see what the working conditions are."

Technology is also enabling the discovery of the true origins of fish, even long after it was caught. Fish are the most diverse group of vertebrates, and their identification can be difficult due to the similar characteristics many of them share. However, DNA tests now offer an effective way of making sure fish are not mislabeled and that endangered species do not enter the supply chain under the name of a different species. In 2005, a Fish Barcode of Life Initiative (FISH-BOL), which aims to create an online DNA catalogue that simplifies fish identification through the use of DNA barcodes, was launched. Similarly, Thai Union launched a pilot project involving DNA barcodes for tuna in collaboration with several universities in 2015.

These new requirements are increasing costs in the supply chain, making Thai seafood products less attractive to a price-sensitive

market. In light of this development, a value-added approach, experts say, may be the way to go. "It should be the natural way. Thailand has the know-how to make value-added products," says Dominique Gautier, director of sustainability at SeaFresh Group. Traditionally, Thailand has been a leading exporter of processed seafood products, notably canned tuna, but in recent years some Thai companies have been diversifying in order to recoup lost profits – there are now spring rolls, dim sum and even sausages made from fish on the shelves.

Technology can also make certification more accessible to small players. "Third-party certification not only requires a clear understanding and alignment of operational entities, but also additional documentation and record-keeping burdens, plus the cost of an on-site audit," explains Emmanuelle Bourgois of FairAgora Asia. "On average, the yearly cost of a standard audit is around US$8,000." To make certification more

CASE STUDY | Thai Fisherfolk Improves Market Access and Livelihoods

While the Fisherfolk Enterprise places catch restrictions on participating fishermen, it has also opened up new markets for them.

THE CHALLENGE: In Thailand, many small-scale fishermen take loans from businessmen to buy new equipment and pay them back by selling them their catch for a cheap price. A large proportion of them get into a vicious cycle whereby they cannot get enough income to support their families or save money for new equipment. They are also impacted by unsustainable fishing practices that have depleted the stocks in areas where they live.

THE SOLUTION: The Association of Thai Fisherfolk Federation realized that a lack of market access for fishermen looking to sell their catch was the main reason for their hardship, and decided to disrupt the market. With the support of Oxfam Thailand, they launched the Fisherfolk Enterprise in 2015, with the aim of connecting them with consumers who are interested in buying fish caught in a sustainable way and happy to pay a premium for it. They have also developed the Blue Brand label, a certification that restricts fishermen from using certain net sizes or fishing in places with a low concentration of targeted fish.

Blue Brand-certified fish is also formalin-free, a chemical substance commonly used to preserve fish in Thailand.

"Most of the clients are first driven by health concerns, and then they start looking into environmental issues," explains Preeyaporn Atthaphong, inclusive business and social enterprise officer for Oxfam in Thailand. According to Preeyaporn, most of the Blue Brand customers are well-educated Thais who live in Bangkok and have high incomes.

The initiative currently uses social media to reach potential clients and gain orders, which are then delivered by partner companies. Blue Brand also suppliers retailers, notably the organic chain Lemon Farm.

THE BENEFITS: In 2016, the Fisherfolk Enterprise had 160 members, including fishermen and people from the local communities who were in charge of processing activities, most of them women. The fishermen now earn between 5 and 20 percent more for their catch and, even though scientific studies have not yet been conducted, fishermen say that stocks are recovering. "If fishermen can earn money more easily, they can also care for the environment," explains Preeyaporn. "In our project, there are three main beneficiaries: the fishermen, who get higher incomes, the customer, that gets healthier fish, and the environment."

TAKE ACTION

To regain consumer trust, fisheries need to:

- **Take seriously the traceability of the supply chain** to instill confidence in consumers and other stakeholders, such as European countries, that fish has been caught legally and minimum environmental and labor standards have been respected.

- **Reduce environmental footprints**, even beyond what is required by international agreements to avoid the further depletion of fish stocks.

- **Improve working conditions**, notably for migrant workers, to avoid any further news reports or research from NGOs linking the Thai fishing industry to slave labor.

- **Consider sustainability certification** a transparent means of achieving better environmental and labor practices.

- **Work together to raise standards.** An industry-wide push is more likely to get lasting results.

The International Labor Organization's extensive guide on Good Labor Practices recommends that companies in the fish-processing sector do the following:

- **Provide a written contract** in the workers' native language.

- **Allow workers access** to their identity documentation.

- **Take steps to ensure workers are not charged excessive fees** by recruitment agencies in order to prevent debt bondage situations.

- **Establish a process to verify age** as part of recruitment of workers to avoid child labor.

- **Establish regular meetings** on workplace matters and encourage workers to choose representatives to talk about issues concerning them.

- **Establish a non-discrimination policy.**

---

attainable, FairAgora Asia has developed Verifik8, an easy-to-use data analytics solution to monitor and verify seafood producers' social and environmental performances. Verifik8, explains Bourgois, benchmarks and ranks producers against the most relevant sustainability standard on the market and includes a unique on-site visit for full compliance reporting. "Our goal is to disrupt the certification market, creating a new way to make the seafood supply chain more sustainable while improving the life of farmers," says Bourgois. As of April 2017, 96 Thai shrimp farms were using Verifik8.

Meanwhile, some companies say that the Sufficiency Economy Philosophy (SEP) can also add strength to the Thai fishing industry. "This has been one of our company's drivers. We are trying to make the best use of local resources for the benefit of local people," says Gautier. SEP, adds Bourgois, can help companies adapt to extreme circumstances, such as the disease

outbreaks that have affected shrimp farming since 2011. "Their self-sufficiency sensitivity helps [them] to introduce new techniques in response to outbreaks."

Despite reforms, many seafood stakeholders are still unwilling to change their ways. "We need everybody in the industry to understand that they have to work differently," says Adisorn Promthep, head of the Thai Department of Fisheries. "It takes a lot of time." Companies and the government are focusing on the most controversial aspects of the supply chain, mainly illegal fishing and human trafficking, but labor issues remain. Exporting companies are aware of the reputational risks, but Asian consumers are often less demanding when it comes to sustainability and many companies are merely reorienting their marketing strategies. But that choice may prove risky – as fish stocks come under increasing pressure, a lack of commitment to responsible sourcing could cause the entire fishing industry to collapse.

Energy

- *Creating competition in the energy sector is vital to sustainability.*
- *More targeted policy and regulation is crucial to ensure that the pace and scale at which renewable technologies are adopted increases.*
- *Technological innovation will enable low-carbon energy and revolutionize the power industry, and data is key to designing the energy system of the future.*
- *Responsibility for meeting Thailand's greenhouse gas emissions reduction targets falls at the feet of energy companies – as well as the state.*
- *The energy industry is not just a major contributor to climate change – over the coming decades, it also stands to be heavily impacted by it.*

Following the historic Paris Climate Accord, Thailand joined the global community in pledging to reduce its greenhouse gas (GHG) emissions. Its nationally determined contribution, or NDC, aims for a 20-percent cut from the projected business-as-usual level by 2030 and leaves the door open for a 25-percent cut should "adequate and enhanced access to technology development and transfer, financial resources, and capacity building support" be in place.

Meeting the NDC targets and addressing longer term challenges will, undoubtedly, require strong action from the energy business sector. According to a joint scenario study by the Tokyo-based APEC Energy Research Center and King Mongkut's University of Technology Thonburi, deep cuts in Thailand's energy-related CO_2 emissions are possible. But that calls for a significant de-carbonization of the power and transportation sectors – which together account for almost 70 percent of GHG emissions in the country – and a greater uptake of energy efficient and renewable energy technologies than current plans.

The good news is that the energy business sector has ample scope and several tools at its disposal for adopting sustainable business practices, be it appropriate policy interventions, energy efficiency programs, or investments in technology and renewable energy businesses. Already a vibrant and fast-growing renewable energy ecosystem finds companies running biofuel production businesses, profitable solar farm operations, and biopower plants. Such actions will also, in the long run, yield significant cost savings and profits, social benefits such as access to clean energy and job creation, and reputational benefits.

Creating a sustainable energy future

Over 60 percent of Thailand's electricity comes from natural gas power plants. Currently, around a third of this natural gas is imported from Myanmar via pipelines and elsewhere in the form of liquefied natural gas (LNG). This number is projected to increase as natural gas production in the Gulf of Thailand declines. Under the Gas Plan 2015, Thailand will more than quadruple its LNG imports between 2015 and 2030. With such high reliance on natural gas, diversification of the power generation mix is imperative. Policy makers and businesses have taken up the challenge. Thailand has become a regional trailblazer in scaling up renewable energy, specifically for solar and bio-based power plants. Investment in renewable energy is expected to top 40 billion baht in 2017. Under the Alternative Energy Development Plan (AEDP) 2015, the government aims to increase the share of renewable energy in the power generation mix to around 20 percent by 2036.

On the transportation front, biofuel promotion programs were introduced in early 2000 with a range of supportive instruments: fuel mandates, biofuel standards, price differentials, and tax incentives, among others. The supporting policies have helped grow the biofuel industry, particularly during a period of high oil prices, slowing the growth of petroleum imports. Many investors and companies have benefited from early government support. A case in point is Mitr Phol Group, a major biopower and bioethanol producer (see *Case Study*, page 96). PTT Global Chemical, a subsidiary of PTT Group, produces methyl ester (B100) for making palm-based biodiesel (see *Case Study*, page 209). As with power generation, the AEDP has set a goal to increase the share of ethanol consumption to 32 percent by 2036.

Efforts must continue unabated. Energy businesses can support the transition to a low (if not net-zero) carbon energy system through a number of actions:

- Improving energy/resource efficiency and energy conservation across the value chain, such as through demand-side management. The Energy Efficiency Plan (EEP 2015) sets a target for reducing energy intensity (energy consumed per GDP) by 30 percent by 2036 (baseline 2010).

- Ramping up efforts to achieve a substantially higher share of renewable energy, and making a sustainable business case for investments in lower-carbon alternatives that are either not yet cost-competitive or linked to immature technology.

- Investing in R&D to prepare for disruptive technologies that could change the energy landscape and business models.

Solar is the most plentiful form of renewable energy in Thailand today.

- Supporting policies that foster a competitive energy market.

These actions come with several key challenges, namely: an inadequate policy and regulatory framework; the need to create a conducive environment for innovation and technology; and multi-stakeholder engagement and good governance.

A favorable regulatory framework

Despite a dramatic decline in the cost of renewable technologies, many are still not as competitive as their conventional counterparts. To overcome this economic barrier to their widespread deployment, a long-term vision and support strategy are required to promote large-scale investments in them. Experiences in Thailand and elsewhere have shown that targeted policy action is crucial.

"Policy and regulatory certainty is the most desirable impetus for scaled low-carbon technology investment," says Juergen Bender, a power sector consultant with extensive international and Thai experience.

The Thai Energy Conservation Promotion Act (1992) and subsequent regulations provided some degree of certainty, though there have been uncertain periods and there exists much room for improvement. The most notable regulatory framework to date is provided by Power Purchase Agreements (PPA), which support grid-connected Small Power Producers (SPPs) and Very Small Power Producers (VSPPs).

> *"A lot of negative aspects of solar or renewable energy occur because of misguided policy implementation."*

Since its inception, the PPA has evolved from offering adders that favored different types of renewable generators to shifting in 2013 to feed-in-tariffs (FiT) for VSPPs and distributed solar systems. A FiT of 6.01–6.85 baht/kWh was offered to solar rooftop projects depending on the system size, and a time-tiered FiT to community-scale projects. Following revisions, renewable energy policy is currently moving toward competitive bidding. A scheme for Small Power Producers hybrid (or SPP hybrid) was further announced in 2017 to support the development of renewable projects utilizing multiple fuels.

However, these instruments may not necessarily coalesce to create a favorable policy environment for renewable technologies just yet (see *The Market Realities of Renewable Energies*, page 203). According to Dr Piyasvasti Amranand, former Minister of Energy and chairman of PTT Group, "A lot of negative aspects of solar or renewable energy occur because of misguided policy implementation."

He explains: "I initiated the policy to provide a high power purchase tariff from these renewable energy facilities ten years ago, at the time when the cost was a lot higher, to stimulate production and supply of renewable energy. Once the cost came down, the tariff should have been reduced. But instead the government kept the tariff at high levels, and imposed what they called targets for solar and wind energy. It was pretty clear from the start that these were really meant to be quotas."

INNOVATION THE ECO-CURE INDUSTRIAL WATER SYSTEM

PTT's Gas Separation Plant processes natural gas into various hydrocarbons, including LPG. Its steam production system requires continuous boiler blowdown, a process whereby water is intentionally wasted to avoid concentration of impurities, causing major energy loss. An optimum blowdown rate depends on the purity of the boiler feedwater.

"So we came up with an innovative, integrative design incorporating a state-of-the-art demineralized water processing unit to produce ultra-high purity water with minimal use of chemicals," says Teerapat Rattanasuwan, a senior process engineer at the plant, and winner of the Petroleum Institute of Thailand (PTIT) Innovation Award 2017–2018. Codenamed 'Eco-Cure,' the system reduces the blowdown rate by up to 30 percent and chemical usage by 99.5 percent. In its first-year pilot, the plant saved about US$770,000 in energy, chemicals, water, and operating costs. The investment was recouped in under three and a half years. When Eco-Cure is applied across PTT Group, it will deliver annual savings of US$50 million in energy and US$110 million in operating costs, plus reductions in chemical consumption and contaminated wastewater of 53,000 tons and 6.5 million cubic meters, respectively.

INDUSTRY SNAPSHOT

TOTAL PRIMARY COMMERCIAL ENERGY DEMAND AND SUPPLY

Total primary commercial energy consumption:

2,093 thousand barrels

per day of crude oil equivalent (kboepd)

Total consumption cost:

1,949 billion baht

(based on final energy)

43%
38%
2% 17%

- Natural gas
- Coal and lignite
- Oil
- Hydro and electricity

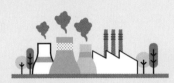

Domestic primary energy production met less than 50% of Thailand's needs, delivering just 1,018 kboepd.

Net imports for 2016 totaled 1,275 kboepd.

Source: Energy Policy and Planning Office (2016)

ELECTRICITY GENERATION

Thailand's total installed power capacity stood at 41,903 MW as of July 2017.

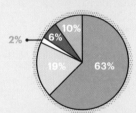

2%
10%
6%
19% 63%

Share of Capacity:
(Total grid-connected electricity generation: 199,567 GWh)

- natural gas
- coal
- hydro and oil
- renewable energy
- imported

Renewable energy also contributed to off-grid generation for residential use and in agro-industrial plants.

Source: Energy Policy and Planning Office (2016)

FINAL ENERGY CONSUMPTION BY SECTOR

Total final energy consumption in Thailand in 2017 (July): 1,442 kboepd

Breakdown by sector:

 40% Transport

 36% Industry

 14% Residential

 7% Commercial

 3% Agriculture and others

Source: Department of Alternative Energy Development and Efficiency (Jan-Feb 2017)

EMISSIONS

The power and transportation sectors account for almost 70% of GHG emissions.

Total energy-related CO_2 emissions by sector:

 38% Power generation

28% Transport

 26% Industry

8% Other

In a BAU scenario, Thailand's total GHG emissions are projected to reach 555 million tons CO_2 equivalent by 2030.

A reduction of 111 million tons would be required for Thailand to meet its NDC pledge to cut CO_2 emissions by 20% by 2030.

Source: Energy Policy and Planning Office (2016)

With some renewable energy costs having come down such that they could be sustainable on their own, it should have been possible to free the market and introduce competitive bidding earlier for some renewable energy technologies. In his view, "The Energy Ministry was out of date, out of touch with the changes in technology and the costs....On the issue of the price, they can and should have been able to do better. We should have gotten more renewable energy at lower prices."

Over the long term, carbon emission trading schemes (ETS) will become a valuable regulatory tool for reducing GHG emissions cost effectively, in addition to fostering a competitive market. As a step towards mandatory ETS, Thailand is currently participating in the World Bank-sponsored Partnership for Market Readiness Program (PMR), and the Thailand Greenhouse Gas Management Organization (TGO) has been piloting the Thailand Voluntary ETS (Thailand V-ETS).

Further factoring into these efforts is the Energy Performance Certificate Scheme (EPC), a voluntary target-and-trade program for energy-intensive factories, commercial buildings, and thermal power plants. The Electricity Generating Authority of Thailand (EGAT), as one example, has earned significant carbon credits through several of its power plant efficiency improvement projects.

For SMEs, the government's role is even more essential. "As a biogas producer, my company has benefited from a range of support schemes by the Ministry of Energy and Ministry of Science and Technology: from grants, to soft loans, to technical assistance," says Somchai Nitikanchana of SPM Farm, which generates three megawatts of electric power from the wastewater of his 250,000-head pig farm.

Innovation & technology

Technological innovation underpins the transition to sustainable low-carbon energy. Although many low-carbon technologies are already available, they are at different stages of development and levels of maturity, and some are far from market-ready.

On one hand, the costs of technologies like solar have come down enough for them to proceed independently of government incentives. Other emerging technologies, by contrast, still require policy and regulatory support to develop their respective industries. For instance, technologies for the processing or conversion of some untapped or underutilized biomass resources, such as rice straw and sugarcane leaves and trash, have yet to be developed or localized. Electric vehicles are not yet competitive with internal combustion engines and continue to rely on government support for mass adoption. Technologies to remove fossil-fuel carbon

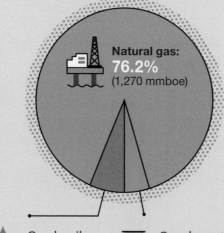

THAILAND'S ENERGY RESERVES

Proven petroleum reserves:
1,666 million barrels of crude oil equivalent (mmboe)

Natural gas:
76.2%
(1,270 mmboe)

Crude oil:
13.1%
(219 mmboe)

Condensate:
10.7%
(178 mmboe)

At the current rate of production (2015), natural gas, crude oil, and condensate reserves could be depleted in 5, 4, and 5 years, respectively. If probable reserves are taken into account, they could be depleted in 9, 7, and 10 years, respectively.

Source: Department of Mineral Fuels (2015)

THE MARKET REALITIES OF RENEWABLE ENERGY

Over the past ten years, the amount of installed renewable energy has grown exponentially. Solar and wind have benefited from policy support, rapid learning of project developers, and technology improvements. All of this has resulted in lower costs of renewable energy, to the point that in many cases they can directly compete with conventional power plants.

A study by Mercator Research Institute on Global Commons and Climate Change found that official models that forecast energy growth, such as the International Energy Agency's (IEA) World Energy Outlook, have consistently underestimated the growth of solar but overestimated the potential for capital intensive low-carbon technologies, such as carbon capture and storage (CCS), and nuclear power.

Indeed, the United Nations' SDG Industry Matrix recommends that companies "invest in non-renewable, low-carbon energy sources, such as nuclear, where appropriate and considered necessary to bridge the transition to a substantially higher share of renewable energy." Thailand's current Power Development Plan

(2015-2036) includes this controversial nuclear power option. However, ambiguity surrounding construction cost overruns, financial risks, and public acceptance is likely to hold it back.

With its past success in developing solar projects, Thailand has tripled its goal of installed solar capacity from 2GW by 2030 to 6GW by 2036. But as we have seen globally, solar has far exceeded policy makers and planners' forecasts due to rapidly declining costs and its low environmental footprint. There is a case to be made for freeing up the market to allow market dynamics to determine capacity generation mix based on current economics and expected long-term marginal costs, where renewables have the long-term cost advantage.

Currently, plans for power generation development in Thailand are dictated by government-set targets, which effectively work as quotas. This implies that businesses looking to invest in solar must compete against other solar developers but not against conventional sources such as coal, natural gas, or large-scale hydropower. Moreover, tariffs are set by the regulator, which provide certainty for businesses, but prices have not adjusted to the rapid decline in the price of solar PV systems or the fall in construction costs that come from experience associated with multiple project developments.

An economics-based long-term forecast conducted by Bloomberg New Energy Finance (BNEF), an energy research firm, forecasts that the renewable energy share in Thailand can be a lot more ambitious than the 30 percent set out in the Alternative Energy Development Plan. In fact, various studies indicate that Thailand's solar power potential ranges from 23–34GW, far exceeding the 6GW target. Under BNEF's market driven forecast, Thailand can receive up to 40 percent of its electricity from renewable sources, thereby reducing electricity imports from neighboring countries as well as LNG from overseas.

In line with global power market development, competition will lead to the development of resources with the most favorable economics. Thailand should take note of the market realities for renewables and continued technological improvements. A power generation portfolio with a high mix of renewables and healthy competition will ensure long-term energy security and sustainability.

CASE STUDY CLP's Long-term Decarbonization Strategy

THE CHALLENGE: CLP Holdings operates a diverse portfolio of energy generating assets based on fossil and non-fossil fuels across the Asia-Pacific region, including Thailand. With large, locked-in carbon-emitting generating assets, CLP has come under increasing pressure to invest in potentially more expensive alternatives while taking care of their shareholders' business interests.

THE SOLUTION: CLP acted early to convince its stakeholders to commit to a long-term decarbonizing strategy. Back in 2004, CLP already set a renewable energy target of 5 percent by 2010, which was successfully met and later boosted to 20 percent by 2020. In its 2016 Sustainability Report, CLP chairman Sir Michael Kadoorie and chief executive officer

Richard Lancaster wrote: "We look forward to working together with governments, businesses and civil society to create new capabilities and solutions needed to achieve a net-zero carbon future." CLP aims to reduce its carbon intensity by 75 percent by 2050 compared to 2007 levels – the cornerstone of its Climate Vision 2050. In 2015, CLP also developed a set of Sustainability Principles that touches on all 17 SDGs, and prioritized the six most relevant to its business.

THE BENEFITS: Currently CLP's portfolio comprises 18,608 megawatts of equity generating capacity, about 17 percent of which is being fueled by renewable energy.

One example that delivers on multiple SDGs is CLP's 63-megawatt joint-venture solar project in Thailand. The Asian Development Bank, which played an assistive role, noted that the project's ambitious CSR program helped transform poor farmlands surrounding the project site into highly efficient and productive organic farms that have become role models. Solar panels are powering electric irrigation pumps, and being donated to local schools and communities.

CASE STUDY EGAT Transforms the Energy-efficient Appliances Market

Label No. 5 rates the energy-efficiency of appliances, with "5" indicating high efficiency.

THE CHALLENGE: Thailand's electricity demand grows typically at the same rate as GDP. Roughly 1,000 megawatts of new capacity is needed each year. The Electricity Generating Authority of Thailand (EGAT), as a major state-owned utility, is obliged to help electricity consumers improve energy efficiency and save energy to reduce demand and public investment.

"Despite being low-hanging fruit, convincing consumers to switch to higher efficiency appliances, such as light bulbs and air conditioners, is never an easy task, as higher efficiency products are more expensive," says Jirasak Mantharngkul,

director of EGAT's Demand Side Management and Planning Division.

THE SOLUTION: In compliance with a government directive, EGAT piloted a Demand Side Management program targeting the residential, commercial and industry sectors. A Global Environment Fund grant and a JBIC loan drove the program from 1993 to 2000, after which EGAT provided it own fund of US$10 million per year. The initial international funding was crucial for infrastructure investment and subsidies to consumers. The cornerstone of the program is Label No. 5, a voluntary energy-efficiency labeling scheme.

THE BENEFITS: To date, 25 products have been labeled. More than 26 million megawatt-hours of electricity, 14 million tons of CO_2, and over 4,000 megawatts of peak demand (equivalent to seven 600-megawatt-sized fossil plants) saved.

The World Bank has hailed the program for changing consumer behavior, transforming the residential appliances market, and strengthening the competitiveness of appliance manufacturers in domestic and international markets. The program has also enhanced EGAT's corporate image and assisted the utility in planning and cost avoidance in system expansion.

MITIGATING CLIMATE CHANGE–RELATED RISKS

The energy industry is not only a major contributor to climate change, but also a sector that climate change will disrupt. Indeed, the Intergovernmental Panel on Climate Change (IPCC) warned that in the coming decades, the sector will be impacted by global warming on many levels.

As global temperatures climb, extreme weather events increase their frequency and severity, and precipitation patterns shift, energy production and delivery will be impacted. Severe drought and water shortages will have strong impacts to thermal power plants such as coal, natural gas, and nuclear, which demand large amounts of water for cooling. Recent storms have become more powerful, downing powerlines, blowing out transformers, and causing extensive financial damage to power utilities.

To mitigate these risks, the energy industry will need to consider how best to adapt. Though, as most energy companies have "locked-in" assets that will continue to emit CO_2 for many years, that might prove easier said than done.

Leading power generation companies in Thailand have already imposed targets for increasing renewable energy assets in their portfolios. For example, Banpu Power has set a target to have renewable energy contribute 20 percent of their power generation portfolio by 2025. Ratchaburi Electricity Generating Holding, one of the largest generators in the country, has set a target to reach a 20 percent share of renewables by 2023. Meanwhile, EGCO Group, which currently has over 20 percent renewable energy, is expected to increase that share to 30 percent by 2026. The Electricity Generating Authority of Thailand, the state-owned power utility, has announced it would strive to cut 12 million tons of CO_2 equivalent by 2030.

emissions through carbon capture and storage (CCS) also remain far off. In addition to economic challenges, many low-carbon technologies must overcome technical issues. The main barrier for renewable energy technologies is that they are not dispatchable, meaning that grid operators cannot request when and how much electricity they want from these sources. Unlike power plants that can be turned on and off, renewable energies are intermittent and cannot be relied on 24 hours a day.

Solving the intermittency problem of renewables presents a large opportunity for businesses in Thailand. Currently, battery technology that can store large amounts of electricity is not commercially viable due to technical and financial constraints. But, as mentioned earlier, that technology is rapidly improving and prices have come down substantially. Various Thai companies, including PTT Group, EGCO, and Energy Absolute, are already investing in batteries to ensure that they do not fall behind on this trend. Bangchak Corporation has also bet on battery technology by investing in lithium mines, as lithium is a major component in a lot of battery technology.

But adding too much renewable energy too quickly could destabilize the electricity grid, because it has not been designed to accommodate a large penetration of intermittent power sources. Therefore, investment in grid infrastructure to make it "smarter" is crucial to decarbonizing the power industry. In this vein, the Ministry of

Investment in grid infrastructure to make it "smarter" is crucial to decarbonizing the power industry.

Energy recently introduced a 20-year Smart Grid Master Plan. Meanwhile, all three of Thailand's utilities entities – EGAT, the Provincial Electricity Authority, and the Metropolitan Electricity Authority – have introduced smart grid pilot projects in selected areas, focusing initially on the installation of smart meters. These actions represent a small yet important step forward.

What is essential over the longer term is an effective innovation policy. Thailand has a lot of catching up to do both in terms of R&D investment and support measures that foster

A banner in Krabi province signals local opposition to a proposed coal-fired power plant.

An additional sustainable energy business example is PTTGC's innovation strategy, which ranges from in-house R&D to contract research, technology acquisition, transfer, and localization (see *Case Study*, page 209). "Still, more government support is needed when it comes to high-risk, high-impact projects," says Dr Chaya Chandavasu, PTTGC's senior vice president for science and innovation.

And the Thai government has taken some positive initiatives forward. It has set targets to boost R&D expenditure (public and private sectors combined) from 0.48 percent to 1 percent of GDP, provided tax incentives to spur private sector R&D, and introduced special investment privileges for foreign direct investments that involve R&D or technology transfer. It is also working to amend relevant laws so that it becomes possible to directly fund innovation activities in the private sector.

innovation among large corporations and SMEs. This covers everything from research on biofuels, bioplastics, and electric vehicles (EVs), to investments in basic science and technology research skills for the current and future workforce. PTT Group has invested heavily in the Vidyasirimedhi Institute of Science and Technology (VISTEC) and Kamnoetvidya Science Academy School (KVIS) for this very reason.

Multi-stakeholder engagement & governance

Thailand requires a mix of technologies to provide reliable and clean energy for the country. Both renewable and conventional power plants will still need to be built. Working toward a sustainable energy future thus entails that company shareholders recognize growing societal demands for less polluting, less carbon-intensive, and more reliable and affordable energy. Shareholders expecting a reasonable return on their investments ought

---

INNOVATION | **SCG RECOVERS WASTE HEAT FOR ELECTRICITY**

Through its subsidiary Cementhai Energy Conservation Company, SCG has developed a waste heat recovery (WHR) system that transforms waste heat from boilers into steam for electricity generation in its cement plants. As about 20 percent of the heat from discharged gases in the cement production process can be used for energy, SCG's WHR system turns it into a source of renewable power.

The system does not emit harmful pollutants such as sulfur dioxide, nitrous oxide, and carbon that would other-wise be emitted from fossil fuel power plants. The electricity generated from the WHR system replaces more than 25 percent of total electricity purchases, reducing annual electricity costs by approximately 523 million baht. To date, SCG generates 107 megawatts of electricity from its WHR system – installed in 3 different production processes across the Group – reportedly reducing more than 300,000 tons of CO_2 a year.

DR PIYASVASTI AMRANAND, *chairman of PTT Group and former Minister of Energy (2006–2008), discusses his leadership and PTT's role in building a sustainable energy future.*

What are the key differences in your guidance for PTT Group compared to your predecessors?
First, the strategy has changed. Previously it was "Big Long Strong" – totally uninterested in the public's view. Now, we want to be the "Pride and Treasure of Thailand." We need to take account of views of the public and civil society, and whatever we do we want to allow communities to benefit with us.

We look at the benefit of the whole country, and we see that creating competition in the energy sector is vital to sustainability. In the past, PTT often resisted liberalization and competition. But over the past three years we have been pushing for liberalization and supporting the government on this. A lot of policies that came out of the Prayut [Chan-o-cha] government came from us, which I think initially a lot of PTT people were not happy with.

For example, we want to see a competitive oil market. We pushed for the inclusion of state-owned enterprises in the Competition Act. There was resistance from other SOEs but not PTT; PTT's oil business will come under the Competition Act. To prepare for that, we have reduced our share in the wholesale oil market by selling shares in Bangchak Petroleum, SPRC refinery.

The other change which we have seen is we are now operating in quite a different environment. Previously we had high oil prices, and profits went up substantially. Inefficient investments were covered up by large profit

that was being made elsewhere. But the price of oil came down very substantially, and now we have to be efficient and prudent about our investment programs. We went through efficiency improvement efforts, cost cutting, and so on. Now we are quite happy as we seem to be doing very well at a US$50 oil price.

Large-scale corruption was found in one project. We have made it very clear that getting rid of corruption is crucial.

What actions is PTT taking on the Sustainable Development Goals? In particular, goal 7 and 13?
Clean energy and climate change, that's something we have been doing for quite some time. If we don't follow the guidelines, we will not survive in the long run.

The energy sector in Thailand has been quite advanced in implementing policies and measures to reduce GHG emissions long before COP21, and before Thailand was ever interested in global warming. I think the Thai government had totally misplaced the responsibility of climate change negotiations by placing it with the Ministry of Natural Resources and Environment, because the Energy Ministry has been doing this work for a long time. And the biggest impact will be from the energy sector.

At PTT, we have been carrying out measures and investments to reduce GHG emissions for quite some time, maybe not enough in certain areas. Renewable energy is a crucial part of this, and now you don't need government incentives, but simply require clear and transparent rules and regulations. Prices have come down and efficiency has gone up to the extent that renewable energy is sustainable by itself, and that's why PTT has been investing in renewable energy. But not enough, I think, too slow, and that is something PTT will have to put more effort into.

What would be your message to critics of PTT?
It's difficult to convince a certain segment of the population of the truth. People who do not like PTT normally write up all sorts of stories, and when you write up something which is dramatic, it's easy to sell to the general public. You just have to keep repeating the message, and I believe it is working. People understand us a lot more.

THE RISE OF RENEWABLE ENERGY

Since 2007, Thailand has been promoting the development of renewable energy through an adder program that offers alternative energy producers long-term contracts to sell electricity at attractive rates. For example, solar producers are eligible for subsidies of up to 6.85 baht per kilowatt-hour paid out over 25 years. Companies that generate power through biomass, biogas, hydro, wind, waste energy, and solar are all eligible for the program. Production has been steadily on the rise, and the government is moving renewable energy policy towards competitive bidding. As of 2016, Thailand's installed renewable energy generating capacity was at 9,552 MW, and new renewable capacity was at 1,435 MW. The government has set the target to increase renewable energy generation in Thailand to 19,684 MW by 2036.

SOLAR POWER

STATUS AS OF 2017
2,656 MW

TARGET IN 2036
6,000 MW

WIND POWER

STATUS AS OF 2017
628 MW

TARGET IN 2036
3,002 MW

HYDRO POWER

STATUS AS OF 2017
3,089 MW

TARGET IN 2036
3,282 MW

BIOGAS

STATUS AS OF 2017
464 MW

TARGET IN 2036
1,280 MW

WASTE TO POWER

STATUS AS OF 2017
171 MW

TARGET IN 2036
550 MW

BIOMASS

STATUS AS OF 2017
3,005 MW

TARGET IN 2036
5,570 MW

NEW ENERGY
(such as geothermal)

STATUS AS OF 2017
0 ktoe

TARGET IN 2036
10 ktoe

TOTAL

STATUS AS OF 2017	TARGET IN 2036
10,013 MW	19,684 MW

Source: Department of Alternative Energy Development and Efficiency (July 2017)

Working toward a sustainable energy future entails that company shareholders recognize growing societal demands for less polluting, less carbon-intensive, and more reliable and affordable energy.

to be aware of the need to comply with all relevant legislation, and uphold nationally and internationally recognized minimum standards relating to energy efficiency and carbon footprints. Likewise, civil society is demanding a greater say in energy sources and plant siting.

Even at the global level, there is a push to make energy businesses more accountable and to accept sustainability as a business priority on par with profit. In fact, they may come under even more intense scrutiny than other sectors because of the large size of investments involved, their contracts with public agencies and extensive impacts on environmental and social sustainability.

From the regulatory perspective, concerned authorities are setting rules and regulations on company reporting to improve transparency, like the Stock Exchange of Thailand's ESG disclosure requirements through Form 56-1 (see *Reporting and Disclosure*, page 144). Investors, with their control of capital, have growing influence on sustainability investments and are seen backing companies with good ESG practices for long-term returns. The SET's Thailand Sustainability Investment (THSI) initiative responds to this shift, featuring companies with outstanding ESG performance on their sustainability assessment. It is encouraging that out of the 55 companies selected for inclusion in the THSI in 2016, 11 of them, or 20 percent, were energy companies.

Finally, customers, suppliers, and business partners are having a bigger impact as well. As part of their sustainability strategies,

companies must adopt a more holistic view of impacts across their entire value chains – across multiple stakeholder groups.

Managing these sometimes conflicting interests and pressures requires multi-stakeholder engagement, partnerships and collaboration. Only this way can businesses enhance corporate sustainability and strengthen stakeholder relations – while keeping pace with policy developments.

A case that demonstrated tangible benefits of multi-stakeholder engagement is EGAT's demand-side management (DSM) program (see *Case Study*, page 204). Resulting from

CASE STUDY   PTT Global Chemical Reduces Its Reliance on Petroleum

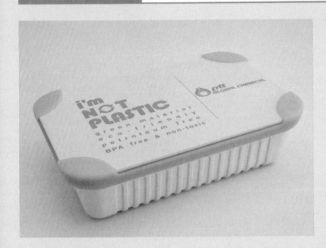

THE SOLUTION: As a company committed to becoming a model for sustainable growth, PTTGC set up a new company dedicated to spearheading green business in 2005. PTT Global Green Chemicals (PTTGGC) focuses on two broad product categories: value added oleochemicals (VAO) from palm oil, and bioplastics/biochemicals from natural feedstock such as sugar, sugarcane, cassava, and corn. Most notable in the VAO group is methyl ester (or B100), which is mixed with diesel to make biodiesel of European biofuels standards.

Many of the products are a direct result of investments in products and process innovation. Out of a total expenditure on research, development and innovation (RDI) of 900 million baht, or 0.26 percent of total revenue in 2016, 32 percent was spent on green business. The acquisition of, or collaboration with, foreign companies with critical technologies is also part of the innovation strategy, particularly in the field of bioplastics.

THE CHALLENGE: PTT Global Chemical's (PTTGC) integrated refinery is one of the most advanced and energy-efficient in the Asia Pacific. However, the company faces increasing local and international pressure to reduce the use of petroleum and petroleum-based products, as customer demands for green chemicals increases. Can the company supply the market at required levels of cost and performance, since not all the technologies are market-ready? Moreover, will it be able to innovate in a field in which it, and the country, is not renowned for?

THE BENEFITS: By the end of 2016, PTTGC's green chemical business reached more than 17 billion baht, or about five percent of total sales revenue. With a quarter share of Thailand's B100 market, PTTGC has made a significant contribution to the government's petroleum fuel substitution drive. Several innovative products with up to 30 percent raw materials and CO_2 savings have already reached the market. As a result, PTTGC has won numerous local and international innovation and sustainability awards, earning the company both financial and reputational benefits.

As battery prices become more affordable in the future, consumers can turn to energy storage.

collaboration with policy makers and appliance manufacturers, the DSM program has effectively changed consumer behavior and transformed the energy-efficient appliance market. Since 1995, DSM has helped save more than 25 billion kilowatt-hours of electricity and avoided more than 4,300 megawatts of installed capacity (roughly equivalent to seven coal-fired power plants). It has now expanded to include the low-carbon, low-cost housing sector.

It is important to note, though, that EGAT has fallen short when it comes to meeting public calls for greater say in decision-making on the building of coal-fired power plants and on compensation to communities affected by its actions.

Moreover, if one considers Thailand's increasing reliance on energy imports from neighboring countries and geopolitically volatile regions, the magnitude of impacts could expand considerably. With economic integration between ASEAN members strengthening, especially Thailand and the Greater Mekong Subregion, public scrutiny will also rise. The main takeaway being that energy businesses should look to minimize sustainability-related impacts beyond our borders as much as within them.

Improved transparency and good governance is critical. Otherwise, the public mistrust of energy companies will continue to haunt future projects.

The future of energy disruption

Solar photovoltaics (PV) have recently become the fastest-growing source of electric power. This is all thanks to the price of solar PV, which has fallen so much that grid parity – whereby the cost of PV-generated electricity is competitive with that of conventional sources – is now a reality in many markets.

In the near future, residential solar PV rooftops in combination with batteries could potentially become transformative. The energy generated by "prosumers" – those who produce and sell as well as consume electricity – is regarded as distributed energy resources (DER). As DER rise, demand on centralized power plants will decline, threatening the revenue of traditional utility businesses which rely on selling power from large power plants and the transmission and distribution of electricity.

Another emerging trend is microgrids: a discrete energy system consisting of DER (including demand management, storage, and generation) and loads capable of operating in parallel with, or independently from, the main power grid. With rapid digitization, especially the rise of the Internet of Things (IoT), microgrids will become smarter, posing direct competition to traditional distribution businesses.

Competition can also be expected from non-traditional players, such as technology service providers and telecom operators. Korea Telecom, for example, is participating in the South Korean government's Jeju island smart grid pilot project along with SKT and LG Telecom, to test smart grid services and solutions for smart homes and buildings, and smart transportation. Additionally, data-related services will enter the market and compete with traditional energy businesses.

"In this scenario, utilities need to transform the role of their distribution business," says Bender. "Many are looking to enhance their

- **Determine your baseline sustainability performance**, such as carbon intensity and other emission factors.

- **Set short- and long-term carbon intensity reduction targets and strategies**, together with subsets such as energy efficiency and renewable energy targets.

- **Identify facilities/areas to improve energy and resource efficiency** by applying cost-effective measures and, wherever possible, best available technology.

- **Evaluate existing portfolios and conduct feasibility studies** for diversifying into a lower-carbon energy mix, particularly deployment of renewables, or fuel switching, such as coal to natural gas, as a medium-term bridging measure.

- **Capitalize on existing support schemes by the government**, whether it is for energy efficiency improvement, investment in renewables, or voluntary emission trading schemes.

- **Formulate aggressive corporate innovation strategies** that will lead to significant energy and resource conservation, performance improvement and cost reduction of low-carbon technologies, high value addition to waste resources, as well as new products or business opportunities.

- **Actively engage and collaborate with stakeholders** to enhance the chances of achieving sustainable business goals, e.g. calling upon relevant government agencies to provide policy and regulatory certainty, and financial institutions to unlock money for climate action.

- **Continuously improve environmental, social and corporate governance (ESG) practices** and transparency in reporting.

- **Prepare for future implementation of mandatory emission trading schemes** by participating in the current voluntary schemes and the design of future schemes.

- **Engage with the Sustainable Development Goals (SDGs)**, where appropriate, to drive large-scale change on sustainability and capture opportunities for value creation. Look to tools such as the SDG Industry Matrix: Energy, Natural Resources and Chemicals.

---

capabilities whereby instead of just planning, building and operating power networks to manage reliability based on their forecasts of customer demand, they are seeking to reinvent a portion of their business model, giving greater prominence to unregulated revenues."

He further states that, "To help manage the inevitable transition, some more advanced grid companies actively engage customers in both their traditional business, e.g. outage apps, and customer-owned tech."

The way forward

Energy businesses in Thailand have become increasingly aware of, and begun acting upon, the commitments expected of them in working toward a sustainable energy future.

The issue is whether they have the will to deepen and scale up their commitments, whether it is carbon-intensity reduction, resource and energy efficiency improvements, or low-carbon and renewables deployment.

Opportunities abound for the sector to invest in sustainable energy, and a strong business case can be made for them. However, there are multiple obstacles ahead. Perhaps defining a common vision and strategy for a sustainable low-carbon energy system at multiple scales – from local community to national and regional, through multi-stakeholder engagement and collaboration – will render the task of finding solutions to all other challenges easier. Success will ultimately depend on the energy business industry's ability to apply creativity and innovation to solving them.

Manufacturing

- *Losing competitiveness within the global marketplace, Thai manufacturers need to reposition themselves and shift from producing low-value components to higher-value products.*

- *As robots take over production lines, basic industry jobs are likely to shrink dramatically over the next 10 to 20 years.*

- *The best chance of sustainable growth may lie in the country's natural and agricultural resources, geographical location, and singular characteristics.*

- *As well as getting better at making things, manufacturers need to find new things to make.*

The manufacturing industry is by far the biggest sector in Thailand, accounting for well over a third of GDP value added and nearly nine out of every ten dollars the country earns from exports. Machinery and transport and 'other manufacturing' (including wood, paper, petroleum, basic metals and minerals, and fabricated metal products) are the biggest segments in a diverse sector fueled by natural resources and driven by foreign investment. An important element of this performance is the country's SME sector, which accounts for over a third of GDP, contributes more than a quarter of all export earnings, and provides eight out of ten jobs.

But performance has been declining. In the decades prior to the Asian Financial Crisis, manufacturing helped Thailand's economy grow at a rapid rate – often at or above 10 percent, with labor productivity increasing at much the same rate. By contrast, between 2005 and 2015, Thailand's economic growth averaged only 3.3 percent and labor productivity about 2.6 percent. Meanwhile, industry's share of GDP value added has slipped from a high of 40 percent to around 35 percent.

Thus the force that turned Thailand from a low-income, mostly agricultural and rural economy into a middle-income industrialized one has faltered. It is imperative that it finds a sustainable way back to growth – and forward to a new and balanced prosperity. Initiatives such as Thailand 4.0 and so-called 'green industry' and 'eco-industrial towns' provide a modernized playing field. Now business needs to provide more suitable players.

In a recent report on Thailand, the World Bank argues that Thai industry needs to undertake more complex functions such as design, research and development, and branding, "moving from the export of low-value parts and components to higher-value products and services and also to final manufactures."

The Asian Development Bank, in a landmark report that analyzes Thailand's manufacturing predicament, concludes: "The technology foreign companies provided [during the period of strong manufacturing growth] has not spilled over to domestic firms, while the domestic business community has invested relatively less in innovation. Research and development (R&D) is weak, with limited patenting activity."

Embracing sustainable manufacturing

Businesses that used to regard the word 'sustainable' as implying an unwelcome brake on profit are now realizing that this is the only viable path to long-term profitability. This means making products in ways that keep environmental harm to a minimum, don't overuse or waste natural resources, don't hurt those who make them or those who buy them – and are economically viable in the long term.

There is no more telling an example of what cannot continue than the country's most economically transformative – but environmentally notorious – estate, Map Ta Phut on the Eastern Seaboard. Manufacturing businesses that hope to take advantage of the incentives contained in government plans for several new industrial zones cannot ignore its lessons. It is not enough that new zones of this nature are being labeled 'eco-this' and 'green-that.' The businesses that become established there will themselves have to pay the kind of attention to environmental considerations that many in Map Ta Phut failed to do. Either that, or they risk condemnation by national and global consumer organizations and other stakeholders, among them Thailand's courts, and could be forced to play catch-up at great financial and reputational expense.

This is the meaning of 'future-proofing' – protecting companies' balance sheets from possible litigation and new environmental regulations that might include high legal and remedial costs, damages and fines. And it applies to the price of funding as well: all over the world more and more asset managers are now requiring companies to provide global environmental, social, and governance (ESG) metrics before they will invest in them.

Alan Laubsch, director of Natural Capital Markets for Lykke Corp, a fintech company, puts it like this: "Instinctively, companies don't like to have to spend money unless it is absolutely necessary. But we now live in a world in which everyone knows everything. Assume there is a CCTV camera in your factory streaming to the Internet and everyone sees everything. Run your business that way….Right

Map Ta Phut in Rayong province is the country's largest industrial estate.

"Assume there is a CCTV camera in your factory streaming to the internet and everyone sees everything. Run your business that way... Right now is the time to come clean."

now is the time to come clean. You could wait until the spotlight turns on you and shames you...or you could step in front of it and say, 'Hey, you know what, we represent the future and not the past and our net costs are going to be stable in the long run.' Any smart businessman will recognize that this is just good business."

That future is made up of the advantages and opportunities that companies will enjoy as a result of putting progressive and sustainable manufacturing procedures at the heart of their operational goals.

The benefits are manifold. There is now an identifiable green space in which technology entrepreneurs and consumers are separately and jointly generating a green marketplace worth trillions of dollars, one in which retailers are demanding that their suppliers respond to the needs of green consumers. Doing so improves the reputations of all concerned and plays a part in attracting young workers who value sustainability in both the workplace and in the products and services they help provide.

The past was less of a miracle than it might have seemed at the time. Most Thai firms that participated in the great industrialization of the economy were suppliers of low industrial sophistication.

This is not just – or even mostly – about greener manufacturing. The challenges are much greater. The pace of robot deployment globally is so great that basic industry jobs are likely to shrink dramatically over the next 10 to 20 years, not just in Thailand but everywhere. That doesn't necessarily mean there will be fewer jobs – there are more likely to be new jobs for people with the skills to do what the robots can't. A worldwide study of the outlook for jobs in the world of greater automation concluded that: "Creativity, emotional intelligence and cognitive flexibility are skills that will tap human potential and allow people to augment robots, rather than be replaced by them."

This means the future is going to have to be very different. Even the past was less of a miracle than it might have seemed at the time. Most Thai firms that participated in the great industrialization of the country's economy were suppliers of low industrial sophistication. Even the much-cited production of hard disk drives (HDDs) relied on imports for the high-value part. What sophistication there was has tapered off since the mid-2000s, largely because of competition from China, and declined between 2008 and 2013, according to the ADB report. In any case, much of it was what the report calls 'technological lending' rather than transfer. This can be very easily 'unlent' as the global supply chain shifts with technology and new competition.

Thailand is still the world's top producer and exporter of rubber.

Robot deployment is likely to displace basic industry jobs.

INDUSTRY SNAPSHOT

Manufacturing accounts for

over **30%** of Thailand's US$395 billion GDP and employs **6.2 million people**.

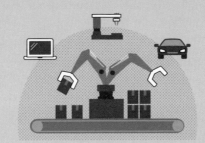

Thailand is **the world's 16th largest manufacturer of goods** and **the 24th largest by export volume**.

Thailand **exported goods** worth **US$222** billion **in 2016** with electronics, machinery, and vehicles accounting for **over 40% of all exports**.

The share of CO_2 emissions from manufacturing and construction (as a percentage of total fuel combustion) in Thailand has declined

from **24%** 2006 to around **21%** 2014

Thailand invests just 0.2% of GDP in R&D.

Thailand produces **approximately** **100,000 graduates**

in **engineering**   **technology**   **science** every year.

GREEN MANUFACTURING

More than **13,000** **factories in 30 key industries** had joined the Ministry of Industry's Green Industry Program as of 2016.

ISO 14001 Some **3,051** **certificates** have been issued to Thai companies for their implementation of environmental impact management systems under **the ISO 14001 standard**.

Thailand can't win this race, neither the one down (offering lower cost production) or the one up (developing cutting-edge technology). That's because its poorer neighbors are in the down game and the up game is impossibly difficult, given how far ahead such countries as Japan, Korea, and Singapore are; and how fast China is catching up to the kingdom.

> **There is a way out. It is to innovate around those things that might be called 'Very Thai.'**

That may sound bleak, but there is a way out. It is to innovate around those things that might be called 'Very Thai' – the country's abundant natural and agricultural resources, including solar energy potential, its geographical location, its digital mobile and logistical connectivity, its relatively high ranking in automobile and electronics manufacturing, its leading edge in medicine and health tourism, and its multi-faceted reputation for welcoming the world.

For example, Thailand grows a lot of rubber trees. When they've stopped producing latex, the trees are usually burned. A toy

manufacturer based in the rubber-growing province of Trang was set up 30 years ago to use the wood from the exhausted rubber trees to make toys (see *Case Study*, page 220).

Another example is the world-beating innovation of biodegradable plastics made from locally available sugarcane feedstock. As the Board of Investment (BOI) said in highlighting this very Thai advance, "Instead of ending up buried for centuries in landfills or washing out to sea, Thai bioplastic containers crumble to worm food in just five weeks." Indeed, the Thai government has made bioplastics a priority area for innovation and growth that opens a wealth of opportunities in a world with an ever-growing demand for alternatives to products made from non-renewable resources. Another company has used bamboo fiber (industrial waste from chopstick production) and tapioca flour to produce a bio-degradable material used in the making of plates, bowls, and other utensils.

An example in a different sector, highlighted by Kasikorn Research, involves Thailand's hard disk drives (HDDs), demand for which is declining in the consumer electronics market. The way forward is to expand its output of solid state hybrid drives (SSHDs) and to respond more robustly to the growing

INNOVATION — THE KALUNDBORG SYMBIOSIS

The Danish industrial town of Kalundborg has lent its name to an environmental policy that might be referred to as "one man's waste is another's treasure." It developed over many years, beginning as cooperation between an oil company and the local municipality for the supply of water. By 1972 it grew into the world's first fully functioning industrial symbiotic relationship (mutually beneficial interaction) that eventually involved around 30 exchanges of water, energy, and by-products

between the municipality and eight other companies.

The process involves the buying and selling of materials or waste streams between companies so that one's waste becomes another's raw material. In Kalundborg, the products traded include steam, ash, gas, heat, sludge, and others that can be physically transported from one company to another. While the environmental benefits of the cooperation are well documented,

the primary incentives for companies to participate in this network stem from economic gains – in the form of resource or monetary savings.

The Kalundborg Symbiosis has been internationally recognized as a role model for industrial environmental sustainability. A critical challenge now is to move the symbiosis away from its fossil fuel dependencies and towards 100% renewable energy. Indeed, the concept has great potential for Thailand's eco-industrial zones.

DR SOMKIAT TANGKITVANICH *is the president of the Thailand Development Research Institute and a leading policy expert in the areas of trade and investment, innovation, education, and information and communications technology.*

Over the past decade or so, Thailand's industrial sector has faltered. What are the main reasons for this slowdown, both global and domestic, and what needs to be done to revitalize the sector?
The lack of innovation is a big problem. Except for a few large companies, most companies in Thailand invest too little in R&D, product design, marketing and branding. Also, public investment in R&D has produced very few commercially-viable results as it is mainly supply-driven.

What role can sustainable development trends such as lean manufacturing play?
Lean production helps increase productivity in Thai manufacturing companies by reducing waste, and increasing labor and capital productivity. Lean production is necessary but not sufficient to lead Thailand to a high-income country status because the increased value added would be too low and would be extracted away by other players, especially large buyers of products made by Thai firms.

Can Thailand draw on the electronics manufacturing base it has built up to move forward to higher value-added electronics and digital technology related products and services? If so, what needs to be done to achieve this?
Thailand 4.0 is a good concept to raise awareness of Thai firms to climb up the value chain. However, it needs effective accompanying programs and projects to help Thai firms to increase their productivity. Attracting foreign direct investment alone without creating linkages between multinational companies and the local economy would not help much in the long run. The electronics and IT sectors are not well positioned to make a big leap forward due to the lack of a skilled workforce.

Many observers of Thailand's economy argue that vocational and on-the-job training is perhaps even more important than broad-based advances in the education system. Do you agree?
Vocational and on-the-job training are "quick wins" because they equip students with practical skills and help link education institutes with workplaces. However, broad-based reform of the education system is unavoidable if Thailand is to equip its students with 21st-century skills.

What are the main benefits that Thai companies will reap by pursuing sustainable strategies?
Pursuing sustainable strategies through lean production helps Thai firms to reduce costs and waste. It is a first step for upgrading. Without such efforts, they would not be able to compete in the global marketplace.

A worker makes silk thread at a traditional workshop in Bangkok.

demand for more HDDs in the enterprise server and online service markets associated with the world of cloud computing and the Internet of Things, rather than the consumer electronics market.

Other 'Very Thai' innovations include a technology that reduces the sugar content in natural juices; a renewable energy company that wants to compete with Elon Musk in lithium ion battery production; and an agri-tech company that seeks to support Thai fruit exporters through online logistical services that save money on transport-related waste.

To succeed in these and other ventures, Thai businesses need to embrace an international mindset, particularly in light of greater inter-regional trade and investment promoted by the AEC and other cross-border agreements, including China's far-reaching Belt and Road initiative. That means they must look to expand abroad more, including through acquisition, and by recruiting global talent and attracting

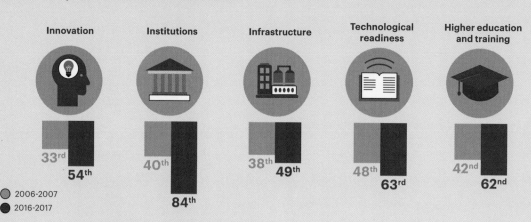

A LOST DECADE

Thailand's Doing Business ranking has slipped in recent years, falling from #18 in 2014 (out of 175 countries) to #46 in 2017 (out of 190 countries). In the 2016–2017 Global Competitiveness Report published by the World Economic Forum, Thailand ranked 34th among 138 nations. However, in key areas that impact the manufacturing sector, **Thailand has experienced a sharp decline in its performance from a decade earlier**.

Innovation	Institutions	Infrastructure	Technological readiness	Higher education and training
33rd / 54th	40th / 84th	38th / 49th	48th / 63rd	42nd / 62nd

● 2006-2007
● 2016-2017

Sources: World Bank's Doing Business Report, 2014; World Bank's Doing Business Report 2017; Global Competitiveness Report, 2006–2007; Global Competitiveness Report, 2016–2017

CASE STUDY | Silicon Craft Trains World-class Computer Chip Engineers

THE CHALLENGE: The real value added in the electronics industry lies in the design of integrated circuits (IC) or 'chips' – the brain inside most digital products. The clever bit is done by electronics engineers, after which the production can be done by semi-skilled workers who follow the blueprint given to them. While Thailand has been one of the world's leading producers of electronics parts, the sector is almost all contract manufacturing of sophisticated products designed by multinational companies. Thailand is the factory, a cost center whose mandate is higher volume and lower cost. If Thailand is to compete in the world, it has to do more of the designing.

THE SOLUTION: The country's only wholly Thai-owned and -run chip design company, Silicon Craft (SC) was founded in 2002 by Manop Thamsirianunt, who had worked as an IC designer for 15 years in the US before returning to Thailand in 2001. The company's CEO, Prong Kongsubto, worked in contract manufacturing both in the US and Thailand before realizing that if Thailand was going to seize the opportunities that its famed role in the electronics sector offered, it needed an innovative company drawing on the cream of Thailand's engineering talent. So he joined Manop, now MD, in 2014.

To find and keep the designers they need, SC has a three-to-five-year horizon. They identify the brightest students at the second-year undergraduate level in the country's university engineering departments. They run seven-day camps at which the students are invited to play with the company's expensive, licensed design technology that they would otherwise never have an opportunity to command. The students move from there to internships, and SC sends some of the brightest to, say, Singapore for work experience. When they graduate, a significant number come and work for

Training talent is an important part of Silicon Craft's business model.

SC, where training continues throughout their employment. "We have not sat back and left it to government to solve our problems," says Prong.

SC's focus is mostly on 'radio frequency identification' and 'near field communications' technology, which allows contactless recognition of and exchanges with objects, animals, or people. Their chips are used in products and devices in the biomedical, Internet of Things, toys, animal identification and tracking, and automotive industries.

THE BENEFITS: SC has won many global customers and runs a representative office in China. It is working toward a stock market listing to raise funds to pay for intellectual property rights and training. The road has been long and hard, but the rewards have been both financial and personal, including the satisfaction of knowing that Thailand has the talent and the capacity to design its own future, as well as its own chips.

Innovation has been hardwired into chip design company Silicon Craft from day one.

CASE STUDY | PlanToys Stays Competitive with a Long-term Game Plan

THE CHALLENGE: Wooden toy maker Plan Creations Company was founded in 1981 in the rubber-producing province of Trang in southern Thailand. At the time, the intention was altruistic and inspired by environmental principles based on the recycling of rubber trees that had ceased yielding latex and were normally just burned. The reward was business success. At the time, China was still a small player in manufactured products and the Internet did not exist, but times have changed.

THE SOLUTION: Not a company to rest on its laurels, PlanToys has maintained competitiveness through differentiation. It is not difficult for others to make similar wooden products. There is no complicated technology involved. So the company concentrated on design and innovation. The most important of these was the development over five years of 'PlanWood' – made from recycling sawdust from the company's existing production process. The new material proved even more durable and cut costs by an enormous 30 percent in its first year of operation, making it possible to provide finished goods at 20-percent lower prices. This far-reaching innovation came out of the company's policy of having a sustainable mindset which it says leads to "sustainable ideas and solutions."

The company has also become more responsive to consumer tastes (including color preferences), which change more quickly these days than ever. That has meant adapting production to minimize waste and unused inventory, shifting to 'just-in-time' operating and quicker delivery. Related to this is the introduction of automation, including more robotic systems.

PlanToys has focused on design and innovation.

While this has meant fewer jobs, it has been managed through natural attrition (around five people leave each month and are not replaced) rather than forced layoffs. Pure automation is in the company's next two-year plan, says Kosin Virapornsawan, Plan Creations' managing director.

The third area of innovation the company has embarked upon is "how we do business," says Kosin. "Online is the future," he says, and that means working more closely with retailers and adapting in other ways, including packaging, which is different for in-store and parcel delivery.

THE BENEFITS: Profitability underpins everything else, and remaining competitive underpins profitability. "Even though we are a company based on sustainability, caring about people and the environment, the first thing we have to do to remain sustainable is to make profit," says Kosin. "And if you do not change internally, how are you going to make profit? You cannot keep raising the price of what you sell."

By innovating and saving, such as with the development of PlanWood, PlanToys can "save money and pass on the benefit to the customer," he adds.

Some toys are made of 'PlanWood' – a material made from recycled sawdust.

know-how, technology, brand recognition and intellectual property.

Thailand already has an enviable open-mindedness. But its businesses need to work harder on turning that into greater fluency in foreign languages and a willingness to lead rather than be led, as well as a willingness to transform corporate culture and governance away from hierarchy and toward meritocracy.

Manufacturing for the future

Is Thailand up to this? Officially, yes. According to the ADB report, "Over the past several years various governments have announced initiatives and development goals designed to meet these challenges. It has established a system of innovation through science parks, research grants, and public research institutions covering areas ranging from metallurgy and food processing to nanotechnology and biotechnology, but the impact of these efforts is yet to be seen." This last remark is a common lament about many of the government's industry initiatives taken over the past decade or more.

As part of the 11th National Economic and Social Development Plan, the Ministry of Industry has promoted green manufacturing and the Green Industry project in Thailand since 2011. The aim has been to reduce the materials and energy involved in the production process and the waste it leaves behind. This is achieved through maximizing efficiency at each stage of the life cycle of a product, from design and procurement, the actual manufacturing process, as well as packaging and distribution, through to the recovery or recycling at the end of a product's life.

As part of these projects, the ministry published a Green Industry Manual aimed at guiding manufacturing companies through five levels of green operating practices. The ministry has also been spearheading the planned launch from 2016 of 'eco-industrial towns' in 15 provinces through to 2026 (see *How Government Makes the Playing Field Greener*, page 222).

More recently, Thailand's BOI, in a series of precision-guided promotion articles on the innovative news and business website Quartz in 2017, highlighted some of the advances the country has already made.

Thailand already has an enviable open-mindedness. But its businesses need to work hard to turn that into a willingness to transform corporate culture, and lead rather than be led.

In 2016 alone, said the BOI, it approved more than 320 agricultural projects valued at over US$4.8 billion, including innovative projects

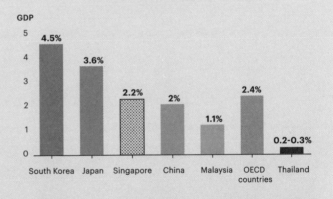

THAILAND LAGS BEHIND ON R&D SPENDING

In Thailand, investment in R&D has been stuck for decades at just 0.2–0.3% of GDP, well below the spending of East Asia's other top economies.

GDP

South Korea	4.5%
Japan	3.6%
Singapore	2.2%
China	2%
Malaysia	1.1%
OECD countries	2.4%
Thailand	0.2-0.3%

The average return on **an R&D investment is 168%** (from a survey of 60 countries).

In countries with below US$12,000 GDP per capita (such as Thailand, where GDP per capita was US$5,775 in 2015), **the return on R&D investment is 333%.**

Sources: *World Bank's Doing Business Report, 2014; World Bank's Doing Business Report 2017; Global Competitiveness Report, 2006–2007; Global Competitiveness Report, 2016–2017*

HOW GOVERNMENT MAKES THE PLAYING FIELD GREENER

Thailand's Ministry of Industry launched a Green Industry project in 2011 to encourage businesses to strive to meet five levels of environmental- and community-friendly operations:

LEVEL 1: Green Commitment through policy goals and action plans.

LEVEL 2: Green Activity that implements Level 1 commitments.

LEVEL 3: Green System, meaning systematic environmental management and accreditation.

LEVEL 4: Green Culture via employee commitment at all levels of the business.

LEVEL 5: Green Network, or extending green practices to supply chain and business partners based on the principle that "we cannot be green alone."

The ministry provides a range of related benefits, including fee exemptions and waivers, eligibility for green loans, awards, certification, and accreditation. The ministry's Office of Green Industry Promotion and Development has since 2011 also published five editions of a detailed 'Green Industry Manual' for Thai businesses to follow its green industry guidelines.

Since 2013, the ministry has also been gradually putting into place a program for 'eco-industrial towns,' following court findings in 2009 against the country's biggest industrial zone, Map Ta Phut, that temporarily halted production based on environmental grounds. Five

provinces were named as those that would be pioneers in the new project by 2016, rising to 15 by 2026. The aim was to identify areas that had the most potential and capabilities for industrial development by "enhancing the people's quality of life alongside environmental care in the area."

The program envisioned three levels of green industrial transformation – factory, estate, and ultimately community. A full range of stakeholders have been, or are due to be, consulted in each of the planned zones, including via public hearings. The ministry's five-level Green Industry criteria provide the guidelines for company participation in the project.

Incentives are the same as for the Green Industry criteria and depend on the type of industry, and commitment to specific investments: five-year exemptions from operational permits and fees, eligibility for green loans, relaxed auditing, exemptions from machine import duties, as well as various exemptions from corporate and other income taxes.

The key indicators for the eco-towns are as follows:

1. A reduction in pollution emissions and waste discharge per production rate.

2. An increase in the growth rate of green products.

3. Greater efficiency in resource and energy consumption rates.

4. An increase in reuse and recycling of solid and industrial waste, with a target of zero waste.

5. More community businesses arising from cooperation between industry and communities.

6. Enhancement of the quality-life of people in the area.

Early assessments of such eco-industrial towns, including through comparison with those in other countries, conclude that the most important factor is appropriate laws and regulations, thereby enabling cooperation between government, industry and community, as well as specific and measurable goals to enhance monitoring and evaluation.

A worker prepares wood at the Eiwlee Industrial factory in Lampang province.

in fruit and vegetable food packaging, biofuel manufacturing, supplements and medical food, rubber science, and extraction of bio-active ingredients.

Significantly, in November 2015, the government approved a plan to promote ten industries as the country's new engine of growth. Five are existing industries that would be encouraged to move up the value chain: (1) next-generation automotive; (2) smart electronics; (3) affluent, medical, and welfare tourism; (4) agriculture and biotechnology; and (5) food for the future. The other five are new industries: (1) robotics; (2) aviation and logistics; (3) biofuels and bio-chemicals; (4) digital; and (5) medical hub.

To achieve this, both public and private sectors have to engage more proactively in the kinds of policies that are essential to make a big difference. More important than any other aspect is education, in which Thailand is a laggard in all respects. It will likely take less time for robots to become good enough to do just about every type of factory work in the world than it will to reform Thailand's education system so that Thais have an even chance of getting jobs in the new global economy. And if private sector business thinks it can leave it to the government to make the necessary changes to the education system, it hasn't been paying attention. What Thai business needs to do is invest resources and time in vocational training on the job, which some development economists see as a more attainable game-changer than an improved general education system.

> ### What Thai business needs to do is invest resources and time in vocational training on the job.

Moreover, if Thailand is going to graduate from low-cost manufacturing to high value-added, then the next most prominent issue is R&D spending. And that isn't just a matter for government either. It is the business

CASE STUDY Thai Summit Invests in People Power

THE CHALLENGE: Being one of the leading auto parts manufacturers in a critical manufacturing base like Thailand is not easy. For Thai Summit Group, competition from international firms looking to establish bases in the country keeps the company on their feet. As competitors bring in cutting-edge technologies, R&D and innovation capabilities, and the skills to adapt to an increasingly disruptive world, Thai Summit, like others in the sector, risks falling behind.

THE SOLUTION: The company's five-year strategy for 2017-2022, V4: Catch Up 195, was developed with a focus on catching up to world-class automotive companies in terms of productivity, profitability, quality, and innovation. To compete in the era of Industry 4.0, the strategy outlines core activities like safety, lean manufacturing, smart factories, and knowledge sharing. Central to all of these are people. Indeed, Thai Summit holds true to its tagline, "Before We Build Parts, We Build People."

"To be competitive does not only mean investing in R&D, it is also about fostering good relations with our employees and labor unions," says Dr Chatkaew Hart-rawung, manufacturing director, Region 1 of Thai Summit Autoparts, a subsidiary of Thai Summit Group. "Sustainability at Thai Summit is about maintaining competitiveness. If the company is not sustainable, its employees will suffer the consequences."

Employees at Thai Summit are urged to keep abreast of emerging tech trends.

Employees are encouraged to demonstrate their capabilities and take charge of their own development. "I always advise my employees to 'Look macro, act micro,'" he says. It is important to be aware of the emerging trends that will shape the industry, but even more so is to use those trends as benchmarks to improve what you have at hand. That could involve something as rudimentary as improving efficiencies on the shop floor and sharing lessons learned and new technologies on Engineering Day, to more formative changes in thought processes.

THE BENEFITS: Investing in people translates to higher employee retention, work satisfaction, and strengthens the company from within. It is common for Thai Summit employees, for instance, to co-design products with their partners and customers, which include bigwigs like Toyota, Nissan, and Honda. The goal is to boost employee confidence and show customers that Thai Summit, too, has R&D capabilities worthy of contribution and can secure their trust. Ultimately, this is part of their effort to reach 100 percent customer satisfaction under the V4 strategy.

Thai Summit is one of the region's leading auto parts manufacturers.

sector that can make the real difference here, and Thailand is nearly at the bottom of the Asian class.

Supachai Panitchpakdi, a former head of the World Trade Organization and of the UN Conference on Trade and Development (UNCTAD) and one-time deputy prime minister, has complained loudly that Thai listed companies pay out too much in dividends – nearly 1,000 billion baht in 2016 – up 30 percent on the year before, while investing too little in strengthening their businesses, especially through much needed R&D.

Looking forward

There is no easy option. Thailand's manufacturing companies can no longer rely on public relations magic and CSR campaigns to try to explain away any environmental or social damage they might cause. In the digital world there is nowhere to hide. Businesses need to make an honest audit of the resources and

operations they employ in their operations and take on the competition in the market by finding new ways of doing the things they do while finding new things to do. This means a shift away from low-value, export-oriented goods towards high-value-added products and services, adopting new technologies and investing in R&D, supporting educational programs and institutions, and partnering with companies at home and abroad that embrace the same mindset and practices. More of the old will not do for the new.

It also means being part of the message that moderation is a better way forward for businesses than irresponsible excess, that better management of resources benefits the nation as a whole, that unethical and corrupt practices in the supply chain as well as labor and human rights abuses need to be eradicated, and that public procurement needs to be transparent and free of the kind of favoritism that fuels inequalities and widespread resentment and injustice.

SMEs

- *SMEs, making up roughly 97 percent of Thai enterprises, have the potential to be the main agent for fostering a dynamic sustainable economy.*

- *Sustainable business practices offer SMEs better risk management, long-term financial growth, and market access.*

- *Networking and sharing information is one of the best things SMEs can do to gain the necessary support and information that enable expansion and growth.*

- *Innovation, top talent, and standardization are keys to competitiveness and can be surprisingly attainable, even for micro-enterprises.*

The importance of small and medium-sized enterprise (SME) to Thailand's development cannot be overstated. SMEs (companies with under 200 employees) make up more than 95 percent of all Thai enterprises and provide about 80 percent of employment in Thailand. Comprising much of the supply chain, SMEs also impact the health and operations of large corporations. Penetrating all regions and industries, SMEs have the potential to be a key agent for change in the private sector.

Although development in Thailand has historically been top-down, incorporating sustainability practices offers an opportunity for development to work from the bottom up – in other words, sustainable practices help SMEs help themselves. This is particularly meaningful when seen in the context of how vulnerable SMEs are to external threats, such as market fluctuations, political unrest, climate change, and natural disasters. This was made evident during the Bangkok floods of 2011, during which some 500,000 SMEs were affected – many of them never to reopen.

SMEs are vulnerable to such external threats because they suffer from internal

shortcomings, says Hatyai University business professor Siriluck Thongpoon. These shortcomings include a low level of competencies, insufficient funds, labor shortages, poor marketing skills, and little knowledge or experience in business operations.

However, forward-thinking SMEs have proven that sustainability strategies can boost competencies and build resilience against such vulnerabilities. For example, when a 2003 study examined 296 Thai SMEs that had survived the Asian Financial Crisis, it was discovered that all had operated using sufficiency business practices described by King Bhumibol Adulyadej. These practices included efficient or frugal use of resources, inexpensive but sound technology, careful manufacturing consistent with capacity, low-risk management, and concern for employees and stakeholders.

In addition to fostering such resilience, sustainable business practices – when implemented correctly – have often led SMEs and startups to experience remarkable growth. When an Akha villager from humble origins founded Akha Ama Coffee in 2010, for instance, he committed to fair trade, efficient resource use, environmental stewardship, and moderate growth. Just seven years later, his company is an internationally recognized brand that has increased its production 15-fold.

SME challenges

Sadly, the adoption of such sustainability practices by Thai SMEs and startups is still quite low. One of the biggest hurdles SMEs face is lack of access to capital and credit. SMEs often have trouble securing bank loans due to insufficient capital, collateral, and bookkeeping. This stymies efforts to scale up, make improvements (such as disaster preparedness), invest in human resources (such as training), and pursue sustainable business practices (such as seeking international standard certification). Even now, more than 15 years after the creation of the SME Development Bank of Thailand, many SMEs cite lack of financial support as the key factor restricting growth.

The public sector is making efforts to address this issue. With the 2015 passing of the Business Collateral Act (BCA), SME owners are now allowed to use movable assets (such as vehicles, equipment, and livestock) as collateral on a loan, removing earlier, prohibitive measures that required immovable assets (such as land or buildings). Now, by using their existing resources, SMEs are allowed greater access to credit, which in turn fosters opportunities for investment and growth. However, to gain such access, SMEs must meet the government halfway: they must leave the informal sector.

Thailand has one of the largest informal economies in the world. While this sector often absorbs the shocks of financial crises and economic downturns, unregistered SMEs and laborers do not enjoy the same legal protections and support as registered businesses, nor can they access the same financial networks. There are also negative impacts on society: while the nation may want to move toward quality jobs, security, and protections for the workforce, labor will always be unstable and workers can easily be exploited in the informal economy – and they often have low bargaining power.

Based in Chiang Rai province, Akha Ama Coffee produces, processes, and distributes organic coffee.

Pulling SMEs out of Thailand's huge 'shadow economy' is tricky at best, but the BCA offers one incentive for SMEs to step into the light and pay taxes. With this move into the formal economy, other resources become available, such as the support of the Office of Small and Medium Enterprise Promotion (OSMEP). While OSMEP offers access to funds, capacity building, and marketing help, these are only available to registered SMEs.

SMEs often have trouble securing bank loans due to insufficient capital, collateral, and bookkeeping. This stymies efforts to scale up, make improvements, invest in human resources, and pursue sustainable business practices.

Then, of course, even if an SME has the funds to spare, would they spend precious resources on sustainability initiatives? According to Dr Sooksan Kantabutra, associate professor of management at Mahidol University, lack of understanding about sustainability and its potential to boost business is a major roadblock to implementation. One common misunderstanding, Dr Sooksan says, is that sustainability ideas such as prudence and moderate growth seem to run counter to the purpose of business – that is, growth and profit. Businesspeople assume that such models cannot compete in a cutthroat world, but this assumption is incorrect. Prudence and moderate growth models improve risk management, he says, helping ensure long-term growth and profit.

Prudence and moderate growth models improve risk management, helping ensure long-term growth and profit.

Dr Sooksan cites the case of Bathroom Design, a Bangkok-based SME reselling imported bathroom furnishings. Launched in 1995, it suffered a major blow two years later with the Asian Financial Crisis. Because 80 percent of

Shophouse businesses are particularly vulnerable to floods.

its business relied on expensive imports at a time when the value of the baht crashed, the company had to survive huge losses during the economic crisis and establish proper risk management for the future.

Owner Wacharamongkol Benjatanachat's solution was to plan for moderate growth, and to focus on innovation instead of short-term gain. By creating his own products, his company began to rely less on imported goods and become more self-reliant. By 2001, Bathroom Design had cut its imports down by half. When it began to seek export markets, the company initially limited exports to Southeast Asia, focusing on innovation and submissions to international awards rather than expansion. In 2007, Bathroom Design won the International Forum (iF) Product Design Award – exactly the kind of international endorsement it needed to break into further export markets. Today, ten years later, Bathroom Design exports to more than 30 countries. It is now a large company, with more than 200 outlets across Thailand and more than 350 staff. In this case, embedding sustainability proved just as effective in building resilience as it did in spurring growth.

Finally, anemic government support and business infrastructure – including a lack of national investment in research and development – presents problems for both Thailand's economic development and SME growth. According to the World Economic Forum on Global Competitiveness, Thailand is less accomplished at innovation than countries with comparable education ratings – national investment in R&D has been stuck at 0.2–0.3 percent of GDP for decades. At the same time, public sector support for SMEs is often piecemeal and difficult to access. While OSMEP, the SME Development Bank, the Thai Credit Guarantee Corporation, and other aid bodies exist, they work independently and do not provide SMEs with a comprehensive, cohesive promotion strategy.

"Currently, the SME promotion environment is not conducive to restructuring the entrepreneur," says TDRI researcher Thanthip Srisuwannaket. OSMEP must be allowed to function as a planning body first and foremost, she says, with the authority to regulate and coordinate efforts by "determining the

INDUSTRY SNAPSHOT

THE IMPORTANCE OF SMEs

There are **2.9 million SMEs registered** in Thailand.

Services make up 33% of SMEs, followed by manufacturing (30%) and trade/maintenance (28%) companies.

- ● Service
- ○ Manufacturing
- ● Trade/Maintenance
- ● Etc.

The government aims to increase GDP from SMEs to

50% of total GDP by 2021

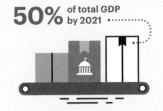

with a special focus on supporting startups.

SMEs account for

more than
95% of all enterprises in Thailand

80% of total employment in Thailand

41% of Thailand's GDP (about 5.56 trillion baht)

45% of total employment in emerging markets

4 out of 5 new jobs

Sources: World Bank and OSMEP

VULNERABILITY TO CLIMATE CHANGE

Across the globe,

78% of SMEs expect risks associated

with climate change to have **a significant effect on their businesses**.

Yet very few have business-continuity plans in place to help them deal with the economic impacts that disasters such as **floods** and **droughts** can have on their business.

In Thailand, some 500,000 SMEs were impacted by the 2011 floods and many never reopened.

500,000 SMEs

Sources: Zurich Insurance Group; OSMEP

direction of SME promotion, examining all SME promotion projects, and measuring other government agencies' successful outcomes."

Ways to implement sustainability

Thailand is fortunate to have a strong, homegrown sustainability framework that reflects and reinforces many deeply-held Thai values. The Sufficiency Economy Philosophy (SEP), while originally designed for smallholders and small-scale farms, is also useful and easily adaptable within the context of sustainable SME business and leadership. SEP's three key values of moderation, reasonableness, and prudence have been proven to help SMEs with their long-term survival, expansion, and risk management. In addition, there are several tried-and-true strategies for moving toward and achieving sustainability that are available even to micro-enterprises and SMEs with limited resources:

Integrate sustainability into SME governance

Sustainable practices are most effective when spearheaded by strong leadership that makes sustainability a key factor in corporate governance. Leaders must set tangible goals and measure progress with KPIs. At large companies, specialized sustainability departments manage progress, but at SMEs and startups, a visionary leader is often the main catalyst that is needed.

"It starts with the leader," says Smith Taweelerdniti, managing director of Nithi Foods, a spice manufacturer that was named the best Sufficiency Economy Small Business in 2007. "It's the duty of the CEO, of the top management, to find out what is best practice. If top management has the belief and the vision, then the rest of the company will adopt it."

Sustainable governance is also at the core of businesses that see a net profit from their

MICROFINANCE, MICROLOANS, AND PEER-TO-PEER LENDING

While the Business Collateral Act of 2015 should make access to credit easier for SMEs, it's important to note that other forms of accessible lending exist. The state-run SME Development Bank offers loans and credit specifically geared to SMEs and entrepreneurs, such as small low-interest loans and credit for imports or exports. The Thai Credit Guarantee Corporation also helps SMEs secure loans by providing credit backing. In addition, recent innovations outside the public sector have given rise to microfinance, microloans, and peer-to-peer lending, which offer tangible benefits to entrepreneurs, SMEs, and farmers, especially in the developing world.

Organizations such as South Africa's RainFin and Care International's lendwithcare.org have taken lessons from crowdfunding to create online platforms that connect borrowers with lenders. In 2015, Beehive Asia became Thailand's first online marketplace for peer-to-peer lending. Following closely behind is PeerPower, which is adapting the model for personal consumer loans. The microloan movement is gaining traction in Thailand and

SMEs stand to benefit – if they are savvy enough to know where to look.

The exterior of MBK shopping complex, a hub of SMEs in the heart of Bangkok.

DR WIMONKAN KOSUMAS *is the deputy director general of the Office of Small and Medium Enterprises Promotion, which offers holistic support to SMEs and runs an SME One-Stop Service Center.*

What is the state of sustainability among SMEs?

According to the Global Entrepreneurship Monitor Report, Thailand has a large SME population but the problem is they're static. Among 3 million SMEs we only have 15,000 medium-sized enterprises, meaning that most businesses stay stagnant. They still struggle to make profits, to catch up with domestic standards, international standards, and to compete on price. But I think we don't want to be too pessimistic. On the other side, our small businesses are very adaptive. Nowadays they are very good at producing green products, organic products, products that meet standards and regulations.

How can adopting sustainable practices help SMEs prosper?

First of all, we have to identify sustainable business practices for Thai SMEs, because we have our own problems. First, the majority of micro-enterprises do not do bookkeeping, so they don't know the structure of costs, income, and profit. And because they try to avoid tax and avoid bookkeeping, there's a cost to that. That's one part of good business practice that we would like SMEs to pursue, because if they don't do bookkeeping, when they go to the bank when their business is doing well, they still cannot get access to finance.

The second thing is innovation. A lot of SMEs still think that innovation is just for big firms. But nowadays it's not. It's a part of competitiveness because everybody else in the world is innovating. It doesn't necessarily mean technology – innovation for SMEs is simply trying every day to make a better product, a better service, and to serve the customer better.

How are social enterprises faring in Thailand? Will there be more in the future?

It's happening already. With the trend of startups in Thailand, you can see young graduates or university professors and scientists coming out of their laboratories and starting businesses. And even if they're not scientists or experts, the new generation knows that in order to come up with new products, they need to address societal problems. You can't just say, "Okay, I like to do this, so I want to make it a product." Now it's a matter of whether this product has a demand and whether it can solve some problems. So with this kind of thinking, it's going to be more sustainable; it's going to be more responsive to society in general.

What is the most important thing that an SME can do to become sustainable?

Another thing that is very important is networking. In Europe and Japan, SMEs belong to business or sector associations – about 80 percent of them belong to associations. They don't stand alone, so they get access to information, standards, marketing networks, best practices, everything. But in Thailand, less than 5 percent of SMEs belong to associations; most stand alone. So what we try to encourage SMEs to do is join their own network, to join their own cluster, so you get information, you get to know best practices, you get to share a cause, order raw materials together, have bargaining power, etc. That's very important.

For medium-sized businesses, or for those who can afford it, we would recommend continued self-assessments or BCP, "business continuity plans." Those SMEs who are in the global supply chain, who work with multinational corporations, they are required to do business continuity plans, to assess themselves, to find what is their weakness, and in emergencies or in crises what would be the alternative, their second and third plans. But I don't think the majority of Thai SMEs can afford to do that. Several government ministries are helping them, like the Ministry of Industry or even our office, OSMEP. We frequently send an expert – we call them *shindanshi* – to check their operations and to identify weaknesses. Sometimes, the insider does not have that insight. But outsiders or industry experts have inspected so many industries before that when they go into the operation, they can spot the problem right away.

CASE STUDY | Nithi Foods Gains Competitiveness through Certification

Workers process spices.

THE CHALLENGE: According to a 2014 survey conducted by Canadian business think tank Network for Business Sustainability, one of the top challenges for SMEs seeking sustainability is how to effectively manage requests for responsible procurement, especially when trying to break into foreign markets. With a growing number of companies requiring suppliers to meet sustainability requirements, SMEs stand to lose out on major accounts if they do not contribute to the triple bottom line.

THE SOLUTION: To attract the business of large corporations, spices and seasoning manufacturer Nithi Foods made ISO certification and sustainability accreditation a priority.

"Nithi Foods voluntarily got certified in the Environmental Management Standard (ISO 14001) in 2007 and the Worker Safety Standard (OHSAS 18001) in 2008," says managing director Smith Taweelerdniti. "These two certifications along with the Food Safety Standard have helped qualify Nithi Foods to become a valued supplier for multinational corporation customers."

Not only did this investment allow Nithi to gain large accounts, but it also provided the quality standards to seek a more robust export trade. While 95 percent of the company's revenue historically came from the domestic market, Nithi Foods has met the standards of Japan – a country with famously stringent requirements – as well as the three countries that have become Nithi's top-growing export market: China, Taiwan, and Indonesia. Nithi has also invested heavily in innovation, building on the company's quality standards to develop value-added products for export, such as East Kitchen and Pocket Chef, Thai spice packets that make cooking Thai food easy for international consumers.

THE BENEFITS: Working toward such sustainability certification and export qualifications has allowed Nithi Foods to gain a competitive advantage over other suppliers, as well as open doors to export markets that spur innovation. Today, this initial investment is paying dividends.

"Before Pocket Chef, our exports were very limited – less than 200,000 baht a year," says Smith. But export revenues now make up roughly 70 percent of Pocket Chef's total sales, which were 4.9 million baht in 2016. This means export revenues have increased to more than 3 million baht – and this from just one export product.

Another benefit has been the spreading of supplier responsibility to the farms Nithi sources raw products from. Because Nithi has already sought international quality standards, it is in a good position to tackle higher standards in sourcing, such as providing fair labor to its suppliers. While this further accredits Nithi and recommends the company highly to international markets and customers with high sourcing standards, it also benefits the farming communities that partner with Nithi in terms of fair wages and working standards.

"Sustainable sourcing from farms has become one of Nithi Foods' key strategies for the next ten years – to learn, improve, and expand our work to touch more farmers in Thailand," says Smith. "We realized that the real value of our work lies in how many farmers we can help."

Nithi Foods interviews a garlic farmer to find ways to improve growing practices.

sustainability efforts. A 2017 MIT Sloan Management Review study found that companies struggle to see monetary payoff from sustainability until a clear strategy is integrated into the corporate mission. This means simply allocating time and money to ad hoc initiatives and CSR programs is not enough – in fact, money is often lost on such efforts. Companies with the most successful sustainability strategies don't view ESG issues as problems to fix, but rather as business opportunities, building solid business cases for sustainability.

Globally, larger companies are proving quicker to integrate sustainability than small ones. Of the large companies included in the 2017 study, 78 percent had sustainability strategies in place, compared to only 54 percent of small companies. Luckily, many large companies publish their sustainability solutions to communicate their efforts to the public.

SMEs can take advantage of this wealth of information to build their own strategies.

Invest in human capital

Human capital is one of a company's greatest assets. Past successes have proven that when SMEs invest in human capital – that is, committing to train and educate staff, investing in innovation and R&D, and prioritizing stakeholder satisfaction – companies increase their competitiveness and corner new markets.

While training and education make up the two conventional types of human capital investment, sustainability principles also encourage investment in developing human resources that already exist, such as traditional or indigenous knowledge; cultural and regional uniqueness (also known as geosocial orientation); long-standing relationships with customers, suppliers, and

---

INNOVATION SOCIAL ENTERPRISES: A NEW WAY TO DO BUSINESS

Across the world, a growing number of entrepreneurs are proving that turning a profit and meeting a social need are not mutually exclusive. Social enterprises are a relatively new business model defined by the US-based Social Enterprise Alliance as having three attributes: they address a social need, they drive revenue through commercial activity, and they benefit the common good.

Until recently, social enterprises enjoyed robust public sector support in Thailand. A National Social Enterprise Committee was established in 2009, and a Thai Social Entrepreneurship Office (TSEO) in 2011. In 2012, the latter spent 30 million baht on a loans-and-equity plan to make funds accessible to social enterprises. However, recent activity has stalled. The TSEO became inactive

in 2016 due to funding issues, and its future is uncertain.

But with the help of independent support networks and organizations,

such as ChangeFusion and the Singapore-based Asian Venture Philanthropy Network (AVPN), Thailand's determined social entrepreneurs continue to fight the good fight. Some, such as Chiang Mai–based Akha Ama Coffee (see *Case Study*, page 235), have become smash successes.

The long term also looks promising for social enterprises, as the pivot toward sustainable businesses in general means that social enterprises stand to be more immune to risk than mainstream SMEs. For more information on resources, funding, and impact investors supporting social enterprises, look to the Skoll Foundation, Asian Venture Philanthropy Network, Thai Young Philanthropists Network, ChangeFusion, and Ashoka Thailand.

other stakeholders; and employee happiness. Happy, knowledgeable workers who are valued for their contribution work more efficiently and make better products, decreasing costs related to turnover, poor quality work, and time wasted on resolving conflict. Moreover, SMEs that are able to invest in their area of expertise can often out-innovate competitors, and SMEs that identify and build on their natural heritage and geosocial orientation offer unique products rich in marketing potential (see *Case Study*, page 235).

Often, such investments are not as costly as managers may fear. Artopex, a Canadian SME manufacturer of office furniture, discovered that providing sustainability education for its workforce resulted in cost savings that offset the initial investment. In a 2013 report commissioned by the Association of International CPAs, Artopex sustainability

director Jean Barbeau stated, "There is some investment of money, and a lot of investment of time for meetings and defining projects. But the savings pay back all of this investment."

Practice ethical sourcing

While ethical sourcing ensures external benefits, such as the proper treatment and payment of workers, the sustainable use of natural resources, and lowered carbon footprints, it also produces two key factors that contribute to profitability: improved public image and decreased risks.

Unethical sourcing threatened the very existence of a major industry as recently as 2015, when Thailand's fisheries sector came under scrutiny for using slave labor. Swift government intervention and reform were required for the industry to recover.

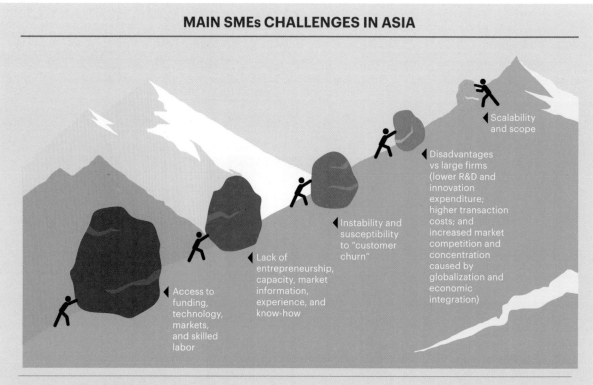

MAIN SMEs CHALLENGES IN ASIA

Scalability and scope

Disadvantages vs large firms (lower R&D and innovation expenditure; higher transaction costs; and increased market competition and concentration caused by globalization and economic integration)

Instability and susceptibility to "customer churn"

Lack of entrepreneurship, capacity, market information, experience, and know-how

Access to funding, technology, markets, and skilled labor

Source: Asian Development Bank Institute, 2016

CASE STUDY | Akha Ama Coffee Helps Indigenous Communities Help Themselves

THE CHALLENGE: The Akha people of Mae Jan Tai Village in Chiang Rai have long suffered from low income, lack of education, and a lack of opportunities. However, they were rich in self-sufficient farming know-how. The villagers knew how to grow coffee, among other crops, but they did not know the true market value and potential of their produce.

THE SOLUTION: Lee Ayu Chuepa, the only person from Mae Jan Tai to attend university, knew there must be a way for his community to use their existing skills and resources to help lift them out of poverty. Making a careful study of their farms, he discovered that coffee was their highest-value crop with the best opportunity for income in both domestic and international markets. He realized the community could add value by processing and distributing the coffee themselves instead of selling it as a raw commodity to middlemen. So in 2010, he founded Akha Ama Coffee: a family-run agribusiness that built on the community's main resource – its indigenous agricultural knowledge – to create a unique product with intrinsic marketing potential.

The Akha's method of coffee cultivation is organic, using agricultural by-products as natural fertilizers and pesticides. Grown among a variety of fruit trees and dried in the fresh mountain air, the flavor profile of Akha Ama Coffee is unique to the highlands of the Golden Triangle. The story of Akha farmers using traditional knowledge lent an engaging backstory to the product, while the company's fair trade, organic business model added value. Realizing this formula set his coffee apart from the competition, Lee submitted Akha Ama Coffee to the Specialty Coffee Association of Europe, who selected the product for inclusion at the World Cup Taster's Championship in 2010, 2011, and 2012. The company began to get international press, including the attention of American celebrity chef Andy Ricker, the creator of Pok Pok Restaurant, which specializes in Chiang Mai cuisine.

THE BENEFITS: By developing and investing in a resource in which the Akha were already abundant, Akha Ama Coffee was able to create a unique product without having to overextend, take risks, or rely on large loans. With low overhead, low debt, and intense customer loyalty, the company is immune to risks, such as bad crop years and market fluctuations.

Lee combined marketing and distribution by opening Akha Ama Café in nearby Chiang Mai. Business was so successful that Lee opened a second location in the heart of the Old City, where the café does a brisk business among tourists seeking regional experiences. In 2010, the year of its launch, Akha Ama produced only 2 tons of coffee. Five years later, production had

Lee Ayu Chuepa harvests coffee beans at the Akha village of Mae Jan Tai.

grown 12 times. In 2017, Akha Ama is approaching a 15-fold increase. The brand has gained international fame, with features by the *Wall Street Journal* and BBC.

From the outset, Akha Ama Coffee was a social enterprise that focused on making a social impact as well as a profit. Since Lee buys the coffee directly from farmers, Mae Jan Tai villagers are seeing margins roughly 5 to 25 percent higher per kilogram than if they were to sell to middlemen. The company's environmentally sound practices cut down on externalities and improve brand recognition, reputation, and customer loyalty, as well as staff loyalty and community buy-in. It has also helped about 15 or 20 monoculture-farming families switch to integrated farming methods, allowing them to get out of debt and improve the fertility of their land.

"How much change can happen in less than ten years is incredible," says Lee.

Traditional craft skills are at the heart of many SMEs, including this Bangkok birdcage maker.

of reputable, ethically minded, low-risk organizations.

The Sustainability Consortium, established by Walmart Stores, offers toolkits, KPIs, and other insights for buyers and suppliers to gauge and improve sustainability throughout their products and supply chains. More than 100 major multinationals – including Walmart, Pepsico, Bayer, Unilver, and L'Oréal – are members of the consortium, committed to buying only from suppliers that meet the requirements of its sustainability guidelines.

Meet compliance standards and sustainability demands of customers

In 2016, the International Trade Centre found that Thai SMEs lag behind their global competitors when it comes to standards certification. As multinational corporations enforce regulatory standards to all of their suppliers, Thailand will be impacted in two ways: domestic regulatory standards will need to change to remain competitive, and suppliers will increasingly have to comply with customer demands if they are to court large accounts.

One way to get ahead of the game is to meet the industry requirements established by the International Organization for Standardization (ISO) and to seek certification. However, this comes at a cost and often means making far-reaching changes in company practices and culture. Thus, we return to the point that the most effective and profitable sustainability strategies are the ones hardwired into a company's core values.

Ensuring ethical practices among suppliers is, admittedly, challenging and complex, especially for companies that deal with multi-tier supply chains. Many companies

A growing number of companies and NGOs are helping SMEs meet sustainability standards, offering tools ranging from audits to training.

fail to look below the first tier (direct suppliers) to the second or third tiers, where many environmental and social risks lie. But with proper monitoring and information gathering, including site visits and audits, companies can protect themselves from damaging practices. Taking such measures will give companies opportunities to cash in on a growing ethical consumerism market – not just in Thailand but globally. SMEs who are suppliers to larger companies, on the other hand, are more likely to attract the business

Thankfully, a growing number of companies and NGOs are helping SMEs meet sustainability standards, offering tools ranging from audits and progress report templates to training and, in some cases, funds for certification. There is no shortage of resources. Fairtrade International, for example, offers a grant to small farming cooperatives and enterprises seeking certification, while Thailand-specific organizations such as the Thai Young Philanthropists Network connects sustainable SMEs and social enterprises to investors.

TAKE ACTION

- **Network, network, network.** Knowledge, shared resources, and power in numbers are essential to SME success. These can all be accessed by joining sector or industry clusters. Also consider joining regional, national, or global sustainable business networks, such as the UN Global Compact or the Sustainable Business Development Institute (SBDI), for access to databases, networking events, forums, and other practical tools to aid integration of sustainability.

- **Micro-enterprises with limited access to formal associations are encouraged, at the very least, to share information** and form bonds with business partners, suppliers, and allies.

- **Make proper bookkeeping and BCPs (business continuity plans) a priority.** Not only does this lead to greater access to finance, but it also gives the entrepreneur greater understanding of the enterprise's strengths and weaknesses. This leads to better contingency plans and greater sustainability overall.

- **Invest in certification.** Being properly certified adds value, eliminates risk, and serves as an integrated form of quality control all in one. In addition, it opens up new markets. Looking beyond domestic standards to ISO certification could open up export markets.

- **Scrutinize the supply chain.** Hire consultants to learn how to look below the first tier of the supply chain, how to set up a supplier compliance code, and how to continue effective management of the supply chain. Micro-enterprises with limited means can apply for such consultancies through academic bodies and university-affiliated SME support programs.

- **Acknowledge the significance of stakeholders.** Many SMEs make the mistake of disregarding the crucial value of human capital. Good employees are the heart of the operation, driving the company forward with new ideas, innovations, and know-how. Begin to nurture human capital first by recognizing the value and potential of employees. Then, offer incentives for workers to commit to the enterprise, such as benefits, bonuses, employee services, and better salaries.

- **Innovate to stay competitive.** Innovation is not a concept that applies only to the high-tech or the publicly traded. It can be applied to SMEs' and micro-enterprises' daily operations. Dr Wimonkan Kosumas, deputy-director general of the Office of Small and Medium Enterprises Promotion, says, "Good business practice is to continually innovate. The keyword should not be 'profit.' It should be 'How can we serve our customers better? How can we produce better products?'" By asking these questions, even micro-enterprises can innovate by continually analyzing how to improve products and services.

Sustainability is not just about caring for ecology and community. It's about doing smart business. It's about analyzing risk, seeking innovative ways to differentiate, finding ways to be resourceful, and treating people fairly. These are all not only sustainable practices, but also sound business principles. The important thing to keep in mind is that true sustainability is not something that can be checked off with annual CSR projects. While such activities certainly make positive contributions, lasting and profitable sustainability needs to dovetail with the business's core mission and be integrated into its corporate strategy (see *Sustainability Strategy*, page 32).

Oftentimes, the main catalyst for such integration is the entrepreneur or company leadership, who holds the power to shape the corporate vision and see through implementation throughout the company's operations. A number of action points (see above) culled from other companies' past experiences and successes can offer a starting point for building an achievable SME roadmap towards sustainability.

State-owned Enterprises

- *Reasons for the poor performance of SOEs include rigid state regulations, lack of skilled personnel due to unattractive remuneration, and corruption.*

- *The public remains largely unaware of the depth and breadth of inefficiencies of SOEs, as credible and rigorous assessments of SOEs and their mandates are rare.*

- *Government attempts to clean up SOEs by consolidating the supervision authority and making procurement more transparent are a step in the right direction.*

- *The rationale behind every SOE should be reviewed. Those that no longer have a meaningful social mandate should be considered for privatization or dissolution.*

Providing public utilities such as water, electricity, energy, and transportation – and even commercial services such as banking and telecommunications – state-owned enterprises (SOEs) play an important role in the Thai economy and the daily lives of Thais. They also impact the country's progress and ability to meet many of the sustainable development–related challenges it faces, including the Sustainable Development Goals (SDGs). Without the commitment of SOEs, for example, it is unlikely that Thailand can meet its commitment to reduce carbon emissions under the Paris Climate Change Agreement.

Moreover, the continued relevance of state-owned enterprises in the 21st century is constantly being questioned. Section 84(1) of the former Constitution of the Kingdom of Thailand 2007, which was enforced until 2016, stipulated that the state "shall not engage in business activities in competition with the private sector unless it is necessary for the maintenance of the security of the state, the protection of public interests, or the provision of public facilities." So, while all SOEs were originally created with a social mandate that would originally have been aligned with the principles of sustainable development for Thailand, many of the SOEs have outlived their original raison d'être and no longer pursue this mandate. For example, the TOT and the CAT PCL were founded to provide local and long distance telecommunications services back in the days when investment in this sector was still too expensive and risky for private investors. Since then, however, advancements in communications technology and increased sophistication of the private sector have rendered this business not only commercially viable, but also hugely lucrative. In a similar vein, the Government Savings Bank (GSB) was originally created to encourage savings among youth. But today many private commercial banks offer attractive savings packages for youth. Hence, the GSB today provides services that are indistinguishable from other commercial banks, be they personal loans, business loans, or deposits that target the mass market.

The increased sophistication of the private sector and advancements in technology are not the only factors that may diminish the efficacy of a state enterprise. SOEs themselves seem to have moved away from or even abandoned their social mandates in a quest for profit, partly due to the SOE incentive schemes that reward financial returns rather than attainment of social objectives. This begs some questions: If SOEs provide services that are no different from those offered by the private sector, what then is the justification for their existence? How can SOEs help promote sustainable development for Thailand if their main preoccupation is with profit?

The trouble with Thai SOEs

Although the number of SOEs in Thailand has remained the same for the last few decades, their size and impact has expanded remarkably. In 2015, their combined revenue was equivalent to 40 percent of the country's GDP, a non-trivial jump from 32 percent in 2010. This is a cause of concern, as the expansion of these SOEs may crowd out more efficient private competitors that do not receive subsidies, soft loans, or tax or exclusive privileges from the state. This concern is evinced by the deteriorating financial performance of many SOEs.

The lackluster performance of SOEs can be contrasted with those of private competitors in the same market. In the telecommunications sector in 2016, the two SOEs, namely TOT and the CAT Telecom, did not perform too badly compared with their private peers (see page 245). However, both have recorded negative sales growth, which raises questions about their future viability. The discrepancy between state and private enterprises in the aviation sector is more glaring. Thai Airways International and its subsidiary, Nok Air, experienced negative sales growth against relatively healthy figures recorded by the private airlines.

Why are the performance results of SOEs inferior to those of their private competitors? There are multiple explanations ranging from corruption, rigid state regulations, lack of skilled personnel due to unattractive remuneration, and social service obligations. Indeed, all these factors contribute negatively to the productivity of SOEs. However, the single most important factor is corruption.

Thais are regularly exposed to news about corruption in SOEs. Most high-profile cases

Thailand Post fulfills its social mandate by serving all citizens, no matter how remote.

are exposed by foreign anti-corruption agencies such as the scandal surrounding Suvarnabhumi Airport's purchase of the CTX Bomb detector from GE Invision, which came under the investigation of the US Department

SOEs seem to have moved away from or even abandoned their social mandates in a quest for profit.

of Justice in 2007. More recently, Thai Airways International and PTT, the national energy giant, were caught in a corruption scandal when Britain's Serious Fraud Office found Rolls-Royce had paid bribes over 30 years to win contracts for aircraft engines and gas plant equipment from the two companies.

Thai SOEs are particularly vulnerable to corruption because they are governed with little accountability and transparency. To begin with, the board of directors of an SOE is usually selected at the whim of the Ministry of Finance, the official shareholder, and the Ministry under which the particular SOE resides. For example, it is customary that the Ministry of Finance and the Ministry of Transport each nominates half of the directors of the Board of Thai Airways International.

Politicians often deal out directorships to their (mostly unqualified) cronies or bureaucrats under their command. Bureaucrats also benefit from the scheme, as a directorship of a prominent or lucrative SOE such as Thai Airways International, Krung Thai Bank, or PTT is often perceived as an entitlement among

SOEs that no longer perform any meaningful social functions should be privatized or dissolved.

top bureaucrats such as permanent secretaries, and those from policy-making and law enforcement agencies such as the Attorney General, the secretary of the National Economic and Development Board, the secretary general of the Council of State, as well as among high-ranking military and police officers.

Besides being vulnerable to political intervention, the presence of high-ranking government officials on SOE boards poses two other major problems. First, government officials are not cut out for business. In stark contrast with Thai state enterprises, the board

A refinery run by the semi-private, national energy company PTT.

of directors of Singapore's Government-linked Corporations is made up of globally prominent business people from well-known multinational companies such as BMW, Li & Fung, and Blackstone Group. Their expertise and innovation is vital to the enterprise. Second, bureaucrats that sit on SOE boards may face conflicts of interest. On the one hand, they need to promote the public interest, and on the other hand, they need to maximize shareholder return. For example, a permanent secretary of the Ministry of Energy who sits on the board of the lucrative national energy company may have qualms about advocating greater competition in the energy market – a move that would certainly dent the company's profit figures.

Besides this flaw in the boards of directors, Thai SOEs are also plagued by rigid rules and regulations designed to prevent fraud rather than promote efficiency. For example, the state-owned telecom operators are not able to participate in frequency auctions because they would have to make a prior budget allocation request, which would have revealed the price they are willing to pay.

Undoubtedly, these shortcomings take a heavy toll on SOEs and the quality of the services they provide. But besides occasional corruption scandals that focus attention on SOEs, Thais are for the most part unaware of the depth and breadth of their inherent inefficiencies, as credible and rigorous assessments of the accessibility and quality of SOE services as well as the output and outcome of their mandates are rare, if not non-existent. This is because the performance evaluation criteria dictated by the State Enterprise Policy Office (SEPO) gives little or no weight to the actual impact of SOEs, but instead values the quality of the organization's governance and its ability to fulfill the policies prescribed by the government.

For example, the assessment criteria for the SME Bank does not include the number of SMEs that received credit for the first time from the bank. Rather, weight was given to the level of non-performing loans and profit figures, which essentially discourages rather than encourages lending to SMEs that were not able to secure funds from commercial banks.

INDUSTRY SNAPSHOT

THAI SOEs AT A GLANCE

58
The number of state-owned enterprises

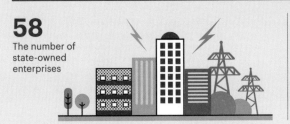

More than 300 subsidiaries

Total revenue in 2015:
5.8 trillion baht
(equivalent to **40%** of GDP)

Total assets:
US$393 billion

270,000 Employees
(roughly **0.7 percent** of the workforce)

TOP 5 THAI SOEs IN TERMS OF PROFIT

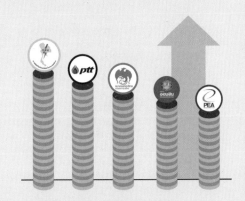

- Electricity Generating Authority of Thailand
- PTT
- Krung Thai Bank
- Government Savings Bank
- Provincial Electricity Authority

SOEs BY PROFIT

SOE by Government Ministry

13 Ministry of Transport

9 Ministry of Finance

7 Ministry of Agriculture and Cooperatives

5 Ministry of Interior

3 Ministry of Natural Resources and Environment

3 Ministry of Energy

16 Others

FINANCIAL RATIOS OF SOEs (2013–2015)

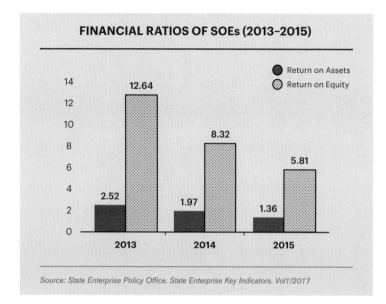

Legend: ● Return on Assets · ◍ Return on Equity

Values — 2013: 2.52 / 12.64; 2014: 1.97 / 8.32; 2015: 1.36 / 5.81

Source: State Enterprise Policy Office. State Enterprise Key Indicators. Vol1/2017

Reforming SOEs

An overhaul of Thai SOEs is urgent and long overdue. Back in the year 2000, former Prime Minister Thaksin Shinawatra, currently in exile, partially privatized PTT, the Airport Authority of Thailand, and the Mass

The performance evaluation criteria dictated by the State Enterprise Policy Office (SEPO) gives little or no weight to the actual impact of SOEs.

Communication Organization of Thailand, and listed these enterprises in the stock market. Although strict disclosure rules imposed by the Stock Exchange Commission helped boost transparency of these publicly listed state-owned companies, the fact that the state continued to hold a majority share and was thus in full control of these companies did not relieve them from political intervention, cronyism, and corruption risks.

The political mayhem that has plagued the country since the military coup in 2006 put the SOE reform agenda on hold until the coup in 2014. Seen as fertile ground for corruption,

the current military government led by Prayut Chan-o-cha was determined to reform SOEs. Shortly after taking power, the National Council for Peace and Order (NCPO) established the so-called 'Superboard' of SOEs chaired by the prime minister (also the leader of the NCPO), two deputy leaders, several permanent secretaries from pertinent ministries, and prominent businessmen and technocrats in finance. The Superboard's immediate task was to solve the dire financial problems of ailing SOEs and to screen large investment projects predisposed to corruption. It also has the mandate to prepare a medium- to long-term SOE reform plan.

The Superboard advocated the establishment of an SOE holding company of the likes of Temasek in Singapore or Khazanah of Malaysia to remove SOEs from individual line ministry control and place them under the authority of an independent central policy and supervisory unit that is managed professionally. In August 2016, the Cabinet endorsed the draft State-owned Enterprise Development Act that would set up the holding company. However, the bill is still under the deliberation of the National Legislative Assembly due to resistance from certain ministries that would like to maintain their grip over the state enterprises that fall under their authority. Skeptics also question the independence of the new governing structure.

As for short-term measures, to boost greater transparency in the procurements and construction projects of SOEs, Thailand joined the CoST (Construction Sector Transparency Initiative) in August 2014. CoST provides support to governments to put systems in place that allow public access to reliable and detailed construction project information. It also provides support to Multi-Stakeholder Groups (MSG) to oversee the validation and interpretation of the information disclosed by the government. The MSG has been formed and is currently undertaking a pilot project to upload key information such as the terms of references of open bids and signed contracts relating to the construction of Suvarnabhumi Airport.

Besides greater public disclosure of details governing SOEs' construction projects, the

DR PIYASVASTI AMRANAND *is the chairman of PTT Group. During a long and illustrious career, he has served as the secretary-general of the Thai National Energy Policy Office, president of Thai Airways International, and Thailand's Energy Minister. During the 1990s, he played a key role in deregulating and privatizing a number of energy-related state enterprises, including PTT.*

What is your view on the role of SOEs on sustainable development issues?

It depends a lot on how the government uses SOEs as an instrument to implement policy or create the wellbeing of the Thai people. In the past we saw the government mixing everything together – thinking 'ok, we want energy security and low energy prices, PTT can go ahead and do it.' That was the policy in the past. And this sort of thinking not only applied to PTT but also to other SOEs.

In the long run, that is not at all good for the country or the SOEs because the SOE would not be in the position to really create value for the country. But the policy is undergoing changes now, with the government policy clearly wishing to make a separation between policy making, regulating, role of shareholders, and operations. That is now very clear.

I believe this is a move in the right direction. It will benefit the country in the long run. It will make SOEs like PTT even stronger and more efficient. We would have no obligation to provide subsidies on any policy. If the government wishes there to be a subsidy, then it will have to find some means of getting funding to provide it. SOEs will have to operate in such a way as to create value for shareholders. And since the government is the major shareholder, the value actually goes back to the government so that it could spend the proceeds on things which are really needed like education, health, and so on.

How do you incentivize the top level to fight against corruption in SOEs?

It is crucial to show that we don't tolerate any kind of corruption. At the same time of course, there are other internal programs and measures to create transparency within the organization such as requirements for registration of representatives or consultants, rules and regulations on disclosures by employees and conflict of interest such as the no gift policy, and creating awareness among employees about corruption. All these are implemented.

The second thing about corruption is this: you have to stop outside interference. If politicians or people outside the company can influence decisions within the company, that could create corruption. Hopefully, the creation of an SOE holding company will help to reduce interference.

The last one is this: there are now various programs which this government has come out with to combat corruption – you have the CAC and we have been working with them on schemes like the Integrity Pact. We have implemented this on a few projects already – large projects. We have outside observers sitting in during the process of drawing up terms of reference, evaluating bids, and making the final decision to purchase the products or services. It's been very useful.

Does SOE privatization help combat corruption?
If you are privatized things are done a lot more transparently. The general public can get a lot more information on listed companies than non-listed SOEs. You see a report in a newspaper, you immediately have to respond by writing explanations to the stock market. Everybody can access information on the SET website.

CASE STUDY | Airports of Thailand's Transparency Initiative

Suvarnabhumi International Airport's expansion was run through a transparency program.

THE CHALLENGE: The expansion of Bangkok's main international airport, Suvarnabhumi, is a mega-project with a budget of 62 billion baht (roughly US$1.7 billion). The project, approved in 2010, was supposed to be completed by 2015. However, due to the unstable political environment at the time that resulted in a military coup in 2014, the project was delayed and revived only in 2015. Given the multiple scandals that plagued the construction of the airport two decades ago, the state-owned Airports of Thailand (AoT) must take measures to prevent history from repeating itself, as well as to prevent corruption in procurement.

THE SOLUTION: In 2014, Thailand announced that it would join CoST, the Construction Sector Transparency Initiative, a country-centered approach to create better value by ensuring transparency in construction projects. Participation in CoST requires the government to commit to a program of full disclosure of information on large, public construction projects and their procurement processes. Participating countries are to produce disclosure reports according to the CoST standard. The report must be approved by a multi-stakeholder group consisting of public, private, and non-government representatives in order to ensure its accuracy.

In 2015, AoT, under the management of Dr Nitinai Sirismatthakarn, volunteered to commit the Suvarnabhumi expansion project to the CoST program. A multi-stakeholder group (MSG) chaired by the Permanent Secretary of the Ministry of Transport was created to oversee the disclosure program. An assurance team responsible for the collection and analysis of information to be disclosed was commissioned to the Thailand Development Research Institute (TDRI), an independent economic policy think tank.

THE BENEFITS: Although the initial phase was difficult, as officials were used to non-disclosure, the level of disclosure improved markedly one year after joining CoST.

At a workshop held to publicize the progress of CoST implementation at AoT, Dr Nitinai said, "Although CoST implementation may have delayed the project for half a year or so, that is much better than the long delay for several years in the past resulting from various scandals surrounding the procurement. It is important to have public trust. Now that all vital information is out in the open, I will have peace of mind after the completion of the project. I need not fear any lawsuit that may arise from any probe into this project hereafter."

If the CEOs of other SOEs embrace the same attitude, then the CoST program can certainly lead to a major change in the governance of Thai state-owned businesses. In early 2017, the Expressway Authority of Thailand, which has received multiple awards for disclosure, announced its decision to join the program. The government has also announced that state offices will join CoST as well. Perhaps CoST can, over time, help change the culture of closed-door operations among the Thai bureaucracy and help root out corruption.

Some of Thailand's international airports, including Koh Samui, are privately owned.

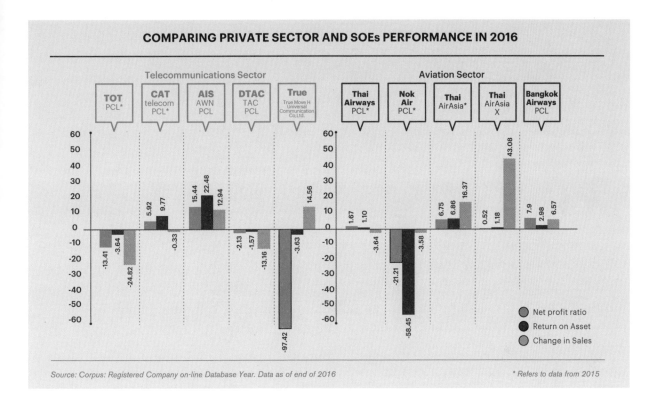

COMPARING PRIVATE SECTOR AND SOEs PERFORMANCE IN 2016

Source: Corpus: Registered Company on-line Database Year. Data as of end of 2016

* Refers to data from 2015

current government also introduced the Integrity Pact (IP) scheme beginning in 2015. The pact consists of a declaration by both the government and private parties to abstain from any form of collusion or bribery and to have third-party experts as observers in the entire procurement process, from the drafting of the specification to the monitoring of the quality of the services or goods procured. Currently, these third-party observers are volunteers dispatched by the private sector anti-corruption outfit, the Anti-Corruption Organization of Thailand (ACT). As a show of its commitment to the scheme, the government has enrolled 44 procurement and construction projects with a value totaling 223 billion baht, including the Suvarnabhumi Airport project. While the initiative is effective in vetting large investment projects, the program imposes a heavy burden on ACT, which must constantly seek expert volunteers to be dispatched as observers to an expanding pool of projects. To sum up, the government has tried to clean up SOEs by consolidating

the supervision authority and making procurement more transparent. However, these measures are temporary and can be

The Integrity Pact compels public and private parties to abstain from any form of collusion or bribery.

easily dismantled by the next government that may not be interested in the reforms. The only exception is the Integrity Pact arrangement, which has been institutionalized in the new procurement law, the Procurement Act of 2017.

What next for SOEs?

Can SOEs play a role in Thailand's sustainable development awakening? Thailand's biggest challenges are that it is an ageing society and one facing the middle-income trap. The country is becoming old but is still not rich. The government has implemented policies

ELIMINATING THE ROT IN STATE-OWNED ENTERPRISES

Recently, an international bribery scandal allegedly involving three of the most prominent Thai state enterprises once again brought the key issue of corruption into sharp focus. In January 2017, Britain's Serious Fraud Office alleged that Rolls-Royce's representatives had paid bribes to intermediaries in order to secure aircraft engine procurement contracts in six countries, including with the national flag carrier, Thai Airways International. It found that the kickbacks between 1991 and 2005 totaled roughly 1.3 billion baht.

Meanwhile, the US Department of Justice and the US Securities and Exchange Commission alleged that the company's employees had paid massive bribes totaling 385 million baht over the course of ten years to secure gas plant equipment supplies contracts with the energy giant PTT and its subsidiary PTT Exploration and Production. Rolls-Royce admitted "extensive systemic bribery and corruption" during the specified period.

The news came as a big blow to the already somewhat tarnished image of Thai state enterprises since both PTT and Thai Airways International – as listed companies – were considered two of the 'better SOEs.' In fact, PTT was named The Best SOE by the State Enterprise Policy Office (SEPO) in 2016, while Thai Airways International is globally renowned. If these two state enterprises that are subject to the stringent scrutiny of shareholders and regulators can be so enmeshed in corruption, what about those unlisted ones whose operations are shrouded in secrecy?

Once the overseas investigations were exposed, anti-corruption outfits like the National Anti-Corruption Commission (NACC), the Anti-money Laundering Office (AMLO), and the Office of the Auditor General (OAG) launched their own probes. Thai Airways and PTT also set up their own special task force to look into the alleged bribery case. The Rolls-Royce scandal is likely to ensnare a large group of people including the SOEs' employees and executives, high-ranking officers and politicians involved with the approval of the procurement at the time, some of whom may still hold much political clout today. The public has yet to witness whether the perpetrators will eventually be brought to justice or go free with impunity.

to upgrade industry; it is promoting a digital economy (Thailand 4.0), promoting foreign investment (SEZ, EEC), encouraging innovation, providing infrastructure, and more. Most of these policies target the domestic or foreign private sector rather than enterprises of the state, bar infrastructure projects such as the

> ### State enterprises are necessary only when the market fails to deliver certain goods or services.

construction of high-speed trains or double tracks that would be under the purview of the State Railway of Thailand. So, what does the future hold for state enterprises?

To identify the role of SOEs in the future Thai

economy, one needs to go back to basic economics. State enterprises are necessary only when the market fails to deliver certain goods or services because of the excessive business risks involved in the provision of such products. This may include, for example, loans to high-risk SMEs and farmers or the production of certain orphan drugs or vaccines that demand large financial outlay with uncertain sales figures. The Ministry of Finance needs to conduct a major review on the rationale of each and every SOE. The social mandate of each SOE needs to be clearly identified and the extent to which the mandate is fulfilled in practice verified. SOEs that no longer perform any meaningful social function should be privatized or dissolved.

Based on the aforementioned criteria, Thailand can afford fewer SOEs. This would lessen the government's supervisory burden and, at the

INNOVATION THAILAND POST

A postal service is often the last bastion against privatization because postal delivery is very costly in terms of labor costs. The US Postal Service, probably the only business operated by the federal government, has 600,000 workers and loses billions of dollars a year. Thai Postal Service was also once a loss-making business unit within the former Communications Authority of Thailand (CAT), an SOE that held a statutory monopoly over international call services. Profits from pricey overseas calls were used to subsidize postal services. When CAT was corporatized in preparation for the planned privatization in 2003, the postal unit was spun off to become Thailand Post Co Ltd. Deprived of the cross-subsidy it used to receive from CAT, the company's prospects were bleak. But in just over a decade, the company, which incurred more than a 200-million-baht loss during the first four months of its operations, was able to turn an operational profit of three billion baht in 2015. Such a turnaround is normally unimaginable for an SOE burdened by rigid bureaucratic rules and prone to political manipulation. So how did Thailand Post do it?

The man behind the success was Teerapong Suthinond, the last governor of the CAT, and the first CEO of Thailand Post. Faced with rising costs due to wage increases for over 20,000 postmen as well as falling postal revenue due to cheaper and more convenient alternative communication channels (such as email and mobile messaging), the company had to rebrand itself as a modern company with modern services.

First, the company asked for an increase in the postage rate from two -to-three baht per item after having assessed that the largest users of postal services are businesses that can afford higher prices than households. The rate increase helped boost revenue but it was not sufficient to cover operational losses at the time.

Second, leveraging its extensive network of post offices and delivery services, the company introduced a variety of new services to compensate for the falling demand for postal delivery service. The first service introduced was the EMS (Express Mail Service) with a state-of-the-art track and trace service on a par with global players such as DHL. Then the company expanded the scope of its track and trace to include parcel delivery and the Logispost service, which provides delivery of large items (such as refrigerators) with a weight up to 200 kilograms. Other services introduced include messenger services for speedy delivery of mail and parcels, and direct mail services for pamphlets and other promotional brochures.

Third, the company also undertook a major organizational reform beginning with the establishment of a new brand that appears modern and efficient rather than bureaucratic. Postal boxes were repainted, postal offices renovated, and staff clad in new outfits. The company also invested heavily in IT. It employed enterprise resource planning software in order to better integrate core business processes, along with customer relationship management and point of sale software to help boost efficiency.

Thailand Post shows that with the right vision, innovation, determination, and better management, a financially distressed SOE can regain its foothold and thrive as a socially conscientious, efficient business.

Through innovation and structural changes, Thailand Post has remained competitive.

CASE STUDY — Singapore Airlines Soars Critically and Commercially

Singapore Airlines shows how an SOE can become a world-class organization.

THE CHALLENGE: Can an SOE be as efficient as a private enterprise?

THE SOLUTION: The Singapore government believes that its state enterprises should be managed more like a private company than a state organization. For starters, there are no government officials on the board. Singapore Airlines' board of directors consists of top-notch local and foreign executives with global pedigrees in marketing, law, investment, finance, accounting, and engineering/technology. Unlike most countries, Singapore does not believe that its state enterprises should be managed solely by its nationals. Selection is merit-based. Hence, the list of the airline's directors includes the founder of Li & Fung, the former CEOs of BMW, and former executives from Blackstone Group.

The company also gives importance to governance. It encourages and facilitates whistle-blowing by employees who come across suspicious situations. It also adopts a suppliers' code of conduct that requires that its suppliers comply with relevant laws and regulations such as those governing competition, labor, environment, intellectual property rights, and information disclosure.

THE BENEFITS: In 2016, Singapore Airlines was ranked the third best airline in the world by Skytrax. It ranked first in 2004, 2007, and 2008. Due to the quality of its service and the efficiency of its management, many people are not even aware that Singapore Airlines is state-owned. Undoubtedly, the Singapore Airlines case goes to show that a hands-off government and meritocratic management style can make a state-owned enterprise as competitive as any private one.

CASE STUDY — Bank of Agriculture Avoids Unwanted Meddling

THE CHALLENGE: When one thinks of 'the people's bank,' one often thinks of the omnipresent Bank of Agriculture and Agricultural Cooperatives (BAAC). With 1,275 branches and offices spread across every province, roughly 95 percent of farming households today have access to BAAC credits that offer low-interest and generous payment periods.

What makes the bank outstanding is not only its ability to fulfill its mission, but also the efficiency with which it did so. A few years after its creation in 1966, the bank was able to become financially self-reliant. At the same time, it has been able to manage its credit risks rather well. But the most formidable risk is that of political interference – how does the bank resist it?

THE SOLUTION: The BAAC has resisted pressure from political interest groups by making its operations as transparent as possible. For example, its annual report provides details about the financial status of its lending under each government-initiated program, whether this fell under debt relief, farm price guarantees, or low-interest loans. On such reports, reckless populist programs would show up as financial losses.

The BAAC offers low-interest loans to farming households in need of credit.

THE BENEFITS: By making full and transparent disclosure a safeguard against political interference, the bank duly received the Integrity and Transparency Award from the National Anti-corruption Commission (NACC). Accolades and prizes are not the only rewards of transparency. In 2016, the bank received a triple A rating from Fitch Ratings (Thailand) and was awarded the title of Bank of the Year by the popular financial magazine *Dok Bia*.

TAKE ACTION

According to PricewaterhouseCoopers, "SOEs are likely to remain an important instrument in any government's toolbox for societal and public value creation given the right context." To build the right context and to streamline current inefficiencies, the following action steps are recommended:

1. The management and supervision of SOEs require a major overhaul to ensure transparency, efficiency, and zero tolerance for graft.

- SOE boards should consist of well-recognized professionals and businesspeople, not bureaucrats.

- The social mandate of SOEs must be clearly described. The extent to which the mandate is fulfilled should be regularly and thoroughly assessed.

- SOEs need to be relieved from the rigid and often byzantine investment, procurement, and hiring rules that are prescribed for state departments. New, streamlined rules should be put in place to maximize efficiency and to allow for innovation.

- Greater managerial flexibility should be balanced with greater transparency.

2. Policy reforms and public communications campaigns will develop a culture of transparency and public value creation.

- The government must enforce SOEs' compliance to the Official Information Disclosure Act of 1999.

- The Ministry of Finance must review the rationale for each SOE. SOEs that do not perform meaningful social functions should be privatized or dissolved.

- The government should communicate to the public the rationale of privatizing SOEs. A public that understands the motivation for privatization is more likely to support innovation and reform.

3. Do the budgetary math. Thailand cannot afford as many SOEs as it currently has.

- Thorough analysis of the public value, cost effectiveness, and governance risks of SOEs will help minimize the government's supervisory burden and the scope of corruption and fraud.

- Utilize a third-party body to solve the financial woes of ailing SOEs and to screen large investment projects that are predisposed to corruption.

---

same time, minimize the scope of corruption and fraud that have plagued the sector. But the notorious privatization of PTT during former Prime Minister Thaksin's government back in the year 2000 – when most equity shares were snatched up in a few seconds by certain politicians, their connections, and their families – has given privatization a bad name. It will be any government's biggest challenge to persuade the public to embrace it once again. But even more of a challenge is convincing SOE employees who do not want to lose the job security to which they have been entitled.

Finally, the management and supervision of SOEs requires a major overhaul if these enterprises are to be sustainable in the long run. First, SOE boards should consist of

well-recognized professionals, not bureaucrats. Second, the social mandate of SOEs must be clearly described and the extent to which the mandate is fulfilled properly and thoroughly assessed. Third, SOEs need to be relieved from the many rigid investment, procurement, and hiring rules designed for state departments in order for them to be able to fulfill their roles effectively, and to be capable of innovating. Greater managerial flexibility needs to be balanced with greater transparency. The government needs to give gravity to SOEs' compliance to the Official Information Disclosure Act of 1999. Without these critical reforms, it is hard to imagine SOEs helping Thailand create truly sustainable, inclusive growth that also tackles the environmental and social problems Thailand is facing.

Tourism

- *This thriving sector is at the forefront of the country's shift to a more service-based economy – and softening the economic blow of a manufacturing sector in slow decline.*

- *Mass tourism is creating water and waste management issues, and contributing to the degradation of nature, in many parts of the country.*

- *Government crackdowns on irresponsible tourism practices have already proven that business-as-usual isn't good enough in many areas.*

- *Most hotels in Thailand are approaching sustainability in a superficial, often ad hoc manner rather than incorporating the concept into their core strategy.*

- *In a sector rife with unverified claims and spin, independent certification offers the best means for tourism businesses to show they walk the sustainability talk.*

Thailand's tourism sector is in fine health. The revenues reaped are staggering; new markets – sports, food – are emerging; and the growth in international arrivals, the vast majority leisure travelers with time and money to spend, appears to be on an unstoppable upward trajectory. Tourism, in its myriad forms, is also at the forefront of the country's shift to become a more service-based economy – and helping to soften the economic blow of a manufacturing sector in slow decline.

But despite these profound and indisputable benefits, the issues facing the world's ninth-most visited tourism destination are deep-rooted and diverse. As well as contributing to greenhouse gas emissions, mass tourism is creating problems related to water and waste management, as well as biodiversity and animal welfare in parts of the country. Tourism can also be linked to a range of social problems, such as community cohesion, regional socioeconomic divides, and rural-urban migration, not to mention an officially excoriated sex industry.

Most industry stakeholders already recognize these issues as risks and challenges. Many also already realize that these risks and challenges are only set to become more urgent in the years to come, as the budget airline industry expands, as integration between ASEAN members increases, and as the Asia-Pacific region's fast-growing middle classes enjoy more and more international holidays.

In addition to advising tourism businesses, the Pacific Asia Travel Association (PATA) is advocating for closer cross-border integration on matters ranging from human resource development to pro-poor tourism, infrastructure development, and ASEAN-wide visas. Meanwhile, the government now pays lip service to the tenets of sustainable tourism about as frequently as it boasts about the seemingly inexorable rise in international tourist arrivals (32.6 million in 2016, a nine percent rise over 2015). Its words are also being matched by concrete actions – from eco-tourism drives and sharply-focused marketing campaigns aimed at high-yield segments, to extreme resource management measures such as island closures and zero-dollar tour crackdowns.

As for the private sector, many niche tour operators are at the vanguard of grassroots sustainability. They dream up new community-based tourism products, they offset the carbon emissions created by their trips, and they generate local jobs and income. Many are among the most evangelical purveyors of sustainable practices operating in Thailand today. The majority of hotels, meanwhile, are either yet to grapple with sustainability or engaging with it only superficially.

Ultimately, aims are diffuse: there is little industry consensus about how best to tackle the issues and disclose progress on them. This dynamic and vital sector is not short of bold claims and fresh ideas, but there currently exists very little of the methodical data collection, capacity building, and buy-in from management and staff necessary to enact lasting change on either an operational or SDG-fulfillment level.

Why tourism needs to change

Many industry leaders instinctively recognize that there is a need to safeguard the communities, sites, culture, and natural surroundings that draw tens of million of visitors to Thailand each year – and upon which millions of livelihoods depend.

For them, it's not just about sustainability – it's also about self-preservation. To put it bluntly, if a country becomes less appealing to tourists, then bottom lines suffer. The tour operator Intrepid Travel, for example, states that growth in demand for its tours is faster in Vietnam, Myanmar, and Cambodia, in part because those destinations are less crowded and offer more authentic experiences than Thailand. Anecdotal reports like this hint at what some armchair commentators say: that the famed resilience of "Teflon Thailand" and this robust sector could, one day, dissipate.

Then there's the political climate. Since the 2014 coup, resorts built on protected land, vendors encroaching onto public beaches, night venues that flout licensing hours or permit indecent acts, and boat operators at ill-managed dive sights have all fallen foul of a government with a carte blanche to address the tourist sector's transgressions in

Northern Thailand's Anantara Golden Triangle Elephant Camp & Resort offers ethical elephant encounters.

a kneejerk manner. In light of this, responsible practices can be a form of immunity, equating to risk management and future-proofing your company.

As things stand, only around five percent of Thailand's tourism market seeks sustainable goods and services. Meanwhile, the huge rise in arrivals from Chinese, ASEAN, and Russian markets combined with a stagnation in the numbers coming from typically more eco-aware Western countries presents a challenge.

Many niche tour operators are at the vanguard of grassroots sustainability. They dream up new community-based tourism products, they offset the carbon emissions created by their trips, and they generate local jobs and income.

However, there are signs that market forces, as well as government intervention, are already helping drive large-scale change.

"Fifteen to 20 years ago sustainability was a niche, but now it is mainstream for Western tourists," says Carl Needham, the Southeast

Tour operator Local Alike strives to create local interactions that benefit everybody.

Asia general manager of Intrepid Travel. He adds that most of the company's 15,000 customers per year want "local interactions, animal welfare and sustainable practices, even for high-end tours." Also sanguine is Somsak "Pai" Boonkam, co-founder of Local Alike, a social enterprise and community-based tourism company with an innovative online platform. He sees latent potential in the East Asian market. "We've seen increasing demand from tourists from Singapore, Korea, and Japan," he says, "as well as some demand from Thai organizations' team-building projects."

Asking guests to hang up their towels or the staff to help plant a few trees is no longer enough for the country's most proactive hotels.

Ultimately, emerging demographics, evolving consumer tastes, and brute economics might be more instrumental in bringing about the wide-scale adoption of sustainable practices in the tourism sector than any ethical or pragmatic argument can be.

How tourism can change

The attempts of the tourism industry's private sector to lessen its negative impacts and foster more positive outcomes can loosely be split

into the following challenges: poverty reduction and social inclusion; employment and training of human capital; and preservation of the natural and cultural environment. But while commercial stakeholders face similar challenges, approaches to them vary markedly.

Hotels

Asking guests to hang up their towels or the staff to plant a few trees is no longer enough for the country's most proactive hotels. In the absence of government incentives or tax breaks for good environmental or social practices, a small but significant number are moving beyond mere CSR initiatives and forging ahead on a range of sustainability-related issues: cutting waste, greening their supply chain, and increasing employee prospects and loyalty.

Reports have shown that the numbers of holidaymakers willing to pay more to stay in a hotel with a proven environmental and social record is rising, albeit slowly. But the main motive among hoteliers in Thailand is the potential savings – not some idealistic desire to help save the world. "People in the hotel industry still believe sustainability is for tree huggers," says Benjamin Lephilibert, founder of Bangkok-based LightBlue Environmental Consulting, which helps hotels reduce their social and ecological footprint. "To get their buy-in, our main focus is how to make the biggest impact on hotel operations so that it has a substantial financial return."

Some hotels have had a true sustainability awakening. Sampran Riverside, a resort in Nakorn Pathom province, has left CSR behind and created a pioneering social enterprise instead (see *Case Study*, page 260). The Sampran Model, as it is known, allows rice farmers and consumers alike to benefit from a short supply chain – farmers get a fair price and guests get an education in the benefits of organic farming. So successful has the model become that it now has wide public-private backing and life beyond the tourism sector.

To tap into Thailand's growing meetings, incentives, conventions, and exhibitions (MICE) sector, Bangkok's Plaza Athenee became the first hotel in the world to earn ISO 20121 certification for sustainable event

INDUSTRY SNAPSHOT

TOURISM BY THE NUMBERS

From 2015 to 2016, Thailand's tourist numbers **increased by 9%**.

Tourist arrivals in Thailand have skyrocketed from 336,000 foreign visitors and 54,000 GIs on R&R in 1967 to some

32.6 million foreign tourists in 2016.

One estimate is that **in 2020 some 60 million tourists** will visit the kingdom.

ASIANS ACCOUNTED FOR 64% OF THAILAND'S TOURIST ARRIVALS IN 2016

BY REGION

EAST ASIA 21.6 million

SOUTH ASIA 1.5 million

EUROPE 6.1 million

THE AMERICAS 1.4 million

BY COUNTRY

CHINA 8.7 million

MALAYSIA 3.5 million

JAPAN 1.4 million

INDIA 1.2 million

Source: Ministry of Tourism and Sports

Chinese tourists accounted for **almost 27%** of the total number of arrivals in 2016 – an **increase of 64%** versus 2013.

Sources: Ministry of Tourism and Sports; Tourism Authority of Thailand; "The Vietnam War and Tourism in Bangkok's Development, 1960~70"

FINANCIAL BENEFITS

In 2016, tourism generated **1.64 trillion baht** in business.

Tourism generates more foreign exchange than any other industry in Thailand (**US$45.7 billion in 2016**).

79% of Thailand's tourism revenue is from international tourists.

40% of revenue in the wholesale and retail sector in Bangkok and other major destinations comes from foreign tourists.

The average spending of a foreign tourist is **around US$150/day**.

JOB CREATION

Direct contribution of travel & tourism to employment

2016	2027
2,313,500 jobs	**4,009,000** jobs
= **6.1%** of total	= **10.4%** of total

Source: Tourism Authority of Thailand

management. The hotel reduces trash by using potted plants instead of floral centerpieces, setting up linenless tables, and donating excess food to charity.

> **Minor International has found that the process of gathering ESG data for all of its hotels has yielded unforeseen efficiency savings.**

Minor International, meanwhile, has found that the process of gathering ESG data for its hotels has yielded unforeseen efficiency savings. The listed Thailand-based hospitality and food company, which operates 155 hotels across 22 countries under its Minor Hotel Group arm, claims to have made significant cuts in water and energy usage across 50 hotels as a result of its sustainability reporting process, which has been conducted annually for five years. Further efficiency gains are also expected off the back of its enrollment in Green Growth 2050, a software-based certification program that tracks the sustainability performance of hotels.

For Lephilibert, every hotel should be embarking on this sort of journey: identifying KPIs, linking them with their strategy, measuring them in earnest. However, most are not. "The way sustainability has been integrated in hotel operations is extremely shallow," he says.

Currently, the hotel initiative du jour is food waste prevention (see *Food and Beverage*, page 172). Hotel management like it because it brings tangible financial benefits and can be leveraged by the PR team. For them, the holy grail is finding an efficiency initiative or pet project that casts a flattering glow, that boosts the hotel's profile as well as its bottom line.

For example, when the Novotel Bangkok on Siam Square hotel agreed to rent its empty rooftop to EnerGaia, a spirulina producer, it stumbled across an attention-grabbing example of Creating Shared Value (see *Collaboration*, page 134). The hotel got a new, if small, revenue stream; EnerGaia got a modular urban farm; and guests got some healthy superfood options. Moreover, the hotel's unlikely association with innovative urban farming has garnered it plenty of effusive media coverage.

INNOVATION — REFILL NOT LANDFILL

The issue of plastic waste in Cambodia doesn't start and end with tourists, but the roughly five million annual visitors are a huge contributor to it. Collectively, they use around 4.6 million plastic bottles per month. That's around 150,000 bottles each and every day. In response, an informal consortium of hotels, tour companies, restaurants, and bars have come up with an alternative: reusable aluminum bottles. Since being launched in 2015, the Refill Not Landfill scheme has gained traction in the tourism hubs of Siem Reap, Sihanoukville, and Battambang by convincing tourism-driven businesses of the marketing and ecological benefits of taking part. The bottles are durable and can be branded to a company's specifications, while tourists can fill them up for free at over 130 refill stations dotted around the country. With 100,000 reusable bottles sold to date, and the use of around 1.2 million single-use plastic equivalents prevented, this innovative campaign is slowing down the pace at which Cambodia's landfills are growing. Partners, meanwhile, are seen to be taking the country's plastic problem seriously.

The founder of one of Thailand's largest hospitality and leisure empires, WILLIAM E. HEINECKE *is the chairman of Minor International, which runs over 155 hotels across 32 countries. His properties support conservation projects for elephants, turtles, dugongs, and coral reefs.*

What about tourism in Thailand keeps you up at night?

I think that my opinion would be like anyone else's: with tourist numbers soaring, this is placing a huge strain on infrastructure and resources. The government has to pay close attention to try to protect them and not allow them to be over utilized.

What needs to change?

We need to be more mindful and to ensure we protect and do not exploit our environment, as that is the country's main attraction. With climate change and visitors now being more environmentally-conscious, Thailand also needs to show that it can be a pro-green destination. However, this doesn't mean visitors have to rough it – luxurious products and services can be eco-friendly too. Sustainability also includes human and labor rights. For example, stringent enforcement is needed for child exploitation and prostitution in the tourism industry. This may mean that some visitors will leave, but it also means we will have better quality visitors in the long run.

Would you approve of more government intervention then?

No, but I think there should be closer cooperation between the private and public sector on these sorts of issues and how to protect the environment. Very often the private sector has good advice that they can contribute while the government has a tendency to do things arbitrarily that may damage businesses or the industry.

What would be an example of that?

Banning umbrellas on the beach. Yes, there were definitely vendors that took advantage and encroached on public areas, but part of the flavor of Thailand is also the interaction with local communities and the local market. By suddenly banning them it got to the degree where people are afraid of having a wedding on the beach. It went beyond what even the government intended to do. And now smoking is banned at the beach; how does this help?

How can the private sector work more closely with the government?

There are a number of associations that advocate or try to have a dialogue with the government but when dealing with bureaucracy, it is a process and it will take time. It is easy to get people to agree with you but much harder for one to take the initiative. While we have great support in some cities, other municipalities are not so supportive, which shows that the practice is not even universal. So part of the challenge is trying to get the government to understand that they're not even doing these things universally, but just doing them in certain places.

Minor International supports turtle conservation in Phuket.

Novotel Bangkok on Siam Square hotel rents its rooftop to EnerGaia, a spirulina producer.

But while these kinds of happy accidents have media appeal, they often only have minimal real-world impact. Instead, hotels big and small need to adopt an overarching

"The move away from hotel certification is a huge step backwards. It's moving away from verified claims and opening the door to self-promotion and greenwashing."

sustainability strategy that helps them adapt to existing trends, overhaul operations, alter staff perspectives and behavior, and, if feasible, pursue sustainability certification. In recent years, some Thai hotel chains have backed away from third-party certificates linked to the Global Sustainable Tourism Council (GSTC) – the UN-backed body that certifies the certification bodies and sets the gold standard – and opted to pursue internal corporate sustainability programs instead. In Lephilibert's opinion, this is a big step backwards. "It's moving away from verified claims and opening the door to self-promotion and greenwashing and the misleading of consumers," he says.

This trend is just one indicator of the big talk but tepid resolve that typifies the hotel industry when it comes to sustainability. "The interest is healthy but the adoption rates are a bit slow," notes Krip Rojanastien, CEO of luxury wellness retreat Chiva-Som, a renowned leader on environmental and social sustainability. "I think it takes time for business people to get convinced of the benefits. They're too busy thinking about competing and finding their niche or new products and markets. What we need is a realignment of focus."

ENVIRONMENTAL IMPACTS

The World Economic Forum's Travel & Competitiveness Report 2017 ranks Thailand

7th
(out of 136 countries) for natural resources

93rd
for enforcement of environmental regulations

100th
for stringency of environmental regulations

122nd
for environmental sustainability

Thailand has **128 national parks** including **22 marine parks** that encompass some 6,000 square kilometers.

Aviation Emissions
Carbon dioxide emissions per person per one-way trip in 2015

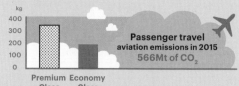

Passenger travel aviation emissions in 2015
566Mt of CO_2

Premium Class   Economy Class

Air travel is the main tourism contributor to global warming: responsible for **40% of total carbon emissions**. Car, rail, accommodation, and activities make up the other 60%.

Sources: World Tourism Organization; PLOS Biology; World Economic Forum's Travel & Competitiveness Report 2017; Griffith University's Global Tourism Dashboard 2016

THE PHI PHI MODEL: SHORING UP SUPPORT FOR TOURISM MANAGEMENT

There is perhaps no more egregious an example of how mass tourism can scar Thailand's natural beauty than busy days at Koh Phi Phi Lay island. Visitors disembark from packed speedboats to run their toes through the fine white sands of Maya Beach, an idyllic cove that rose to fame after featuring in the Hollywood film *The Beach*. In high season there can be up to 5,000 visitors a day. All of this places huge stress on the marine environment – but is also hugely lucrative: entry fee revenues for the marine national park in which Koh Phi Phi resides make up almost half of total revenues from all national parks in the country.

However, soon this textbook case of patently unsustainable tourism may become a role model. In mid-2016, a proposal that Koh Phi Phi Lay be closed each low season (June to September) to allow the environment and ecology to recover found favor among a loose coalition that includes the local community, conservationists, businesses, and, most importantly, the park authorities. The Phi Phi Model, as it is known, also includes tighter enforcement of boat registration, fee collection, and waste management by hotels and restaurants on neighboring Koh Phi Phi Don.

The hope is that the Phi Phi Model will become a test case that proves that commercial tourism and nature conservation can coexist. "If the Phi Phi Model works, it means we can apply it to other marine parks across the country," assistant professor Thon Thamrongnawasawat of Kasetsart University, the marine biologist who proposed the model, told the *Bangkok Post* on its announcement. "It's about raising questions about what kind of tourists we need in national parks: Do we need mass quantity, or do we want small numbers with quality?" However, whether a pilot project that calls for stakeholders to act selflessly can succeed remains to be seen – as of writing, the crux of the Phi Phi Model, seasonal closure, is yet to become a reality.

Tour companies

Tour operators see the problems with their own eyes. They see the litter in the national parks, experience the traffic caused by tour buses, and hear locals lamenting the changes tourism has brought. In response, many offer tour products that are precision-tooled to minimize social, environmental, and cultural impacts.

For example, Intrepid Travel employs local LGBT, hill tribe, or minority people as guides and drivers in an effort to spread benefits to marginalized folks. Andaman Discoveries connects villagers with conscientious travelers interested in authentic experiences like eco tours and homestays (see *Case Study*, page 116). And Local Alike offers hill tribe treks with a twist near Chiang Rai. Guests learn how

to prepare their own food, help locals pick up trash, and learn how farmers have interpreted the late King's Sufficiency Economy Philosophy.

The best of these socially conscious endeavors help to sustain Thai culture, be it through textiles, *muay thai,* or cooking, rather than to eradicate it. They also dovetail with tourism minister Kobkarn Wattanavrangkul's push to create community-based tourism projects that allow tourists to "come away with a better under-standing of the country's culture and heritage and also help narrow the rich-poor income gap."

But while these products attest to the ingenuity and good intentions of a niche but growing segment, they give little clue as to the deep-rootedness of sustainable practices within the companies themselves. Some tour

BENJAMIN LEPHILIBERT is *the founder of the Bangkok-based LightBlue Environmental Consulting, which helps hotels reduce their social and environmental footprint by offering guidance on everything from green meetings to food waste.*

What is your approach to achieving sustainability within hotels?

There are companies helping companies on CSR and communities, but our approach is more human-centered. We're focused on tackling low-hanging fruits to improve efficiency rather than demanding investments in expensive machinery. There is so much that can be done by working with humans. It's about moving from awareness to changes in behavior.

What are your recommendations for hotels just starting out?

Identifying KPIs that relate to all the different subcategories you put under sustainability is fundamental. You need to understand where you are now to know where you want to go. Then you need to work out which KPIs are most important to you and how you can work toward those new objectives within your team, because a one-man sustainability approach won't work. "Why" is also often overlooked: Why is sustainability important? Why are you asking staff to reduce energy consumption? I also recommend working closely with human resources. Most of the time they're neglected in implementing change but they're a good department to work with as they can reach out to everyone, they know internal

communications channels, and they know what leverage and rewards can be used. Finally, it's important to keep track of the KPIs, to keep communicating improvements to your staff and ideally to try and tie those improvements with incentives or bonuses.

Is there a hotel sub-sector that is leading the way?

The hotel groups that are doing better are usually the smaller ones. The larger ones tend to make a lot of noise and to build partnerships with the other big guys so that they build their credentials. But there is no transparency there.

How important are sustainability certification programs to hotels?

There are so many degrees in sustainability, but if you go for proper, third-party certification then there are no question marks. I have been an auditor myself. You don't mess around. You have a certain buffer but if you're not compliant you don't qualify.

Are any local certificates emerging?

We're working on our own certification related to food waste prevention. It's called The Pledge on Food Waste and is third-party audited. It measures detailed financial KPIs to see what the financial impacts of your new measures are on your bottom line, the implications for your staff, the ways in which you engage customers to reduce plate waste, and how you distribute or transform your food excess.

What do you hope to see less of in the future?

Hotels are very slow at adapting to shifting trends. They're not early adopters of new practices. Innovative thinking, challenging their model, adapting – in these areas they're so conservative.

And what do you hope to see more of?

An area where I see potential is in new hotel projects starting from scratch. That's the direction the industry should take if we want to start moving forward: comprehensive approaches. Embed sustainability in every step: branding, values, architecture, construction, interior design, pre-opening, operations, everything.

companies feel that, as one owner puts it, sustainability is a state of mind that doesn't need formulating or articulating: "We don't want to spend time and energy promoting something that's inherent in our core values."

However, those that do try to measure their externalities find it eye-opening. "You can never say that you're truly sustainable," says Willem Niemeijer, the founder and CEO of Khiri Travel, a B2B travel company that went down the certification route and then found itself working through a GSTC-approved checklist that spans everything from office waste to idling passenger vans. To help them stay on top of their KPIs, the company, which employs around 130 staff, has a full-time sustainability guru. "We need to have a sustainability manager to really stay on the cutting-edge," he says.

Other tour companies are more focused on fine-tuning staff skills. In the case of Smiling Albino, a luxury adventure tour company, they go beyond simple job training in an attempt to improve the prospects of their team. "We do things like speech training, emergency rescue training, how to deal with difficult situations – enrichment programs where we send them to learn about things that aren't necessarily connected to their jobs," explains co-founder Daniel Fraser. As for their supply chain, the company willingly pays extra in an effort to foster long-term, healthy relationships. "We're proud to say that we pay our guides and suppliers far more than any other company in travel," says Fraser. Doing this, he explains, improves safety and increases guest enjoyment. "As soon as you bargain it down, the driver is going to drive the boat faster, and

Out in the field, some tour companies are striving to measure their social and environmental impacts.

| CASE STUDY | Sampran Riverside Pioneers Organic Tourism and Helps Rice Farmers |

THE CHALLENGE: Nakhom Pathom province's Sampran Riverside Resort, a center for traditional cultural activities located an hour's drive west of Bangkok, was in need of a consistent supply of organic rice, fruits, and vegetables. But it wanted to create a supply chain that would do more than just put rice on the table. The goal was to also establish a long-term arrangement that creates shared value – empowers Thai rice farmers, who often subsist near or below the poverty line, while sating guests.

THE SOLUTION: The resort's owner decided to start buying the organic produce it needed directly from small-holder farmers. This humble arrangement has gone from strength to strength. To meet its needs, Sampran Riverside now sources approximately eight tons of organic vegetables, fruits and herbs, and three ton of organic rice per month from local farmers.

THE BENEFITS: The farmers can count on guaranteed sales and more reliable incomes. Sampran Riverside gains a more reliable supply of healthy food, as well as an enhanced brand image that gives it a winning edge over its other eco-friendly competitors. Tourists gain something too. "I want to use tourism as a tool to inspire people to become smarter consumers," says the resort's managing director Arrut Navaraj.

Before the deal, there were times when farmers couldn't sell all their rice, and middlemen took some of the profits. Eliminating middlemen also created jobs, as the community started to operate its own rice mill. The by-product of such production, chaff, is used as a natural fertilizer for the rice. Now the

Sampran Model farmers learn about sustainable farming and marketing.

farmers earn additional profits of around 400,000–500,000 baht per year. Also, farmers now avoid using pesticides or chemical fertilizers on the 9,000-rai area they cultivate. Before, such chemicals would end up in water sources such as canals and irrigation ditches. Using fewer chemicals also protects the health of farmers and consumers.

In addition, the arrangement has kickstarted what is today known as the "Sampran Model": a multi-faceted, collaborative project linking organic farmers directly to consumers via a value chain based on fair trade. Its scope also includes a weekend farmers' market, Talad Sookjai, where organic farmers sell their produce and delicacies, and monthly workshops about organic farming and holistic health for visitors. Sampran Riverside's managing director Arrut Navaraj uses the term "organic tourism" to describe what he has created.

The Sampran Model has also inspired Farm to Functions, an alliance between nine hotels, convention centers, and the Thailand Conventions & Exhibitions Bureau whereby they purchase organic products directly from farmers, and promote sustainable agriculture and healthy eating. The first phase of the initiative linked about 300 farmers in Thailand's least developed region, the northeast, to large businesses in Bangkok. And in late 2016 the initiative added an agreement between 13 hotel operators in Bangkok. The operators have committed to purchasing seven tons of jasmine rice per month.

The Sampran Model connects organic farmers directly with tourists at Talad Sookjai.

CASE STUDY   Khiri Travel Fine-Tunes Operations through Certification

For the team at Khiri Travel, sustainability is a moving target.

THE CHALLENGE: For Willem Niemeijer, founder of the Nonthaburi-based destination management company Khiri Travel, it boiled down to this: "How can we be certain we are doing what we say we are doing when it comes to giving back and ensuring fair work practices?" Since its creation, the B2B-focused tour provider has strived to be ethical, but as the years wore on, the need to be held to a standard became more and more apparent. "We knew we were doing good things – educating, training, and raising awareness for projects, etc. – but we wanted to understand ourselves better," he says. "We create and sell tours but on the sustainability part we were amateurs."

THE SOLUTION: Khiri Travel opted for Travelife certification, one of the most respected certification bodies in the travel industry. Niemeijer also decided to aim for the highest level of certification, Travelife Certified, which entails undergoing a full on-site audit every other year.

It was no walk in the park. "We did it in three countries simultaneously, Thailand, Vietnam, and Myanmar, and it was very rigorous," says Niemeijer. Initially, he had expected it to focus more on daily in-the-field operations, where "everything you do has directly to do with the environment and other sustainability issues," but that was only one part of it. Included on Travelife's list of over 200 sustainability criteria, which is approved by the UN-backed Global Sustainable Tourism Council, are many relating to office and labor practices. Suddenly they were forced to consider questions such as:

Do all the staff have contracts and insurance? Are the air conditioners energy-efficient? The questions were simple but their magnitude within the context of Khiri Travel, which employs around 130 staff across its three offices, were huge.

Out in the field, things were even more challenging. Quickly it dawned on Niemeijer and his team that the whole sustainability policy of a company often rests on the actions of one person: the tour guide. "How much can you do to influence that person? What can we fairly ask of them when they already have a tough job? These are things that we have to tackle incrementally."

THE BENEFITS: Despite the hurdles, Niemeijer views the process as invaluable. As well as bringing the staff together on a whole new level, Khiri Travel gained a great deal of training, operations and management advice, plus a roster of measurable KPIs that dovetail with its core principles. Internal processes they had never even considered before – such as the emissions caused by idling vans as they wait for guests to arrive, the disposal of batteries, and more – are now within Niemeijer and his staff's line of sight.

They also gained by observing their rivals. "Other tour operators on Travelife have their own initiatives," explains Niemeijer, "so you basically learn from your competitor what else you can do to become better." While he notes that the commercial benefits and cost savings have been minimal, he strongly believes that other tour operators and destination management companies should follow suit, partly because of the pressure it will exert on the industry's supply chain. "The more of us that are certified the more our suppliers will see there's a competitive advantage to doing more."

Khiri Travel measures its impacts on every environment.

THE GOVERNMENT'S ROLE: FINDING THE RIGHT BALANCE

In May 2017, the Minister of Tourism and Sports, Kobkarn Wattanavrangkul, gave a frank speech in which she acknowledged that "short-term gain has all too often been the driving force in the tourism industry" and that it "stands at a critical juncture." A balance needs to be struck, she said, on three fronts: heritage must be preserved, tourism revenues shared more evenly around the country, and the environment safeguarded. However, she also made it clear that the government believes it can achieve all of these goals while still welcoming higher numbers of tourists each year.

The reasons the government is trying to have its cake and eat it are obvious. Tourism revenue hit a high of 1.64 trillion baht in 2016 (an almost 13 percent rise over 2015), bringing the sector's GDP contribution to ten percent. This money improves the lives of millions of people.

The government knows the number of visitors is creating problems. Back in 2003, it established the Designated Areas for Sustainable Tourism Administration initiative to increase the spread of tourists to underserved provinces such as Loei and Trat. The Tourism Authority of Thailand (TAT) also now fosters community-based projects and high-yield segments such as weddings, health, and food tourism. It also encourages international tourists to stay longer and spend more, and domestic tourists to travel at off-peak periods to less congested areas. "Our marketing plan is focused on quality tourists in all markets because quality tourists do not destroy the environment," explains Tanes Petsuwan, deputy governor for international marketing at the TAT. "We also want to promote the decongestion of popular tourist spots, as well as motivate tourists regarding sustainable tourism."

There have also been drastic measures. Tourists were banned from Koh Tachai, Koh Khai Nui, and Koh Khai Nai indefinitely in May 2016. This came about after motorboats and clumsy snorkelers were found to have damaged coral reefs and accelerated the coral bleaching caused by rising sea temperatures. There has also been a crackdown on "zero-dollar" Chinese tours, which cut corners and prevented money from trickling down to local businesses. But are these measures and policies enough to strike the balance? Can ever-higher numbers of tourists coexist with a policy that claims to prioritize environmental and sociocultural concerns as much as economic ones?

With Thailand's strained infrastructure – hours-long immigration bottlenecks at the airport for example – and the pressure concentrated in tourism enclaves such as Krabi, Chiang Mai, and Phuket, the government has its work cut out – and acknowledges it. "We are totally aware of the backlash against 'over-tourism' in some cities, such as Barcelona and Venice," says Tanes. "We can, should, and must learn from those experiences."

Policy options to foster sustainable practices may include:

- Regular carrying-capacity and environmental impact assessments of popular sites

- Caps on visitor numbers, or tourist group sizes, at popular sites during peak hours

- Incentives or tax credits for hotels and operators investing in energy efficiency or underserved markets

- Closer consultation with tourism stakeholders, so they know where they stand legally and can help sculpt change rather than merely react to it

- Avoid kneejerk interventions that create negative publicity and throw the tourism sector into disarray

- Fuse Thailand 4.0 with the tourism industry, so that Thai startups harness technology and lead the market

- Create an institute of tourism studies to train tour guides and other related human resources

- Train local guides to better deal with international visitors, or revise labor laws so foreign guides can work here legally and become more attuned to local sensitivities

- Launch public-private partnerships that foster the sustainable management and upgrading of tourism zones

- Closer ASEAN cooperation on a range of tourism-related issues, from visas to sex tourism

- Fast-track the infrastructure the industry needs, so that holiday enjoyment-sapping inefficiencies are eliminated

TAKE ACTION

Some key actions for all tourism-industry businesses to consider:

- **Embrace verified certification as a means of developing quantifiable sustainability-related KPIs,** ensuring transparency and helping create pressure to change along your supply chain.

- **Cut your environmental impact by any means possible,** be it by offering reusable water bottles in your hotel, offsetting carbon emissions, or repurposing food waste.

- **Raise awareness of sustainability among tourists** through educational campaigns, marketing, training, and special events.

- **Partner with other businesses to share best practices** and identify local sustainability priorities.

- **Look to tourism industry associations** such as PATA for sector-specific tools that will help you better understand, measure, and mitigate impacts.

- **Urge local and national governments to enforce regulations,** partner with sustainable businesses, and make policies that further sustainable tourism.

- **Harness the power of technology** to improve operations, craft new products, and reach the masses.

Key operations-level actions for hotels:

- **Conduct thorough waste reviews** and energy and water efficiency audits.

- **Raise employee awareness on sustainability** and resource-efficient practices.

- **Develop green meeting facilities** that demonstrate your leadership in sustainability.

- **Involve guests in your green policies.**

Key operations-level actions for destination management companies and tour operators:

- **Expand into new market niches** that sustain local culture and natural heritage rather than taint it, such as adventure, activity-based or community-based tourism.

- **Train staff so that your sustainability shines** in the field as well as in the office.

- **Craft tours that create value for the community** as well as your company and clients.

- **Foster the dispersion of tourists** by creating new tours that tap into the charms of little-visited regions or take them off the beaten track in popular ones.

ultimately they're going to be looking at ways to recuperate that money." For him, it boils down to this: "Am I contributing to an evolving stronger middle-class by the way I treat my suppliers? Or are they merely cogs in a wheel that enriches my entrepreneurial endeavors? If the answer is the latter then there's no way you're sustainable."

Sustaining success

Thailand's charms may be unique, but the quandary the country's tourism industry finds itself in is not. All across the world, governments, tour operators, hoteliers, and the wider public have realized that mass tourism brings with it negatives as well as huge benefits.

As elsewhere, the government bears the ultimate responsibility for implementing regulatory policies that minimize those negatives. Yet, they alone should not and cannot be relied upon to promote social harmony, or to offer lasting protection of Thailand's ecological and cultural riches, or to ensure that the huge rise in tourists visiting the country is matched by a rise in their geographic spread. Instead, each and every stakeholder should take responsibility by phasing out bad practices, sharing their experiences, and assuming a stewardship role of the places they impact upon.

Retailing

- *To remain competitive in the coming decades, retailers must maintain enough flexibility to adapt to the rapid evolution of technologies, consumer demands, and public expectations.*

- *Digital retailing will change the dynamics of customer relations, making them more personalized and empowering for the consumer, while physical retail spaces will also have to change to offer added value beyond simply being a distribution channel.*

- *Cost, style, and range of choice are still the main factors that inform the purchasing decisions of Thai consumers. 'Responsible consumption' brands that address these factors are the 'sustainable products' most likely to perform well in the domestic market.*

- *Systemic change is ultimately dependent on a shift in consumer behavior. Retailers possess both the responsibility to educate consumers about sustainability and the opportunity to profit from it.*

These are dynamic times for the retail sector. Retail conventions that have held true for decades are rapidly being turned on their heads by disruptive new technologies and changing mindsets about consumption. While factors such as price, choice, and convenience still remain relevant among consumers, experience and ethics are becoming bigger drivers of how and what people buy. As the World Economic Forum put it in a 2017 report, "The key drivers of success over the next decade will be centered on building a deep understanding of and connection to the empowered consumer, promptly incorporating transformative business models in both the offline and online space, and establishing key capabilities." Simply put, this is a prime time for retailers to adapt and evolve.

There is also growing public awareness about the dark side of retailing, especially among more developed countries. FoxComm's employee suicides, H&M's sweatshops, WalMart's labor exploitation, L'Oréal's animal testing – in the West, media coverage of such tragedies have become commonplace and

shaped consumer mentality. According to a report on grocery retailers by the Boston Consulting Group, 'responsible consumption' (RC) brands are on the rise. Between 2010 and 2013, sales of RC brands outpaced conventional brands by almost 200 percent in Europe. The group concluded, "RC products are upsetting established market shares in the industry. 'A' brands – those with the high-volume, quality-oriented products that dominated most categories in the past – are now losing out."

It's particularly important for such changes in consumer and retailer behavior to happen here, in Asia. Home to 40 percent of the so-called consumer class, Asia is the center of the global shopping spree and holds significant influence on global retailing trends. And while Thailand has been slower on the uptake than Europe or America, the trend is likely to grow here as well, offering retailers a new way forward to be both ESG-sound and profitable.

Awareness of the environmental impacts of overconsumption, for example, is growing and becoming trendy in some circles, with the rise of organics and ethically minded retail spaces like Osisu, a home furnishings store devoted to upcycled items. Malls, too, have also swiftly identified ways to add value, redefining their role as merely a distribution channel to a space offering healthy experiences and lifestyle choices. Projects such as Thailand Knowledge Park and Central Festival Eastville have renovated the conventional mall space to include work and study areas, libraries, projection rooms, and jogging paths. While these shared spaces support social sustainability, from a business standpoint such changes may prove crucial for offline retailers to remain viable. In these incremental ways, forward-thinking customers and retailers are assigning value to more sustainable spending and shopping habits.

This trend is not something to be feared or avoided: many sustainable solutions – such as the growing popularity of RC products, the rise of the circular economy, curbed waste, and ethical sourcing – all offer opportunities for profit, lowered costs, and improved efficiencies in the retail sector. Moreover, reining in rampant overconsumption has become an environmental and social imperative. Sustainable Development Goal 12: Responsible Consumption and Production tasks the world with curbing consumption even as the population mushrooms. Many of Goal 12's targets call on retailers – in particular, large and transnational companies – to adopt sustainable practices and to report their efforts.

Retailers must note that sustainability and consumption are not mutually exclusive. Joining the growing movement of responsible consumption does not require scaling back or closing up shop. A retail sector tempered with ethics, environmental stewardship, and social consciousness may prove just as profitable and robust as one based on runaway consumption – and, in the increasingly forward-looking, green-tinted future, perhaps more so.

Key risks and challenges

Overconsumption and debt: In Thailand specifically, rampant overconsumption presents real risks not only to the region and the environment, but also to the national economy:

A moving art installation at Central Embassy in downtown Bangkok.

Thailand's high household debt spurred by a consumer mentality that assigns status to material goods has created a shaky economic landscape. This state of indebtedness has given rise to a culture of loan defaults, scant savings, and little immunity in times of financial crisis. It also causes a dangerous level of social

Home to 40 percent of the so-called consumer class, Asia is the center of the global shopping spree.

insecurity – according to a National Institute of Development Administration study, half the Thai population does not have enough savings to retire comfortably. If such a financial scenario turns into a recession, it is bound to hit the bottom line of local and global retailers.

Ethical supply chains: Here in Thailand, public awareness of responsible consumption is still nascent. As a result, many retailers believe that ensuring an ethical supply chain is an unnecessary expense. But with every new exposé of labor exploitation, contamination, environmental atrocities, or unethical practices, Thailand will become less immune to consumer outcry. The international community has already condemned Thailand's fisheries for being complicit in exploitative labor practices, which impacted major global retailers that sourced seafood from Thailand, including Walmart, Woolworths, Coles, and Aldi.

Currently, domestic markets seem either unaware of such abuses through the supply chain or are still unwilling to pay a premium for RC brands. In 2016, researchers at Verdict Retail found that 60 percent of Thai consumers felt that a retailer's sustainability was important to them when buying clothing and footwear, but only 20 percent were willing to pay extra for sustainably sourced products.

Thai consumers "demand style, range, quality, and value for money alongside ethical credentials."

The survey concluded that the driver for this behavior was not complacency per se, but actually a variety of other qualifiers that sustainable products did not meet, such as style, cost, range of choice, and availability. They concluded that Thai consumers "demand style, range, quality, and value

for money alongside ethical credentials, as evidenced by the fact that the clear winners in the sustainability stakes are collections such as Asos Africa, H&M Conscious and Topshop Reclaim, which put style at the forefront of their proposition along with sustainable credentials."

Because style, choice, and cost are the main factors driving Thai consumer behavior (at least in the clothing industry), responsible consumption is likely to increase in Thailand once these needs are met. Furthermore, this is bound to happen as more companies – influenced by louder global consumer outcry – begin improving the designs, variety, and cost of sustainable products to remain competitive. It's only a matter of time until such changes begin to impact the domestic market, and ethical sourcing becomes a priority on a par with cost and style.

The environment: You see it all over Thailand – styrofoam food containers being used by street vendors, supermarket produce and groceries swaddled in unnecessary packaging, clerks at 7-Eleven and Family Mart distributing unnecessary straws and single-use cutlery. Even the physical aspects of Thailand's retail landscape fly in the face of sustainability: big-box stores, mega-malls, and air-conditioned environments burn through electricity most hours of the day. It seems that for most retailers and consumers, the environment is the last thing on their minds.

The overuse of plastics, the prevalence of 24-hour air-conditioned buildings, the disregard for harmful pollutants used in the manufacture of fast-moving consumer goods (FMCG), the propagation of a wasteful consumer mentality – these are the very issues a responsible retail sector should lead the world in addressing. By getting ahead of the game and innovating to support a more sustainable pattern of consuming and producing, retailers can earn a trailblazing reputation, become trusted leaders in the industry, foster new customer loyalty, and create myriad marketing opportunities, as well as benefit from financial and policy incentives, such as green loans for energy efficiency renovations. On the other hand, waiting for environmental penalties and external pressures may save on short-term investment but damage operations long-term.

WE'RE CLOSED TODAY.

Join us outside. Bring friends.

#OptOutside

A shopper in the US outside a storefront promoting the successful #optoutside campaign.

INDUSTRY SNAPSHOT

RETAIL CONSUMPTION

The Thai retail market has a value of

$84.3 billion as of 2015, with grocery sales of

$52.56 billion

Total retail consumption is about **25%** of total GDP

70% of all food retailing

Modern trade such as **hypermarkets, supermarkets,** and **convenience stores** now accounts for roughly

More than **90%** of urban Thais visit convenience stores, on average 13 times per month

WASTE & ENERGY

61 million

Styrofoam boxes are used by Thais per day

Source: Pollution Control Department

1.15 kg

The average amount of waste produced by each Thai daily

Source: Pollution Control Department

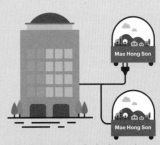

A major Bangkok shopping complex uses almost twice as **much electricity** as Mae Hong Son province

Source: Mekong Commons

The family-owned Central Group operates many of Thailand's biggest malls and department stores, and also has a growing retail presence in Europe. Executive director PICHAI CHIRATHIVAT talks about the conglomerate's sustainability strategy, 'Centrality,' and how it impacts its shopping-related subsidiaries.

How did your 'Centrality' strategy come about?

It started two years ago when Khun Tos [Chirathivat] became the CEO of Central Group. We were thinking: how can all the business units work together, because we have more than 20 companies. In the past, we weren't really connected to each other. Strategy is very, very important and this one gives us synergy, not only in terms of business sense but also in terms of sustainability, creating shared value, and other aims.

Why come up with a new strategy?

We felt like we were doing a thousand things but that no one could really see what we're doing. So all the CEOs came together and we asked ourselves, "What do we really want?" Sustainable development has so many areas but we narrowed it down to four pillars. The first is social equity: we want to improve education, improve quality of life, improve healthcare, and contribute to community wellbeing. For the second, economic prosperity, we want to improve local products and support local SMEs. These two pillars were almost 80 percent of what we've done in the past, but in the past year or two, we have been shifting our focus onto the third column: environmental quality. How to save energy? How to have a clean energy shopping mall? Lastly, the fourth pillar is cultural heritage: we want to reconstruct important temples and bring benefits to all the stakeholders in the provinces.

How does the first pillar, social equity, inform your relationship with staff?

We are currently very focused on the elderly and hiring seniors, because Thailand's population is an ageing one. We also want to hire more handicapped people to work for our company. My dream is to staff one location with only handicapped people except for the manager, starting maybe with a Tops Family Mart.

What is the aim of the economic prosperity pillar?

We are trying to help SMEs develop products. We want to share what we know. We can help them with product development, design, funding, and we can also support them with skills, such as how to work with big companies. We also know what products consumers want and do not want, so we can advise them what to make.

How are Central malls reducing their environmental footprint?

We have installed solar rooftops on three malls and plan to do it for six more. Currently, the amount of energy produced might not be that high compared to the amount of total energy consumption, but we are trying to reduce it and use equipment to make it more efficient. Later on, we plan to try to get tenants interested in energy saving because that plays a big part.

Is it hard to educate consumers about their impact?

We have a 'no bag' day but it is not really working. We are thinking about how we can really make people aware of this. I think we have to educate people.

How else are your malls evolving with the times?

In the old days, people went to a department store, which became a one-stop retailer, then a shopping mall. But now we think this model is not going to work in the future. A lot of shopping centers around the world are dying because they are pure shopping centers. They have to become more than that.

Online disruption: There's no getting around it – digital retailing is changing the game, blurring the line between online and offline retailers, as well as the line between consumer and retailer. The World Economic Forum forecast that e-commerce penetration will grow from ten percent today to more than 40 percent over the next ten years. Similarly, Euromonitor International reported that the digital trend increased significantly among Thai retailers in 2016. As such, those who are not swift to adapt to new digital platforms will lose their competitive edge.

However, digital retailing and marketing still remains a Wild West of dizzying potential and pitfalls, and these new technologies present both risks and opportunities for brick-and-mortar retailers. Hasty transitions made without a deep understanding of digital platforms, their varying uses, and their potential applications can lead to bad investments. "Industry participants will only succeed if they have a relentless focus on using technology to increase the value added to consumers," the World Economic Forum stated in 2017. But the forum added a cautionary note: "They must, however, do so with a realistic assessment of their costs and benefits."

Solutions

Cashing in on the circular economy:
Diminishing resources and evolving consumer ethics could change the very nature of our economy. According to a 2016 report published by business consultants McKinsey and Co, the circular economy has the potential to replace our current, linear economy's trajectory of "make-use-dispose." As its name implies, a circular economy is one in which resources are used for as long as possible to extract maximum value, and then reused or regenerated at the end of service life. The circular economy purports to reduce waste and environmental impacts, increase value captured in supply chains, and improve con-sumption habits. And, according to McKinsey's modeling on the EU, "the net benefit of applying circular-economy principles could be as much as 1.8 trillion Euros annually by 2030." Although this model has yet to make significant headway in Thailand, it presents ample opportunities for profit and differentiation.

The good news is that small – though scattered – steps toward a circular economy are being made here. 'Upcycled' items are coming into vogue, with sustainability-minded customers drawn to the unique provenance of such products, the innovations involved in manufacturing and retailing, and the social good the product represents. One local success story is Chiang Mai-based Rubber

> *"The net benefit of applying circular economy principles could be as much as EUR1.8 trillion annually by 2030."*

Killer, led by architect-turned-product-designer Saroengrong Wongsavun. The studio offers a line of bags, backpacks, wallets, and shoes made from inner tubes. After opening a flagship store in Chiang Mai, Rubber Killer has quickly expanded its distribution to Bangkok, and now also exports to Japan and the United Kingdom.

While small-scale designers and retailers may have the agility to cash in on the circular

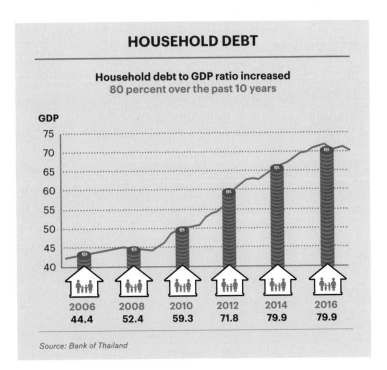

HOUSEHOLD DEBT

Household debt to GDP ratio increased
80 percent over the past 10 years

GDP

2006	2008	2010	2012	2014	2016
44.4	52.4	59.3	71.8	79.9	79.9

Source: Bank of Thailand

CASE STUDY | Tesco Lotus Makes the Physical Retail Space Carbon Neutral

Asia's first zero-carbon Tesco Lotus store was opened in 2011 in Thailand. Tesco plans to become a zero-carbon business by 2050.

THE CHALLENGE: Tesco, a UK-based company, set a goal to utilize 100 percent renewable energy across all its stores and distribution centers globally by 2030, reduce CO_2 emissions by 50 percent by 2020, and to become a zero-carbon business by 2050. Tesco Lotus entered Thailand as a joint venture, thus inherited stores that had been launched since 1996. The continual upgrades of older stores for better energy efficiency have resulted in some significant milestones.

THE SOLUTION: In 2016 Tesco installed solar rooftops at five distribution centers and eight stores for on-site solar power generation, and it plans to continue installing more. The store is utilizing more efficient technologies, such as LED lights and more efficient cooling and refrigeration systems.

The company underwent the first independently certified carbon footprint audit in Thailand in 2009, in cooperation with the Ministry of Natural Resources and the Environment. The first 'green' store was opened in Thailand in 2004 with more than 6,000 square meters of photovoltaic panels on the roof, which generates 12.5 percent of the store's electricity requirements and saves approximately 15 percent of carbon emissions compared to a regular store. From 2006 to 2008 Tesco cut carbon emissions by 14.4 percent, then 19.54

percent from 2006 to 2009. In 2008 they opened their second 'green' store with a goal to increase energy savings to 30 percent and reduce carbon emissions by 40 percent through the use of new technologies, such as wind turbines and a solar cooling system.

Tesco opened its first zero-carbon store in 2010 in the UK, followed by the first in Asia in 2011, in Thailand. The store utilizes natural refrigeration with hydrocarbon, and a biogas system collects leftover vegetables and bread to make biogas used to cook food.

THE BENEFITS: A solar farm generating 264 kW reduces power consumption by 489,000 kWh per year, leading to significant cost savings. Smart engineering, such as porous concrete that reduces reflected heat, a double airlock entrance, rammed earth walls, a natural skylight, LED lighting, a wind turbine, and a rainwater capture system has lowered expenditures on water, HVAC, and energy systems.

The store has achieved 100 percent offset average emissions from carbon and energy saving initiatives, and Tesco Lotus was awarded the Green Retailer Award by the Prime Minister on the Thai Environment Day in 2015.

economy, it may be harder for large retailers to make the switch. One useful strategy to make the transition is to approach it incrementally. Analyzing which products or materials have the biggest impact will help prioritize the most effective changes, whether it be the potential of certain materials to contribute to a closed resource loop, or the replacement of low-performing products with more durable materials. For example, when the footwear company Timberland decided to reduce its environmental impact, it developed a Green Index that measures the carbon footprint, chemicals, and resources consumed by each material. Using this index, Timberland could analyze which products were the most harmful, which were the least, and which had the best profit margins. This made it possible to prioritize the use or disuse of certain products, making the transition to sustainability methodical and rooted in profit analysis.

Fostering culture and community: It's a trend you see across the nation: cities are becoming saturated with large stores, and each new development tends to displace existing businesses and communities. After Thailand's deregulation of trade in 1996, the number of hypermarkets and convenience stores skyrocketed, increasing its share in food retailing from 5 percent to over 50 percent. Meanwhile, according to retailing researcher Randall Shannon, the number of mom-and-pop shops decreased by a third, dropping from 400,000 to 280,000 within a decade.

The emergence of modern trade formats has given rise to a bittersweet mixture of social gains and losses. While major retailers such as Tesco Lotus have provided communities with newfound conveniences, better prices, consumer protections, and employment opportunities, they have also led to the closure of many traditional trade formats, such as mom-and-pop shops and fresh markets. At the same time, in high-density urban areas, rent has become so high that entire neighborhoods have become devoid of traditional retailers that once served as community gathering places. In many ways, these developments are breeding a landscape of one-size-fits-all consumption and cultural homogenization, in addition to the loss of a sense of community and the livelihoods provided by Thai SMEs.

But at the same time, major retailers and malls are filling gaps, providing needed services, such as public spaces, entertainment, access to international brands, and secure employment.

According to retailing experts Boonying Kongarchapatara and Randall Shannon, one strategy that large discount stores can adopt to ease tension with local retailers is to partner with them. Makro offers an excellent

After Thailand's deregulation of trade in 1996, the number of mom-and-pop shops decreased by a third, dropping from 400,000 to 280,000 within a decade.

example: the Makro Retail Alliance (MRA) program, launched as part of Makro's CSR, offers assistance to small, traditional retailers to stay competitive. Participants receive training in managerial skills and accounting, in addition to tools like seminars and shop decorating tips. While traditional shops benefit from such training, Makro is able to act as a wholesaler for them, sourcing products for resale at competitive prices. Consequently, Makro has met with less resistance from local retailers in

Inside CentralWorld's Thailand Knowledge Park. Retailers are increasingly offering community spaces.

Outside Siam Paragon shopping complex in downtown Bangkok. Mobile phone usage is rapidly changing the shopping experience.

its expansion upcountry. Similarly, Unilever – about as global a consumer-goods company as it gets – is combining the survival of local mom-and-pops with an effort to reach previously untapped markets. Through its Platinum Store program, Unilever has

> ## *Unilever is combining the survival of local mom-and-pops with an effort to reach previously untapped markets.*

successfully rebranded traditional shops to stay competitive with retailing giants like 7-Eleven and Family Mart, while also ensuring promotional and sales opportunities for its products (see *Case Study*, page 275).

Partnerships between local stores and manufacturers also exist, such as SCG's

program to help local home construction shops become authorized Cement Thai Home Mart stores. According to Kongarchapatara and Shannon, thousands of construction material shops have joined the program and successfully become more competitive. Many other retail sectors – including electronics, bookstores, coffee shops, and toy stores – have used such franchise solutions and partnerships to make small retailers more competitive with modern trade formats. Indeed, strong partnerships will become ever more essential as rapid changes in technologies and expected services necessitate streamlined collaboration among retailers, suppliers, distributors, and other industry players.

Government participation can also play a crucial role in the survival of small-scale retailers. Deputy director general of the Office of Small and Medium Enterprises, Dr Wimonkan

Kosumas, says countries like Japan and Korea have set public policy precedents that protect the work and livelihoods of traditional shops, or help them retain employees with valuable skills.

"In Korea or Japan, if employees have rare expertise, or if high-demand expertise is at risk of being bought out by large enterprise, then the government intervenes," says Dr Wimonkan. "Small business and micro-enterprises normally cannot afford to have a provident fund scheme for their employees, but in order to attract qualified employees to stay in small businesses, the government will intervene. They put up maybe half the cost, and the owner pays half. But in Thailand we don't have such schemes yet."

'Going local' in terms of inventory, aesthetics, and supply is another way retailers are evening the playing field and profiting at the same time. Global brands that take a more local,

THE RISE AND RISE OF ECOMMERCE

As things stand, online shopping only accounts for

about 3%

of total retail sales in Thailand

Cash on delivery (COD) is still the preferred payment method for

70% of Thai ecommerce shoppers.

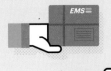

And Thailand boasts the unique claim to being the biggest social commerce market in the world:

51%	Thailand
31%	Malaysia
27%	China
6%	Canada

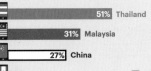

51% of online shoppers in the kingdom purchase products using social networks.

Fast forward to 2025, and Thailand's ecommerce landscape will look markedly different:

Thailand is projected to be the **second biggest ecommerce market in the region,** after only Indonesia.

Online shopping's share of total retail sales should have **surpassed 15%**

Its total value is expected to have increased 12-fold to

US$11.1 billion

from the current figure of US$900 million.

And, judging by today's fast evolving and hyper-competitive marketplace, **new online giants** will have dislodged the old ones.

Sources: ECOMScape: Thailand, PwC Total Retail survey 2016

CASE STUDY | Whole Planet Foundation Alleviates Poverty through Microfinance

THE CHALLENGE: US-based Whole Foods Market is an organic grocery retailer sourcing products from all over the world, procuring items as wide-ranging as wool from Mongolia and chocolate from Tanzania. As such, its operations have significant impacts on developing countries, producers, and consumer behavior. And, while fair labor practices and promoting environmental sustainability are both integral parts of sustainable retailing, Whole Foods wanted to go one step beyond: to alleviate poverty wherever they source products outside the direct supply chain.

THE SOLUTION: In 2005, under the vision of CEO John Mackey, Whole Foods launched Whole Planet Foundation (WPF), a nonprofit that uses microfinance to aid income generation in vulnerable communities, integrating entrepreneurship with CSR.

"WPF believes that the most effective role we can play in creating a world free of poverty is to invest in entrepreneurs and entrepreneurial solutions that alleviate poverty now and for future generations," says Daniel Zoltani, global programs director of Whole Planet Foundation. "This is a bottom-up approach. Give a hand up, rather than a hand out."

While many retailers limit social responsibility to fair labor practices among its suppliers (which Whole Foods also does), WPF is committed to serving communities outside the market's supply chain. As a private nonprofit foundation, it is careful to avoid 'self-dealing' by financing or assisting Whole Foods' suppliers and growers. Instead, the foundation donates money to local microfinance institutions (MFIs) working on the ground in countries where Whole Foods does business. These funds are disbursed to farmers, artisans, and other micro-entrepreneurs almost exclusively outside the supply chain. Supporting their businesses, in turn, supports a wider community that is not restricted to the market's operations.

"Our simple strategy is to direct subsidized capital to the loan pool of partner MFIs to support greater outreach to high-risk, more vulnerable, remote, low-income communities which are often more expensive to serve," says Zoltani. To this end, roughly 88 percent of WPF-funded entrepreneurs are women. The foundation currently supports 2.3 million micro loans which support 3.9 million beneficiaries across 69 countries and to date has authorized roughly US$75 million globally.

The program is also unique in how it is integrated into the stores' daily operations. One percent of proceeds from all products labeled 'Whole Trade Guarantee' is donated to Whole Planet Foundation. This covers 100 percent of the foundation's overhead so all other revenue goes directly to subsidize microloans. Customers are incentivized to purchase Whole Trade Guarantee products through the label's added value of meeting strict environmental, fair trade, and quality standards.

THE BENEFITS: While WPF's microfinance activities do not cross paths with Whole Foods' supply chain, the retailer still reaps tangible business benefits, such as enhanced image and marketing opportunities. The foundation provides key ways to promote the store's Whole Trade Guarantee label, adding another incentive for customers to buy. The foundation has also strengthened relationships between the retailer and its partner suppliers, many of which participate in WPF's efforts by making annual donations. In addition, an annual Prosperity Campaign, a two-week fundraising campaign encouraging customers, suppliers, and staff to donate, raises awareness about impoverished communities around the world and creates meaningful dialogue between the retailer and its customers.

Then, of course, there's the question of furthering Whole Foods' mission as a conscious company and living by its core values. Zoltani notes that committing to these values in action creates purpose-driven staff, as well as a more conscious and responsive consumer base. "These do not directly impact the bottom line of Whole Foods Market per se," he says, "but they definitely contribute to the success of the company."

Whole Foods strives to boost incomes in vulnerable communities.

CASE STUDY | Unilever Partners with Small-Scale Retailers

Platinum Store participants pose together with Unilever representatives. Unilever is partnering with some smaller retailers to help them remain competitive.

THE CHALLENGE: Although giant, multinational retailers, convenience stores, and manufacturers are displacing traditional 'mom-and-pop' shops around the world, these small, usually family-owned shops still make up a significant part of global retailers' consumer base. Rather than displacing Thailand's general trade, some giant consumer goods companies have been looking for ways to partner with them – to help them become more competitive, and therefore maintain a mutually beneficial relationship as wholesaler.

THE SOLUTION: In accordance with Unilever's stated mission to 'make sustainable living commonplace,' the company launched the Platinum Store program to help traditional retailers in Thailand compete with global-brand convenience stores and discount stores. Mom-and-pops that become Platinum Stores receive management training on merchandising, marketing, advertising, and running promotional campaigns. The stores are given a blue star logo that signifies 'star quality,' or services on par with global convenience stores, such as better lighting, attractive displays, community washing machines, and customer loyalty programs. Sometimes Unilever is able to bring in added services through partner companies, such as ATMs. In return, all Platinum Stores must ensure that they have high-visibility displays of Unilever products.

A study conducted by Unilever found that Platinum Stores increased sales by an average of ten percent. What started as an effort to help one flood-stricken mom-and-pop shop in Bangkok in 2011 has become a nationwide program, with more than 10,000 stores participating to date.

THE BENEFITS: The first Platinum Store increased its sales by 400 percent within six months of opening, and the added value and enhanced customer experience of Platinum Stores have successfully warded off displacement by large convenience stores such as 7-Eleven and Family Mart. Mom-and-pop shops whose businesses were once threatened have been able to not only increase profits, but to also keep competition at bay.

For Unilever, the Platinum Store program (part of a larger, global scheme called the Unilever Sustainable Living Plan) is an opportunity to fulfill the company's mission of providing livelihoods to the underprivileged. It also reaps quite tangible business benefits in terms of distribution and profit: because many small retailers service hard-to-penetrate urban enclaves and remote rural areas, partnering with these mom-and-pops allows Unilever to promote and sell its products to previously untapped markets. Rob Rijnders, vice president of customer development of Unilever Thai Trading Limited, told the *Bangkok Post* that Platinum Store sales contribute six to seven percent of the company's total sales.

THE OPPORTUNITIES OFFERED BY THE EXPANDING AGEING MARKET

The rising elderly population means more demand for personalized services.

Growing awareness about responsible consumption is not the only thing changing consumer behavior – Thailand is undergoing a major demographic shift as well. Euromonitor International reports that an ageing society will be the next big trend in the Thai retail sector. People aged 65 and older made up 11 percent of the population in 2016.

This number is forecast to grow to 14 percent by 2021, then double to 27 percent by 2050. Along with this comes another telling trend: the percentage of older people who can use the Internet almost doubled from five percent to nine percent between 2010 and 2015.

Together these statistics point toward a major shift in spending power: a lot more elderly people will be shopping in the coming years, both online and offline. Retailers will have to give more thought to this across several dimensions. On one hand, the physical accessibility of stores – such as wheelchair access, rest areas within stores, and stock display – will become a growing consideration. Added services catering to the elderly, such as delivery, carry-out, or personal shopping services may increase competitiveness. Demand for certain products or types of stores are expected to grow, including dietary supplements, pet supplies, and home furnishing products that cater to limited mobility. To meet the growing demands of the elderly, retailers may need to reconfigure both inventory and how they offer it.

CAPTURING THE RISING SENIOR MARKET

Food and Beverages

Stock organic food products

Offer diet and nutrition advisory services

Open restaurants with healthy choices and delivery services

Serve nutritious ready meals with suitable portion size and clear labeling

Retail Trade

Provide home delivery service

Add space for elderly to meet up and socialize

Choose small community malls, as preferred by older consumers

Increase sales and distribution via online channels

Sources: Insight: Staying Ahead of Thailand's Graying Society, SCB Economic Intelligence Center

region-centric approach actually add value to product lines. This is because brands and retailers are able to better serve and cater to local tastes, as well as preserve culture and identity in the face of globalization. Additional benefits are that local products rack up fewer food miles, shorten the supply chain, and foster stronger relationships with suppliers. This reduces emissions, cuts transportation costs, and puts value and livelihoods back into local economies. Big C, for example, promotes the local entrepreneurship and craftsmanship of OTOP (One Tambon, One Product) producers. The store's 'Taste OTOP, Taste of Thailand Zone' launched in 2013 to promote OTOP food products as souvenirs for tourists.

According to Central Group executive director Pichai Chirathivat, a key strategy to build a more inclusive retail sector is to shift from CSR to CSV, or 'creating shared value.' This means creating economic and social values simultaneously. "People's lifestyles are changing, so we need to be alert all the time. The way we do business, the way we treat our customers and stakeholders, the way we get more involved with people and communities – the whole thing comes down to the word 'sustainability,'" Pichai says. Creating shared value often means collaborating with competitors. "In the past, if you were competitors, you didn't talk to each other. But now it's changing as we are working together. I think this is the future of doing business."

Rather than launching ad hoc sustainability initiatives such as, say, one recycling drive per year, CSV works to establish corporate policies that ensure sustained social impacts in addition to economic benefits for the company. The proper payment and treatment of staff and suppliers is a good example. This not only helps increase the quality, yield, and value of goods, but also improves the livelihoods of all those involved, from the supply chain to the administrative office. Such measures also go far to reinforce brand image and reputation. To this end, Tops and Tesco Lotus supermarkets are highly active in educating and improving practices among their suppliers. In 2016, Tesco Lotus received 183 Best Workplace for Labor Relations and Welfare awards. These types of commitments do not just improve the lives and communities touched by the company;

Entertainment, both real and virtual, is now a part of the Bangkok retail experience.

they also go far in shifting public awareness and dialogue about what responsible consumption and production looks like.

With analysts forecasting online sales to grow 15 to 20 percent year-on-year, digital retailing cannot be ignored.

Tapping into tech: With analysts forecasting online sales to grow by 15 to 20 percent in Thailand year-on-year, retailers cannot ignore the scale and reach with which digital markets will revolutionize the sector. In addition to changing the way people buy and sell, technology can accelerate the move toward sustainable consumption in other ways.

For one, digital markets democratize the retail sector, offering opportunities for small retailers to reach global markets. Social media, too, provides platforms with unprecedented reach to reinforce brands and educate the customer. The major sporting goods retailer REI offers a prime example of how social media can benefit the bottom line while promoting sustainability: rather than participate in Black Friday, the biggest shopping day of the year in the US, REI became one of the few retailers

US retailer REI closed its stores on the year's biggest shopping day to make a statement against consumption.

which allows retailers to track consumer tastes and behavior, can help develop more efficient forecasting of supply and demand to enhance freshness or reduce waste.

Then, of course, there are the innovations taking place within the physical retail space, making offline retailing more sustainable. Tesco launched its first zero-carbon store in the UK in 2010, followed by the first in Thailand in 2011 (see *Case Study*, page 270). Such initiatives will only become more common as retailers renovate brick-and-mortar stores in an attempt to heighten efficiencies and minimize waste.

Educating the customer: At the end of the day, everything comes down to the consumer. Retailers may make incremental changes toward sustainability but, perhaps in this sector more than in any other, systemic change depends ultimately on shifts in consumer behavior.

In 2016, Simon Mainwaring, CEO of WeFirst branding consultancy, told *Eco-Business* that there is considerable push and pull between retailer and consumer in regards to changing consumption patterns. "Consumers are voting with their hard-earned dollars for companies authentically investing in making our world a better place socially and environmentally," he said. "On the latter, brands are realizing that to maintain their relevancy they must shift towards making positive change. Further, the competitive landscape is nudging these efforts forward and, in the future, we will see a shift towards brands competing to be the most purposeful."

to take a stand against overconsumption and close all its stores during the annual event. Instead, it used Twitter to encourage staff and customers to take photos of themselves spending time amid nature rather than shopping on Black Friday. This resulted in 1.4 million unique participants, heightening REI's visibility, reinforcing their brand, proving commitment to the company's core values, and earning REI prime publicity during peak shopping season.

Currently in Thailand, the most relevant digital trends are the direct sale and marketing opportunities provided by the chat application Line (which, according to Euromonitor International, is used by 33 million people nationwide) and the social media platform Facebook. While programs like Line official and Line@ allow retailers to communicate directly with their consumers, Facebook has introduced new ways to expand reach through viral marketing. Adapting to and integrating such digital tools are not only necessary to remain viable, but are also a way to boost efficiency and sustainability. Digital retailing,

Some retailers have begun to take concrete action to curb unsustainable attitudes, such as charging customers a fee to use a plastic bag to carry their purchases. Some retailers in Thailand, such as the sporting goods store Decathlon, already do this. However, beyond such practical measures, retailers must also help nurture key shifts in perspective. Public consciousness should not automatically assume disposability of material goods but, rather, acknowledge their life cycles. To this end, the value of a product should be put on its provenance, quality, and 'narrative' over its convenience, disposability, or the

TAKE ACTION

- **Practice ethical sourcing** to foster responsible consumption, make stronger ties with local suppliers, and profit. Market and stock responsible consumption products to take advantage of growing market share, and forge partnerships with artisan brands that can help differentiate and build the social capital of the business.

- **Address social needs to differentiate from competition.** For enhanced efficiency, make sure the social need integrates well with the corporate mission.

- **Run shared-value initiatives** that foster community development, spur new domestic markets, allow for knowledge exchanges, and shorten supply chains.

- **Use tech, digital, and online tools and social media** to cater to underserved markets, interact with consumers, publicize ethical products and initiatives, track supply and demand, and boost efficiencies.

- **Curb waste and unnecessary packaging**, and use sustainable packaging where possible. Incentivize recycling among employees and customers (such as stocking and selling canvas shopping bags or tote bags), and publicize all such efforts.

- **Instate measurement matrices that will help improve efficiency.** All retailers should strive to track energy and waste in order to set goals and develop improvements in environmental impacts. Similarly, proper bookkeeping, inventory, and stock management is required to boost efficiency and remain competitive.

socioeconomic status it brings. It is becoming easier to assign such sustainable values as manufacturers, designers, and artisans realize the marketability of responsible production and begin to publicize these aspects of their products.

Siam Discovery, a department store in Bangkok, is an example of this kind of new, narrative-driven retailer. In particular the mall's Objects of Desire store promotes homegrown, Thai production and design, providing alternatives to high-emissions imports. Marketing local products as chic or as on par with international products also shifts consumer mentality to a more sustainable one that values local heritage, local products, and local artisans.

Looking forward

Whether through online formats, mall complexes, outdoor markets, or small retailers, the simple activity of purchasing goods powerfully shapes our habits, our mindsets, and the world around us. So imagine the positive impacts of a responsible retail sector – one that thinks beyond high volume sales and breakneck growth, and

addresses the inherent contradictions and flaws in its business model. It could be revolutionary – instrumental in changing what we buy and maybe even how much of it we buy.

"Consumers are voting with their hard-earned dollars for companies that are authentically investing in making our world a better place."

With much of the West already making grand gestures and significant headway towards responsible consumption, such a future is certainly within our grasp. But Thailand's retail sector must now step up to the challenge, realize its position of power, and begin to affect incremental change. How retailers facilitate trade, how they interact with consumers, and how they behave as buyers themselves – these are all crucial factors in the fight to ensure the planet can continue to meet our needs. But also at stake is the health of the nation's fragile communities, culture, and economy.

Finance

- *Thai financial institutions should recognize the growing demand for ESG-based investment and make sure they are geared up to provide the expertise and the platforms needed to meet it.*

- *Rather than leaving matters to the government, Thailand's financial services industry must take a leadership role in establishing policies regarding hot topics like responsible lending and transparency.*

- *Fintech can represent a threat or an opportunity to traditional financial institutions, depending on whether or not they choose to incorporate this rising trend into their business services model.*

- *"Green" lending should not be viewed as a cosmetic measure to glam up a bank's reputation, but rather as a real opportunity to be harnessed for profit.*

Thailand's financial sector is one of the most advanced and resilient among developing countries. Lessons learned from the 1997 Asian Financial Crisis have helped the country navigate the global crisis of 2008 and beyond. But financial services businesses now face the most profound challenges since the country's economic recovery at the turn of the century.

The biggest come from technology and, powered by that, innovative and disruptive forms of competition. But others, while less dramatic, will also play a part in determining the outlook for the sector in the coming years. These include a changing mindset among policy-makers and customers alike that places sustainable products and services at the center of any discussion about business strategy.

Thailand's financial businesses, in particular the country's banks, are well placed to rise to these challenges. They still enjoy an enviably high level of public trust, which they must now use as a platform on which to embrace the opportunities these challenges offer – to support those environmental, social, and governance (ESG) policies and projects on which a more sustainable economy are built.

This involves doing the following:

- **Avoid reckless risks that, when they don't pay off or go as planned, can negatively impact other actors – and sometimes entire economies**

- **Stop rewarding employees for high-risk, high-return behavior for which, in the end, shareholders and customers may have to pay the price**

- **Offer responsible retail products where the costs and potential losses, not just the potential gains, are transparent**

- **Protect the security and privacy of customers' data**

- **Stop allowing (or in some cases even helping) corrupt people to hide their money**

- **Adopt a recruitment policy that reflects the diversity of Thai society**

- **Make services available to all sections of our society, not just the well-off**

- **Stop lending to enterprises that are**

reckless about the environmental and social consequences of their business practices, and support those that invest in industries and products that actively improve or mitigate damage to the environment or society

- Pay more than cosmetic attention to the environmental costs of the use of energy and other non-renewable resources

Thai financial institutions do not have an outstanding record on these issues, much to the dismay of policy makers and regulators. A recent comprehensive study by Sarinee Achavanuntakul, et al, on sustainable banking in Thailand, observed that: "Thai banks still conduct haphazard social or environmental activities through their CSR (corporate social responsibility) campaigns which are largely unrelated to their expertise and normal business operations. Social, environmental, and governance (ESG) risks are still seen mainly as 'compliance risks,' with the implicit assumption that such risks are sufficiently contained in relevant legal and regulatory frameworks." (See *How Green Is Your Bank?*, page 285.)

Thailand's financial services businesses cannot leave matters in the hands of the authorities when it comes to setting the agenda regarding what is right or wrong. Likewise, they should not think that customers and clients can be appeased by charitable contributions.

There are always going to be difficult trade-offs between financial and non-financial factors. But the sector must acknowledge the high costs of having to overcome the damage done to balance sheets and reputations by imprudent lending or opaque financial products and practices that are sooner or later likely to be unmasked. But it goes further than that – there is an overwhelming business case for the financial sector to seize the many opportunities that reside in a strategy that responds positively to the priorities listed above.

Financing for sustainable development

The role of finance in sustainable development involves all parties – policymakers, financial

A boy caught in the 2011 floods holds money aloft to keep the notes dry.

institutions, borrowers, and society at large. The private sector cannot rest on its laurels by pointing to past achievements and wait for the government to forge policy in areas that are either untouched or inadequately attended to. These include:

- Better access to banking services for the marginalized and poor (see *Case Study*, page 287)

- Greater access to (sometimes unsecured) funding for small enterprises (see *A Gift Thai Banks Need to Appreciate*, page 288)

- More transparent products that highlight their risks, not just the potential benefits

- Recruitment and human capital management practices that are attuned to Thailand's diversity

- More consideration of the environmental and social consequences of the projects they finance

- A willingness to find ways to fund projects and industries that are themselves inspired or driven by sustainability principles

On the policy front, the Bank of Thailand (BoT) is in the process of strengthening its so-called "market conduct" regulatory framework aimed at consumer protection and governance for banks. Part of this involves policy guidance on sustainable banking, which, among other things, will seek to promote more financial literacy as part of a campaign against indebtedness, a perennial weakness in the Thai economy.

Financial illiteracy and ill-considered borrowing by the poor are not just development issues for the government and the central bank to address.

However, financial illiteracy, ill-considered borrowing by the poor, and financial inclusivity are not just development issues for the government and the central bank to address. They threaten macro-economic stability and therefore the wellbeing of all, not least the financial services sector, which is the first line of resource-consuming defense when debt threatens to become unmanageable. The BoT introduced a "Debt Clinic" in mid-2017 to assist commercial banks in steering troubled borrowers back to financial health.

Where policy leads the way, enforcement and compliance will, of course, be the ultimate test of a market conduct regulatory framework, but financial institutions cannot afford to wait until Thailand's other public institutions manage to catch up with them. In many cases, it is still a common practice for banks to trumpet their financial literacy seminars as evidence of CSR while practicing opaque and aggressive hard sell techniques on unsuspecting customers in their retail departments. In mid-2017, the BoT introduced new curbs on credit card lending as one part of its efforts to rein in household debt.

Consumer protection in Thailand is still a work in progress. There is, for example, still no legal requirement for any service – public or private – to inform stakeholders when there has been a privacy breach, such as data being stolen through computer hacking. The private sector should not wait for a government remedy to this serious shortcoming in Thai law.

In the longer term – if developments elsewhere serve as a guide – policymakers are likely to move toward setting up frameworks

INNOVATION A CLINIC FOR THE UNWEALTHY

With oversight from the Bank of Thailand (BoT), 16 Thai and foreign banks began piloting a "Debt Clinic" in 2017 to help individual debtors turn more than 100 billion baht in unsecured loans into performing assets. "The clinic is aimed at helping those who have debts with multiple creditors to pay off their debt, while at the same time strengthening good financial discipline to prevent social and economic issues that could arise," said Bank of Thailand governor Dr Veerathai Santiprabhob. He added that National Credit Bureau figures suggest that about 500,000 people are qualified to participate in the program.

The 16 banks are Bangkok Bank, Krungthai Bank, Siam Commercial Bank, Kasikornbank, Bank of Ayudhya, Kiatnakin Bank, Citibank, CIMB Thai Bank, TMB Bank, Tisco Bank, Thai Credit Retail Bank, Thanachart Bank, UOB Thai, Land and Houses Bank, Bank of China and Industrial, and Commercial Bank of China (Thai).

Assistance was made available to regular income earners who failed to repay credit and cash cards and personal loans with at least two banks for more than three months before 1 May, 2017.

Participants are to pay back their debt through the company that operates the clinic, Sukhumvit Asset Management (SAM), a wholly-owned subsidiary of the Financial Institutions Development Fund. The latter was set up by the BoT in the 1980s to provide assistance to troubled financial institutions and played a vital role in nursing the sector back to health after the 1997 financial crisis. Debt is paid back at rates far below the central bank's ceiling interest rate for credit cards, and participants are required to sign an agreement that they will not run up additional debt for at least five years.

INDUSTRY SNAPSHOT

The combined net profits of Thailand's four largest banks totaled **151.9 billion baht** in 2016, while their total assets amounted to **11,392 billion baht**.

SIAM COMMERCIAL BANK

Net Profit	Total Assets
47.6 billion	**2,913** billion

KRUNG THAI BANK

Net Profit	Total Assets
32.3 billion	**2,689** billion

KASIKORNBANK

Net Profit	Total Assets
40.2 billion	**2,846** billion

BANGKOK BANK

Net Profit	Total Assets
31.8 billion	**2,944** billion

KASIKORNBANK was the **1st** commercial bank in ASEAN selected for the DJSI World Index and DJSI Emerging Markets Index.

Number of financial institutions on Thailand's ESG100 list in 2017: **11**

FINTECH

Projected transaction value of Thailand's fintech market:

US$11.5 billion in 2017 → **US$23.4** billion in 2021

By mid-2017, **3 major Thai banks** had set up dedicated Venture Capital subsidiaries with combined funds of **US$110** million to support fintech projects.

CONSUMER TRENDS

92% of **Thais** have a high level of trust in banks.

Household debt in Thailand has increased drastically from 54.6% in 2007 to **84.2% of GDP** in 2015.

Thailand's ratio of debt to income is 121%, on par with levels in the US and UK.

Some 20% of 29-year-old Thais have debt that has lapsed into non-performing loans.

28.3 million individuals and **30,000 juristic persons** have registered to use Thailand's new national digital-payment system, PromptPay.

Increased use of electronic payments, including credit, debit, and prepaid cards, added **US$3.18 billion (0.19%)** to Thailand's gross domestic product from 2011-2015, the largest weighted average increase in Asia.

Sources: Long-Term Issuer Default Ratings by Fitch Ratings, 2017; Krung Thai Bank Annual Report 2016; KASIKORNBANK Annual Report 2016; SCB Annual Report 2016; Bangkok Bank Annual Report 2016; Nikkei Asian Review; DJSI; Thaipat Institute ESG100, 2017; Provincial Administration Department; 2015 McKinsey Report; Bangkok Post; TechCrunch, Bloomberg; Krungsri; Statista; Bank of Thailand, Moody's Analytics; National Credit Bureau

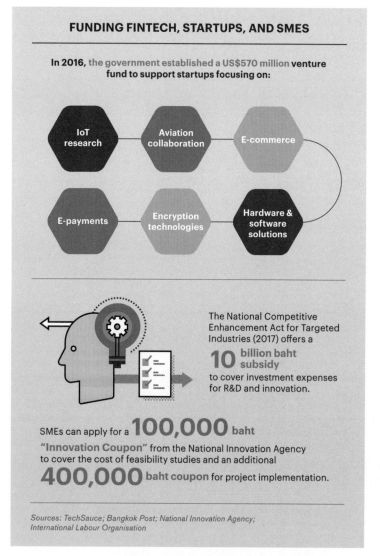

FUNDING FINTECH, STARTUPS, AND SMES

In 2016, the government established a US$570 million venture fund to support startups focusing on:

- IoT research
- Aviation collaboration
- E-commerce
- E-payments
- Encryption technologies
- Hardware & software solutions

The National Competitive Enhancement Act for Targeted Industries (2017) offers a 10 billion baht subsidy to cover investment expenses for R&D and innovation.

SMEs can apply for a 100,000 baht "Innovation Coupon" from the National Innovation Agency to cover the cost of feasibility studies and an additional 400,000 baht coupon for project implementation.

Sources: TechSauce; Bangkok Post; National Innovation Agency; International Labour Organisation

over the world. Lending institutions need to re-examine their risk and prudential rules on a consistent basis and desist from incentivizing high-risk, high-reward practices.

This lesson has been repeatedly and expensively learned by global banks that have been forced to pay vast sums in fines for violating regulatory guidelines and laws by not adequately supervising employees who turned a blind eye to money laundering or market manipulation. If Thai banks wait for the regulators to move before they act, they risk being expensively behind the curve in the same way.

Meanwhile, advances in financial technology (commonly known as "fintech") offer many potential benefits on both financial inclusion and cost. However, for now the established institutions are focused on how to harness these technologies to better deliver traditional services mostly to existing customers.

This is a lost opportunity, particularly in light of the fact that the big corporate market is near saturation with thin margins and all the big players have access to similar technological capacity. However, new and less explored opportunities exist among smaller enterprises and minor entrepreneurs. One example is the Thailand-based payments startup Omise, which in July 2017 raised US$25 million in new financing in an 'initial coin offering (ICO).' An ICO is like an IPO (initial public offering), except the investor doesn't receive shares or ownership rights but rather 'digital coins' or tokens that can be traded on digital currency (sometimes called 'cryptocurrency') platforms (see *Case Study*, page 290).

Moreover, Thailand's urban middle class tends to regard electronic financial services with suspicion if those services are not provided by their bank. But there is a large potential customer base beyond them. It is an anomaly that Thailand has one of the highest per capita social media usage rates in the world, but comparably low e-finance usage. Financial businesses need to enhance Thailand's comparative advantage in this area.

PromptPay, an initiative of the BoT and supported by the two main bankers'

in which the negative externalities (everything from pollution to bank bail-outs) of many businesses are accounted for in some way so that they become internalized as part of an enterprise's costs. An example outside the financial sector is carbon pricing, whereby companies are charged for their greenhouse gas emissions. But the financial sector is surely just one more major crisis away from finally being forced to pay for the toxic fallout from the kind of irresponsible lending and market behavior that has occurred many times all

HOW GREEN IS YOUR BANK? THE FIVE LEVELS OF RESPONSIBLE BANKING

Academics at the Massachusetts Institute of Technology (MIT) have drawn up what they call "Five Levels of Socially Responsible and Green Banking," with the fifth being the most advanced. They are summarized as follows:

LEVEL 1: Banks sponsor superficial "green" events and undertake public relations activities that are not related to the core business of the company (in other words, "greenwashing").

LEVEL 2: Banks develop a small percentage of isolated and token products or activities that they add to their conventional banking portfolio, not as part of a company-wide application of socially responsible and green business principles and practices.

LEVEL 3: Social and green principles and practices underlie most of the banks' products and processes.

LEVEL 4: Activities are broadened from a banks' own direct client interactions to include the larger system through networks, alliances, and public conversations that broaden the movement of conscious investors and

regulatory changes that redefine the banking industry.

LEVEL 5: Banks are not driven by a strategic response to external challenges (e.g. avoiding a negative scenario), but by a desire to address the core challenges of our time by innovating at the level of the whole financial system.

A recent comprehensive study of green banking in Thailand, 'Business Case for Sustainable Banking in Thailand' by Sarinee Achavanuntakul, found that the majority of commercial banks and specialized financial institutions (SFIs) were operating at Level 1. "A few commercial banks, namely Krung Thai Bank, KasikornBank, and to a lesser extent Krungsri Ayudhya Bank, TISCO, and Bangkok Bank, can be said to be at Level 2 due to their products and services being in line with sustainable development and/or improving financial access," the study noted.

It added: "No Thai bank has yet integrated environmental and social risk assessment and management into their lending process, which is one of the first steps toward 'responsible wholesale lending' practice."

---

associations, has provided early evidence of how technology can boost efficiency of the payments system while also improving financial access through convenience and lower costs. The banks need to log the lessons of this project and feed them into further applications so that financial inclusion benefits both businesses and society as a whole.

There are also many new possibilities created by the "big data" element of fintech, not least the ability to gather credit information beyond the limits of what the National Credit Bureau (NCB) is currently able to glean. Electronic payment platforms allow the monitoring of a range of financial activities not recorded by the NCB, such as informal borrowing, trade credit, payment of utility bills, and other small items.

Similarly, with improved big data-facilitated credit information, secured lending can be

widened in scope beyond just physical collateral, including "non-possessory" security as well as such credit-like transactions as leasing and factoring.

Thailand has high social media usage but comparably low e-finance usage.

Thailand's mainstream financial institutions appear to be confident that they are protected by the regulators from full-scale competition from fintech firms. Cyrus Daruwala, a leading consultant and adviser to the industry and the managing director of IDC Financial Insights, recently told bankers at a regional conference: "It is only the gaps they will steal from you and the gaps are peer-to-peer lending, community lending, and a couple [of others]. Other than that, there is no real threat."

GREEN BONDS: BANKROLLING THE SUSTAINABLE REVOLUTION

The still largely underdeveloped green bond market in Thailand provides a huge opportunity for domestic financial institutions to expand in a market characterized by strong demand and weak supply.

Areas of interest include funding for renewable energy projects, eco-friendly farms, clean water initiatives, infrastructure projects aimed at limiting flood damage and the impacts of extreme weather patterns – as well as social and sustainability projects such as anti-corruption and good governance initiatives.

It is expected that more than US$120 billion in green bonds will be issued globally in 2017 (up from US$94 billion in 2016). That's an impressive figure when you consider that only about US$200 billion has been issued since the green bond market was launched less than a decade ago. Of course, this is still only a tiny fraction of the total amount of bonds issued globally by companies and governments.

In this relatively small but fast-growing market, China is a trendsetter. Its green bonds account for two percent of all bonds issued in the country, more than any other nation, and accounted for 40 percent of all green bonds issued globally in 2016. By contrast, India's green bonds amounted to less than two percent of the world's total.

There are still many hurdles to overcome. One is the lack of common benchmarks and ground rules for what constitutes a green bond. In most parts of the world there are two voluntary frameworks (the Green Bonds Principles and the Climate Bonds Standards), while China has its own.

The main problem, however, is supply. The International Finance Corporation (IFC), part of the World Bank, which is putting more than US$300 million into a new green bond fund, points out that few banks in emerging markets have issued green bonds, leaving a large gap in the market. In fact, the IFC is partnering with giant European asset manager Amundi to launch the world's biggest green fund aimed at emerging markets. Developing country bankers – including those in Thailand – cannot afford to let this opportunity pass them by while they plod on in a traditional lending capacity.

The BoT is playing its part in monitoring and guiding any technological changes that can have a big impact on the financial institutions it oversees. In 2017, it set up a "regulatory sandbox" for firms wishing to experiment with innovative financial products and services in real world conditions under its watchful eye, which many have taken up with enthusiasm.

However, so-called disrupters relish the fact that some of the established players are complacent and limiting their technology improvements mainly to existing services and customers. All the better for us, they say, because once we've won market share outside these areas we will slowly but surely come and eat their lunch.

These are familiar themes to BoT governor, Dr Veerathai Santiprabhob, who told leaders of the country's financial institutions in June 2017: "Now it is your turn as the drivers of the business world to devise and decide how to best navigate and move ahead toward our common goal of sustainability. How to invest in new technology to increase productivity; how to build a cushion against rising competitors with new and unexpected business models; and, lastly, how to enhance inclusivity of the public at large in benefiting from our economic growth, which can, in turn, benefit your business in the longer run."

Bridging gaps to sustainability

Banks are run by people who know there are non-financial risks in much of what they do, including some that will turn out to be financial, such as ending up with "stranded" (prematurely obsolete) assets in the "dirty" sectors of power generation, for instance. But they still have big clients who right now are looking for financing

Ngern Tid Lor staff teach customers about micro-finance.

Many consumers in Thailand lack financial literacy.

THE CHALLENGE: If around eight million Thai households have outstanding illegal loans of five trillion baht, wouldn't it make sense for financial institutions to try harder to win some of that business? The problem, of course, is that the vast majority of those households suffer from all the weaknesses that got them into the "loan shark trap" in the first place: unpredictable and unstable incomes, little or no collateral, and low financial literacy. If these problems could be sustainably addressed, the opportunities would surely be considerable.

THE SOLUTION: When Bank of Ayudhya bought Ngern Tid Lor from AIG in 2009, the business model of the micro-lender was essentially to tap into the only collateral poor people had – their "wheels" (*ngern tid lor* translates as money attached to wheels), i.e., motorcycles and pick-ups. Many Ngern Tid Lor customers were trapped in an illegal lending cycle, borrowing large high-interest amounts from loan sharks for "life events" – such as medical or school fees – and then using their smaller, lower-interest motor vehicle loans to pay off the loan sharks.

"We had no idea that this is what was happening; but now we discovered the true purpose of our business," says managing director Piyasak Ukritnukun. That purpose was to turn the company's vehicle-based lending business (with around 230,000 clients) into a micro-lending one, essentially providing an escape from the loan-shark trap. Micro-finance at its best is about lending to those who have been hitherto

excluded, explains Piyasak. If a small loan is secured against a vehicle, it's still a micro-loan.

In time, the company expanded its branches to 500 and cut the wait for its auto loan service from two hours to 30 minutes. Moreover, it offers the sector's lowest margin interest rates, which it posts online, and gives clients copies of their loan agreements and receipts for payments. It also provides clients with financial education, which has led to the company becoming an insurance broker offering policies with each loan, the kind of protection and security many low-income clients never imagined possible. Ngern Tid Lor has received criticism from some parties, however, for its seeming promotion of consumption, spending, and borrowing.

THE BENEFITS: Over the past few years, the company's average loan size has come down, while its client base has gone up. The company's bad loan ratio is also low, at just 1.5 percent. "When people don't have credit, they work hard to preserve it. Most people are well-intentioned and are willing to pay back their loans," explains Piyasak.

When marginalized people are empowered financially and treated with respect, it can also lead to more business opportunities for the lender. "The next step is when they migrate into a full bank account....We provide the gateway for that," says Piyasak. "In our business, we used to say we produce loans; now we say we deliver opportunities."

A GIFT THAILAND'S BANKS NEED TO APPRECIATE

Not often is a company offered a service that they don't have to pay for, especially when that service "guarantees" to win them more business. But that's exactly what Thai banks get out of the Thai Credit Guarantee Corporation (TCG).

For 25 years the TCG, a non-profit state enterprise, has supported small-scale businesses by providing guarantees for non-collateralized (unsecured) loans from commercial banks. There are about 2.9 million small- and medium-sized enterprises (SMEs) in Thailand, accounting for around 40 percent of the country's total economic output and eight out of ten jobs. Yet, only half are able to access finance – a dismaying case of neglect.

The TCG was set up under the supervision of the Ministry of Finance in December 1991 to try to address that neglect. Since then, it has issued more than 300,000 letters of guarantee for SME loans totaling some 600 billion baht (of which just more than half are still outstanding), helping to create about half a million jobs.

This kind of credit guarantee agency is common in market economies. They are better than direct government subsidies, which "are not cost effective because of mistargeting, rent-seeking, and lack of fiscal sustainability." Briefly – and simply – it works like this: An enterprise goes to a bank and asks for a loan but doesn't have collateral (a physical asset against which to secure the loan). The bank asks the TCG to guarantee the loan. The TCG has

a close look at the would-be borrower and offers the bank a package based on one of the guarantee products already agreed upon with the Ministry of Finance. ("The banks are our customers," says TCG president Nitid Manoonporn.) The package is usually a guarantee for a specific period to pay the bank a certain percentage of the loan (around 20 to 25 percent) should the borrower default. (The TCG often provides some financial literacy training for the borrower.) The borrower must pay a premium to the TCG of around 1.75 percent of the loan per year. If the bank is happy, it gives the enterprise the money. If the latter fails to pay it back, the TCG draws on the funds it has amassed from the premiums it has charged other borrowers, plus a previously agreed (recently diminishing) amount from state funds, and pays the bank the agreed percentage of the loan. What this means is that, other than the risk involved in making the loan in the first place, the bank puts up nothing.

It does not have to be like this. In Japan and Korea – often singled out as models regarding support for the kinds of vital small businesses that underpin most economies – the funds for reimbursing the lender come from a bigger state subsidy to the credit guarantee agency, plus a contribution (less than half a percent of the total of such loans) from all banks that make use of its services. That's not a big chunk, but it's enough (in Japan, providing around 25 percent of the credit agency's funding), and it puts the banks' money where their mouths should be.

Credit guarantee services underpin economies especially at times of "increased tightness of credit markets and can be an effective countercyclical tool to support and restore a sustainable level of financing for credit-constrained SMEs." Moreover, they contribute "in the form of better conditions in accessing credit for SMEs, such as higher loan volumes, lower interest rates, or longer loan maturity."

Thailand's banks should not wait for the government to change the way such credit guarantee facilities provide for the economy's most important, and financially neglected, sector. By playing a greater role in providing sustainable backing for this important part of the economy, Thailand's private sector financial institutions will strengthen that economy while widening their customer base. A win-win by anyone's definition.

for projects and whom the banks can't desert because of an imprecise and immeasurable risk with an indeterminate timescale.

All banks have risk management departments, and that is where these issues need to be addressed. "The purpose of risk management is not to minimize risk. [It] is to make sure that risks are priced appropriately," says Bob Litterman, a former head of risk at Goldman Sachs.

Indeed, risk mitigation is the most often cited reason for investors taking ESG into consideration, with climate demand second. This is as true for financial services companies as it is for any other.

Thailand has its fair share of ESG issues confronting this sector. Corruption and lack of enforcement remain rampant throughout the economy, undermining trust in government, politics, and public services. Everything from wealth management to infrastructure investment is exposed to these ills.

Thai banks are also becoming more active in neighboring countries where ESG risk is often greater. At the same time, however, they want to be recognized as responsible global corporate citizens. Highly visible projects, such as the Xayaburi Dam on the Mekong River in Laos, have exposed several leading Thai banks to considerable global reputational risk.

Highly visible projects, such as the Xayaburi Dam on the Mekong River in Laos, have exposed leading Thai banks to considerable global reputational risk.

Sensitivity to this changing ethical mood is a growing aspect of global investment behavior. This is evident from the fact that most big investment banks now have ESG research and banking departments to cater to institutional clients, including some sovereign wealth funds and hedge funds, that have strict guidelines regarding the ESG measures of companies they invest in. Thai financial institutions need to recognize the growing demand for ESG-based investment and make sure they are geared to provide the expertise and the platforms to meet it (see *Fund Managers and ESG*, page 292).

DIRTY BANKERS: LESSONS FROM A PALM OIL DEBACLE

Lenders hoping to win over critics of their ESG policies by simply announcing financing guidelines should take notice of HSBC's recent palm oil debacle. The key takeaway from this cautionary tale should be that strict implementation matters.

By the end of 2016, the UK-based HSBC was already a high-profile participant in the "green bonds" market (see *Green Bonds*, page 286). In 2014, the bank had adopted guidelines on financing palm oil companies, dropping more than 100 clients for failing to meet its sustainability standards.

However, in January 2017 the environmental watchdog Greenpeace published a report entitled "Dirty Bankers" in which it accused HSBC of providing more than US$18 billion in financing over the previous five years to palm oil companies whose activities included widespread destruction of forests in Indonesia. Greenpeace then launched a campaign that was joined by 30,000 of the bank's own customers urging it to stop providing funding to companies "associated with the most unsustainable aspects of palm oil development."

HSBC was forced to react quickly, and within a month had adopted even stricter guidelines in keeping with its policies on other agricultural commodities, including cocoa, coffee, and cotton.

In return, Greenpeace welcomed HSBC's decision and the fact that several of the bank's remaining clients had signed up to the new industry guidelines. Greenpeace added: "This also sends a clear signal that other banks must follow suit."

CASE STUDY | Worldview International's Blue Carbon Forestry Credits

The program allows investors to finance the reforestation of coastlines.

THE CHALLENGE: While there is no shortage of well-meaning projects that benefit the environment, usually such ecological enterprises rely on a charitable benefactor or crowd-funding. Probably the most exciting example is the Norwegian government pension fund's financial support for the protection of rainforests, a far-reaching endeavor by the world's biggest sovereign wealth fund. But how do you launch an environmental project that is based more on investment opportunities than goodwill? In other words, how does an institution raise money for sustainability projects without relying on charity?

THE SOLUTION: Worldview International Foundation (WIF) is spearheading a project to plant eight million mangrove trees in Myanmar's Thor Heyerdahl Climate Park, which is named after one of WIF's founders. Mangroves play a significant role in protecting the environment, partly by sequestering or absorbing carbon from the atmosphere (turning it into so-called "blue carbon") and partly by providing a rich habitat and protecting coastline. Each mangrove is expected to sequester one tonne of CO_2 over 20 years. Similar projects are possible in Thailand, where – like Myanmar – vast areas of mangrove forests have been destroyed to make way for shrimp farming.

After a hefty upfront donation, WIF launched an investment vehicle called "TREE" coins, which serve as Blue Carbon Forestry Credits. Each mangrove tree costs US$1 to plant – 50 cents pays for the tree and 50 cents goes to the community involved in the planting. This means an investor who buys one TREE coin for US$1 is providing the funds to plant one mangrove tree.

But that's not the end of it: the element that makes this project stand out as a model is that the TREE coin the investor holds is an asset whose value is likely to increase and which can be exchanged for conventional currency (or another non-conventional asset, such as Bitcoin) at a time of the investor's choosing. In other words, it is a real investment with real prospects (and risks, of course) of increasing value.

The project is due to be underpinned in late 2017 by a verified carbon standard (VCS) audit, which should make TREE coins eligible for purchase to offset the carbon footprints of companies anywhere in the world. This means that the value of TREE coins will be influenced by demand for carbon credits at a time when public policies are increasingly mandating that enterprises – covering all sectors and industries, from energy producers to airlines – offset their carbon footprint by purchasing blue carbon credits. In preparation, WIF has partnered with Lykke, an independent trading platform, to launch TREE assets, which can be traded on Lykke's platform with no brokerage or trading fee, 24 hours a day, seven days a week.

THE BENEFITS: There are three winners in this game. First, there are the physical and community environments near the new trees, as well as the planet as a whole because of the massive increase in carbon sequestration capacity. WIF and other enterprises seeking sustainable funding solutions also benefit from such an initiative. Finally, the financial community is provided with new markets and opportunities. The latter includes both investors themselves and fintech operators such as Lykke that offer real and profitable alternatives to traditional – and less sustainable – investment portfolios and trading vehicles.

Participants plant mangrove trees.

| CASE STUDY | Kasikornbank Bolsters Sustainable Business with Green Loans |

Kasikornbank financed 60 percent of the launch of Solar Power Company Group.

THE CHALLENGE: The 'green' world can be as impenetrable as a rainforest: there are acronyms everywhere you look and incentives, conditions, and exemptions aplenty. This can make the difficulty of coming up with a financial strategy for supporting energy conservation and efficiency almost as tricky as persuading your stakeholders that it is a good idea.

To most Thai observers and participants, the government's energy conservation plans around 2007–08 appealed to those of an environmental frame of mind. Finance was at most a supporting act. How could a financial institution identify opportunities that squared not just with its "corporate social responsibility" objectives, but also with its business goals?

Kasikornbank, encouraged by its president at the time, Prasarn Trairatvorakul, an engineering graduate, looked closely at what opportunities the Ministry of Energy's policies offered and set about mapping a strategy that addressed both the expectations and reservations of all its stakeholders. "Most people at the time thought it wasn't really serious, more a CSR kind of thing, but we provided the living example that 'this can be done,'" says Obboon Vonguriya, Kasikornbank vice president and corporate business sector head.

THE SOLUTION: After a year of research prior to the January 2010 launch, two key goals emerged as essential to Kasikornbank's green finance initiative: (1) to grasp the policy incentives that made sense from a clear financial business perspective; and (2) to find a trusted private sector partner with the entrepreneurial skills and passion to make it work.

For the first, the Ministry of Energy's Department of Alternative Energy Development and Efficiency (DEDE) provided the soft loan support that Kasikornbank saw as most viable; and for the second, the founder of a solar

energy company met the policy requirements of an ESCO – an energy services company that doesn't just make equipment, but can guarantee the savings that come with installing their product. The latter was no routine decision. The entrepreneur the bank put its trust in was (a) a woman, (b) retired, in her 50s, and (c) someone who had run many businesses, but not an energy company and whose business plan had already been turned down by nine banks.

And so in April 2010, with the help of a Kasikornbank loan for 60 percent of the project, Wandee Khunchornyakong Juljarern launched her Solar Power Company Group's (SPCG) first solar farm in Korat in the country's northeast. Soon the International Finance Corporation, the World Bank's private-sector arm, and the multilateral Clean Technology Fund also provided funding. By 2014, SPCG, now listed, was generating nearly a fifth of the country's solar production.

THE BENEFITS: Having felt its way with soft loan incentives, Kasikornbank got to know the alternative energy sector and the 'pay as you save' logic of the energy conservation-lending model. It wasn't long before Kasikornbank, now more experienced in the sector, was providing 100 percent of the loans for companies installing energy savings, not just for equipment but for the consultancy and other services involved. This created a firm foothold in a fast expanding market. It also meant the bank was well placed to take advantage of further advances in the sector – including rooftop solar – and also to forge a partnership with a "sort of icon of the solar industry," as Ittiporn Intravisit, Kasikornbank's first vice president in the Corporate Credit Product Management Department, puts it. All of this has greatly enhanced Kasikornbank's reputation for being the country's leading "green" financial services company – a reputation that is well worth having as the world pivots more towards environmental sustainability.

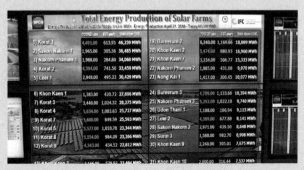

SPCG now generates nearly a fifth of the country's solar electricity production.

Thai financial institutions have made few strides in this regard. Kasikornbank is the only one to have made it into the Dow Jones Sustainability Index and the FTSE4Good Emerging Index. Only three (Kasikornbank, Bank of Ayudhya, and Bangkok Bank) were listed on the Stock Exchange of Thailand's Sustainability Index in 2016. Meanwhile, all banks explicitly maintain that they have ethical standards and procedures to counter corruption and to encourage whistleblowing, but the efficacy of anti-corruption measures are by definition unknown except when those measures are found to have failed.

Examples in Thailand include Krungthai Bank and Bangkok Bank's Bualuang Green Loans aimed at improving the environmental impact of small- and medium-sized enterprises; and Kasikornbank's K-Energy Saving Guarantee Program, which supports energy efficiency projects by energy service companies. This is sometimes referred to as 'impact investing' and can bring reputational and moral rewards to the investor alongside the financial return.

Green finance is further facilitated by the growing presence in the financial markets of green bonds, complete with credit ratings, that are used to finance development projects that mitigate climate change or its social impacts (see *Green Bonds*, page 286).

FUND MANAGERS AND ESG

These days, a growing number of asset managers around the world are being guided by environmental, social, and governance (ESG) principles. This provides a major opportunity for Thai financial institutions, which sadly lag behind other developed markets, to provide research and investment guidance for a growing number of potential 'impact investment' clients.

This view is supported by industry research in 2016, which found that some 300 global fund managers managed assets with ESG strategies totaling more than US$8 trillion, nearly twice what it was just two years earlier. Already 40 percent of the world's major companies include significant ESG metrics in their shareholder reports, and investments in companies with improving ESG scores are outperforming those with lagging scores, according to HSBC.

The push comes not just from the private sector, but also from policy-makers and regulators. In June 2017, the Bank of England announced that it would look closely at banks' exposure in the face of climate change as part of its efforts to tackle the "significant" financial threats posed by global warming. Ben Caldecott, director of the sustainable finance program at Oxford University's Smith School of Enterprise and the Environment, commented, "This is ground-breaking. It is the first time a financial regulator has looked at climate risk in such a comprehensive way and at the banking sector in particular."

Articulate voices are being added to the growing perception that asset management needs to connect with ESG values and that making that connection makes investment sense. For example, well-known Wall Street investment fund manager, Joshua M. Brown, wrote immediately after US President Donald Trump withdrew the country from the Paris Climate Change accord:

"People who have accumulated wealth or are in the process of doing so may wish to express their beliefs and hopes for the future in the way that they allocate their portfolios."

"It isn't…true that conservation is antithetical to profits and jobs. Further, there is no necessary tradeoff between stewardship of our land and good paying jobs – it's just that the nature of the jobs themselves will need to change. And they already are."

"…There is a massive movement underway being driven almost entirely by the desire of the end-investors to have a portfolio that is in sync with their values."

"One very intelligent way I've heard it phrased is that if a corporation qualifies as an ESG allocation (as a majority of the Fortune 500 do, by the way) then it means the company is being managed by people who care and are paying attention."

TAKE ACTION

The financial services industry provides an indispensable enabling role for the wider economy. According to a jointly produced study by the UN Global Compact and KPMG on the application of SDG principles in business, there are four opportunities for shared value (defined as "the coming together of market potential, societal demands, and policy action") involving the financial services industry:

- **Access:** Increasing financial inclusion, including access to secure payment and remittance facilities, savings, credit, and insurance.

- **Investment:** Financing and insuring renewable energy and other infrastructure projects, including so-called "impact investing."

- **Risk:** Bringing risk expertise into the open to directly influence customer behavior and public policy through innovative pricing and risk management.

- **Cross-cutting:** Positively influencing and actively guiding the ESG practices of corporate customers and investors.

In addition, there are a number of best practices that can help underpin the financial sector's commitment to achieving sustainability. These include the ten Equator Principles aimed at assessing environmental and social risks; the Green Bond Principles, which provides guidance to issuers and investors; UNEP's Principles for Sustainable Insurance; the UN-supported Principles for Responsible Investment; and the Sustainable Stock Exchanges Initiative aimed at better corporate transparency, governance, and ESG performance.

Today, these steps are voluntary. They may remain that way for some time, but not for long. When regulation, policies, and public opinion align with the imperatives of innovation and the need for sustainable strategies, signing up to these principles will not be optional.

However, Thai financial institutions have so far failed to seize these opportunities.

Indeed, apart from China, all Asian countries have been slow to rise to the green financing opportunity, galvanized more by a 'regulatory-push' factor rather than an 'investor-pull' factor. However, the Asean Capital Markets Forum recently announced that it was looking to promote ASEAN green bonds to global investors by adopting the Green Bond Principles and exploring pan-ASEAN issuance guidelines for the asset class.

These opportunities constitute the business case for sustainable banking practices as mapped by Sarinee Achavanuntakul:

- **Responsible wholesale lending delivers better risk management by reducing legal, reputational, and financial risks, and opens up new market segments**

- **Responsible retail lending delivers greater consumer protection and financial literacy, thereby reducing repayment risk and over-indebtedness while making it possible to raise market share among existing clients by generating consumer approval**

- **Improving financial access, especially through electronic innovation, opens up opportunities in an under served market**

Lead, don't follow

Only when non-financial risk moves up the priority lists of financial institutions will sustainability take a central place in the market. But those that wait for others – or the regulators – to take the lead are likely to find themselves scrambling to catch up while at a massive competitive disadvantage. This is the point at which non-financial risk converges with financial risk and which ultimately will be the decisive factor that separates the leaders from the losers.

Healthcare

- *An emphasis on treatment rather than prevention is driving up medical costs, overburdening public hospitals, and often leading to substandard care.*
- *The high number of medical personnel focusing on specialized care and gravitating to private healthcare operations has led to a shortage of qualified primary physicians to care for the majority of the population.*
- *Uneven distribution of medical resources across geographical and socioeconomic lines is widening the gap between the haves and have-nots. This is also exacerbated by the tendency of healthcare institutions to prioritize profits over serving the greater social good.*
- *With the national healthcare budget already under significant strain, Thailand must find innovative ways to care for an increasingly ageing population.*

Healthcare in Thailand has made great strides over the past century. Since the 1930s, the country has drastically cut the infant mortality rate and extended life expectancy by decades. The government has insured 99.7 percent of the population through a three-pronged insurance system, and Thailand surpassed the UN's health-related Millennium Development Goals in 2004, well ahead of the 2015 deadline. At the same time, the private healthcare industry is also a major success story, with hospitals in Thailand attracting an ever-growing number of overseas visitors.

Yet despite its achievements, the sector today is facing new and severe threats to its own health. The current model of healthcare in Thailand – as in most of the world – is increasingly a reflection of the social and economic inequalities plaguing the nation. A shortage of nurses and primary doctors, and a dearth of community care and preventive care initiatives are placing more and more pressure on a poorly funded public health system, while a new generation of medical staff are drawn to the higher salaries of specialized services, better working conditions, superior resources, and prestige of private hospitals. In addition,

the influence of pharmaceutical and insurance companies distorts the relationship between doctor and patient, incentivizing doctors to prescribe certain medications or procedures by offering covered costs, freebies, and, at times, funding for conferences, continued education and hospital support. Major marketing and advertising pushes by drug companies also cause bias among caregivers, while the limits to what insurance companies are willing to cover also restrict healthcare providers' options. In these ways, the interests of drug and insurance companies are often advanced over the interests of the public. As a result, critics say that both the public and private sectors struggle to uphold the traditional values and mission of the healthcare profession.

The industry's focus on specialized care has proven problematic for several reasons: first, specialized care is more expensive than prevention and ends up costing the government more than it can afford. Second, the rate of preventable, non-communicable diseases (NCDs) – such as cancer, respiratory infections, alcohol-related disease, obesity, and diabetes – continue to rise without proper public health education. And finally, the mass exodus of medical personnel from public to private institutions has led to a glut of specialists and resources in the private sector catering to the wealthy few, but not enough primary physicians to care for the vast majority of the population.

Much of what is giving rise to such problems has to do with the current value systems bred by medical schools, says Dr Thep Himathongkam, CEO and founder of Bangkok's Theptarin Hospital.

"The supply does not meet the demand," he says. "While the country needs community and preventive care, the production of doctors in medical schools focuses on tertiary care. The biggest consumer (the government) does not talk to the supplier (medical schools) to plan together for personnel production that fits the country's needs."

Flaws in the current system are exacerbated by the health insurance system. Public health insurance, which was originally conceived as a service to share health costs between patients and the government, was reformed in 2002 as the Universal Coverage Scheme (UCS), requiring only a 30-baht co-pay (in 2007, the co-payment was abolished and the UCS became free). While this, in addition to the Civil Service Medical Benefit Scheme and the Social Security Scheme, succeeded in covering 99 percent of the population, it has proven unsustainable for the national budget, spiked the number of outpatient visits, strained the system, and placed the burden on taxpayers. The emphasis on curative care over prevention also drives up medical costs and ends up overburdening public hospitals, leading to long queues and inferior service. Meanwhile, private insurance companies and the superior services they offer are only accessible to the wealthy.

The uneven regional distribution of medical care also widens the gap between the haves and have-nots: as of 2017, roughly a third of all private hospitals (98 out of 351) were concentrated in Bangkok; the rest were located in other major urban hubs. Medical tourists, too, divert Thailand's attention and treatment from the have-nots: in 2015, foreign patients contributed to 27 percent of total income at private hospitals listed on the Stock Exchange of Thailand. That figure is projected to reach

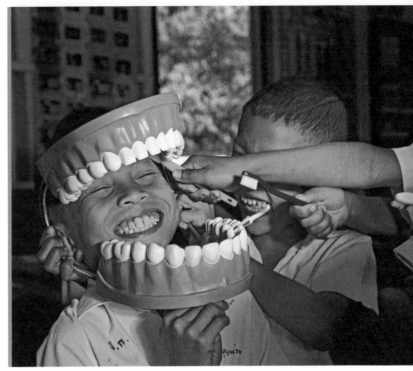

The benefits of basic healthcare education can last a lifetime.

30 percent in 2017. This inefficient distribution of money and resources ultimately hurts the vitality of the nation as a whole.

Future complications also hover just over the horizon, with huge implications for the national economy. Thailand is already straining under the weight of its ageing population, and is

"While the country needs community and preventative care, the production of doctors in medical schools focuses on tertiary care."

forced to make annual increases in the national healthcare budget to help address the issue. With rising costs, a shortage of healthcare professionals, and a heavily overburdened system, Thailand faces an uphill battle in keeping its populace healthy and well cared for. In the eyes of the free market, these problems may seem unexceptional. But does that mean they should be normalized? Or is there another role to be played by the private healthcare sector to help remedy some of these alarming trends and show the way forward toward a more sustainable healthcare system?

A sustainable healthcare model should focus on prevention and a holistic approach to wellness.

While the Thai model focuses primarily on expensive treatments of individual symptoms, a sustainable healthcare model should focus on prevention and a holistic approach to wellness – including diet, exercise, proper shelter, a sense of community, education, a work-life balance, and mental and emotional wellbeing. Indeed, major medical establishments around the world are trying to push for a change of mindset along these lines. The UK's public provider, the National Health Service, for

example, is partnering with local governments, communities, and Public Health England to instigate a system-wide overhaul that prioritizes three things: a clean environment, resilient communities, and a self-reliant approach to health.

Sustainability in the medical industry also includes the impact of its operations on the environment. Operating 24 hours a day, hospitals are thought to be the second-highest energy consumer of any industry. Yet, as purveyors of health and wellbeing, hospitals have a responsibility to promote environmental health, especially in light of how many ailments stem from environmental factors. In 2014, Institute for Health Care Improvement co-founder Don Berwick said, "Hospitals, places of healing, can model healthier behavior. Leaders that integrate environmentally sustainable operations at their facilities create a culture of nurturing and demonstrate sincere commitment to all people."

INNOVATION | APPS FOR ACCESS

According to the World Economic Forum, the smartphone is in a position to become one of the most powerful tools for creating better access to healthcare. Smartphone apps allow patients to instantly store or share medical records, get

consultations from doctors anywhere in the world, learn about symptoms and diagnoses, track lifestyle behaviors and vital signs, and more. These revolutionary services have the potential to democratize patient care, boost efficiency, and lessen carbon footprints and paper waste.

Singaporean startup RingMD, for example, has already made remote consultations a reality in Asian markets, including Thailand. The app provides a videoconferenc-

ing platform via website or mobile app for patients to communicate with doctors and specialists located anywhere in the world. During these digital consults, patients can receive routine health check-ups or take care of preliminary work needed to treat serious health issues.

In South Africa, which is home to more HIV-positive citizens than any other country in the world, Project Masiluleke sends text messages to the general public to connect people living with HIV to call centers staffed by trained operators who can give health information, counseling, and referrals to local clinics. The private text messages help patients sidestep the stigma surrounding HIV and find equitable access to care.

INDUSTRY SNAPSHOT

UNIVERSAL HEALTHCARE

99.7%
of Thailand's
population

is insured through the Universal Healthcare Scheme (UCS).

Thailand has

 **0.4 doctors per
1,000 people**

 **2.1 nurses per
1,000 people**

 **21 hospital beds per
1,000 people**

Thailand produces just **2 doctors and 12 nurses
per 100,000 people** annually (which is one-third
to one-fourth the rate of Singapore).

SUSTAINABILITY CHALLENGES

Thai hospitals
produced more than

52,147 tons
of infectious
waste in 2014.

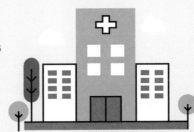

Hospitals are estimated
to be the

2nd

highest energy
consumer of all
industries.

MEDICAL TOURISM

Foreign patients
account for almost

30% of total
spending
at private hospitals.

Thailand treated

2.91 million foreign
patients
in 2015.

AN AGEING SOCIETY

By 2035, people aged

65 or older
are estimated to make
up one-fourth of the
population.

Sources: National Health Security Office; World Health Organisation;
World Bank; UN Population Prospect, 2015; SDG Index; Joint
Commission International

Pathways to sustainable healthcare

Prevention over profit

Treating disease, rather than providing preventive care, has become the norm since Thailand's adoption of Western medicine in the early 1900s. But prevention is the cornerstone of sustainable healthcare, and with rising NCD rates, it's more important now than ever. While prevention promotes early detection and healthy lifestyle choices that can curb many of Thailand's leading causes of death, it also affords more efficient management of medical resources – all of which are imperative in a nation with an ageing populace. Moreover, an emphasis on medication rather than prevention has become a matter of life or death in Thailand: according to research by Chulalongkorn University, roughly 38,000 Thais die from antibiotic resistant bacteria every year due to over-prescription and the prevalence of antibiotics in the nation's food and water supply.

The National Health and Security Organization (NHSO), which oversees the national health-care budget, is beginning to see prevention programs as a necessary part of public policy and has made significant efforts in the field. In the 2018 fiscal year, for example, the NHSO plans to include free screening for colon cancer and the human papillomavirus (HPV) vaccine to reduce the risk of cervical cancer.

Education is also an effective way of addressing healthcare inequalities. Many state-owned hospitals promote prevention by educating the public through health campaigns and outreach initiatives. In recent years, a number of publicly funded TV commercials highlighting health woes, including cancer and smoking, have gone viral. The impact of such initiatives shouldn't be underestimated; they are a particularly important tool for marginalized communities with inadequate access to medical services.

FORMULA ADS BANNED IN THAILAND

Thailand now has one of the world's lowest rates of breastfeeding. This shift provides a concise analogy for how society has moved away from common sense, and traditional and affordable methods of maintaining health, to more commercialized methods. It also shows how the Thai healthcare industry as a whole has facilitated this transformation. While breast milk is free and important to a baby's development, formula companies have successfully marketed the convenience of their products. They have also offered so many free samples at hospitals that today only 12.3 percent of Thai mothers exclusively breastfeed.

For optimal development, the World Health Organization recommends exclusive breastfeeding for at least the first six months of a baby's life, with continued breastfeeding until two years of age. While the culture of using formula does offer busy or working parents necessary relief – and for some mothers, less pain – it comes at the cost of the essential health benefits of breast milk.

Meanwhile, critics say hospitals are not doing enough to actively promote the benefits of breastfeeding. As such, the government has had to step in to curb the profiteering of formula companies at the expense of public health: as of September 2017, instant milk formula advertisements had been banned in Thailand.

In Bangkok, the Bhumirajanagarindra Kidney Institute Hospital is setting a unique example in preventive care. The hospital is Asia's leading kidney institution, but as a nonprofit it focuses on health education, patient outcome, affordability, and resource-sharing among academics and medical professionals. Built through funds donated by the food and beverage conglomerate ThaiBev, the state-of-the-art hospital has the capacity to serve 1,000 patients a day, yet its core mission is to lessen the number of patients seeking treatment.

For private hospitals, implementing preventive measures offers ample marketing and public relations opportunities that can help differentiate socially-conscious institutions in a competitive – and often uncompassionate – market. Gerard Lelande, physician and founder of CEO Health, said, "The private sector uses the wellbeing approach as a way to promote their services." While this may be interpreted as disingenuous, it's a tactic that offers social benefits while boosting business – a win-win. Furthermore, a 2016 Deloitte report found that health promotion among staff is also cost-effective: one study found that for every US$1 spent on employee wellness programs, medical costs fell US$3.27 and absenteeism costs fell US$2.37.

More primary caregivers

The shortage and high turnover of nurses is a telling trend in Thailand. According to the World Health Organization, Thailand's ratio of nurses to population at 2:1,000 is higher than that of neighboring countries, however, that pool is shrinking. In 2016, Permanent Secretary to the Ministry of Public Health Dr Sopon Mekthon stated that his office loses about four percent of its nursing staff every year. Many reasons can be attributed to this: a general lack of interest in the profession; career interruptions caused by pregnancy or motherhood; the proliferation of higher-paying jobs such as pharmaceuticals, beauty clinics, and health-related direct sales; the demanding nature and hours of nurses' shift-based work; and a lack of robust recruitment and training. However, the main reason for this shortcoming may be found in the cultural change influenced by an increasingly capitalist

SOCIETAL ILLS

Thailand ranks **1st among ASEAN countries in alcohol consumption.**

Around **1.4%** of Thais are addicted to **amphetamine-type stimulants.**

Around **11.4 million** Thais smoke **cigarettes or tobacco.**

Thailand ranks **2nd in global traffic fatalities** with more than **24,000 road deaths per year.**

Thailand's **teenage pregnancy** rate is the **2nd** highest in Southeast Asia.

Around **38,000 Thais die from antibiotic resistant bacteria** each year due to over-prescription and the prevalence of antibiotics in the water supply.

The prevalence of HIV among adult Thais has fallen from **a high of 2% in 1996 to 1.1% in 2015.**

1 in 3 Thais over age 15 struggle with obesity.

The number of Thais with diabetes is expected to rise from **3.2 million in 2013 to 4.3 million** by 2035.

Sources: SDG Index; National Statistical Office of Thailand; World Health Organisation; Chulalongkorn University's Drug System Monitoring Mechanism Development Center; World Bank

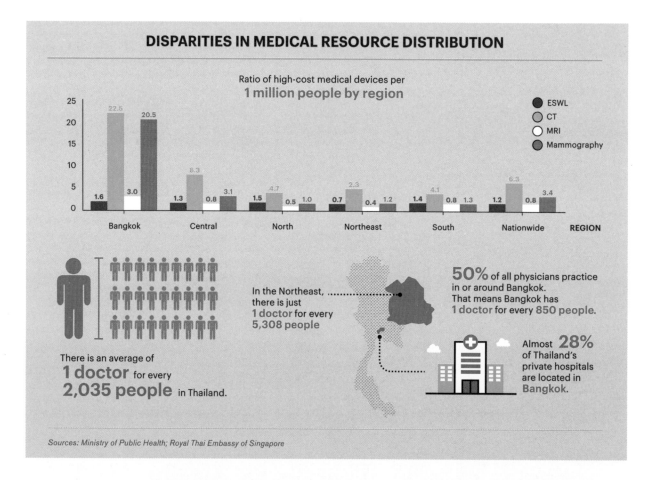

DISPARITIES IN MEDICAL RESOURCE DISTRIBUTION

Ratio of high-cost medical devices per
1 million people by region

- ESWL
- CT
- MRI
- Mammography

Bangkok: 1.6, 22.5, 3.0, 20.5
Central: 1.3, 8.3, 0.8, 3.1
North: 1.5, 4.7, 0.5, 1.0
Northeast: 0.7, 2.3, 0.4, 1.2
South: 1.4, 4.1, 0.8, 1.3
Nationwide: 1.2, 6.3, 0.8, 3.4

REGION

There is an average of
1 doctor for every
2,035 people in Thailand.

In the Northeast,
there is just
1 doctor for every
5,308 people

50% of all physicians practice
in or around Bangkok.
That means Bangkok has
1 doctor for every **850 people.**

Almost **28%**
of Thailand's
private hospitals
are located in
Bangkok.

Sources: Ministry of Public Health; Royal Thai Embassy of Singapore

medical sector. The mindset in the health industry as a whole has shifted from one based on performing a social service to one more focused on earnings and profits.

"The tertiary care focus in medical schools leads to young doctors' desire to become specialists," says Dr Thep. "Specialists are seen as superior and earn much more compared to general doctors. This skewed value leads to the lack of doctors who wish to be community doctors." Unfortunately, community doctors and nurses are exactly what Thailand needs.

A new mindset is needed among the new generation of caregivers, adds Dr Thep, who strongly believes in the principles of the Sufficiency Economy Philosophy (SEP). In his opinion, the runaway profiteering of the health

industry could be checked and balanced through SEP's emphasis on moderation and reasonableness. "For the Thai healthcare system to become sustainable, the current dysfunctional situation would benefit from adopting the Sufficiency Economy mindset. This involves basing decisions on virtuous goals rather than just on profit," he says.

Another way to adjust the distribution of medical resources could be addressed by the public sector: if the insurance system were rewritten to allow integration between public and private insurance plans, the excess capacity of private institutions could be better accessed by the public. However, the government currently does not allow holders of public insurance to pay additional fees to access services at private institutions.

CASE STUDY | Theptarin Hospital Prioritizes Diabetes Prevention

THE CHALLENGE: Although the current medical norm is to provide treatment, preventive care is increasingly recognized as the more socially conscious and efficient way of promoting health. But prevention is often at odds with the private-sector mandate to seek profit. When Dr Thep Himathongkam founded Theptarin Hospital he integrated the Sufficiency Economy Philosophy principles of moderation, reasonableness, and prudence into the corporate vision, not only to guide operations, but also to support his patients' lifestyle choices. Over 30 years, Dr Thep has created a successful model that prioritizes diabetes eradication over short-term profits.

THE SOLUTION: Dr Thep used leadership skills – such as investing in human capital, using the latest innovations in the field, developing strong teams, collaborating with competitors, and prioritizing patient outcome over profit – to create Thailand's first multidisciplinary diabetes care team. Because the team's work focused on patient education and self-care, the model was too unconventional to receive support from a state-run hospital. So, in 1985 Dr Thep joined the private sector, which allowed him the freedom to set the corporate mission and provide the kind of care he envisioned.

Although the startup costs and challenges were daunting, Dr Thep weathered the difficult times. He trained his staff in preventive care and instilled strong ethics in management. While the hospital nurtured a culture of prevention, education and self-empowerment, staff and patients saw a reduction in health risks, symptoms, expenses and resources used. They also saw an increase in patient-doctor relations, patient trust, hospital efficiency, and impact. In addition, the hospital emphasized sharing of knowledge and collaboration with

Founded in 1985, Theptarin Hospital is a regional leader in diabetes prevention.

partner institutions to increase the number of medical personnel who understood diabetes care.

THE BENEFITS: Theptarin Hospital, known for showing how the principles of the Sufficiency Economy Philosophy can be applied in the business sector, has greatly benefited from its reputation as an innovator and leader in diabetes prevention. The hospital created additional income streams through the lifestyle services it offers to numerous firms, providing health education to clients. Collaboration with competitors also allowed Theptarin to cut costs. Rather than invest in expensive equipment, the hospital refers patients to partner institutions for high-tech tests and care. Rather than losing customers to competitors, Theptarin retains patients by building good relationships and providing quality care through primary physicians.

The hospital also emphasizes developing the moral behavior of its personnel by promoting from within and encouraging teamwork rather than individual success. This has resulted in greater employee satisfaction and low turnover. In fact, some of the current staff have been at Theptarin for more than 20 years. Meanwhile, the employee engagement policy helps to provide better care to patients.

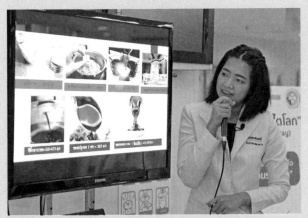

Theptarin emphasizes preventive care training and continues to invest in research.

Environmental sustainability

When Bangkok Hospital replaced its air conditioning system with an energy-efficient central system, energy consumption was reduced by 40 percent over the course of four years, drastically lowering electricity bills. This kind of financial benefit is only one example of how environmental sustainability can improve and support the healthcare sector. Consuming less, extending the life of equipment, and improving efficiency are all activities that can reduce costs.

In addition to energy use and water use, waste management remains a major environmental issue in the medical industry. In Thailand, hospitals created more than 52,147 tons of infectious waste in 2014. Yet, with a growing population and demand for healthcare services increasing, this number could rise considerably. According to Kathy Gerwig, environmental stewardship director at California-based Kaiser Permanente, one of the most cost-effective solutions is simply to cut down on waste. Waste processing is costly for hospitals, so programs that reduce waste often see quick returns on investment.

Although 'greening' an entire industry might seem like a Herculean effort, efforts to do so can, and perhaps should, start small. Hospital staff – from porters to surgeons – can and should all play a part. The simple act of employee engagement has proven a successful way to brainstorm and flesh out ideas, run trials, and implement greening efforts that can be scaled up and lead to industry-wide trends.

CASE STUDY | Wellness City Offers Holistic Care to the Elderly

Exercise helps the residents of Wellness City stay fit and healthy.

THE CHALLENGE: With Thailand straining to meet the needs and cover the costs of an ageing population who require round-the-clock medical care, hospitals face the threat of becoming overburdened. Meanwhile, the business-as-usual method of treating NCDs with prescription medication is coming under fire not only as wasteful, but also ineffective and harmful in an increasing number of cases.

THE SOLUTION: Wellness City, located in Ayutthaya province, houses a retirement community, a several-thousand-unit condominium to accommodate patients and visitors, an organic farm, a health spa, and an on-site 24-hour hospital staffed with doctors and medical personnel.

The hospital offers natural remedies, such as diet and lifestyle counseling, in addition to integrated medical services that include care for diabetes, hypertension, hepatitis, and more. It also offers detox and rehabilitation programs, spa treatments, and wellness courses such as massage, yoga, anti-ageing therapy, and preparation for retirement. All of this is offered in a comfortable, natural environment.

THE BENEFITS: Wellness City has successfully responded to growing demands for elderly care and medical tourism to build a private and profitable enterprise that eschews non-sustainable health practices such as over-medication and reactive treatment. Wellness City's mission, vision, and range of holistic services are so popular that it has successfully expanded its operations and customer base. It recently opened a second branch of its wellness center and is constructing a third housing complex that will add another 70 homes.

Innovating through collaboration

Technology-assisted service can be a cost-saving measure that reduces clinical and administrative waste and improves operational efficiency. Thailand has a robust medical technology industry, and it is positioned to grow as manufacturers shift toward a value-based economy for Thailand 4.0. It's a golden time for private-public cooperation for sustained growth in this industry.

In Thailand, medical R&D projects and the use of state-of-the-art medical technologies have been initiated and supported primarily by public university hospitals, but other public agencies are also supporting these efforts. The Thailand Center of Excellence for Life Sciences (TCELS), for example, is a government-run agency focusing on advanced medical robotics projects. It supports private sector players by providing a network of researchers, logistics support, and investor liaisons. One project supported by TCELS is the Dinsaw Mini, an artificial intelligence robot that has been trialled since 2009 in hospitals in Japan and Thailand – two countries struggling with the issue of an ageing population. In an effort to help tackle the shortage of caregivers, the robot helps assist the elderly in serving meals, picking up items, and reporting emergencies through phone contacts.

Preecha Bhandtivej, president of the Thai Medical Device Technology Industry Association, says that several manufacturers are also focusing on medical devices made of locally sourced materials. For example, Thai Centri, a natural rubber latex tubing manufacturer, is making medical-grade resins from locally sourced rubber to produce saline tubes, blood bags, dental dams, catheters, and other medical equipment. Domestic manufacturing like this helps reduce imports of medical devices, thereby lowering costs and nurturing R&D within the industry.

Continued innovation of medical technology in the Asia-Pacific region is forecast to earn the regional market upwards of US$190 billion over the next decade. Not only will this industry prove to be one of the most profitable in the region, but its innovations also have the

A condom mascot offers leaflets to Thai teenagers.

potential to break the constraints of the fee-for-service based healthcare system and expand new business models that deliver care in ways previously not thought possible.

Finally, collaboration among public and private hospitals and the government can offer solutions with wide-ranging impacts. For example, the government can affect necessary change in the Thai medical curriculum by

Thailand has a robust medical technology industry, and it is positioned to grow as manufacturers shift toward a value-based economy.

collaborating with private and public hospitals to assess needs and prioritize prevention over tertiary care. Precedents for such collaborations exist – since 2013, Thai hospitals have cut down the incidence of diabetes-related foot amputation by 80 percent due to years of collaboration between private institutions and the government. While private practitioners spearheaded research and training initiatives,

CASE STUDY | M.R. Sa-ard Dinakara Clinic Revives Thai Medicine

THE CHALLENGE: The practice of traditional medicine was prohibited by law during the early 1900s and, although it has been reintroduced, has become somewhat of a lost science. Today, many Thais are not aware of their culture's wealth of holistic and natural remedies. M.R. Sa-ard Dinakara Clinic offers health services based on Thai traditional medical knowledge that has been passed down in the founder's family for six generations.

THE SOLUTION: Komson Dinakara na Ayudhaya established the family-run clinic in the heart of Bangkok to provide easy access to urban patients. Traditional medicine is known to ameliorate or cure many conditions caused by modern lifestyles, such as gastroesophageal reflux, migraines, fatigue, insomnia, diabetes, high blood pressure, low blood pressure, arthritis, erectile dysfunction, herniated nucleus pulposus, and allergies. The clinic also manufactures herbal medicines that have been used by Komson's ancestors, who have served Thailand's royal families since the beginning of the Chakri Dynasty.

Treatments at M.R. Sa-ard Dinakara Clinic are rooted in Thai medicinal herbs.

The clinic's traditional remedies and cures provide an additional income stream.

To contribute to the country's self-reliance, Komson has helped Dr Banchob Junhasavasdikul, dean of the College of Integrative Medicine at Dhurakij Pundit University, draft a curriculum and establish a program on integrative medicine. Komson gives lectures in Thai medicine and wellness at Dhurakit Pundit and several other universities. Over the past ten years, the number of public and private universities that offer programs in Thai medicine has continued to grow. Komson believes this is because traditional approaches in medicine – with their focus on diet, peace of mind, and spiritual wellness – could serve as models for sustainable healthcare practices.

THE BENEFITS: Although traditional Thai medicine is not yet mainstream, the clinic's existence in a commercial area has reminded people of the value of traditional medicine, and awareness is on the rise. Today, several leading medical schools allow students to major in traditional medicine. The clinic successfully attracts ailing urbanites, and among his patients Komson is able to deliver holistic healthcare based on self-sufficiency and prevention. The clinic also serves as an outlet for the herbal remedies that his family has been concocting for generations, supporting a medical legacy that might otherwise be lost, as well as adding an income stream. Among those who value traditional medicine, the clinic is a rare and invaluable cultural and medical institution.

TAKE ACTION

• **Top management must take ownership** to effectively identify and develop opportunities that will benefit both business and sustainability. Instating a corporate sustainability board will ensure that the hospital's sustainability goals are integrated with business goals.

• **Promote preventive care** to curb health issues before they become serious problems that necessitate expensive treatment and overburden hospitals.

• **Facilitate better communication between medical schools, hospitals, and government.** Close cooperation between the public and private sector is required to assess the reality of the country's medical needs, tailor curricula to meet these needs, and ensure new generations of professionals meet the demand.

• **Restrict engagement with pharmaceutical sales representatives,** or refuse to accept gifts. Doctors can cite professional integrity as a reason to limit being courted by pharmaceutical representatives.

• **Encourage employees to share ideas for green practices** and allow them to be creative. Not only does this generate ideas for greater sustainability, but it will also foster better employee engagement and could lead to cost-saving practices.

• **Utilize designs that conserve energy.** Like Bangkok Hospital, which saw a 40 percent reduction in electricity bills after installing a new air conditioning system, all hospitals stand to gain by renovating buildings and introducing systems that are more energy-efficient.

• **Support quality domestic medical equipment manufacturers.** This reduces imports of medical equipment, fosters industry independence, and saves costs related to procurement and transport.

• **Take advantage of innovation incentives.** There's no better time for medical innovation, as the Board of Investment and other economic planning bodies begin to offer attractive incentives for investing in medical R&D, and as the government passes pro-public-private partnership policies to meet Thailand 4.0.

• **Consider the principles of the Sufficiency Economy Philosophy.** Train young doctors and nurses to value social rather than monetary payoffs and pursue career paths that contribute to the greater social good.

---

the government supported these efforts by including foot training in public personnel development plans. Today, some 67 percent of diabetes patients receive complete foot exams and more than 72 percent receive foot self-care education.

Changing mindsets

Sustainability-minded hospitals and healthcare services are not outliers, but are increasingly becoming the norm. In 2014, Johnson & Johnson and Harris Poll conducted a joint survey among global healthcare professionals about sustainability. More than half (54 percent) of the respondents said that their hospitals incorporate sustainability into purchasing decisions, and 80 percent believed this would be the case in two years. Sixty percent said "green initiatives" are an important factor for patients when choosing a hospital, and 55 percent said that such initiatives help to improve health outcomes.

Early adapters stand to gain the most from differentiation, marketing opportunities, and reputational benefits. All adapters – whether early, late, or in between – stand to gain from the substantial cost savings that improved efficiencies offer. However, such advancements cannot be achieved without the collaboration of the public sector. If public insurance schemes were altered to cover preventive care, this could go a long way in fomenting demand for prevention and primary doctors, as well as promoting a shift in behavior by patients. The support of the government is also crucial in encouraging stakeholders in the health system to work for the greater good. Ultimately, changing the focus of the healthcare industry is largely about changing mindsets – admittedly a difficult change to enact.

Real Estate

- *Nearly 50 percent of the value of global real estate holdings is vulnerable to climate-related market shifts.*

- *The lack of a green supply chain, lack of public awareness, ongoing labor issues, and the prevalence of corruption still make sustainable solutions in this sector challenging.*

- *Visionary leaders and unified efforts by industry players are needed to make the real estate sector sustainable.*

- *Demand for sustainable buildings is growing among multinational corporations, which increasingly must justify their carbon footprint.*

- *Despite higher building costs, the improved efficiencies and lower energy costs of green buildings mean investments are recouped in an average of seven years.*

They say that the buildings of a nation are a measure of its wealth. In Thailand, both historically and in modern day, the lion's share of real estate development has been concentrated in Bangkok and the surrounding Central region, making up an annual average of roughly 60 percent of the nation's land and building transactions, according to the Bank of Thailand. The next largest concentration of real estate deals is in the Eastern region, which in 2015 accounted for 10 percent.

Globally, construction and real estate is responsible for more than 20 percent of the world's carbon emissions and contributes significantly to waste, pollution, and the use of non-renewable resources. Meanwhile, building damage caused by extreme weather events presents a massive risk to the global economy. According to the University of Cambridge Institute for Sustainability Leadership, nearly 50 percent of the value of global real estate holdings is vulnerable to climate-related short-term market shifts. According to the Global Risk Institute, almost half of those losses cannot be prevented unless there is coordinated action on climate change.

But the environment isn't the only issue at play. The real estate and construction industry factors into a wide range of sustainability issues, including land acquisition, the ethical sourcing of materials, urban planning, labor practices, health, and safety. Not only does the environment we build shape the physical world around us, but it also impacts our human relationships.

Studies have shown that compared to other industries, construction, and real estate has been sluggish to adopt new sustainability demands and goals. But with new drivers for change – such as the ratification of the Paris climate agreement, increasing government regulations on energy efficiency, growing awareness of labor exploitation, and rising demand for green-certified buildings – the industry has come to a tipping point.

The barriers to better buildings

Lack of government support: One of the major barriers to sustainable real estate development is the lack of incentives for green buildings. While Thailand's Building

Energy Code of 1995 outlines requirements for energy efficiency, it is outdated and only applies to commercial and government buildings.

Several initiatives and tax incentives are available, but industry professionals are not necessarily aware of them. Many incentives – such as the Board of Investment's promotions for green projects – have not been made permanent. One existing incentive is the bonus Floor Area Ratio granted by the city of Bangkok to TREES-certified buildings (the nation's own green-building certification, TREES, or Thai's Rating of Energy and Environmental Sustainability, is based on the US Green Building Council's widely-used LEED, or Leadership in Energy and Environment Design, ratings system.)

The Ministry of Energy also offers a revolving loan program that supports energy efficiency in construction. But compared to other countries, Thailand's green incentives are small potatoes. In the US, for example, a wide range of financial incentives such as tax breaks and subsidies are available to developers proposing green buildings. Singapore requires all residential and non-residential buildings exceeding a floor space of 2,000 square meters to meet stringent energy-efficiency standards. If Thailand is to measure up, more permanent and aggressive incentives are needed to drive growth in green building.

Lack of public education/awareness:
The overall lack of awareness about green buildings and their benefits hinders the development of this sector. It remains difficult to find knowledgeable architects, contractors, and consultants who are familiar with sustainable solutions. In addition, with the public's lack of awareness of the benefits of green real estate, there is little incentive for developers to make the investment.

Samphop Bunnag, president of the Property Management Association of Thailand, says that condo developers do know the advantages of long-term, eco-friendly construction but are under consumer pressure to keep prices down. "If you [spend more for sustainable buildings] then the price will be higher than the competition,"

Bangkok, where most of Thailand's real estate is concentrated, is yet to start significantly 'greening' buildings.

he says. If consumers were to think long-term and recognize the value added by energy efficiency – even when such upgrades are not immediately visible – that would certainly change the industry. But this takes time. "Change the attitude first and that takes education. That might take a generation."

Compared to other industries, construction and real estate has been sluggish to adopt new sustainability demands and goals.

Lack of a green supply chain: Even if industry professionals envision a more sustainable real estate sector, they will need sustainable materials to make it happen. However, in Thailand such materials have not made it into the mainstream. This is why property developer Magnolia Quality Development Corporation (MQDC) is spearheading a shift toward sustainable materials with the launch of a Materials Library in Bangkok. Open to industry professionals as well as the general public, the library showcases the latest findings in

The fastest-growing alternative energies, like solar and wind, unfortunately offer inconsistent power supply. Storing the energy harnessed by such sources with hydrogen storage systems is one solution starting to move from theory to practice. In

Thailand, Chiang Mai–based CNX Construction has built the world's first 24-hour solar-powered hydrogen-energy storage multi-house residence in an effort to bring completely self-reliant hydrogen-storage houses into the mainstream.

"The Phi Suea House is a sustainable residence project fully powered by photovoltaic panels harvesting the sun's energy," and storing it in a "hydrogen house" for use 24 hours a day, says owner and developer Sebastian-Justus Schmidt. "We believe that in ten years everyone will understand the different energy storage technologies as they understand the use of solar panels today," he adds.

The 10-by-15 meter "hydrogen house" sits in a corner of a 17-rai property six

kilometers northeast of Chiang Mai. Schmidt's son designed and runs the hydrogen system. The solar arrays include 101 kilowatts of solar panels, which cost nearly US $50,000. They provide more than enough electricity to take the entire property off the grid.

Because solar arrays only produce power during the day, the property needs some power source during the night. The hydrogen fuel cell stores the power and allows access only when needed. The system can store about 130 kilowatt-hours of electricity, enough for about a week.

Altogether the hydrogen system costs about US$50,000 and includes three 1,000-liter storage tanks. Another US$50,000 investment was needed for electricity inverters.

innovative construction supplies, materials, and solutions. Known as LIBRA-RISC, the project is based on a model established by Materials ConneXion, a network of material libraries that stretches from downtown New York to Bangkok's Thailand Creative & Design Center. The facilities serve as go-to resources for many manufacturers, designers, architects, engineers, and students.

> *The costs of constructing a certifiably green building are often too heavy for individual, residential tenants to bear.*

Already, many sustainability-minded companies and developers such as SCG, Starbucks, and Toyota are turning toward natural bio-products and energy-efficient materials for their construction projects, demanding innovation and sustainability

from their suppliers. But it may take some time before such materials become accessible, affordable, and mainstream.

Higher construction costs: Although building materials and solutions vendors may be pushing the industry to adopt ecologically sound products, the cost and limited availability of solutions can be prohibitive. According to Solidiance, a marketing consultancy group focused on Asia, the additional cost to build a LEED Certified building is roughly 3 to 10 percent higher than a normal building.

High costs also mean that with a few exceptions, green buildings in Thailand are limited largely to commercial buildings. The costs of constructing a certifiably green building are often too heavy for individual, residential tenants to bear. This presents a conundrum for the coming years, when an estimated population boom is projected to create a great demand for affordable,

INDUSTRY SNAPSHOT

GLOBAL PERSPECTIVE

The real estate sector uses more energy than any other sector, consuming 40% of the world's energy annually.

The construction and maintenance of buildings uses 40% of the world's raw materials (3 billion tonnes annually).

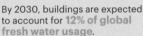

Building construction and demolition generates as much as 40% of the world's solid waste.

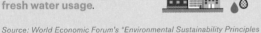

By 2030, buildings are expected to account for 12% of global fresh water usage.

Source: World Economic Forum's "Environmental Sustainability Principles for the Real Estate Industry" report

CLIMATE CHANGE IMPACTS

Construction and real estate are responsible for more than 20% of the world's CO_2 emissions.

The concrete industry alone accounts for 5% of all global CO_2 emissions.

By 2030, the World Bank estimates that the real estate sector's CO_2 emissions could increase by 56% due to increasing population, housing, and industry.

Yet, a 35% reduction in real estate CO_2 emissions is required by 2030 to stay within the 2-degree Celsius global temperature threshold established by the Paris Agreement.

Sources: "Environmental Sustainability Principles for the Real Estate Industry," World Economic Forum, 2016; University of Cambridge Institute for Sustainability Leadership

GREEN BUILDINGS

Thailand has some 140 certifiably green structures around the country today. The Thailand Green Building Institute has issued eco-friendly certification to 76 buildings since 2009.

Working at optimum efficiency, green buildings can:

- use up to 50% less energy
- use 60% less potable water
- produce 70% less solid waste
- emit 35% less CO_2
- save around 21% on the operating costs of new buildings over five years.

MIGRANT LABOR

1 of every 5 legally registered migrants in Thailand is employed in the construction sector.

There are more than 200,000 women from Cambodia, Myanmar, and Laos working in Thailand, accounting for almost 40% of all registered migrant construction workers.

Source: International Labour Organisation

UNEQUAL DISTRIBUTION OF LAND AND DEVELOPMENT

The top 10% of landholders in Thailand (roughly 1.5 million individuals and juristic organizations) hold 61% of all land, while the bottom 10% hold just 0.7%.

60% of Thailand's real estate development is concentrated in Bangkok and the surrounding central region.

Source: Land Development Department

sustainable housing. Because residential tenants often cannot absorb the cost of green buildings, luxury condominiums are the most common type of residential developments going green.

"Approval of land, construction, opening bids – a million different steps can give way to corruption."

Corruption: Thailand boasts one of the world's most efficient land administration systems and low-cost construction permits. However, many other institutions and abuse of legal frameworks allow for rampant corruption, including public procurement, customs, public services, and financial services. Unsustainable loans and licenses for construction projects, many of them bought through bribes and kickbacks, played a large part in bringing about the Asian Financial Crisis of 1997. This serves as proof positive that corruption in real estate development poses great risks not just to the sector, but also to stakeholders and the health of the national economy as a whole.

Risks and opportunities

Preparing for climate change: In 2015, a report by the University of Cambridge Institute of Sustainability Leadership published a stunning figure: about 45 percent of the value of all real estate investment portfolios worldwide could be lost due to climate-related short-term market shifts. This is equivalent to US$34.5 trillion, or the entire GDP of the European Union. The same report estimated that real estate insurers lose an average of US$50 million every year due to weather events. In light of these figures, retrofitting old buildings for disaster preparedness, cutting the energy consumption of existing buildings, and erecting new buildings to sustainable standards becomes a financial imperative.

Eliminating social and reputational risks: It's no secret that the real estate sector is rife with corruption and labor exploitation – two major risks to corporate image and the bottom line. While a labor shortage makes the construction industry heavily reliant on migrant workers, the legal framework governing migrant employment is fraught with

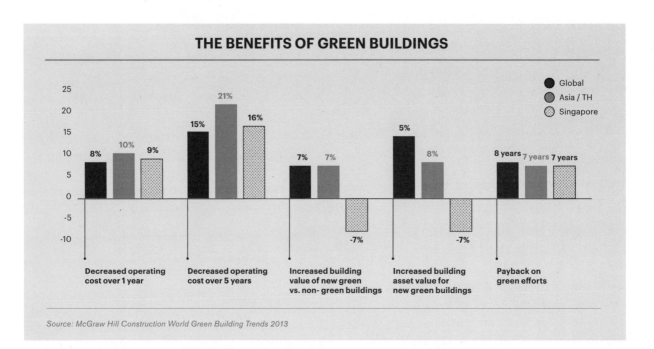

Source: McGraw Hill Construction World Green Building Trends 2013

Tiki Eco-resort Minimizes Its Carbon Footprint

The low-impact bungalows will be constructed from local materials and are designed to harmonize with the surrounding environment.

THE CHALLENGE: Elmar Kleiner founded Office for Interior and Architecture (OIA) in Germany in 1995 and moved his base to Thailand in 2002. Since then he has been involved in many sustainable development projects in Asia. While Kleiner has always excelled at designing green buildings, with TIKI Eco-resort, he has taken it one step further: he has engineered a construction process with minimal environmental impact.

THE SOLUTION: "No generators. No diesel. No pollution during construction or operation," Kleiner says. This is how he plans to reduce the environmental impact of the construction of TIKI Eco-resort in southern Myanmar, near Dawei. The entire project will be built only using clean, renewable energy, with no combustion engines involved in the transportation or building process, or in the operation of the building.

TIKI Eco-resort will be built of wooden structures pre-assembled at a local factory, which will be light enough to be transported to the site via solar-powered catamaran. From there, the parts will be manually carried into place and assembled with light machinery fuelled only by a 10-kilowatt solar array. No heavy machinery requiring an access road or generators will be used at all. Materials and labor will be sourced locally as much as possible to cut down on transportation emissions and promote urgently needed sustainable development in the region.

The eco-resort itself will be a study in clean energy and self-sufficiency. Starting with two bungalows, the resort will expand over a ten-year plan that will eventually comprise 36 units. It will run completely on "fire and ice" technology: solar power provides electricity during the day, and generates power to fill up water and ice storage tanks. These 'ice boxes' will supply most of the cooling energy needed for air conditioning. When the solar panels cannot supply power, water stored at a higher elevation is released to generate electricity through turbines similar to a hydroelectric dam.

Such cutting-edge technologies can be surprisingly simple and cost-effective but still require know-how in sustainable engineering. Kleiner says the resort's electricity-generating capacity will provide extra power that will be available for free to nearby villagers – thereby fulfilling a social good as well.

THE BENEFITS: By tackling sustainability issues that go beyond the obvious, OIA has become an undisputed leader in sustainable building vision and design. The reputational benefits of such projects have helped OIA garner a number of high-profile projects, such as the Pandora Industrial Campus in Lamphun and the Häfele Design Center in Phuket. The surprising cost-effectiveness of holistic designs integrated with cutting-edge technologies can be attractive to budget-conscious developers and clients, as energy consumption and other running expenses for sustainable solutions can be far below standards. That applies not only to hospitality projects but also commercial, industrial, and even residential buildings.

"Contrary to public opinion, you can, but don't have to spend more of your budget to get better results," says Kleiner. "We prove that in each of our projects."

Bangkok's Unilever House was designed to be as energy efficient as possible.

Although the initial investment for green buildings can be high, buildings end up paying for themselves over the long run.

loopholes and inconsistencies, making alien workers vulnerable to discrimination, wage theft, extortion, harassment, and collusion among employers and government agencies. Thus, developers who do not ensure proper labor practices on construction sites face significant social and reputational risks posed by such labor exploitation.

Corruption, on the other hand, is so systemic in the Thai real estate sector that it is difficult to root out. Dr Wit Soontaranun, executive vice president of the Social Contribution Office of DTGO Corporation, says that the only way to combat it is by sticking to your principles. "Approval of land, construction, opening bids – a million different steps can give way to corruption," he says. "So transparency must be a principle of the company. If you allow any corrupt practices, it creates a whole culture of bribery."

Improving corporate image: According to Solidiance's 'Thailand's Green Building Goals' white paper, a key factor cited by companies who have invested in green buildings is improved corporate image. Paying higher rent is increasingly worth the cost for companies who can benefit from a reputation of sustainable buildings and operations. Toyota, for example, has successfully launched a global initiative to build new green facilities and retro-fit all dealerships to green-certified standards.

Meeting rising demand: Growing demand for sustainability in Thailand is also changing the priorities of real estate professionals. Simon Landy, executive chairman of Colliers International in Bangkok, says, "The demand comes from multinationals that have to justify their carbon footprint." In 2015, *The Nation* reported that more office-space tenants in Bangkok now prefer LEED-certified buildings because many are required by corporate policy to occupy green buildings. While multinationals such as HSBC, Shell, and Johnson & Johnson require LEED certification for all projects worldwide, Unilever, Citibank, and L'Oreal have retrofitted their Bangkok offices to LEED standards. Thai companies are also following the trend – for example, Kasikornbank's Phahon Yothin headquarters was awarded LEED Gold certification in 2011.

"We feel that LEED certification is essential to attracting and retaining blue-chip organizations like Google, Stanford University, Canon, and Mizuho Bank," Urasate Navanugraha, managing director of Univentures REIT Management, told the *Bangkok Post* in 2016.

Low operational costs and improved efficiency: Although the initial investment for green buildings can be high, buildings end up paying for themselves over the long run through improved energy, water, and waste efficiency.

CASE STUDY   Retrofitting Inefficient Buildings on a Budget

THE CHALLENGE: Building owners and developers who are interested in moving toward sustainability are often scared off by the initial investment required to build a new green-certified building. However, retrofits provide a way to 'green' buildings – and even achieve LEED certification – without breaking the bank. By taking incremental approaches, one could feasibly create a sustainable building out of an old structure at a much lower cost.

THE SOLUTION: Owners can start with small measures that don't require altering the building. Appliances can make a big difference – even such small changes as switching to LED lights or installing energy-efficient air conditioners. Replacing old, inefficient refrigerators with new, efficient ones can pay for themselves within a couple years, says Acharawan Chutarat, an architect and lecturer at King Mongkut's University of Technology Thonburi School of Architecture & Design.

Home automation systems can also regulate the use of energy with timers and sensors, automatically lowering or shutting off lights and air conditioning during low-use periods, such as at night or when the building is empty. More substantial

Baan Chaan Modular Home is a traditional Thai home retrofitted for maximum sustainability.

measures, such as additional insulation, better windows, solar power, water collection, added green space (such as on a rooftop), and additional parking space for bicycles also contribute to meeting the green standards for LEED certification.

"Limit it to what you can do," says architect Soontorn Boonyatikarn, who built one of Thailand's first totally solar-powered homes. "Think of a big old car. You can put in a new engine, new tires and a solar roof, but you'll still have a heavy bulky body."

THE BENEFITS: Many sustainable design aspects can be added to existing buildings, with most paying for themselves over time and improving the inhabitants' quality of life. Research shows that renovated buildings will recoup their investment in six to ten years, mostly through savings on electricity bills, which can be 30 to 50 percent lower than before renovation.

Because green-minded tenants are willing to pay a premium for sustainable spaces, higher rents can also be charged to help shoulder the burden of the retrofit. The newly green building will simultaneously benefit from improved image, reputation, and differentiation, and proper marketing of these green efforts will attract more interest and customers.

Dr Soontorn Boonyatikarn built one of Thailand's first solar-powered homes.

CASE STUDY · Magnolia Builds a Smarter, Socially Enriching Mixed-use Space

Green space covers 30 percent of the WHIZDOM 101 complex.

THE CHALLENGE: In light of the UN's figures that cities consume 75 percent of the world's natural resources and 80 percent of the energy supply, and produce 75 percent of carbon emissions, buildings that model 'smart cities' have great potential to make far-reaching impacts. In Thailand, Magnolia Quality Development Corporation (MQDC) is attempting to go beyond the usual green building standards to combine environmental gains with positive social impact.

THE SOLUTION: In addition to minimizing the energy consumption of its residents, WHIZDOM 101 is designed to promote better health, foster sustainable development, and serve as an innovation hub. Located near a BTS line and combining both residential and commercial spaces (including shopping, dining, office space, and green space), the complex aims to cut down on both urban commuter carbon footprints and the buildings' CO_2 emissions, while also supporting a sense of community. Each residential and commercial unit will be equipped with advanced automation systems for smart heating, ventilation, and air conditioning management, as well as energy recovery ventilation technology that works to improve indoor air quality by reducing the amount of CO_2.

"Our research shows that in a typical Thai one-bedroom apartment, CO_2 will almost double overnight to 1,500 parts per million, far higher than the 800 ppm that the World Health Organization recommends," says Dr Jittapat Choruengwiwat, vice president of MQDC's Research & Innovation for Sustainability Center (RISC). Studies have shown that concentrated levels of indoor CO_2 can lead to disrupted sleep and poor work performance. Long-term exposure can cause

more serious adverse effects, such as developmental problems in young children or dementia in the elderly. In total, WHIZDOM 101 is estimated to save carbon emissions of 15,000 tons per year.

The complex also provides space for the general public and is designed to promote health and exercise, including a 1.3-kilometer elevated biking and jogging lane and a 3-rai elevated park. Green space covers 30 percent of the complex.

THE BENEFITS: WHIZDOM 101 fetches higher prices than other mid-range developments in the area, with units in the condominium tower starting at 120,000 baht per square meter. Yet higher prices have not been a deterrent to tenants: within two weeks of the tower opening for booking, 60 percent of the units were reserved. In addition, the complex is expected to reduce energy consumption by 30 percent compared to other building projects in the same category.

The project is located on Sukhumvit Road, close to Punnawithi BTS station, and is due to be completed in mid-2018. In 2017, WHIZDOM 101 was shortlisted by the Ministry of Energy as one of seven business models that turn urban areas into smart city ecosystems that minimize environmental impacts, save energy, and reduce carbon emissions.

The WHIZDOM 101 project is expected to cut carbon emissions by 15,000 tons per year.

Higher savings as a building ages is a key driver for going green.

One study conducted by McGraw Hill Construction estimated that in Asia, operating costs decrease by 21 percent within five years of constructing a new green building. Renovated green buildings also saw significant reductions of 13 percent. For green buildings in Thailand, investments are recouped on an average of seven years – on par with Singapore and faster than the global average.

But energy efficiency is not the only thing that can recoup costs: a green building provides a work environment that leads to greater efficiency and employee wellbeing. The same companies that are seeking improved corporate images are also finding benefits in increased productivity and lower turnover.

Green loans and future subsidies: Although government subsidies and tax breaks have yet to be created in Thailand, the financial sector has stepped up its involvement in supporting green development. Numerous low-interest loans and financial incentives known as 'green loans' are helping the construction of green buildings, investments in energy-efficient upgrades, and retrofits of existing buildings for better environmental impact. Some well-known green loans include Bangkok Bank's Bualuang Green Loan, Kasikornbank's K-Energy Saving Guarantee Program, and Krungthai Bank's Green Loan. Green subsidies offered by the government may also come in due time.

Green buildings translate to higher asset value: Green-certified and ESG-conscious buildings yield higher profit margins. Across the board, sustainability-minded companies and individuals are willing to pay a premium for LEED and TREES-certified buildings. According to Solidiance, the monthly price per square meter of floor in Bangkok can be up to 30 percent higher than non-green buildings. According to 2012 figures, Park Venture and Sathorn Square – both green-certified commercial buildings – charged monthly rents of 1,000 and 875 baht per square meter respectively, as opposed to an average of 629 baht for non-green buildings.

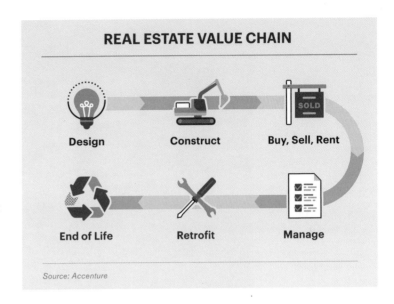

REAL ESTATE VALUE CHAIN

Design → Construct → Buy, Sell, Rent

End of Life → Retrofit → Manage

Source: Accenture

Better city planning: Until recently, lack of oversight among provincial and municipal planners led to freewheeling urbanization of greenbelts with little regard for environmental or social concerns. But the Thai government passed a new Town Planning Act in 2015 that aims to improve the integration of national, regional, and municipal planning.

Between 2014 and 2017, the Department of Public Works and Town and Country Planning of the Ministry of the Interior put in place 'general province plans' across 73 provinces and 'general town plans' in the heavily urbanized provinces of Bangkok, Samut Prakarn, Phuket, and Nonthaburi. These streamlined plans for all 77 provinces take into account public infrastructure, drainage, and environmental concerns, including disaster preparedness. They also include stricter controls for buildings, while presenting ample opportunities for developers to capitalize on the country's newfound interest in sustainable urban development.

The solutions

Reducing environmental footprints: Since Thailand erected its first LEED-certified building in 2007, green designs and energy-efficient technologies have come a long away. The

Many construction workers in Thailand are undocumented migrants.

World Economic Forum notes that globally 40 to 50 percent of all commercial buildings being built today are 'green' – a significant rise from only 2 percent in 2005.

One of the key elements of greening the industry is to nurture more sustainable supply chains. The sector would benefit from the adoption of a

Although lack of awareness and access to sustainable materials might limit or slow down green development, it's imperative to forge ahead.

'cradle-to-grave practice,' which considers the life cycle of materials, where materials come from, how they are manufactured, and how they fit into a circular economy. Globally, suppliers and manufacturers are focusing more on developing sustainable construction materials; however, in Thailand many of these materials must be imported and come at a higher cost. Some key local players, such as SCG, the country's largest construction materials company, are developing ecologically friendly materials.

Although lack of awareness and access to sustainable materials might limit or slow down green development, it's imperative to forge ahead. A World Economic Forum report published in 2016, 'Environmental Sustainability Principles for the Real Estate Industry,' clearly lays out specific action points, stresses the importance of creating a corporate strategy for environmental sustainability, and offers a framework for monitoring impacts. Industry professionals should consider:

- Do you have policies in place concerning sustainability and climate change?

- Do you have clear environmental efficiency targets throughout the value chain? Do these cover suppliers' and contractors' performance?

- Do you engage in partnerships with governments and civil society to ensure effective communication on projects and environmental management?

- Will you use innovative technologies in data management or smart solutions to manage your performance and monitor impacts?

- Will you assume leadership in raising awareness about environmental impacts for residents and suppliers/contractors?

Addressing social needs: Real estate greatly impacts social wellness – particularly in areas of affordable housing, land acquisition, labor practices, and urban planning. Developers are responsible for the fair compensation and resettlement of communities affected by land acquisition and ensuring the health and safety of all employees, suppliers, and contractors. Currently, the Thai construction sector employs 80 to 90 percent migrant workers, many of whom are illegal, and working without any legal protections. Safety management and

adherence to labor regulations is a must.

Residential developments also touch upon issues of income disparity and affordable housing. While there are admirable projects aiming to provide positive, health-conscious social impacts (see *Case Study*, page 314), currently only the rich can afford to live in these buildings, reaping all the benefits of energy cost savings, green spaces, and community health. So how can developers offer this kind of improved living space to lower-income people?

Sadly, without government subsidies, grants, tax credits, and other financial support for

INSIGHTS

DR SINGH INTRACHOOTO *is the chief adviser for the Research & Innovation of Sustainability Center at Magnolia Quality Development Corporation.*

What do you see as the challenges for sustainable real estate development?
When the customer hasn't requested sustainable features and when your own people are resistant because of cost restrictions. With any new idea or innovation, you can't expect it to be the cheapest. Laws and regulations are

another challenge, since the government doesn't support sustainable real estate at all. Also, how to communicate to the customer? You design or create a sustainable building but the customer doesn't know its value. The industry doesn't have visionary developers. Everyone is doing business as usual.

How should the sector tackle lack of demand and public awareness about sustainability?
We need to educate the public. For example, some time ago I set up a company that recycled and reused bioproducts and waste from export products. At the beginning I had zero Thai customers. But now there are so many people talking about waste, about a circular economy. So if a small company can do it, then a large company can do it and make a much bigger impact.

What role does the real estate sector play in the global sustainability movement?
In most countries, construction is an indicator of economic health. So we should do something because it's in this sector's hands. When we wipe out forests and mountains and take their resources – wood, iron ore, limestone, flagstone – it all goes to buildings. So we really have to think about this. Our actions really mean a lot to sustainability.

Public sector tax credits and incentives are needed to spur developers to invest in low-income housing.

green affordable housing, it's difficult for developers to create such spaces. In the US, for example, the Low Income Housing Tax Credit is one continuously successful subsidy that has made many social-impact developments possible. Although Thailand's

Unifying sustainability principles among property developers would help the industry shape the agenda, rather than simply reacting to regulations.

Government Housing Bank (GHB) offers accessible home loans for low- and middle-income groups, the nation has yet to establish such wide-reaching tax credits and subsidies.

Internationally, innovative developers and

construction companies have found successful and profitable business models to address affordable housing, as well as a spectrum of other social issues throughout the supply chain. For example, LafargeHolcim, a leading building materials and solutions company, has developed ways to offer microfinance and technical assistance to individual builders in impoverished regions around the world, distribute high-quality, sustainable building materials to the slums of India, and build collective social housing in Nigeria.

Looking forward

The real estate industry has a tough road ahead: by 2030, the World Bank estimates that the sector's CO_2 emissions are expected to increase by 56 percent. Yet, a 35 percent reduction in real estate CO_2 emissions is re-

TAKE ACTION

PLANNING PHASE:

Think local, design holistic. To find out what is sustainable or energy-efficient in a particular region, look to vernacular homes, says Malina Palasathira, an urban designer who co-runs Bangkok-based Design Qua Ltd. Buildings need to harmonize with their surrounding environment to be sustainable.

Elmar Kleiner, a German architect based in Thailand, recommends a holistic, integrated design approach that includes design, ecology, economy, technology, sociocultural aspects, and process quality.

Hire a green designer or consultant. Find a designer with deep understanding of truly sustainable living and design, and get them involved in the project from the very beginning. The cost will ultimately pay for itself through return on investment.

A professional sustainable building consultant will be able to assess the best practices and features for a building in its unique location. Sustainability consultants will also be able to offer the latest technical knowledge, such as solar power, HVAC assessment, and material efficiency.

Actively market green building projects. Developers need to be more proactive in marketing the unique selling points of green buildings. Outline the actual benefits for the tenants, emphasize the return on investment, and clearly show how companies can gain a competitive edge by going green.

CONSTRUCTION PHASE:

Seek green certification. LEED, TREES, and other green certifications can be a helpful tool during construction. Certification standards can help fine-tune the building plan, and receiving certification early will allow for marketing of the building's green features ahead of project completion.

Practice process efficiency and quality. Make sure the construction process is being assessed for energy efficiency and material quality every step of the way. This will bolster labor practices, improve waste management, lower emissions, and minimize energy and resource use.

USE PHASE:

Practice green leasing. Landlords and managers can use a 'green lease' to get tenant buy-in for sustainability efforts. Depending on the lease's green clauses, the landlord and tenants will agree to share responsibilities regarding energy efficiency, waste management, water use, and other property management issues in exchange for cost incentives. The government of Australia offers a Green Lease Handbook for free, online.

Be efficient with waste management. Sort all recyclable waste – such as paper, metal, and plastics – for easier recycling. Compost biodegradable waste. When dealing with e-waste, give them away through online groups such as Freecycle, or look into manufacturers' take-back programs.

---

quired by 2030 to stay within the two-degree celsius global temperature threshold agreed in the Paris Agreement. Simultaneously, as the region ramps up ASEAN integration and more migrants seek opportunities in Thailand, the industry is bound to face more labor challenges, including legal employment, fair wages, and worker safety.

Such challenges can be found everywhere in sustainability planning, but this should not make industry professionals lose heart.

According to the World Economic Forum, unifying sustainability principles among property developers would help the industry shape the agenda, rather than simply reacting to regulations and other external pressures. While sustainability will ultimately help bottom lines, a sense of human-centered purpose must come first, believes Dr Wit. "Try to think of others instead of self first," he says. "Always ask, 'What's in it for others?'" And then, once corporate vision is aligned with this sense of purpose, "You have to fight for it," he adds.

Transport

- *Inefficiencies in Thailand's logistics sector, and potential for growth in petrol-fueled vehicle sales, could prevent Thailand from meeting its 2030 emissions reduction target.*

- *Investment in rail – including high-speed passenger, dual-track freight, and urban mass rapid transit – is a major part of the government's US$64 billion infrastructure plan. Many communities and sectors stand to benefit.*

- *Transport sector businesses need to take a leading role in the three accelerating and reinforcing shifts shaping today's transport landscape: on-demand services, the Internet of Things, and electric vehicles.*

- *In Bangkok, on-demand mobility and the neglected sectors of water transport, non-motorized transport, last-mile mobility, and bus and minibus transport provide the biggest potential for change.*

The Thai economy is shifting gears. The recently launched Thailand 4.0 strategy seeks to establish a firm footing for a new knowledge-based economy and a value-based sustainable future. It is grounded in promoting foreign investment in ten high-tech super clusters, with tax incentives for high-innovation companies that establish R&D and advanced manufacturing operations, such as the automobile industry. Meanwhile, state spending on infrastructure, which is largely aimed at establishing Thailand as a logistics hub, is set to be one of the main drivers for growth over the next few decades – and sorely needed. Since the 1997 Asian Financial Crisis, investment in infrastructure has been marked by a steady decline, but a whopping US$64 billion infrastructure plan (2016–2022) aims to reverse that trend.

Several global trends may accelerate this transport transformation. A 2016 report by a high-level UN advisory group, appointed by former UN secretary-general Ban Ki-moon, emphasized that greener transport is essential for meeting the ambitious Sustainable Development Goals (SDGs). Just looking at the bottom line, it projected savings of up to US$70 trillion and an additional US$2.6 trillion of global GDP gains by 2050. The 2030 Agenda identifies five targets (such as road safety and energy efficiency) where transport has a direct impact, and another seven indirect targets (including agricultural productivity, air pollution, and climate change). However, that list can easily be expanded to include all SDGs – improved mobility for vulnerable populations, for example, contributes to getting more kids to school (Goal 4: Inclusive and Quality Education for all).

Intergovernmental consensus is not the only factor driving change. Growing urbanization – today 54 percent and set to reach 66 percent by 2050 – is increasing pressure on infrastructure, driving up congestion and pollution, and creating new opportunities for providing high-quality services to billions of people. Meanwhile, ageing societies across the developed world are increasingly coming to rely upon on-demand services, home deliveries, public transport, and assisted mobility. Technological innovation targeted at these areas will continue to drive prices down, provide new solutions and efficiency gains, and create new service-oriented markets. Massive infrastructure investments – China alone spends US$158 billion annually in 68 countries under its Road and Belt Initiative – will reshape trade routes and connect a globalized world even more tightly.

Theoretically, the confluence of these local and international shifts should help position Thailand at the forefront of the transport revolution; however, this outcome is far from certain. These new global markets are yet to mature, while here in Thailand, structural weaknesses continue to pose barriers to competitiveness: corruption concerns plague new projects, and foreign companies still struggle to find skilled staff.

Thailand also has its work cut out when it comes to meeting its Nationally Determined Contributions (NDC) target. While not a major contributor in terms of total global emissions (0.82 percent), the kingdom has agreed to reduce the amount of emissions it does produce by 20 to 25 percent by 2030. Together with the energy production sector – the largest emitter – the transport sector holds huge sway in whether it meets that target or not. The country's first Biennial Update Report to the UNFCCC reveals that the transport sector emitted 61.1 million tons of GHG CO_2 equivalent in 2011 (20 percent of total emissions), the majority from the road segment. This percentage is similar to the European Union's 19.5 percent and close to world levels of 23 percent for 2013. However, the strong potential growth in Thai vehicle ownership – due to economic development and the relatively low motorization rate (241 cars per 1,000 inhabitants, approximately half of the EU rate) – and inefficiencies in the logistics sector are potential roadblocks to it reaching its NDC.

Along with the ambitious government goals and the measures outlined in Thailand 4.0, the Thailand 20-Year Energy Efficiency Development Plan (2011–2030), and National Transport Master Plan (2011–2020), additional efforts are clearly needed. For one, regulators need to up their game – to fine-tune legislation and incentives to promote electric vehicles (EVs) and temper car ownership growth, as well as engage with business to explore ways to safeguard the domestic manufacturing base and

Bangkok's subway, or Metropolitan Rapid Transport, network is expanding in an effort to increase commuter mobility and reduce road traffic.

support the repositioning of SMEs in the e-mobility landscape. Businesses, meanwhile, should not shy from taking a lead on sustainability and the innovation that drives it. Dr Chatkaew Hart-rawung, managing director of Thai Summit Automotive, expresses this sentiment well: "We cannot wait for the government. The industry must act by itself if it wants to remain competitive."

Urbanization – today 54 percent and set to reach 66 percent by 2050 – is increasing pressure on infrastructure.

Tech drives progress

Can Thailand's transport sector undergo a low-carbon transformation? On paper, yes, but such an outcome also hinges on visionary leadership by Thailand's private sector. First, businesses should strive to improve current road freight efficiency, while the major rail and port projects mature. Second, they need to take a leading role in the three mutually accelerating and reinforcing shifts that are shaping today's transport landscape.

THE LONG ROAD TO SELF-DRIVING CARS

For most people, artificial intelligence (AI) in transport is a fully automated car. Passengers get in, push a button, read the news or even take a nap, and get out at their destination. These so-called 'Level Five' vehicles are still 15-20 years away according to experts. The big change happens at 'Level Three,' when the vehicle directly interacts with the environment, using sensors and onboard computers. The Lidar technology currently tested by Google and others uses a laser beam to scan the entire surroundings, in addition to cameras that detect traffic lights and recognize moving objects, sensors that measure distance between vehicle and all objects, and GPS positioning and maps. The onboard computer combines all this data and makes split-second decisions.

Drivers today are already using many assisted-driving features: collision avoidance, self-parking, enhanced cruise control, blind spot warning, drift countermeasures, built-in smart assistants, impact detection. In 2015, 17.8 million new vehicles had either embedded or tethered connectivity, and this number will climb rapidly. The road to fully automated cars will be long. The technology is already there but legislation, high costs, safety concerns, liability questions, and other issues still need to be resolved.

Most self-driving cars will likely be sold first to large companies or on-demand mobility providers to be used as service fleets. This could result in so-called zombie cars (empty cars that are running errands or cruising waiting for a customer), which need to be addressed with de-incentivizing pricing measures. In the ideal scenario, fully automated fleets of EVs could reduce environmental impacts, drive more safely and efficiently, and provide detailed driver behavior statistics, reducing insurance premiums.

These are:

Transport as an on-demand service. The proliferation of on-demand service providers is making it very convenient and cost-effective to move around seamlessly from origin to destination, and now even outcompetes car ownership and public transport in some large urban centers. Car-sharing and ride-sharing companies are at the center of this new mobility paradigm – and growing rapidly. Despite its management troubles and regulatory challenges, for example, Uber

> *Uptake of electric vehicles is poised for explosive growth in the next decade, and will most likely surpass industry projections.*

boasts a US$69 billion valuation as of 2017. And it is not only cars. Chinese companies like Mobike and Ofo have rolled out hundreds of thousands of bikes in dockless bike sharing systems. In addition, the growing on-demand delivery of goods and services segment (Indonesia's Go-Jek has 200,000 motorcycles in 25 cities that can take you places, deliver packages and even bring a masseuse to your door) will ride on the expansion of the maturing online retail business, which is set to reach three billion consumers by 2021.

Transport as a connected network (the Internet of Things). Advances in multiple technological innovations like battery capacity and electric powertrains – and especially in ICT, sensor, GPS, AI, and digital payment systems – have made on-demand mobility a reality. These hardware and software elements enable vehicles to interact with the environment in real time. Delivery trucks can be rerouted and monitored to ensure peak performance and optimum loads. GM, Google, Uber, and others are pursuing the coveted prize of the fully autonomous vehicle. The sector is riddled with high-volume acquisitions of, and partnerships with, ICT companies.

Transport by electric vehicles. Uptake of electric vehicles is poised for explosive growth in the next decade, and will most likely surpass industry projections. EVs are not only all-around more efficient, safer, roomier

INDUSTRY SNAPSHOT

SHARE OF GHG EMISSIONS

Share of GHG emissions from transport sector by mode

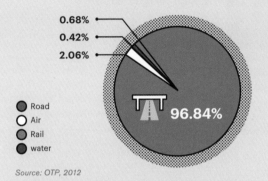

0.68%
0.42%
2.06%
96.84%

- Road
- Air
- Rail
- water

Source: OTP, 2012

LOGISTICS AND INFRASTRUCTURE RANKINGS

The World Bank's 2016 Logistics Performance Index of **160 countries:**

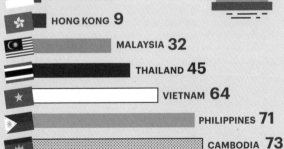

SINGAPORE **5**
HONG KONG **9**
MALAYSIA **32**
THAILAND **45**
VIETNAM **64**
PHILIPPINES **71**
CAMBODIA **73**

Thailand's infrastructure was ranked 49th
(out of 138 countries) by the 2016–2017 Global Competitiveness Report, behind just Singapore (#2) and Malaysia (#24) in ASEAN.

Source: World Bank Logistics Performance Index, 2016; Global Competitiveness Report, 2016–2017

COMMUTING

The Bangkok Metropolitan Area has 3 mass transit rail networks comprised of 5 lines that span over 112 km.

7 new mass transit rail lines covering 240 kilometers of new track are slated to be completed by 2022.

On an average day in Bangkok

900,000 people use the mass transit rail network

40,000 passengers use the Chao Phraya River ferry service

25,000 riders use the Bus Rapid Transit system

64 Average number of hours Bangkok **drivers** spent in traffic congestion in 2016

The government has vowed to boost **the number of electric vehicles** on Thailand's roads to **1.2 million**, supported by **600–1,000 charging** stations, by 2036.

Traditional transport companies must keep pace with the latest innovations.

vehicles that require less maintenance; they are set to outcompete the conventional equivalent on price alone by 2026. Traditional manufacturers are pushing hard to catch up to vanguard companies like Tesla, and many

Major car manufacturers are transforming into all-around energy and transport service providers.

already have, or are poised to roll out, mass production models in all price categories. Battery prices – the biggest cost barrier – are dropping rapidly, and will continue to fall. All major car manufacturers are taking a leaf from Tesla's playbook and transforming into all-around energy and transport service providers, breaking ground on their own battery factories, marketing stationary storage packs, and partnering with PV companies.

Venture capitalists bet on innovation

Some of these trends are already percolating through the engine of Thailand's economy. In particular, capital-rich Thai companies

and banks are looking to capture the value of innovation through investments in startups and research facilities. These efforts dovetail with many of the drivers behind the ongoing transportation revolution.

Siam Commercial Bank's subsidiary Digital Ventures (DV) has been supporting ETRAN e-scooters from the very beginning, and is behind other startups that facilitate cashless payments, important for uptake of on-demand services. The car-sharing startup is another interesting prospect for DV. "I see mobility as the next big trend following fintech," says Charle Charoenphan, head of DV Accelerator. "These startups create their own market from zero. Their main activity is changing behavior. It's small; that is why companies like Toyota and Honda are not concerned, but what if ETRAN has 1,000 vehicles on the street? People will be concerned."

Another example is provided by SCG, the country's largest industrial conglomerate. It established AddVentures in 2017 to invest in e-commerce, automation, energy efficiency, and B2B platforms for construction products, logistics, and other services. The fund's yearly disbursement of US$9-15 million is financed from SCG's R&D budget (US$132 million).

PTT, the state-owned oil and gas company, acquired an 18-percent stake in US battery producer startup 24M Technologies, via its subsidiary Global Power Synergy, to capitalize on innovative lithium-ion technology. The factory, to be constructed in 2018, will make batteries for EVs and stationary home and grid storage. PTT also set up a US$169 million research park in Rayong to kick-start a domestic Silicon Valley. In 2017, the government announced that it will establish a complementary R&D center, Eastern Economic Corridor of Innovation (EECi), on the site.

The future is electric

Sales of electric vehicles stood at under one percent of total sales in 2015, putting Thailand in the neighborhood of China (one percent) and the US (0.7 percent). While absolute volumes are still small (80,000 vehicles in 2016, almost all hybrids), the

SOLVING THE CHALLENGES OF A CAR-CLOGGED CAPITAL

The Thai capital is widely acknowledged to be one of the most congested cities in the world, but with several sector shifts underway – the bus system being improved, global players like oBike looking to break into the market with dockless bike sharing, and on-demand mobility widespread – the ingredients are there for a significant, transport-led improvement in livability, economic growth, and sustainability.

In particular, the expansion of mass rapid transit looks set to create new pockets of economic development (and speculation), reduce traffic, and improve accessibility. Thanks to public-private partnerships with international sector leaders, Bangkok is currently following a development path similar to the mega-cities of East Asia: a multi-modal, connected city with a rapidly expanding backbone of rail mass rapid transit, both elevated rail and metro. The network spans 112 km and has five lines currently in operation. Another six new lines or extensions are expected to open within the next three years. If the entire planned network is completed, Bangkok will reach a distribution of rail kilometers per capita similar to Tokyo.

Like the mega-cities of East Asia, Bangkok is rapidly expanding its rail mass transit.

Thailand has yet to instate planning that promotes non-motorized transport.

However, despite the US$2.2 billion price tag of Bangkok's urban rail upgrade, certain things look set to remain the same. Short trips will probably continue to be provided to hardened locals by around 200,000 motorcycle taxis – often driven by migrant workers from the provinces – and the staple tuk-tuks. Walking and cycling will remain possible, but not particularly pleasant. And unless strong regulatory measures or incentives are introduced, the city's snarled traffic, resistance to non-motorized transport, and piecemeal planning will continue to hobble the push for Bangkok to become smart and sustainable.

But businesses can still bring about incremental change. On-demand mobility will continue to grow and provide new opportunities for innovators, with multiplier effects in other sectors. Similarly, the neglected sectors of non-motorized transport, water transport, last mile mobility, bus, and minibus also provide high potential for transport-sector disruption.

TOWARDS A SUSTAINABLE TRANSPORT INFRASTRUCTURE

RAIL TRANSPORT	LAND TRANSPORT

Overview

Investment in this sector – including high-speed passenger, dual-track freight, and urban mass rapid transit – accounts for 77 percent of the government's planned US$64 billion infrastructure investment.

Highlights

- 17 double-track projects are planned, providing efficient freight connectivity to the distant regions of Chiang Mai, Isaan and further to China via Laos.
- Additional broad gauge (1.435 m) will be laid for medium- and high-speed trains to streamline freight and passenger traffic.

Sustainability trends and business opportunities

▸ With rail freight currently at only 2% of the total, the planned upgrades should deliver a significant mode shift, reducing truck traffic and its impacts.

▸ Economic spinoffs will be most strongly felt in the distant provinces, traditionally neglected and with many times lower GDP and income per capita. New investments should flow into the regions; new storage and distribution facilities as well as local production will be stimulated.

▸ Significant potential knock-on effects to regional trade with northern neighbors, which account for 10% of Thai current exports, more than with Europe.

▸ The massive capital injection will have immediate impacts on the construction and materials businesses. As projects mature, the transport and logistics sectors, retail (especially large hypermarket operators), and a host of other industries will benefit (hospitality, tourism, small retail, food and beverage).

Overview

Highway construction is the second priority in the agenda of the grand infrastructure spending plan (13% of the planned US$64 billion). National and especially regional road connectivity is still a major bottleneck for growth due to poor regional accessibility and congestion in urban areas. Building better and more roads is only one part of the puzzle, and can have sharply diminishing returns due to congestion.

Highlights

- Priorities are improving links in the congested industrial core around Bangkok and the 535-km stretch from Bangkok to the border with Laos.
- In 2016, the number of registered vehicles in Thailand stood at more than 37 million. Around 40% were cars and trucks, while 50% were two-wheelers.

Sustainability trends and business opportunities

▸ The logistics sector is estimated to generate US$96.5 billion in revenue by 2019. Local companies are looking to maximize market share by working together with industry leaders (e.g. Saha Group has partnered with Japanese Seine Holdings).

▸ Improving road links to the provinces will have a knock-on effect on local incomes and industries.

▸ Measures like the 2016 overhaul of the excise tax scheme to advance lower-emission vehicles and 2015 electric vehicle promotion scheme should be promoted. EV manufacturer industry incentives need to be streamlined to support e-mobility uptake and the government's goal of making Thailand an EV production hub.

WATER TRANSPORT

Overview

While smallest in volume (US$1.1 billion of a total US$64 billion), the investments in ports, freight handling facilities, and inland waterways can generate the most direct 3P added value of multimodal transport. The country's two main ports, Bangkok and Laem Chabang (94 million tons of freight in 2014), are overcrowded and have weak multimodal links. Laem Chabang stands to benefit from numerous improvements including the construction of a coastal and multipurpose berth for river barges and coastal vessels, as well as the planned Single Rail Transfer Operator (SRTO), which will directly connect ships to rail.

Highlights

- Water transport is the cheapest freight mode – 45% less than rail and 300% less than road – but accounts for only 15% of domestic transport.
- The government's plan to upgrade ports and develop more efficient multimodal connections between port and railway transport will reduce costs and boost transport and logistics businesses. Business operators could shift nearly 1.1 million TEUs (twenty foot equivalent units) of shipments to rail (rather than road) transport by 2032.

Sustainability trends and business opportunities

▶ Developing facilities, navigable river waterways, and multimodal connections would have a significant effect in reducing transport costs, increasing global competitiveness of Thai goods, and reducing CO_2 emissions.

▶ Agricultural produce like rice and tapioca could be shipped via barges from the heartland to the coast, while coastal transport could deliver heavy, non-perishable goods like rubber and furniture more efficiently.

▶ Logistics service providers, suppliers, and producers need to show initiative and seize the emerging transport hub opportunity.

AIR TRANSPORT

Overview

The air industry is growing rapidly but stands on shaky footing. Completed overhauls of key airports (Phuket and Bangkok's Suvarnabhumi and Don Muang) cannot keep up with demand, which doubled between 2010 and 2016. Airports of Thailand (AOT) has started a three-phase upgrade of Suvarnabhumi to double capacity to 90 million passengers by 2021. In total, it is set to receive 60% of the US$6 billion, 10-year airport investment plan.

Highlights

- The US$5.7 billion upgrade of U-Tapao Airport, in the industrial eastern Gulf of Thailand, aims to relieve Suvarnabhumi and hopes to take a slice from Singapore's aircraft maintenance, repair, and overhaul business.
- Low-cost carriers (notably Thai Air Asia and Nok Air) are behind the explosive rise in passenger volumes and dominated the domestic market in 2015 with an 80% share. This push exposed vulnerabilities in this sub-sector in both liquidity, asset management, and safety as well as operations.

Sustainability trends and business opportunities

▶ Thai airlines and AOT should take more ambitious steps to green airplane fuel efficiency, facility energy efficiency, waste management, ground operations, supplier performance, and other aspects. For example, AOT has committed to restoring natural and water resources around airports, reducing CO_2 footprint per passenger by 20% by 2019, and reducing energy consumption by 18% by 2020. These and other measures need to be further enhanced with more ambitious goals as well as complemented by robust actions by airlines and suppliers.

Sources: Bangkok Post, Nikkei Asian Review, Airports of Thailand, Airline Network News and Analysis, SCB Economic Intelligence Unit (2015).

domestic goals are ambitious. The National Energy Policy Council Roadmap calls for 1.2 million electric vehicles, supported by 600–1,000 charging stations by 2036. The Ministry of Finance has earmarked 76 million baht for charging stations. The implementation roadmap would follow three phrases: pilot schemes (200 electric buses in Bangkok, for example); a focus on public fleets between 2017-2020; and a post-2020 roll-out to consumers, plus investments in charging infrastructure and vehicle-to-grid systems.

Considering the domestic market, technical know-how and production capacities, Thailand has substantial potential in terms of both hosting the manufacture of EV primary parts and assembly, and a unique opportunity to lead in home-grown brands. The pioneering and ongoing collaboration between the e-bus market leader BYD and Thailand's Loxley Group, which put the first Thai-assembled

INSIGHTS

DAVID HENDERSON *is the founder, business leader, and product developer of DRVR. Over two years, DRVR has established itself as a rising player in the fleet management software market in Southeast Asia.*

What is the potential impact of information technology, on-demand transport and demand management tools on logistics operators?
I see it revolutionizing the industry, and changing how these industries work. It is a huge opportunity for cost savings, but also for growth of their businesses. It gives businesses who are early adopters of this technology a huge advantage over their competitors.

Which advantages does AI provide for improving efficiency?
In Southeast Asia and Thailand it can be difficult for someone to make a decision. For example, a 40-year-old woman sitting in a logistics center in Sayaburi may pass on the decision instead of acting. This is where we feel that AI is valuable, by actually having the system make the decision on behalf of the user. So, things like routing, identifying fuel theft. Instead of having a fleet manger stare at a screen all day, we have an event-based system that tells them what they are going to do. The system needs input from the users initially, but over time learns what the expected behavior is and starts to deliver that.

How do you assess the Thai and Southeast Asia markets for fleet management services?
The government is very serious about improving logistics infrastructure in Thailand. We've also seen the Malaysia 2020 transport infrastructure program; we were invited to contribute to that. It is a high-entry cost, flexible market, that is easier to penetrate with a startup. If you have developed a solution for the EU it is not going to work here. It does not work with the local regulations, driver behavior, its more expensive, etc. If you have an algorithm that is based on driver behavior, it's more expensive in the EU. It will not work in Southeast Asia.

We are globally focused. We have no competitors in the region who are interested in business outside their country. For example, a competitor in Thailand has a map for the country, but once you cross the border it's blank.

What recommendation do you have for streamlining logistics in Thailand?
Part of the problem here is that there are many different departments that are involved in this process, and if there was one consolidated department it would be much more beneficial. For one of our projects we work with the Department of Industrial Works, the Department of Land Transport, and the Department of ICT. Let's say you deliver industrial waste from point A to point B, there are six different forms you need to complete, and they are all paper-based forms.

| **CASE STUDY** | ETRAN E-scooters Electrify Last Mile Transport in Bangkok |

ETRAN has developed an electric scooter that can be printed with a 3D printer and has zero tailpipe emissions.

THE CHALLENGE: Scooters are a ubiquitous sight in Thai cities. They easily whiz through traffic, take up little space, and are cheap to own and operate. These qualities also make them very attractive for "last mile" public transport journeys and short trips in the neighborhood. On the flip side, air-polluting older models dominate the streets and the motorbike taxis eek out a living with ten hour-plus workdays. The riding experience can be dangerous and generally is not very comfortable. Still, scooter taxis will remain the most attractive daily transport option for many commuters and will only grow in importance as cities expand and become denser.

THE SOLUTION: The story of ETRAN is a great example of how the combination of new maturing technologies and new mobility business models can provide a comprehensive solution that advances the triple bottom line. The vision was to develop a transport service that bridges the last mile gap with an environmentally friendly, superior product. The CEO and founder, Soranun Choochut, says of their creative journey: "We are industrial designers, and there were no opportunities to do original design in the Thai automotive sector, so we decided to start our own."

The company designed an electric two-wheeler from the ground up, specifically for the scooter taxi sector. Starting with customer-oriented design, the e-scooter maximizes comfort by providing ample space for both rider and passenger. By 3D printing the body, ETRAN could maximize testing and shorten the development cycle. The powertrain and battery provide a maximum range of 70 km and speeds of up to 80 km/h. The body and final assembly of the mass-production series will take place at Thai Summit Automotive, a leader in sustainable

automotive manufacturing in Thailand. "They supported us by helping us do R&D, to scale the model, to do serious automotive design for production," says Soranun.

In fact, a strong relationship with industry players and partners has propelled ETRAN from idea to working prototype in less than two years. Microsoft supplied cost-free cloud services. Siam Commercial Bank's Digital Ventures provided key seed funding – a 300,000 baht initial injection for prototypes and another one million baht for the first fleet of five bikes and two charging stations to be tested in November 2017 (for a six percent stake in the company). The Engineering Department of Thammasat University is working on the charging stations, where motorbike taxis will be able to swap used batteries for new ones in seconds.

THE BENEFITS: Under its business model, ETRAN will rent these safer, low-carbon vehicles to individual operators under full-service agreements. A monthly flat fee of 3,500 baht covers everything – vehicle rental, batteries, and maintenance. Drivers can stay with their local neighborhood crew, and continue driving their usual routes, at greatly reduced costs. The monthly fee is only half of the usual fuel costs, not to mention vehicle purchase and maintenance. The additional projected 36,000 baht yearly income would greatly improve livelihood security for this vulnerable group.

The inclusion of leg space within the body of the vehicle should also greatly increase passenger comfort and improve safety – especially for women who often have to balance on the passenger seat. E-scooters are quiet and have zero tailpipe emissions, which improves quality of life in cities.

CASE STUDY | DRVR's Fleet Management System Improves Freight Efficiency

Thailand's challenging road conditions call for creative logistics solutions.

THE CHALLENGE: Freight operations are riddled with inefficiencies. Trucks cover hundreds of kilometers empty on their return journey. Fuel theft or drivers using trucks for side businesses is common practice. Service providers overcharge clients, claiming excess capacity to contracts. The costs of these phantom vehicles can mount, as many large companies are increasingly outsourcing their freight to small operators. For example, the Thai electronics retail chain Power Buy recently switched from a single provider to 500 different providers.

THE SOLUTION: DRVR (pronounced "driver") helps companies optimize their freight services via a fleet management system that combines telematics with powerful algorithms and a user-friendly interface. The company set up operations in Bangkok in April 2015, due to the large auto original equipment manufacturer base, available skilled workforce (both international and domestic), good flight connections, and business climate.

Telematics monitors vehicle performance using on-board diagnostics (sensors for fuel consumption, speed, impact, etc.) combined with GPS positioning, maps, and linked via a 3G network to an operations center. DRVR's comprehensive Transport Management System (TMS) allows the client to plan and optimize their routes and allows them to see where their vehicles are in real time. According to CEO David Henderson, "The solution is inexpensive (approximately US$100 of upfront hardware costs), low power, low bandwidth, simple to use, and relies on powerful algorithms specifically developed for the Southeast Asian market." An event-based AI system identifies routing opportunities, fuel theft, reckless driving, and automatically contacts drivers via text message. With very low upfront costs and monthly service fees, most clients see a return on investment within a few months.

DRVR uses gamification as a strategy to stand out from their competitors (most staff are game developers). It also works very well in the local context. For example, rewarding best-performing drivers with points and pay incentives, instead of punishing underperformers is a much more effective intervention strategy in the structured, conflict-adverse ASEAN work culture.

THE BENEFITS: In August 2015, the company launched in Myanmar, and within a few months, one of their clients, PSL, a cold chain logistics company, marked a five-fold increase in deliveries with the same 60-vehicle fleet. Their biggest Myanmar customer, YOMA Strategic Holdings, has improved routing and billing to their leasing clients, covering 700 vehicles and adding 100 vehicles each month.

Building on these early successes, Thailand operations started in November 2016. DRVR is helping the Metropolitan Waterworks Authority of Bangkok manage the dispatch of service technicians to fix burst water pipes. The network is expanding across Bangkok (it now has a total fleet of 300 vehicles), and they are exploring ways to improve operations, customer care (reporting via photo sharing and tracking progress via the MWA app), and response times.

The 30-vehicle pilot with Siam City Cement Group (SCCG) launched in early 2017. With 1,400 vehicles and 27 different GPS providers, SCCG needed a single dashboard view of the entire fleet in their control center. "They were at war with themselves in the war room and needed help," quips Henderson. SCCG also wants to use its excess capacity to build an online marketplace for logistics. For example, trucks that deliver cement, chemicals, or industrial waste from Bangkok to another province usually return largely empty. Using a distributed ledger (a more advanced version of blockchain), plus a tracking application showing the capacity of each vehicle, various deliveries along the path could be commissioned and paid via cashless micropayments.

CASE STUDY | Somboon Advance Technologies Puts SEP to Work

A Honda factory in Thailand. The presence of Honda, Toyota and other car makers in the kingdom creates demand for parts, skilled labor, and innovation.

THE CHALLENGE: The Sufficiency Economy Philosophy (SEP) places a focus on sustainability and long-term benefits for all stakeholders, with three pillars (moderation, reasonableness, and prudence) and two enabling conditions (knowledge and virtue). Somboon Advance Technologies took on the challenge to design a comprehensive business strategy that facilitates action along these principles and engages all stakeholders while securing a strong position in the cost-driven and competitive original equipment manufacturer supplier market.

THE SOLUTION: Somboon Advance Technologies has shaped its operational approach around SEP principles. The company manufactures parts – disk brakes, springs, engine components, and axles – for vehicles as well as agricultural machinery and has 2,800 employees in three business units. Its Sustainable Development Master Plan (2013-2017) outlines the ambition to advance balanced triple bottom line impacts by creating "smart people," "business trust," and "societal growth."

Somboon Advance Technologies established a mechanism to encourage and further good governance and ethics from the shop floor up to the board of directors with integrated reporting on detailed GRI indicators.

Participatory product development encourages innovation and co-creation with customers and staff. The newly designed agricultural machinery (cassava planters) and green products (axles, turbo chargers) are lighter and more efficient, ultimately reducing fuel costs for final consumers. Production processes are continuously being streamlined, increasing reuse and recycling of materials during manufacturing, reducing waste and water use, and increasing energy efficiency. In 2016, ten new energy conservation projects were launched.

That same year, 7.7 million baht was invested in an education project to help employees develop their full potential. The Somboon Learning Academy provides training for all staff levels in production, management, supervision, engineering, HR, and foreign languages. Employee wellbeing is a key pillar and further strengthened through Buddhist ceremonies, a savings cooperative, regular medical check-ups, sports facilities, scholarships for children of employees, and other initiatives. Employees provided 17,000 hours of volunteer work in 2016, forging closer bonds with their communities.

THE BENEFITS: Despite the ongoing challenges and cost-cutting pressures in the sector, Somboon Advance Technologies has maintained steady profitability of over 600 million baht per year, and maintained overall customer satisfaction at over 80 percent (tracked via regular surveys). For several years in a row, the Stock Exchange of Thailand has recognized their performance through awards for corporate governance, social responsibility, and sustainability.

All of the environmental goals for 2018 have been surpassed, yielding reductions in water consumption (nine percent), CO_2 emissions (ten percent), and industrial waste (40 percent). The 13 ongoing energy conservation projects reduce electricity consumption by 2.6 million kWh per year, saving 1.5 tons of CO_2 equivalent. The combined value of the materials, oil, and water recycling efforts reached an estimated two million baht.

The surrounding communities have also greatly benefited from the volunteering culture nurtured. For example, the Thai Red Cross Society collected 107,000 cubic centimeters of blood donations, and staff renovated a temple and three schools. The Sufficiency Economy principles have helped shape a motivated and committed workforce, as evidenced by the lowest accident level in four years and low staff turnover rate (just 13 percent).

e-buses on the road in 2016, could provide a domestic supplier base.

Vanguard countries like Norway and the Netherlands provide a few valuable lessons. Strong end-consumer subsidies encourage early uptake, while incentives like free parking and charging shape consumer behavior in the long run. Substantial charging infrastructure coverage is essential for boosting consumer confidence. The charging infrastructure in the country is in its infancy and largely limited to pilot projects by government institutions or state companies. In 2016, PTT signed contacts with six major automakers to build a network of 20 charging stations. Current government priorities focus on wooing automakers to set up e-vehicle operations in the country (for example, via favorable tax and investment incentives), but in the short term, more robust actions are needed on consumer incentives and charging stations.

INSIGHTS

SORANUN CHOOCHUT *is founder and CEO of ETRAN Group, a startup that provides an environmentally friendly alternative for the daily urban commute with motorcycle taxis. The company has designed an electric scooter to be deployed throughout Bangkok.*

How did you arrive at the idea of developing an e-scooter from the ground up?
We wanted to do something in the public sector to change people's minds about new, clean energy. Like with natural gas taxis. When people saw that taxis use alternative energy, LPG, a lot of people started using it in their cars. They trust it, because the public service started using it first. Also, as industrial designers there were no opportunities to do original design in the Thai automotive sector, so we decided to start our own.

Which innovations distinguish the ETRAN scooter?
Current motorcycle design focuses on the driver, the passenger seat is a bonus. We started with the passenger. Taking out the engine gives a lot of space to utilize to create comfort and safety for the passenger. Especially for women with skirts, who have to sit sideways, it's dangerous. We also want to reinvent production. We'll use rotation molding, like for kayaks, instead of the traditional injection molding. It's very strong. We will integrate payment with the public transport rabbit card to provide an integrated clean journey. 30 percent of one million daily BTS users have to take a last mile trip.

Which collaborations helped the company develop?
The swapping station is currently being developed together with students from Chulalongkorn University, and Chula also invested half a million baht. We are testing it to provide a proof of concept of 1,000+ charges per battery. Thai Summit supported us by helping us do R&D, to scale the model, to do serious automotive design for production. The prototype is 3-D printed using an ABS plastic polymer at Thai Summit. We are also discussing with the BMA, with banks, with real estate agencies, and 7-Eleven to select locations for charging stations.

What are the goals of the company?
Our goal is to provide public transport in cities across the globe, to convert all transportation services into environmentally good products. For the motorcycle taxis in Bangkok, we want to convert 30 percent in three years. That is my mission. In Thailand, 1.8 million motorbikes are sold each year, so it's a very small percentage. Then, we also want to do three-wheelers and then expand into four wheels. The traditional tuk tuk design does not fit future public transport. The risk is on me; if I fail, I fail, but if I succeed it's about the country, the world. They will see that this works.

TAKE ACTION

Visionary Leadership

Early entry is crucial for capturing value, and large companies in particular need to lead by example (such as Somboon Advance Technologies adopting Sufficiency Economy Philosophy principles). Early entry improves performance, opens up new areas of growth, and creates opportunities in – and shapes – supplier operations up the value chain. Startups and SMEs can provide a fresh, new approach to addressing longstanding structural challenges by taking greater risks and exploring new markets.

Embracing Innovation

The new transport paradigm is being driven by new technologies and business models. Thai companies that heavily invest in research and development can expect stronger returns on investment and competitive advantages (e.g. PTT's tech park). Nurturing in-house innovation and aggressively seeking acquisitions or investment in cutting-edge technology leaders (both at home and abroad) can open up new business horizons.

Thinking Globally

Scalability and global reach is a defining trait of the new transport ecosystem, both for market share and business development. Thai companies, both big and small, can secure diverse gains by looking to ASEAN and beyond, from initial concept to post-IPO. Focusing on operations that show the biggest scalability potential should be a priority. While operating out of Thailand, ETRAN, DRVR, and PTT's project with 24M Technologies Co are aimed at global markets.

Partnerships

The shared part of the new transport economy underscores the importance of collaboration, and the Thai private sector needs to leverage experience through partnership. Companies can open up their R&D facilities to explore added value creation and collaboration potential (yielding new products or even entire divisions). Stronger business incubator support will help nurture startups through the growing pains of the initial years. The ideas that prove viable will benefit all partners and the country as a whole.

The long road ahead

Thailand has reached a fork in the road. It is well placed to take advantage of the emerging and exciting opportunities in the global transition towards sustainable transport, but whether it will do so remains unclear. There is sufficient domestic political and budgetary support, as well as access to capital markets and expertise (albeit foreign) for major infrastructure projects that can provide the backbone of an integrated system. As a base for domestic and export-oriented production of motor vehicles, it has long-standing relationships with most global car manufacturers, parts suppliers, and entire vehicle production ecosystems.

Some domestic conglomerates are already looking to optimize operations, reduce exposure to resource risks, and capitalize on new business models. Meanwhile, a vibrant, local startup scene – powered by the imagination of some of Thailand's brightest and best

A vibrant, local startup scene is bringing new mobility and Made in Thailand solutions online and onto the roads.

– is bringing new mobility and fresh Made in Thailand solutions onto the roads, albeit only in small numbers. The country is crying out for more of them. The Thai private sector actors, both large and small, who realize this and capitalize on such opportunities stand to reap the benefits of the emerging new mobility reality – and create tremendous added value for both their bottom lines and for the country.

REFERENCES

PART 1

Kantabutra, S. (2014). Measuring Corporate Sustainability: A Thai Approach. *Measuring Business Excellence, 18 (2),* 73–88.

Kantabutra, S. and Siebenhüner, T. (2011). Predicting Corporate Sustainability: A Thai Approach. *Journal of Applied Business Research, 27 (6),* 123–134.

Kantabutra, S. (2012). Research to drive the Sufficiency Economy Philosophy in Business. In Apichai Puntasen (Ed.), *Looking Back to Drive the Sufficiency Economy over the Next Decade (2013–2022).* Bangkok: The Thailand Research Fund.

PART 2

Sustainability Strategy
Achavanuntakul, S. (2016, June 20). Myths about CSR. *ThaiPublica.*

BSR. (2016). *The Future of Stakeholder Engagement.* San Francisco, CA: Enright, S., McElrath, R., and Taylor, A.

Corporate Reporting Dialogue. (2016). *Statement of Common Principles of Materiality.*

Datamaran. (n.d.). *Seven Secrets to the Perfect Materiality Assessment in Record Time.*

Global Reporting Initiative, United Nations Global Compact, and World Business Council for Sustainable Development. (2015). *SDG Compass: The Business Guide to the SDGs.*

Lowitt, E. (2011, July 26). Why you shouldn't have a sustainability strategy. *The Guardian.*

MIT Sloan Management Review. (2017). *Sustainability at a Crossroads: Progress Toward Our Common Future in Uncertain Times.* Cambridge, MA: Kiron, D., Unruh, G., Kruschwitz, N., Reeves, M., Rubel, H., & zum Felde, A.M.

RobecoSAM. (2016). *CSA 2016 Annual Scoring Methodology.*

Sustainability. (2015). *Sustainability Incorporated, Integrating Sustainability into Business.* London: Mosher, M., & Smith, L.

United Nations Global Compact. (2015). *Roadmap for Integrated Sustainability.*

World Business Council for Sustainable Development. (2017). *CEO Guide to the SDGs.*

Corporate Governance and Leadership for Sustainability
King, M., & Atkins, J. (2016). *Chief Value Officer: Accountants Can Save the Planet.* Sheffield: Greenleaf Publishing.

Organisation for Economic Co-operation and Development. (2015). *G20/OECD Principle of Corporate Governance.*

Securities and Exchange Commission of Thailand. (2017). *Corporate Governance Code for listed companies 2017.*

Risk Management
AON. (2007). *Sustainability – Beyond Enterprise Risk Management.*

Committee of Sponsoring Organizations of the Treadway Commission. (2013). *Demystifying Sustainability Risk: Integrating the triple bottom line into an enterprise risk management program.*

Committee of Sponsoring Organizations of the Treadway Commission. (2012). *Understanding and Communicating Risk Appetite.*

Nacaskul, P. (2017). Financial Risk Management and Sustainability – the Sufficiency Economy Philosophy Nexus. *Social Science Research Network Working Paper,* https://ssrn.com/abstract=3057886

Nacaskul, P. (2015). Sufficiency Economy Philosophy: Conceptual Background & Introduction. *Social Science Research Network Working Paper,* https://ssrn.com/abstract=2625967

Nacaskul, P. (2013). Sustainable Development – Calling for Policy Analytics and (Wittgensteinian Turn Towards) Economics of Moderation. *Social Science Research Network Working Paper,* https://ssrn.com/abstract=2334765

PricewaterhouseCoopers. (2013). *The New Face of Risk: Uncovering the Hidden Risks.*

RobecoSAM. (2017). *Corporate Sustainability Assessment Companion.*

Saardchom, N. (2013). Enterprise Risk Management under Sustainability Platform. *Journal of Business and Economics, 4,* 32–41.

World Business Council for Sustainable Development. (2013). *Getting Sustainability Risks onto Management's Agenda: Moving from Theory to Opportunity.*

World Business Council for Sustainable Development. (2017). *Sustainability and enterprise risk management: The first step towards integration.*

Human Resources and Organizational Culture
Bafaro, F., Ellsworth, D., & Gandhi, N. (2017). The CEO's guide to competing through HR. *McKinsey Quarterly.*

Cohen, E. (2010, October 25). HR and sustainability: partner or pioneer? *The Guardian.*

Garton, E. (2017, September 4). The Case for Investing More in People. *Harvard Business Review.*

Lawler III, E. E., & Mohrman, S. A. (2014, November 5). The Crucial – and Underappreciated – Role of HR in Sustainability. *MIT Sloan Management Review.*

McKinsey & Company. (2017). Getting ready for the future of work. *McKinsey Quarterly.*

Kantabutra, S. et al. (2012). *Study on the development of indicators and assessors in line with Sufficiency Economy Philosophy business standards.* Bangkok: The Thailand Research Fund.

Resource Management
Aldersgate Group. (2017). *Amplifying Action on Resource Efficiency.*

The Nation. (2013, January 27). Green procurement ideas inspire Thai businesses. *The Nation.*

Supply Chain Management
Bové, A., & Swartz, S. (2014). Starting at the source: Sustainability in supply chains. *McKinsey.*

Fish, L. (2015). *Managerial Best Practices to Promote Sustainable Supply Chain Management & New Product Development.* New York: Department of Management, Canisius College.

Hanifan, G., Sharma, A., & Mehta, P. (2012). Why a sustainable supply chain is good business. *Accenture.*

Massaroni, E., Cozzolino, A., & Wankowicz, E. (2015). Sustainability in supply chain management – a literature review. *Sinergie Italian Journal of Management, 33 (98).* Verona: Fondazione Cueim.

PricewaterhouseCoopers. (2013). *Going beyond philanthropy?: Pulse-check on sustainability.*

SCB Economic Intelligence Center. (2017). *Insight: Keeping ahead of the new supply chain dynamics.*

Tozan, H., & Erturk, A. (2015). Applications of Contemporary Management Approaches in Supply Chains. *InTech.*

United Nations Global Compact and BSR. (2015). *Supply Chain Sustainability: A Practical Guide to Continuous Improvement.*

United Nations Global Compact and EY. (2016). *The State of Sustainable Supply Chains: Building responsible and resilient supply chains.*

Products and Services
Charter, M., & Tischner, U. (2001). Sustainable product design. In Charter, M., & Tischner, U. (Eds.), *Sustainable Solutions.* UK: Greenleaf Publishing.

Department for Environment, Food and Rural Affairs. (2003). *Changing patterns: UK Government Framework for Sustainable Consumption and Production.* London: Defra Publications.

Hanssen, O.J. (1999). Sustainable product systems – experiences based on case projects in sustainable product development. *Journal of Cleaner Production (1999), 7,* 27–41.

Maxwell, D., & Sheate, W. (2006). Enabling sustainable development through sustainable consumption and production. *International Journal of Environment and Sustainable Development (2006), 5 (3),* 221–239.

Maxwell, D., Sheate, W., & van der Vorst, R. (2006). Functional and systems aspects of the sustainable product and service development approach for industry. *Journal of Cleaner Production (2006), 14*, 1466–1479.

Maxwell, D., & van der Vorst, R. (2003). Developing sustainable products and services. *Journal of Cleaner Production (2003), 11*, 883–895.

Nielsen Global Survey. (2015). *The sustainability imperative: New insights on consumer expectations.*

Roy, R. (2000). Sustainable product-service systems. *Futures (2000), 32*, 289–299.

National Science Technology and Innovation Policy Office. (2014). *Thailand Science Technology and Innovation Profile.* Bangkok: STI. ISBN: 978-6161203740.

TPSO. (2016, June). CLMV + T as our home market. *TPSO Journal, 59.*

United Nations Environment Programme. (2004). *Why take a life cycle approach.* United Nations Publication.

United Nations Environment Programme and World Business Council for Sustainable Development. (1999). Eco-Efficiency and cleaner production: Charting the course to sustainability. Paris: UNEP and WBCSD.

van Weenan, H. (1997). Sustainable product development: opportunities for developing countries. *UNEP Industry and Environment Review (1997), January-June.*

Technology
Asian Development Bank. (2015). *Thailand Industrialization and Economic Catch Up.*

Bussi, M. (2017). Thailand Must Invest in Its Workers. *International Labour Organization.*

Balea, J. (2016, April 25). Thailand plans $570m venture fund for startups. *TechAsia.*

Ekvitthayavechnukul, C. (2016, 22 July). Thailand: Siam Commercial Bank sets up $50m fund to invest in fintech startups. *Deal street Asia.*

Grossman, N., Baxter, W., & Algie, J. (2017). *Thailand's Sustainable Development Sourcebook.* Bangkok: Editions Didier Millet.

Jamrisko, M. & Lu, W. (2016, January 17). These Are the World's Most Innovative Economies. *Bloomberg.*

Makower, J. (2017). *State of Green Business 2017.* GreenBiz Group Inc.

Nash, T. (2012). *Ethical Markets: Global Green R&D Report.*

Navigant Research. (2016, March 22). *Technology and Substance in Sustainability.*

Office of Industrial Economics. (2017). *The general situations of industrial production in Thailand.*

Sachs, J. (2013, December 19). Technology is key to new era of economic growth. *Financial Times.*

Schwab, K. (2016). *The Fourth Industrial Revolution.* UK: Portfolio Penguin.

United Nations Conference on Trade and Development. (2015). *Science, Technology and Innovation Policy Review: Thailand.*

Collaboration
Accenture Consulting. (2017). *Building and Sustaining a Successful Public-Private Partnership.*

Albani, M., & Henderson, K. (2014). *Creating Partnerships for Sustainability.* McKinsey & Company.

Albrectsen, A. (2017). *Why collaboration will be key to achieving the Sustainable Development Goals.* Geneva: World Economic Forum.

Baxter, W., Grossman, N., & Wegner, N. (2016). *A Call to Action: Thailand and the Sustainable Development Goals.* Bangkok: Editions Didier Millet.

C&E. (2016). *Corporate-NGO Partnerships Barometer 2016 Report.*

Ethical Corporation. (2016). *State of Responsible Business 2016 Report.*

Gray, B., & Stites, P. (2013). *Sustainability Through Partnerships: Capitalizing on Collaboration.* Network for Business Sustainability.

Hamilton, G. (2017). *Public-Private Partnerships for Sustainable Development* (PowerPoint presentation). United Nations Economic Commission for Europe.

Janvatanavit, K. (2017, 17 May). *Corruption – an impact on business operations and reputation.* Sharing Session at the Thai Institute of Directors.

PPP Knowledge Lab. (2016). *Thailand Country Profile.* Washington, D.C: World Bank Group.

PricewaterhouseCoopers. (2015). *Make it your business: Engaging with the Sustainable Development Goals.*

Sachs, J., Schmidt-Traub, G., et al. (2016). *SDG Index & Dashboards – A Global Report.* Bertelsmann Stiftung and Sustainable Development Solutions Network.

Tilleke & Gibbins International Ltd. (2016, December 9). Public-private partnerships in infrastructure projects. *Bangkok Post.*

United Nations Global Compact. (2017). *Why Partner – and How.*

World Economic Forum. (2016). *Common Best Practices across Public-Private Partnership Organisations.* Geneva: World Economic Forum.

Reporting and Disclosure
Allison-Hope, D. (2016, July 18). The Future of Reporting is Triangular. *BSR Blog.*

Corporate Register. (2017). *The CR Reporting Awards 2016.*

Global Reporting Initiative and SustainAbility. (2017). *Insights from the GRI Corporate Leadership Group on Reporting 2025: Future Trends in Sustainability Reporting.* Amsterdam: GRI.

Global Reporting Initiative and United Nations Development Programme. (2016). *Measuring Business Impact on the SDGs.*

Kahn, M. (2017, February 26). Requiring Companies to Disclose Climate Risks Helps Everyone. *Harvard Business Review.*

Kerai, R. (2017). Impact: What's it worth?. In *The Sustainability Yearbook 2017.* Zurich: RobecoSAM.

Kering Group. (2016). *Environmental Profit & Loss (EP&L) 2016 Group Results.*

Koehler, D. A., & Hespenheide. E. (2014, January 28). How materiality drives improved sustainability reporting. *GreenBiz.*

Makower, J. (2017). *State of Green Business 2017.* GreenBiz Group Inc.

Mosher, M. (2015, February 16). How Dow, Novo Nordisk and others own their indirect impacts. *GreenBiz.*

PricewaterhouseCoopers. (2014). *Learning from early adopters of integrated reporting: Five themes to drive improvement.*

PricewaterhouseCoopers LLP. (2016). Sustainability reporting and disclosure: What does the future look like? *Point of View.* USA: DeSmith, S., & Paul, B.

SustainAbility. (2014). *See Change: How Transparency Drives Performance.* London: Mosher, M., Smith, L., & Wicker, J.

SustainAbility. (2015). *Sustainability Incorporated, Integrating Sustainability into Business.* London: Mosher, M., & Smith, L.

Task Force on Climate-related Financial Disclosures. (2017, June). *Recommendations of the Task Force on Climate-related Financial Disclosures.*

Unruh, G. (2016, December 12). Sustainability Reporting: One Size Fits Nobody. *MIT Sloan Management Review.*

World Business Council for Sustainable Development. (2016). *Reporting Matters.* Geneva and London: WBCSD and Radley Yeldar.

PART 3
Agribusiness
Food and Agriculture Organization of the United Nations. (2017). *Regional Workshop on Participatory Guarantee Systems (PGS) for organic agriculture in the Greater Mekong Sub-region (GMS): Lessons Learnt and the Way Forward.*

Poapongsakorn, N., & Chokesomritpol, P. (2017, June 30). Agriculture 4.0: Obstacles and how to break through. *Bangkok Post.*

Pretty, J., et al. (2006). *Resource-Conserving Agriculture Increases Yields in Developing Countries*. Department of Biological Sciences and Centre for Environment and Society, University of Essex.

Sachs, J. (2015). Chapter 10: Food Security. *The Age of Sustainable Development*. New York: Columbia University Press.

Food and Beverage
Business Wire. (2016, April 4). Thailand Convenience Store Market Outlook to 2020 – Research and Markets. *Business Wire*.

Food and Agriculture Organization of the United Nations. (2014). *Food Waste Footprint: Impacts on natural resources summary report*.

Hervio, J. (2017). *Thailand 2017, Beyond the Concerns*. Thailand: Ipsos Flair.

Sattaburuth, A. (2016, April 27). Sugar tax for public health: Soft drinks 20–25% price rise. *Bangkok Post*.

Singha, C. (2016, March 31). Leaf bowls to replace Styrofoam takeout food boxes. *Bangkok Post*.

Thaitrakulpanich, A. (2017, February 21). New Labels and Tax Take on Thailand's Junk Food Problem. *Khao Sod English*.

Fisheries
Anantanasuwong, D. (2001). Shrimp Farming in Coastal Areas in Thailand and the Proposed Economic Instruments for Sustainable Shrimp Farming. *Ritsumeikan Annual Review of International Studies, 13 (3)*.

Hodal, K., Kelly, C., & Lawrence, F. (2014, June 10). Revealed: Asian slave labour producing prawns for supermarkets in US, UK. *The Guardian*.

Morgan, G., & Staples, D. (2006). *The History of Industrial Marine Fisheries in Southeast Asia*. Bangkok: Food and Agriculture Organization of the United Nations, Regional Office for Asia and the Pacific.

Department of Fisheries, Ministry of Agriculture and Cooperatives of Thailand. (2015). *Marine Fisheries Management Plan of Thailand: A National Policy for Marine Fisheries Management (2015–2019)*.

United Nations Environment Programme. (2009). *The Role of Supply Chains in Addressing the Global Seafood Crisis*.

Marine Stewardship Council. (2014, November 11). *New research shows increasing appetite for sustainable seafood*.

Energy
Bloomberg New Energy Finance. (2017). *Thailand Country Profile*.

Fungtammasan, B., Tippichai, A., Otsuki, T., & Tam, C. (2017). Transition Pathways for a Sustainable Low-carbon Energy System in Thailand. *Journal of Renewable and Sustainable Energy, 9*, 021405. doi: 10.1063/1.4978496

Office of Natural Resources and Environment.

(2015). *Thailand's Nationally Determined Contributions (NDCs): A communication to UNFCCC*.

World Bank (2006). *World Bank GEF: Post-Implementation Impact Assessment Thailand Promotion of Electrical Energy Efficiency Project*. Washington, D.C: World Bank Group.

United Nations Global Compact and KPMG. (2017). *SDG Industry Matrix: Energy, Natural Resources and Chemicals*. New York: United Nations Global Compact.

Manufacturing
Asian Development Bank. (2015). *Thailand: Industrialization and economic catch-up*.

Brinded, W. (2017, January 26). This is how robots are going to change employment. *Business Insider*.

Charusilawong, N. (2015). *Thailand Hard-disk drive industry: impending challenges and opportunities on the horizon*. Kasikorn Research Center.

Hausmann, R. (2015, May 31). The Education Myth. *Project Syndicate*.

Kim, J. (2017). Case Study: *Thailand's Community-Based Eco-Industrial Town Development*. Global Green Growth Institute.

ManpowerGroup. (2017). *The Skills Revolution*.

Office of the National Economic and Social Development Board. (2017). *NESDB Economic Report: Thai Economic Performance in Q2 and Outlook for 2017*.

Organisation for Economic Co-operation and Development. (2017). *OECD Sustainable Manufacturing Toolkit*.

Teeravaraprug, J., & Podcharathitikull, T. (2016). Factors for Success in Eco-Industrial Town Development in Thailand. *World Academy of Science, Engineering and Technology International Journal of Economics and Management Engineering, 10 (7)*.

World Bank. (2017). *Thailand Systematic Country Diagnostic: Getting Back on Track, Reviving Growth & Securing Prosperity for All*. Washington, D.C: World Bank Group.

SMEs
Avery, G., & Bergsteiner, H. (2016). *Sufficiency Thinking: Thailand's Gift to an Unsustainable World*. Australia: Allen & Unwin.

International Trade Centre. (2016). *SME Competitiveness Outlook 2016: Meeting the Standard for Trade*.

MIT Sloan Management Review. (2017). *Sustainability at a Crossroads: Progress Toward Our Common Future in Uncertain Times*. Cambridge, MA: Kiron, D., Unruh, G., Kruschwitz, N., Reeves, M., Rubel, H., & zum Felde, A.M.

The Office of SMEs Promotion. (2015). *SME White Paper*.

Thoonpoon, S. (2012). *Sustainability of SMEs in

Southern Thailand: The Roles of Sufficiency Economy and Strategic Competency. Thailand: Hatyai University.

United Nations Global Compact. (2015). *Support Your SME Suppliers*.

Tourism
Amornvivat, S., Charoenphon, V., Pruedsaradch, P., Bunsupaporn, K., & Akaraphanth, L. (2016). *Insight: Thai Tourism, Sustaining Success*. Bangkok: SCB Economic Intelligence Center.

Crosbie-Jones, M. (2014). Holiday Time in Thailand. *Bangkok Post The Magazine*.

Denman, R. (2013). *Sustainable Tourism for Development Guidebook*. World Tourism Organization (UNWTO).

Kongkrut, A. (2016, August 8). New Plan Calls for Sustainable Tourism on Koh Phi Phi. *Bangkok Post*.

Oxford Business Group. (2017). *The Report: Thailand 2017 (Tourism Overview)*.

Tourism Authority of Thailand. (2016, January 19). Thailand advancing towards sustainable tourism in line with global trend. *TAT News*.

Wattanavrangkul, K. (2017, May 5). Sustainability key to avoiding pain while ensuring long-term gains in tourism. *The Nation*.

World Economic Forum. (2017). *The Travel & Tourism Competitiveness Report 2017*. Geneva: World Economic Forum.

Retailing
Euromonitor International. (2017). *Passport: Retailing in Thailand*.

Global Agricultural Information Network. (2016). *Thailand: Retail Foods*.

Greenpeace. (2016). *Timeout for Fast Fashion*. Hamburg: Cobbing, M, & Vicaire, Y.

Scott, A. (2015, October 15). Cutting Out Textile Pollution. *Chemical & Engineering News*.

Siegle, L. (2017, July 30). Fashion must fight the scourge of dumped clothing clogging landfills. *The Guardian*.

World Economic Forum and Accenture. (2017). *Shaping the Future of Retail for Consumer Industries*. Geneva: World Economic Forum.

Verdict Retail. (2016, September 15). Ethical Sourcing? Most shoppers won't pay for it. *Inside Retail Thailand*.

Finance
Achavanuntakul, S., Khlongakkara, S., Paveenchana, S., Tanangsnakool, K., & Ingsakit, R. (2015, March). *Business Case for Sustainable Banking in Thailand*. Bangkok: Sal Forest.

Brown, J. (2017, January 21). How You Can #Resist With Your Portfolio. *The Reformed Broker*.

Cheng, E. (2017, March 17). Some on Wall Street are making a new bet on investors' consciences. *CNBC*.

Chonlaworn, P., & Pongpirodom, P. (2015, April 1). Can Nano Finance unleash the grassroots from loan shark problems?. *SCB Economic Intelligence Center*.

Greenpeace. (2017). *Dirty Bankers: How HSBC is Financing Forest Destruction for Palm Oil*.

International Capital Market Association. (2017). *The Green Bond Principles 2017*.

Kaeufer, K. (2010). Banking as a Vehicle for Socio-economic Development and Change: Case Studies of Socially Responsible and Green Banks. *Global Alliance for Banking on Values*.

Organisation for Economic Co-operation and Development. (2013). *SME and Entrepreneurship Financing: The Role of Credit Guarantee Schemes and Mutual Guarantee Societies in supporting finance for small and medium-sized enterprises*.

Panyanukul, S., Promboon, W., & Vorranikulkij, W. (2014). *Role of government in improving SME access to financing: Credit guarantee schemes and the way forward*. Bank of Thailand Symposium 2014.

Parpart, E. (2015, March 20). Our Fintech Future. *Bangkok Post*.

Santiprabhob, V. (2015, June 21). *Navigating through Uncertainties for Thailand's Sustainability* (Interview Transcript).

Ward, P., Miller, E., Pearce, A., & Meyer, S. (2016). *Predictors and Extent of Institutional Trust in Government, Banks, the Media and Religious Organisations: Evidence from Cross-Sectional Surveys in Six Asia-Pacific Countries*. PLOS ONE.

Real Estate

Research & Innovation for Sustainability Centre. (2017, April 10). *Libra-RISC10 presentation*.

Magnolia Quality Development Corporation. (2017, May 30). *WHIZDOM 101 Shortlisted for 'Smart Cities-Clean Energy Award' from the Ministry of Energy*.

Solidance. (n.d.). *Thailand's Green Building Goals: Aspirations and Realities*.

Oxford Business Group. (2016). *The Report: Thailand 2016 (Construction & Real Estate)*.

Willis Towers Watson. (2017). *Real Estate Climate Risk Report 2017*.

World Economic Forum. (2016). *Environmental Sustainability Principles for the Real Estate Industry*. Geneva: World Economic Forum.

Transport

Attavanich, W. (2017). *Impact of the First-Time Car Buyer Program on the Environmental Cost of Air Pollution in Bangkok*. Bangkok: Faculty of Economics, Kasetsart University.

Bouton, S., Knupfer, S., Mihov, I., & Swartz, S. (2015). *Urban Mobility at a Tipping Point*. McKinsey & Company.

International Energy Agency. (2016). *Global EV Outlook 2016: Beyond one million electric cars*.

Greater Mekong Subregion Information Portal. (2017). *Vehicle Motorization Index*.

Office of Natural Resources and Environmental Policy and Planning. (2015). *Thailand's First Biennial Update Report: Under the United Nations Framework Convention on Climate Change*.

Olivier, J., Janssens-Maenhout, G., Muntean, M., & Peters, J. (2016). *Trends in Global CO$_2$ Emissions: 2016 Report*. The Hague: PBL Netherlands Environmental Assessment Agency.

Oxford Business Group. (2016). *The Report: Thailand 2016 (Transport)*.

Partnership on Sustainable Low Carbon Transport. (2016). *Sustainable Development Goals and Transport*.

United Nations Global Compact and KPMG. (2016). *SDG Industry Matrix: Transport*.

United Nations Secretary-General's High-Level Advisory Group on Sustainable Transport. (2016). *Mobilizing Sustainable Transport for Development*.

PICTURE CREDITS

Every effort has been made to trace copyright holders of images in this book. In the event of error or omissions, appropriate credit will be made in future editions of Thailand's Sustainable Business Guide.

Akha Ama Coffee: 227, 235
Alan Laubsch: 69
Andaman Discoveries: 116 all
Anek Farm: 106
Anthony Watanabe: 132
Bangkok Post: 206
Bank of Ayudhya: 287 (left)
Benjamin Lephilibert: 258
Betagro Group: 160, 167 all, 169 all, 173
BBOXX: 129
Central Group: 79, 141 (top left), 268
Charoen Pokphand Foods: 159, 194
Chiva-Som International Health Resorts: 36 all, 41 all
Chulalongkorn University School of Agricultural Resources: 164 all, 168
CLP Holdings: 204 (top left)
Coca-Cola Thailand and Laos: 184
Community Organization Development Institute: 318
Dario Pignatelli: 214 (right)
David Henderson: 328
Dhanabadee Ceramic: 82 all
Donato Calace: 42
Earth Net Foundation: 190 (bottom right)
Electricity Generating Authority of Thailand: 204 (bottom left)
Elmar Kleiner: 311
EnerGaia: 256
Etran Group: 329
Fisherfolk: 13, 188, 196
Getty Images: 5, 9, 10, 24 (left and right), 27, 29, 35, 52, 63, 70, 88, 89, 101, 110, 122, 126 (bottom left), 145, 166, 176, 178 all, 187, 191, 192, 213, 214 (left), 218, 228, 230, 236, 239, 244 (top left and bottom right), 247, 248 (top left), 257, 265, 266, 271, 272, 277, 278, 281, 303, 307, 316, 321, 324, 325 (top right), 331
HiSo Snack: 182 (top left)
Insects in the Backyard: 182 (bottom right)
Interface Carpets: 39 all
IKEA Southeast Asia: 91, 94
John Thøgersen: 115
Kasikornbank: 68 (bottom left)
Kering Group: 152
Khiri Travel: 261 all
Khon Thai Foundation: 138

King Mongkut's University of Technology Thonburi (KMUTT) School of Architecture and Design: 313 (top right)
Krating Poonpol: 131
Local Alike: 252, 259
Mae Fah Luang Foundation: 137 all, 233
Magnolia Quality Development Corporation: 314 all
Mick Elmore: 313
Minor International: 55, 251, 255 all
Mitr Phol Group: 22, 96, 163, 170, 222
M.R. Sa-ard Dinakara Clinic: 304 all
Nicholas Grossman: 180, 298
Nithi Foods: 232 all
Phi Suea House: 210, 308
Piyasvasti Amranand: 207, 243
PlanToys: 73, 113, 220 all
PTT Public Company Limited: 200, 240
PTT Global Chemical Public Company Limited: 209
Refill not Landfill: 254
RingMD: 296
Robert McLeod/Lantern Photography Co., Ltd.: 57 (bottom left)
Sa Paper Preservation House: 68 (top left)
Sampran Riverside Resort: 162, 260 all
SCG: 33, 103 all, 120
SCG/Athit Perawongmetha: 119
Silicon Craft: 219 all
Singh Intrachooto: 317
Shutterstock: 87, 203, 248 (bottom right), 287 (right), 312, 325 (bottom left), 330
Solar Power Company Group: 199, 291 all
Somkiat Tangkitvanich: 217 all
Sooksan Kantabutra: 83
Soranun Choochut: 332
Steps with Theera: 80
Taylor Weidman: 92 (bottom right), 223
Techfarm: 126 (top right)
Tesco Lotus: 102, 174, 270
Thai Beverage: 105, 141 (bottom right), 183
Thai Credit Guarantee Corporation: 288
ThaiHarvest-SOS: 181
Thai Institute of Directors: 47, 51 all, 53, 57, 58, 59, 60
Thai President Foods: 92 (top left)
Thai Summit Group: 224 all
Thai Union Group: 147, 193
The Anti-Corruption Organization of Thailand: 135
Theptarin Hospital: 301 all
Thon Thamrongnawasawat: 190 (top left)
Ticketmelon: 78
United Nations Global Compact Network Thailand: 108
Wellness City: 302
Wimonkan Kosumas: 231
Whole Planet Foundation: 274, 276
Worldview International Foundation: 290 all

INDEX

Principal coverage of a topic is entered in **bold**.
Illustrative material is entered in *italics*.

Thai names are alphabetically entered as written
under the first name. Other names are inverted
and alphabetically entered under the second
name.

EDITORIAL TEAM

Adis Israngkul (writer, "Resources Management") is an advisor on natural resources and the environment at the Thailand Development Research Institute. His areas of expertise include natural resource and environmental economics, project cost benefit analysis, economic instruments for natural resource and environmental management, and sustainable development.

Bandid Nijathaworn (writer, "Corporate Governance") is the president and CEO of the Thai Institute of Directors, and secretary general of Thailand's Collective Action Coalition against Corruption. He was formerly the deputy governor of the Bank of Thailand. A reputable economist and governance advocate, he regularly contributes to local and international media outlets on topics of economy, corporate governance, and anti-corruption.

Benjapa Sodsathit (art director) received an MFA from Minneapolis College of Art & Design in Visual Studies and a BFA from Silpakorn University. She is a co-founder of Palotai Design Co. Ltd., which services clients locally and internationally.

Bhimsupa Kulthanan (editor and writer, "Sustainability Strategy," "Risk Management," "Human Resources and Organizational Culture," and "Reporting and Disclosure") previously worked as a sustainability consultant at ERM-Siam, advising corporate clients on sustainability strategy and reporting. Her background is in international development and environmental policy.

Bundit Fungtammasan (writer, "Energy") is currently the senior vice president for research and innovation at King Mongkut's University of Technology Thonburi, and a faculty member of its Joint Graduate School of Energy and Environment (JGSEE).

Deunden Nikomborirak (writer, "State-owned Enterprises") is a research director at the Thailand Development Research Institute. Her areas of expertise include competition policy, sectoral regulations, governance, anti-corruption strategy, and services trade and investment.

Graham Watts (writer, "Manufacturing" and "Finance") was a journalist at the *Financial Times* for 21 years. He was an editor on the *FT*'s world news desk responsible for coverage of economics, trade, and global policy issues.

Grissarin Chungsiriwat (researcher) is a freelance translator, researcher, and interpreter. She has completed research and edited several books for EDM, including *King Bhumibol Adulyadej: A Life's Work*. She is currently the festival manager for BangkokEdge Festival, Bangkok's first idea festival.

Janjarang Kijtikhun (writer, "Collaboration" and "Technology") is a social performance and international development consultant specializing in social risk management, social investment, and economic development-related issues. She has previously worked for the ILO and UNCTAD, and consulted for energy sector companies and startups in Thailand and abroad.

Jeff Goldman (writer, "Tourism") has worked across six continents implementing programs on education, cultural exchange, health, social enterprise, energy, and environmental policy. He has been an executive director of the Fair Trade Resource Network in Washington, D.C., and CEO of Mango Tree Education Enterprises in Uganda. He is a graduate of the Massachusetts Institute of Technology.

Krittinee Nuttavuthisit (writer, "Products and Services") is an associate professor of marketing at Sasin Graduate Institute of Business Administration. Her research focuses on consumer experience and wellbeing, contemporary marketing, and sustainable development.

Laura Villadiego (writer, "Fisheries and Marine Resources") is a freelance journalist focusing on the environmental and social impacts of global supply chains. In Thailand, she has extensively researched the fishing, sugar, and palm oil sectors. Her work has been published in *The Guardian, Al Jazeera,* and *The South China Morning Post*, among others.

Luxana Kiratibhongse (art director) graduated with a Fine Arts degree from Macalester College in the USA. A graphic designer for more than ten years, she has been commissioned by clients in Thailand and around the world for marketing, advertising, and editorial projects.

Max Crosbie-Jones (editor and writer, "Tourism"and "Supply Chain Management") is a Bangkok-based journalist and editor covering art & culture, design, travel, and business. Formerly the managing editor of *Bangkok Post The Magazine*, his work has appeared in *CNN Travel, ArtReview,* and *Monocle,* among others.

Mick Elmore (writer, "Real Estate") is a journalist with over 30 years of experience. He has filed stories and photos for nearly 100 publications from more than 20 countries. He earned a Masters in Southeast Asian Studies from Chulalongkorn University in 2014 and teaches there. Mick paid his last power bill in 2012, since then relying totally on solar energy.

Nichapat Chaokchaingamsangh (designer) earned her BFA from Bangkok University.

Nicholas Grossman (editor-in-chief) has produced over ten books on Thailand, including *Thailand's Sustainable Development Sourcebook, A Call to Action, Thailand: 9 Days in the Kingdom, Chronicle of Thailand, Americans in Thailand, A History of the Thai-Chinese,* and *King Bhumibol Adulyadej: A Life's Work.*

Nikola Stalevski (writer, "Transport") is currently based in Tbilisi, Georgia. He works across the globe promoting sustainable urban transport, e-mobility, livable cities, and all other interventions that move people and goods in smarter, more environmentally-friendly ways.

Nina Wegner (editor and writer, "Agribusiness," "Retailing," "Real Estate," "Healthcare," and "SMEs") is a freelance journalist who writes about indigenous issues and corporate responsibility in developing countries. Her work has been published in *The Wall Street Journal*, *Al Jazeera*, *The Atlantic*, and *The Huffington Post*, among others.

Patima Klinsong (writer, "Healthcare") has been a journalist, writer, and translator for over 15 years. She graduated in Technical Communication from the Illinois Institute of Technology.

Patinya Rojnukkarin (art director) earned her MFA from Minneapolis College of Art & Design in Visual Studies and BFA from Silpakorn University. She has 17 years of graphic and motion graphic experience.

Peta Bassett (writer, "Food and Beverage") is a freelance writer focusing on food transparency and sustainability. She co-founded the former Spring Epicurean Market for consumers to meet their butcher, baker, and salted caramel-maker and continues to profile food makers via the website Seed and Tell while also contributing to regional publications.

Randall Shannon (writer, "Retailing") is an associate professor at the College of Management, Mahidol University. His specializations are in retailing, shopping behavior, branding, private label brands, and consumer behavior.

Siree Simaraks (designer) has over eight years of experience in graphic design. She holds a bachelor's degree in Graphic Design from the Faculty of Architecture, Urban Design, and Creative Arts at Mahasarakham University.

Sirikul Raddudsadee (designer) earned her BFA from Silpakorn University.

Sompong Sirisoponsilp (writer, "Agribusiness") is an associate professor at the Chulalongkorn University School of Agricultural Resources. His specializations are in logistics and supply chain management, transportation planning, and transportation engineering.

Sooksan Kantabutra (writer, "Introduction") is an associate professor and director of the Center for Research on Sustainable Leadership at Mahidol University College of Management. His areas of specialization include organizational innovation, sustainable enterprises, organizational competitiveness, and sustainable leadership.

Sumet Ongkittikul (writer, "Supply Chain Management") is the research director for transportation and logistics policy at Thailand Development Research Institute. His prior experiences include roles as a PhD researcher and research consultant at the Erasmus University Rotterdam, and an advisor on various government sub-committees on transport and logistics.

Supawan Visetnoi (writer, "Agribusiness") is a full-time instructor at Chulalongkorn University School of Agricultural Resources. Her current research interests are sustainable agriculture education, and national policy on extension services to farmers that focus on sustainable agriculture and development.

Tanakorn Pornratananukul (writer, "Corporate Governance") is the CG supervisor for director development at the Thai Institute of Directors. He leads the curriculum development team, which develops content and training materials to enhance board of directors' understanding of the importance of corporate governance.

Will Baxter (contributing editor) is a journalist and photographer based in East Africa since 2017. Previously he was based in Southeast Asia for 14 years. His work focuses on human rights, conflict, climate change, and social issues.

Wirawan Munnapinun (writer, "Corporate Governance") is the assistant vice president for research and policy at the Thai Institute of Directors. She oversees corporate governance projects including the Corporate Governance Report of Thai Listed Companies, ASEAN CG Scorecard Project, Board of the Year Awards, and organizes seminars and forums promoting corporate governance best practices.

Woranuj Watts (writer, "Manufacturing" and "Finance") has worked as a business journalist for 15 years, and is now a freelance writer and translator.

ACKNOWLEDGEMENTS

The publishing team is grateful to the following individuals for their assistance and advice: Dr Chirayu Isarangkun Na Ayuthaya whose belief in this project and support was essential to its realization. A special thank you to Ongorn Abhakorn Na Ayuthaya, Thatri Likanapichitkul, Orawan Yafa, Visarute Vironjanawat, and the entire team at the Thailand Sustainable Development Foundation for their continued support throughout the project.

In addition, we thank Achara Wisuttiwongrat, Adam Saytanides, Alan Laubsch, Anand Panyarachun, Arayan Trangarn, Arisa Xumsai Na Ayuthaya, Apasiri Kulthanan, Ar-tara Satraroj, Christopher Hughes, Daniel Zoltani, Elmar Kleiner, Ian Craine, Ingo Puhl, Jonathan Grossman, Linda Kaewrak, Nattaya Lourvanij, Pantamas Krikul, Parames Krairiksh, Paul Choong, Pimjai Hoontrakul, Pinta Punsoni Macdougall, Piti Sithiamnuai, Piyawan Prayuksilpa, Polpiya Thitivesa, Poomjai Nacaskul, Prae Piromya, Priyanut Dharmapiya, Radeethep Devakula, Raksina Chirawanich, Ratchada Sungkeetanon, Sansanee Wanamatin, Sopitta Chotechuang, Sutinee Phukosi, Syamol Lumlongrut, Taechat Apichit, Thantika Bodhisompon, Tanya Vannapruegs, Taylor Weidman, Teerana Paradornuwat, Thep Himathongkam, Tom Beloe, and Yonchailai Jaturatis.

"A balanced approach combining patience, perseverance, diligence, wisdom, and prudence is indispensable to cope appropriately with critical challenges arising from extensive and rapid socioeconomic, environmental, and cultural change occurring as a result of globalization."

From the written statement on the Sufficiency Economy Philosophy provided to the public by His Majesty King Bhumibol Adulyadej in 1999 [unofficial translation from the Thai]